D1083423

THE GOLDEN AGE OF BATTLEFIELD PRESERVATION

ALSO BY TIMOTHY B. SMITH

*The Untold Story of Shiloh:*
*The Battle and the Battlefield*

*Champion Hill: Decisive Battle for Vicksburg*

*This Great Battlefield of Shiloh:*
*History, Memory, and the Establishment of a*
*Civil War National Military Park*

# THE GOLDEN AGE OF BATTLEFIELD PRESERVATION

*The Decade of the 1890s and the Establishment
of America's First Five Military Parks*

ʕ   •   ʔ

## TIMOTHY B. SMITH

*With a Foreword by Edwin C. Bearss*

THE UNIVERSITY OF TENNESSEE PRESS / KNOXVILLE

Copyright © 2008 by The University of Tennessee Press / Knoxville.
All Rights Reserved. Manufactured in the United States of America.

First Edition.

This book is printed on acid-free paper.

Smith, Timothy B., 1974–
The golden age of battlefield preservation : the decade of the 1890s and
the establishment of America's first five military parks / Timothy B. Smith;
with a foreword by Edwin C. Bearss. — 1st ed.
    p. cm.
 Includes bibliographical references and index.
 ISBN-13: 978-1-57233-622-3 (hardcover : alk. paper)
 ISBN-10: 1-57233-622-6
1. United States—History—Civil War, 1861–1865—Battlefields. 2. Battlefields—Conservation and restoration—United States—History. 3. Military
parks—Government policy—United States—History. 4. National parks and
reserves—Government policy—United States—History. 5. Chickamauga
and Chattanooga National Military Park (Ga. and Tenn.) 6. Antietam National
Battlefield (Md.)—History. 7. Shiloh National Military Park (Tenn.)—History.
8. Gettysburg National Military Park (Pa.)—History. 9. Vicksburg National
Military Park (Miss.)—History. 10. United States—Cultural policy. I. Title.
  E641.S64    2008
 973.7—dc22                          2007033770

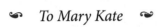 *To Mary Kate*

# CONTENTS

# ILLUSTRATIONS

MAPS

# FOREWORD

MORE THAN HALF a century ago, on September 28, 1955, I entered on duty as park historian at Vicksburg National Military Park. Although a longtime Civil War aficionado, I was unfamiliar with the park's administrative history or that of its relation to and interaction with the other four great national military parks established by the United States Congress in the last decade of the nineteenth century. The parks had been established in response to campaigns by veterans and their politically active leaders to commemorate their war years, which they saw as the defining years of their lives and of the nation. These flagship parks, along with other national military parks established in the first third of the twentieth century, were administered by the United States War Department until August 1933, when they were transferred by a presidential executive order to the National Park Service (NPS), a bureau of the Department of the Interior.

During my years at Vicksburg, first as park historian and then as regional research historian, I became knowledgeable about the park's administrative history. A need to expand my horizons in this field became apparent in my second year in the NPS. It was then that I became a member of a team of professionals assigned to study and recommend boundaries for the recently authorized Pea Ridge National Military Park. My colleagues on the team were NPS veterans who had joined the bureau in the early New Deal years. They possessed a collective memory (dating to 1933–34) of park administrative history that proved invaluable to me subsequently. Four years later, in the summer of 1960, I was detailed as a member of another team, this time to study and recommended the boundary of what has since become Wilson's Creek National Battlefield.

Meanwhile, in the mid-1950s, the NPS entered on a ten-year program known as Mission 66 to upgrade facilities, staffing, and resource management throughout the system by the fiftieth anniversary of the NPS in 1966. NPS senior management by then recognized a need for a comprehensive park administrative history program. The program soon foundered because of higher priorities associated with the Mission 66 project and a lack of oversight by Washington and regional officials. Among the best products emerging from this ill-starred undertaking was Charles E. Shedd's *A History of Shiloh National Military Park, Tennessee.*

It would be 1983 before NPS management again recognized the need for and revived the administrative history program. Funding and centralized oversight were provided. Meanwhile, Ronald F. Lee, a senior NPS employee who had entered on duty two score years before as a historian at Shiloh National Military Park and had served as chief historian and recently retired as the director of the Middle Atlantic Region of the NPS, authored in 1973 *The Origin and Evolution of the National Military Park Idea.* Until then neither the NPS nor the public possessed a comprehensive history of our national military parks, which, like our great natural parks such as Yellowstone, are unique to America. Lee's limited but pioneering and much-quoted in-house publication endeavor was invaluable in furthering our understanding of the role of the veterans and their allies in the creation of a vital element of today's NPS.

Then, thanks to Timothy B. Smith, Ph.D., who honed his research, analytical, and writing skills under the tutelage of Dr. John Marszalek at Mississippi State University, addressed this subject in a masterful fashion. Dr. Smith had cut his teeth at Shiloh National Military Park, where he immersed himself in becoming familiar with all facets of the campaign and its personalities.

As I had done at Vicksburg more than forty-five years before, he became fascinated with Shiloh's administrative history, the whys and wherefores of its establishment and development. It was during this time that I became acquainted with Tim Smith, when I visited Shiloh with tour groups. Our discussions frequently focused on the role of veterans in memorializing themselves and their deeds at Shiloh as well as at the other four flagship military parks. I was impressed by the young historian's enthusiastic questions, and I shared with him my knowledge of Shiloh personalities and my perceptions of the park and its history since my first stop there in July 1954 as a visitor.

Therefore, I was not surprised that in 2004 the University of Tennessee Press published *This Great Battlefield of Shiloh: History, Memory, and the Establishment of a Civil War National Military Park* by Dr. Smith. I was impressed by the depth and quality of the research and writing style. Particularly enlightening was the treatment given to the "old soldiers" in the park's development and how they wished the battle actions of themselves and their units interpreted in the monumentation. My long-deceased friends Charles E. Shedd and Ronald Lee would have been justly proud and would have appreciated Smith's publication.

At this time the author discussed with me his plan to expand his horizons. He would build on what he had learned about Shiloh into a comprehensive history focusing on the establishment and development of the five flagship national military parks under the War Department. Impressed by what I heard and long cognizant of the need of NPS management and the interested public for such a publication, I encouraged Dr. Smith to proceed.

My NPS years had satisfied me that such a publication would be invaluable. Although the subject flagship parks were under oversight of the War Department, each was headed by its own three-man commission composed of veterans of the battle. Two of these old soldiers on each commission wore blue and one gray. The commissioners were proud and independently minded. The commissions enjoyed far more autonomy than today's park managers. They were able to put their stamp on how the parks were to be interpreted and monumented.

I was honored, in view of my more than half a century of interest in the administrative history of the NPS, especially that of the War Department parks, when Dr. Smith asked if I would consider preparing a foreword for *The Golden Age of Battlefield Preservation: The Decade of the 1890s and the Establishment of America's First Five Military Parks.* I asked to review a draft manuscript. Upon reviewing the manuscript, my response was an enthusiastic yes.

Smith provides a masterful overview of the dynamics leading to the establishment of these parks. Our nation's greatest nineteenth-century generation was more than twenty-five years removed from the four years when they stood tall. A number had become leaders in politics and business, and they desired to set aside national military parks to commemorate themselves, their long gone comrades, and the war as they saw it. How they did this was as remarkable then as it is today. Smith addresses the administrative and developmental history of the five flagship parks in an informative manner without overwhelming his audience in detail and minutia. We get to know the movers and shakers whose contributions shaped how the NPS and other park systems, both here and abroad, have looked and continue to look, and how the parks were planned, interpreted, and developed. The story of these 1890s military parks will enlighten and appeal to a much broader audience than the Civil War and parks communities.

I wish that *The Golden Age of Battlefield Preservation* had been available back when I joined the NPS family. It would have given me an invaluable crash course in the background and evolution of America's military parks as well as a perspective on how we interpret, protect, and preserve this important facet of our heritage today.

Edwin C. Bearss
*Historian Emeritus*
*National Park Service*

# PREFACE

STANDING IN THE middle of the famous Sunken Road at Shiloh National Military Park, the group asked why the road was not sunken today. I explained to them that there was no contemporary evidence that the road was sunken at the time of the battle, that 1880s- and 1890s-era photos show the road relatively flat, and that the term "Sunken" had not even appeared in Shiloh literature until the 1880s. Even with all the evidence, the entire group still exhibited a confused and perplexed look, as if they were thinking, "But it's *called* the Sunken Road!" Then I told them, "And, you know the old joke—every battlefield has to have a sunken road, a church, a peach orchard, a wheat field, a bloody something, and . . ." A hearty chuckle ran through the crowd, and it was as if I could see lightbulbs coming on inside their heads.

It is a joke of course, but there is some truth to it. Granted, Civil War battles had been fought on regular land that had been farmed, cleared, and planted with orchards and crops and contained churches, residences, and other structures. And sadly, so much blood was shed in many battles of that war that it did run into creeks and stand in ponds. But there is still a sense that when developing these first battlefields, park creators worked together, playing off each other's ideas, and there is a tinge of suspicion that the veterans preserving those battlefields may have competed with one another—a kind of "my sunken road is deeper than your sunken road" effect. The results may not have distorted history, but they may have produced minor myths such as belief in the existence of a multi-foot-deep sunken road at Shiloh.

The enlightening experience in Shiloh's sunken road exhibits many interesting attitudes, such as the desire for a good story and the necessity to reconcile what we see today with what happened during the Civil War. Most notably, however, it shows the general public's interest in how these battlefields came about. Who built them? When did all this happen? Why are they here? Modern Americans seem to be interested in this avenue of history, and academia has also turned its attention to the matter. Working at Shiloh, I became pleasantly surprised at the interest of battlefield trekkers and even common visitors in the story of how Shiloh National Military Park came to be. And reactions to my Shiloh establishment study, *This Great Battlefield of Shiloh*, have been rather heartening, showing a deep interest on the part of modern Americans in battlefield preservation of the past.

This book seeks to build on that interest and help answer the questions many visitors have today. But to do so, there are a few words of explanation that need to be given about organization and structure. There is no good way to organize a book of this nature. I have chosen to deal with each park individually after a chronological chapter that places the work on the individual battlefields in context. As a result, there is admittedly some general repetition because the five parks were similar in many ways and were constructed in related manners. Likewise, much of the activity occurred at the same time. The only conceivable alternatives would be either to treat the subject in a purely chronological fashion or in a topical manner, both of which would require the reader to jump back and forth between five different parks—and more importantly between five different commissions made up of numerous characters—as events occurred simultaneously all over the nation. That seemed too much to ask of the reader. I am firmly convinced that the majority of those interested in this book will be those who come to the topic from a specific park background and will want to read primarily about that park. I also believe there is enough uniqueness in each park to make each different chapter new to the reader and thus not so repetitious. I can only hope the reader will agree.

Likewise, I have chosen to study only the veteran commissions and the establishment phases of each battlefield rather than the entire histories of each park. The 1933 transfer of all five parks to the National Park Service thus seems to be a perfect stopping point. Such a view will spare the reader of later monotonous maintenance and administrative history in what is already, by definition, a rather tedious topic. It is my contention that the commission years were the formative years of each park, and while new developments have occurred at each site since then, the original veteran commissions formulated the main structure and nature of each park early in the parks' history. And that the veteran-dominated commission era at each park was the strongest memorialization period also needs no explanation.

With those parameters set, then, there are several themes developed in this book that need illumination. One revolves around the memory and reconciliation argument so prevalent in today's Civil War historiography. Ranging from the argument that the two sections rejoined only in the 1890s over racial issues to the equally important assertion that not all in the North and South were reconciled even in the 1890s, this school of research has produced important and interesting results that will help shape our own memory of the war. This book seeks to look at the first five military parks' role in the process and heavily leans toward the reconciliation school of thought. Although there was undoubtedly continuing animosity over the war, there was also undoubtedly much reconciliation taking place, and I argue that the military parks were central to that phenomenon. In fact, commemoration was the common denominator of all the parks. There is no doubt that a feeling of brotherhood and reconciliation permeated the memorialization and remembrance activities the veterans performed on their battlefields.

Although subscribing to the reconciliationist school, this book, as part of a growing subfield of battlefield preservation, wanders from that parent thesis in several important ways. Some historians such as David Blight and Edward Linenthal fault the early veterans for taking too narrow a view of the Civil War and preserving the battlefields only as military conflicts and not as racial, cultural, or social battlegrounds as well. The National Park Service is even now fighting this battle once again, but in the 1890s, the modern context was not in existence. These historians argue that the reconciliation of the 1890s was a result of a retrenchment from racial advances in the Civil War and Reconstruction. With a step back from these cultural advances, Civil War veterans were not going to emphasize those aspects, but rather honed in on the militaristic honor and glory on which both sides could agree. Thus this book argues that, yes, what the veterans produced was an editorial on their times, emphasizing the militaristic and not the social, but that it was also a highly advantageous and successful embryonic start at battlefield preservation. The fact that it did not reach full maturity initially does not mean that the entire period must be disregarded as a failure or as unimportant. Such an attitude would be synonymous with branding the foundational period of our United States government as a morbid failure just because it did not settle the issue of slavery, which had to be dealt with numerous times in later decades and finally in the Civil War. In the 1890s, the nation was simply not interested in a discussion of the racial legacy of the Civil War. But what the veterans did in terms of preservation in the 1890s would be impossible today; they laid the firm groundwork that has been refined through the years, and is even still being refined today, into our collective memory of the Civil War. Our modern memory of the Civil War could not, and did not, develop over night or even over a decade. It has literally taken more than a century. Without the veterans' actions in the 1890s, it would have been much more difficult today to be where we are in the evolution of Civil War memory. They laid the foundation upon which modern preservationists as well as modern academics build.

A second theme is an interest in the people who actually built and preserved the battlefields—from Congress to the veteran commissioners. Rather than studying the philosophy behind the process and battlefield preservation theory, I seek to look at the people and the process itself and see how and why it worked. Admittedly, the veteran generation's papers (what few of them there are) and speeches are normally dry and administrative in nature, but perhaps readers can gain a sense of the men who built the parks. If intricate personality descriptions are not available, then I hope that at least the passion with which they preserved their battlefields will become evident, because it was these men, I argue, who literally institutionalized, physically on the ground, what was important at each site. We are still today working off of the interpretations that these veterans fashioned with their emphasis on places such as the Hornet's Nest at Shiloh and Little Round Top at Gettysburg.

The major theme of this book, however, must be battlefield preservation (or, in some cases, the lack thereof) and how the 1890s-era parks fit into the overall context of the conservation movement that began during the war itself and is still going on today. I argue that the corner that was turned in 1890 with the establishment of America's first national military park was a watershed event. The pre-1890 Gettysburg style of commemoration, which was one-sided, divisive, and state-based, was shelved in preference for a drastically different federal effort, which was inclusive of both sides (if not of all society) and helped reunite the sections. And the 1890s effort was the epitome of the physical preservation movement. We must remember that only five battlefields were preserved in the 1890s, and those at varying levels. But we also must realize that these 1890s-era battlefields were the climax of battlefield preservation in America. Everything that has resulted since then has been marred by social and economic factors beyond preservationists' control, but fortunately those obstacles have not stopped preservationists through the years.

We are still fighting to save battlefields today, just as our forefathers in the effort did over one hundred years ago. And what we do now is all based on the foundation they set in place in the 1890s. As we go about our efforts to preserve, administer, and broaden our understanding of the Civil War, we would do well to remember the veterans' concerns and actions as we carry on their work today. Although the veteran generation did not have all the answers, admittedly made some wrong choices, and took too narrow a view of the Civil War, no decision on any battlefield should ever be made without first asking the question of what the veterans would have done in the same situation. We owe that much to them. Chickamauga, Shiloh, Gettysburg, and the many other battlefields are not our parks; they were and still are the veterans' parks. We are mere stewards of them. After all, they paid for them with their own blood.

# ACKNOWLEDGMENTS

NO HISTORIAN WORKS in a vacuum, particularly when writing about such a diverse topic as five national parks. Many people from many different places have supported this project and have only made it better. Any remaining weakness in fact or interpretation is strictly my own.

The staffs of numerous institutions have aided in my research. The people who work at repositories such as the Library of Congress and the Tennessee State Library and Archives are a treasure. Particular thanks must go to the staff of the National Archives and Records Administration, whom I worried to no end to find obscure documents and files. Their professionalism and courtesy are part of what makes research and writing such fun. Others likewise made material available to me, in particular Christopher Waldrep, who has published a study of memory and race relations at Vicksburg.

Also highly deserving of thanks is the special cadre of friends and former coworkers in the National Park Service who not only administer these sites with a passion and devotion similar to that of the veterans who established them but also took time from their busy schedules to aid my research, help round up the wonderful illustrations, and look over various drafts of the book. Dr. Richard Sellars, who is working on a cultural history of the National Park Service, has been a great adviser and is always ready to share any material he comes across. Jim Ogden at Chickamauga and Chattanooga provided much insight into his park, opened the park files for my research, and came to my rescue by providing several great illustrations. Elizabeth Joyner courteously facilitated my research at Vicksburg, while Virginia DuBowy aided in collecting images for the book. My colleague at Shiloh, Stacy Allen, made beneficial comments on Shiloh's history in an earlier draft. Greg Goodell at Gettysburg guided me through the vast Gettysburg archives and collections and provided several images, while Scott Hartwig and John Heiser answered questions and located material for me. Gettysburg licensed guide Garry Adelman read the Gettysburg chapter and caught quite a few misinterpretations of the actions there. Ted Alexander at Antietam opened his research files and provided very beneficial newspaper material he was even then in the process of copying. Perhaps the most thanks should go to Susan Trail, superintendent at Monocacy National Battlefield, who made her raw dissertation research material from the National Archives available to me. I think the way she put it was: "There is plenty work to do without reinventing the wheel." Her generosity, as well as her dissertation, greatly aided the Antietam chapter.

Making the book-writing process enjoyable are the historian friends that read and critiqued the manuscript. Dr. John F. Marszalek courteously and courageously reads everything I write, and somehow never complains but always does so with the eagerness and tact that is truly illustrative of a mentor and friend. The ever-publishing Steve Woodworth, who had his own deadlines and research activities, likewise courteously took time to read through the manuscript and provide many useful comments.

Two National Park Service stalwarts, however, deserve special thanks. Terry Winschel has been a true friend and mentor through the years. He offered keen insights into the park preservation movements, provided a lot of good material, fact-checked the Vicksburg chapter, and then served as a reader for the University of Tennessee Press. They don't make 'em any better than Terry.

Ed Bearss, who perhaps knows more about the history of the parks than anyone else, generously allowed me to pick his brain for several hours and also went through the book in manuscript form. He also served as a reader for the University of Tennessee Press and kindly wrote the foreword to the book. Ed is a national treasure.

Working with the University of Tennessee Press has again been a pleasure. Jennifer Siler's outstanding team of Scot Danforth, Gene Adair, Stan Ivester, and Tom Post, along with freelance copyeditor George Roupe, is among the best in the business.

God has truly blessed me with such a loving and caring family, for which I cannot give enough thanks. My parents, George and Miriam Smith, continue to support my every endeavor with love and encouragement, as do my favorite in-laws, Bennie and Barbara Castleman. I could notd ream of a sweeter, more beautiful, or more loving wife than Kelly, who supports and loves me in whatever direction my professional career takes. And I thank her for having the most blessed little bundle of joy in the world.

Mary Kate Smith, to whom I have dedicated this book, only recently discovered America, and thus was not around for most of the research and writing. Still, she has brought more joy than I ever could have imagined and, at less than a year old, is already helping dad on other projects.

Timothy B. Smith
*Adamsville, Tennessee*

# INTRODUCTION
## *The Context of Civil War Battlefield Preservation*

ALL OVER THE United States, groups of every shape and size are fighting, scratching, begging, and borrowing to preserve Civil War battlefields. The Siege and Battle of Corinth Commission, the Iuka Battlefield Commission, the Friends of Raymond, the Brices Cross Roads National Battlefield Commission, the Mississippi Civil War Battlefield Commission, the Mississippi Department of Archives and History—all are hard at work and represent such efforts only in the state of Mississippi. Many national organizations are intensely laboring there as well, entities such as the National Park Service, the Civil War Preservation Trust, and The Conservation Fund. And the example of Mississippi is illustrative of other states as well. Since battlefield conservation defeats in the early 1990s and the resulting boom in preservation consciousness, millions of Americans seem to be rekindling a long-lost belief in the need to preserve America's hallowed ground.

Yet there was a time in the not-too-distant history of the United States when battlefield preservation was in its prime. Four generations of conservation have existed since the Civil War. The first was a disjoined and purely local attempt at monumenting and preserving isolated scenes of conflict. Then the "Golden Age" of Civil War battlefield preservation took place in the decade of the 1890s. Unfortunately, the next wave of protection did not occur until the late 1920s and 1930s, when it was already too late to properly save the fields of conflict. The most modern attempt is a century late but doing what it can to preserve and protect.

In the years during and after the Civil War until 1890, veterans and local citizens marked several important sites such as the Round Forest at Stones River, the Vicksburg surrender site, Henry House Hill at Manassas, and even remote Pea Ridge in northwest Arkansas. Although not specifically built for preservation purposes, silent national cemeteries also marked the sites of many battlefields. The battlefield that received the most attention in this period, not surprisingly, was Gettysburg, where a memorial association oversaw the marking of that site in a precursor to what would come later. But even at Gettysburg, the phenomenon was primarily non-Federal, non-Confederate, and non-reconciliatory.

The shift from the Gettysburg style of commemoration to what came in the 1890s was thus a major turning point. The Golden Age of Civil War battlefield preservation took place in the decade of the 1890s. Several factors came together to produce a once-in-a-lifetime opportunity in which the old battlefields could properly be saved. These factors included veterans returning to the fields to document what had happened, the opportunity to preserve almost pristine fields that had not yet experienced the development that would later come in the second industrial revolution, and massive government support from Congress and state legislatures dominated by veterans. Under an overarching umbrella of sectional reconciliation, the 1890s saw five battlefields set aside as parks—Chickamauga-Chattanooga, Antietam, Shiloh, Gettysburg, and Vicksburg—and today they are considered the biggest and best preserved. More importantly, these parks were created with federal monies for *both* sides and thus were strongly reconciliatory in intent and exemplified an institutionalized interpretation of each battle, which is still primarily applied today.

Unfortunately, budget constraints and fiscal responsibility prevented the veteran generation from completing its work. The next wave of preservation did not occur until the late 1920s and 1930s, when it was already too late to save the fields of conflict. By that time, growing cities and towns had taken their toll, and there was less of each battlefield to preserve. There was also less emphasis on and support for preservation from nonveteran legislators in both Congress and statehouses. There were also fewer surviving veterans to mark important positions on the battlefields, and those who were still around were aged men whose mental faculties were not always crisp and clear. The result was a series of much smaller, less monumented, and highly urbanized parks such as Fredericksburg and Spottsylvania, Kennesaw Mountain, Petersburg, Stones River, and Fort Donelson.

Today, many groups are trying to remedy a situation that only the veterans themselves could have prevented in the 1890s and early 1900s. Numerous small local battlefield commissions are struggling to buy land, and national organizations are lending their considerable weight to the effort, but their efforts today can never equal what was done in the 1890s when all the factors lined up to produce unmatched success.

Just as modern preservation groups are becoming interested in Civil War battlefields again, the idea of memory tied to battlefield preservation is also becoming more important to historians. A vast new field devoted to memory is gaining popularity, with Michael Kammen's *Mystic Chords of Memory: The Transformation of Tradition in American Culture* (New York, 1991) and John Bodnar's *Remaking America: Public Memory, Commemoration, and Patriotism in the Twentieth Century* (Princeton, NJ, 1992) providing context for further study. Regarding Civil War memory specifically, G. Kurt Piehler's *Remembering War the American Way* (Washington, DC, 1995) offers a broad examination of how our nation has looked at its wars, with David Blight's *Race and Reunion: The Civil War in American Memory* (Cambridge, MA, 2001) serving as the standard-bearer for the Civil War years and John R. Neff's recent *Honoring The Civil War Dead: Commemoration and the Problem of Reconciliation* (Lawrence, KS, 2005) shedding light on a different aspect of the reconciliation thesis and reminding us all that there was still animosity between the sections even during the 1890s and the wave of reconciliation sweeping the nation. Other recent works by William Blair and Alice Fahs have contributed to the discussion as well.

A subfield of this new Civil War memory discipline is the history of battlefield preservation. For years, only the National Park Service was interested in such study. Various park administrative histories and Ronald F. Lee's *The Origin and Evolution of the National Military Park Idea* (Washington, DC, 1973) provided site-specific histories and a short overall analysis. In more recent years, academia has become more involved, with Edward T. Linenthal's *Sacred Ground: Americans and Their Battlefields* (Urbana, IL, 1991) first examining how the United States has used its battlegrounds as memorial tools.

The past few years have seen an explosion in battlefield preservation-related research. Michael W. Panhorst's dissertation, "Lest We Forget: Monuments and Memorial Sculpture in National Military Parks on Civil War Battlefields, 1861–1917" (1988), as well as Mary Munsell Abroe's dissertation "'All the Profound Scenes': Federal Preservation of Civil War Battlefields, 1861–1990" (1996), shed light on the military parks and their monumentation. Richard Sellars's "Pilgrim Places: Civil War Battlefields, Historic Preservation, and America's First National Military Parks, 1863–1900," published in *CRM: The Journal of Heritage Stewardship* (Winter 2005), develops the background of the first five battlefields preserved in America. This important article has since been published in booklet form as *Pilgrim Places: Civil War Battlefields, Historic Preservation, and America's First National Military Parks, 1863–1900* (Fort Washington, PA, 2005).

Individual park studies are represented by Vicksburg park historian Terry Winschel's "Stephen D. Lee and the Making of an American Shrine" in the *Journal of Mississippi History* (2001): 17–32, which offers insight into Vicksburg's establishment, as does Christopher Waldrep's *Vicksburg's Long Shadow: The Civil War Legacy of Race and Remembrance* (New York, 2005). My own *This Great Battlefield of Shiloh: History, Memory, and the Establishment of a Civil War National Military Park* (Knoxville, TN, 2004) offers insight into Shiloh's history, while a later volume, *The Untold Story of Shiloh: The Battle and the Battlefield* (Knoxville, TN, 2006), delves deeper into some of the topics broached in the earlier book. Monocacy National Battlefield superintendent Susan Trail's dissertation, "Remembering Antietam: Commemoration and Preservation of a Civil War Battlefield" (2005) covers the Antietam park's history. James Kaser's case study of the 21st Ohio at Chickamauga, *At the Bivouac of Memory: History, Politics, and the Battle of Chickamauga* (New York, 1996), provides an interesting look at that park. Gettysburg of course has received much attention, including Thomas Desjardin's *These Honored Dead: How the Story of Gettysburg Shaped American Memory* (Cambridge, MA, 2003), Amy Kinsel's dissertation "'From These Honored Dead': Gettysburg in American Culture, 1863–1938" (1992), and Jim Weeks's *Gettysburg: Memory, Market, and an American Shrine* (Princeton, NJ, 2003).

Although Herman Hattaway and A. J. Meek in *Gettysburg to Vicksburg: The Five Original Civil War Battlefield Parks* (Columbia, MO, 2001) had a tremendous opportunity to explore the subject, they rather produced an illustrated history that unfortunately does not evenly address the history of each park and is riddled with errors. Fortunately, there are currently numerous other historians working on specific battlefield histories, examining how their individual stories helped build a collective memory of the Civil War.

Thus support for battlefield preservation is gaining momentum both in preservation circles as well as academia, but that support is underfunded in today's world. We can only look back fondly to the days when battlefield preservation was the national trend, when Americans grandly honored a passing generation for its accomplishments and when the Golden Age of battlefield preservation produced results the likes of which we will never see again.

❧ • ❧

The decade of the 1890s saw amazing changes in the United States that benefited some sections and races but were hindrances to others. The 1890s saw a budding reconciliation of the North and South, split in ideology since before the Civil War and literally since 1860. As tempers cooled after the fact, as old men reconciled, and as younger generations took up new issues, the old wounds of the Civil War began to fade into memory as the North and the South developed new issues other than the racial questions that had so divided them. White Americans thus began displaying unity while emphasizing the courage, bravery, and honor of Civil War soldiers with monuments, statues, and joint reunions. But the chief symbols of this reconciliatory and commemorative era were the military parks. "These Military Parks," the veterans declared, "are not designed to commemorate either victory or defeat, but as monuments to the heroism of the American citizen soldier during the most trying period of our Nation's existence, and as object lessons of the struggles for the maintenance of the Union, and their cost." Of course, not all aspects of American life demonstrated this reconciliation so blatantly as the military parks. The downside for blacks was that the modest gains made since the Civil War were left behind in the effort to get beyond the disruptive issues over race. Decades of segregation and racism thus emerged. Likewise, recent research also indicates that Americans still felt the tinges of animosity when celebrating the dead, such as on Memorial Day. But as far as celebrating their mutual history and increasing nationalism was concerned, growing Northern and Southern unity was evidenced nowhere better than on the military parks established in the decade of the 1890s.[1]

The 1890s was the best and only real opportunity the nation had to preserve their battlefields effectively. Such a unified movement was not possible before 1890, with all the lingering hatred left over from the war itself and Reconstruction. And the time was also fast approaching when battlefield preservation, on the scale it was done in the 1890s, would be an impossibility. Congressmen who in the 1870s and 1880s were drawn into vehement sectional Reconstruction debates were suddenly loosed from those differences in the 1890s, and their impending departure from this life was very much on their minds. By 1890, the window of opportunity for reconciliation had opened, but it would close due to the passing of that generation in a very short time—in a matter of only a few years.

Unfortunately, the veteran generation mostly missed that opportunity. There was a brief chance to preserve many of the battlefields, but the veterans only preserved five sites. They could have accomplished so much more that is now impossible, despite the present generation's efforts. Fiscal responsibility ate away at any chance to preserve all the major battlefields, but the total cost would have been proportionately less then than it has turned out to be now. In the long run, spending more money in the 1890s would have saved many of the battlefields that are simply too expensive to preserve now.

Fortunately, the veterans did not completely miss their chance. Led by pioneering battlefield preservation thinkers such as nationally known newspaper correspondent Henry Van Ness Boynton and War Department battlefield authority George B. Davis, the veterans were very cognizant of the fact that their generation was quickly fading away. One battlefield preservationist remarked that "the work of restoring these battlefields has not been undertaken too soon. Those who have personal knowledge of positions and movements are rapidly passing off the stage." The aging soldiers also had a definite desire to preserve and mark the battlefields while they still retained their mental faculties and memories. "Time and its influences are rapidly clouding the memories of the participants and effacing and destroying the present existing evidences of their patient toil and heroic accomplishments," noted one veteran of the Union Army of the Tennessee. In the 1890s, the veterans realized that if they did not do it then, no one would be around later to mark the battlefields accurately. Their history would be lost forever. If the veterans were to tell their story, they had to do it then.[2]

At that time, the veterans had a brief opportunity to preserve almost pristine battlefields. By 1890, many changes had occurred on the fields, to be sure, but none of a lasting or destructive nature. One Civil War veteran and park builder remarked that the field of Chickamauga, "under the ownership of the unprogressive natives, remained practically unchanged." All the battlefields were, in the 1890s, still very much untouched, but that would not be the case for long. Unknown to the veterans, a time of economic and industrial expansion would soon be sweeping the nation. The second industrial revolution would see many rural people move to cities and towns, and urbanization was the key threat to battlefields. Most Civil War battles had been fought around cities and towns, because the armies were primarily fighting over transportation routes. Of course, most transportation routes crossed in cities and towns. Expansion and urbanization during World War I would forever destroy the battlefields. Industrialization and the mobility made possible by the automobile also ate away at the pristine condition of the battlefields. If the battlefields were to be saved in totality, they had to be protected in the 1890s, before the wave of a second industrial revolution swept over the fields of conflict.[3]

Equally important, the veterans also had to save the battlefields at a time when appropriations would be comparatively forthcoming. Even in the reconciliation-rich and patriotic 1890s, some opposition to spending massive amounts of money on battlefields developed in Congress. But it was still a time when Civil War veterans dominated Congress (who would fund the parks) and state legislatures (who would appropriate money for monuments to their states' units). The veterans realized that future generations might not share their affinity for their fields of conflict and might not spend the necessary money to preserve them. Thus it was a critical time to appropriate money for battlefield preservation.[4]

These three factors all combined to make the 1890s the optimal time to preserve Civil War battlefields. Of course, the men could not see into the future and know what would come and how any changes would affect the battlefields, but they were reasonably sure that as time passed, less emphasis would be placed on the battlegrounds. And they were certain that their generation would soon pass, thus taking a major primary source away from preservationists. As a result, the veterans saved five battlefields in varying degrees, but in the long run, it is unfortunate that they did not do more. Still, the veteran generation is to be applauded for its preservation work. Indeed, what the veterans accomplished on just five battlefields far exceeds anything later generations have done or can do, and serves as the basis for modern historic preservation policies.

The work of the veterans was clearly a labor of love. The old soldiers wanted to save their battlefields for a number of reasons, not the least of which was to memorialize their fallen comrades, some of whom still lay buried on the battlefields in question. "There is nothing in this broad land of ours more sacred than the soil which has been wet with the blood of its patriotic sons," one veteran wrote. They also wanted to preserve the battle sites in order to allow future generations a glimpse into the battles they had fought. Other reasons were to equip the modern military with actual battlefields for study, to commemorate the actions of their particular armies, and to offer future historians the best source of all in writing the various histories of the engagements.[5]

The process by which the veterans desired to preserve the battlefields was also clear in their minds. They wanted the battlefields preserved in the state and configuration of the war-era fields, and any modern construction to provide access, they argued, should be kept to a minimum and should not alter the terrain or historical remnants of the battles. One veteran argued, "It is not intended that these parks will be ornamental pleasure grounds. The real object is to restore these historic fields to substantially the conditions they were in at the time of the battles." Significantly, the last thing the veterans wanted was for the battlefields to be landscaped and made into recreational parks. One veteran, in fact, reminded his hearers in a speech that

> a park for health-seekers, for esthetics or pleasure-seekers, with fine drives and shady walks, beautiful flowers, and flowing fountains, can be made any-where with money. But there is the one and only place in the world where there can be a "Chickamauga." There will be no place here for the gaudy display of rich equipages and show of wealth; no place for lovers to bide tryst; no place for pleasure-seekers or loungers. The hosts that in the future come to this grand Park will come rather with feelings of awe and reverence. Here their better natures will be aroused; here they will become imbued with grand and lofty ideas; with courage and patriotism; with devotion to duty and love of country.

To the veterans, the battlefields were hallowed ground that deserved to be treated as such.[6]

An outgrowth of this desire to restore and preserve the battlefields in their battle-era configurations was the use of tablets and monuments. The veteran commissions that built the parks wanted to keep the land as close as possible to the battle terrain. But they went further than that and placed hundreds of tablets and monuments on the fields. Some argue that these commemorative features take away from the Civil War–era battlefield look, but one must remember that these veterans were preserving the battlefields as they looked on the day or days of battle. Such a desire would include restoring or recreating thousands upon thousands of soldiers on the battlefields. Replacing the soldiers themselves on the various lines of battle was of course impossible, but the next best thing was to commemorate those lines of battle with monuments and markers. Veterans of Vicksburg declared: "The stage setting of the implements of war, for which this obsolete ordnance serves now only a suggestion, and the shafts and blocks of granite and marble that everywhere attract the vision of the visitor are, it is to be hoped, a proper suggestion, or so many sad reminders, of the hot contest that covered these hills and valleys forty-four years ago." To the veterans, those monuments, tablets, and artillery pieces represented the soldiers that had fought those battles and thus were an inherent part of returning the battlefields to the war-time look and feel. That is why so many soldiers held their monuments and markers in such high esteem. The monuments were the reincarnated soldiers, honoring not only those still alive to place them, but also memorializing those who were killed on those exact spots.[7]

The veterans also wanted the parks to have certain other traits. They deeply wanted the parks to be a joint venture between Northerners and Southerners. The budding reconciliation being felt in the 1890s would be hollow in terms of preserving battlefields if both sides were not involved. Therefore, from the start, the Federal veterans asked for, and frankly insisted upon, Confederate help—all without reopening the wounds of the causes of the war. "These parks will be devoted strictly to the illustration of the great struggles which rendered them famous," one veteran argued. In the same all-inclusive vein, the original builders of the parks desired the participation of states, which was key to making the parks a united effort.[8]

All together, the desire of the veterans is clear; they wanted the parks to be reconciliatory items, object lessons, patriotic icons, and most of all, memorials to the living and the dead that had fought in the war. And that generation deserves all the honor heaped upon them, as well as the courtesy of taking their desires into account today. The battlefields of the 1890s, unlike most others, were developed, built, and maintained by the veterans, and modern policy makers would do well to remember that fact. Perhaps Ed Bearss has said it best: "No Park Service employee was ever shot at on those grounds."[9]

So the decade of the 1890s was the most important period in the battlefield preservation movement, the Golden Age of battlefield preservation. It came at a time when all the elements lined up to produce unmatched possibilities, and the veterans took advantage of that opportunity by turning the corner in a federally funded, two-sided effort at preserving five battlefields. In the process, the veterans institutionalized the accepted memory of the Civil War that is still primarily being applied even today.

Despite a limited vision, the veteran generation did excellent work, indeed better work than is even comprehensible today. Modern preservationists, as admirable as they are, can never preserve pristine battlefields, can never acquire enough money to completely save even one major battlefield, and can never accurately locate all the lines of battle on a specific field. The optimal time to preserve battlefields was in the 1890s, when a combined series of events allowed the veterans themselves to spawn the Golden Age of Civil War battlefield preservation.

# 1

## BATTLEFIELDS, CEMETERIES, AND EARLY PRESERVATION

### *The Prelude to the 1890s-Era Parks, 1861–1890*

THE CIVIL WAR left thousands of battlefields in the United States, and even some abroad. Most battlefields had uncommon and almost unremembered names such as Bulltown, Snicker's Gap, and Inman Hollow, while other names such as Shiloh, Vicksburg, and Gettysburg ring with mysticism and honor. The climactic events in the American Civil War cannot be looked at in a vacuum, but there were several dominant battles that determined the outcome of the war. In fact, most historians, if asked to enumerate the most important engagements in the Civil War, would probably agree on ten or so of the most salient battles fought between 1861 and 1865. Obviously, the veterans themselves thought some battles more important than others and preserved five battlefields for future generations. It is no coincidence that the five battlefields preserved in the 1890s were five of the most important, if not the five *most* important, among all Civil War battles.

In April 1862, the first big battle in the war came at Shiloh. As the Union Army of the Tennessee awaited the arrival of the Union Army of the Ohio at Pittsburg Landing, Tennessee, Confederates of the Army of the Mississippi struck in a surprise attack on April 6, 1862. Catching the Federals off guard, General Albert Sidney Johnston and the Confederates drove northward all day long on April 6, only to be halted in front of Pittsburg Landing at nightfall. Major General Ulysses S. Grant tenaciously defended the landing throughout the day, thus allowing an avenue of conjunction for his and Major General Don Carlos Buell's army from Nashville. With Buell's arrival, Grant counterattacked on April 7, driving the Confederates off the battlefield, but only after vicious fighting. Producing more than 23,000 casualties, the Battle of Shiloh doomed nearby Corinth, Mississippi, and its important Confederate railroads, thus setting the stage for farther Union movement into the Mississippi valley. Casualties at Shiloh totaled more than in all of America's wars to that date.[1]

Later in 1862 came America's bloodiest day. After defeating several Union attempts to reach the Confederate capital at Richmond, Virginia, General Robert E. Lee and his Confederate Army of Northern Virginia advanced into Maryland in September 1862. Although spread out, Lee was able to concentrate before meeting Major General George B. McClellan's Army of the Potomac on the eastern outskirts of Sharpsburg, Maryland. On the banks of the Antietam Creek raged an all-day battle on September 17, 1862, one that produced more than 23,000 casualties in that single day. The results of Antietam were significant. Not only was Lee forced to withdraw into Virginia, but President Abraham Lincoln was also able to use the Union victory as a reason to issue his Emancipation Proclamation, which freed all slaves in areas still in rebellion against the United States. That event, coming on the heels of the dramatic thwarting of Lee's invasion, served to transform the war into a moral crusade against slavery, which helped reduce the chance of foreign intervention on the side of the Confederacy.[2]

During the next summer came dual events that, if they did not cause mortal wounds to the Confederacy, wounded the South to a point that defeat was likely. In November 1862, Grant and his Army of the Tennessee began their push southward into the Mississippi countryside, intent on sweeping the Mississippi valley clean of Confederate resistance. After some six efforts to reach Vicksburg, the Confederate Gibraltar, Grant was little closer to taking Vicksburg than when he had begun. But beginning with a dramatic crossing of the Mississippi River south of Vicksburg in late April 1863, Grant led a brilliant campaign for the next three months, one that saw five pitched battles and a siege. The Battle of Champion Hill on May 16, 1863, doomed Vicksburg, to which Grant laid siege only days later. Finally running out of food and time, Lieutenant General John C. Pemberton surrendered his Confederate garrison of nearly 30,000 men on July 4, 1863. The surrender opened the Mississippi River to Union traffic along its entire length, cut off the entire trans-Mississippi from the Confederacy, and effectively took Mississippi out of the war.[3]

Meanwhile, the largest clash in the Civil War raged at Gettysburg, Pennsylvania, during those turbulent first few days of July 1863. After yet another series of startling victories, Robert E. Lee had determined the time was once again right to invade the North. Such a maneuver would produce a Southern victory on Northern soil, and perhaps relieve some of the pressure on Vicksburg. Lee advanced into Pennsylvania in late June, followed by the Army of the Potomac under Major General George Gordon Meade. The two armies clashed on July 1, 1863, west of Gettysburg, and the battle spread to the east and south as both armies concentrated around the small town. Heavy fighting took place on July 2, and the climactic event, the massive Confederate assault on July 3, ended the battle with the Union victorious. Producing more than 53,000 casualties, Gettysburg marked the geographic high watermark of the Confederacy. Lee had to retreat once again back into Virginia with a broken army. Never again would the Confederate Army of Northern Virginia go on the strategic offensive.[4]

The fall of 1863 saw the Confederacy's optimism fading fast. A small flicker of hope returned with the victory of General Braxton Bragg's Army of Tennessee on the banks of the Chickamauga Creek in northwestern Georgia on September 19–20, 1863. Defeating Major General William S. Rosecrans's Army of the Cumberland in two days of vicious fighting, Bragg followed the retreating Federals to Chattanooga and laid siege to the city. The half-starved and morale-deficient Army of the Cumberland received a major infusion of life from reinforcements in the form of the Army of the Tennessee and the Army of the Potomac. Also arriving in Chattanooga were new commanders. Grant came from his Vicksburg victories, took command, promptly drove Bragg away, and secured for the Union the gateway to the deep South and Atlanta. The battles of Chickamauga and Chattanooga produced horrific casualties (more than 35,000 at Chickamauga alone), but they more importantly put the Confederates on the defensive once and for all in the pivotal western theater.[5]

There were, of course, many other important battles. The snow-covered ridges of Fort Donelson, Tennessee, in February 1862, the grueling afternoon sun at Corinth, Mississippi, in October 1862, and the trenches filled with ice water at Stones River, Tennessee, in December 1862, all attest to the horrible conditions the soldiers faced on the battlefield. The day-after-day battles of the Peninsula campaign in Virginia in May and June 1862, "Stonewall" Jackson's Valley Campaign in March and April 1862, Grant's Overland Campaign and drive on Richmond in May and June 1864, and the grueling Atlanta Campaign between May and September 1864, all attest to the massive amount of fighting and maneuver in the Civil War. And the charges against the Crater, the Mule Shoe, the Stone Wall, and at Cold Harbor and Franklin all demonstrate the courage and bravery of Civil War soldiers.

In terms of importance, however, five battles stand out for determining the outcome of the war. The largest battle in the Mississippi valley and then the opening of that valley; the turning back of two separate Confederate invasions of the North; and the opening of the door to the interior of the South all stand as the most important battles of the Civil War. It is no wonder that when the veterans decided to preserve their most important battlefields, those were the five they first selected: Shiloh, Antietam, Vicksburg, Gettysburg, and Chickamauga/Chattaooga.

Preservation and remembrance at these battlefields actually began during the Civil War itself. Soldiers placed monuments on several fields to commemorate what had taken place there and to commemorate the dead, a dual theme that would become prevalent in later Civil War remembrance. Soldiers during the war and veterans afterwards pre served battlefields or portions thereof not only in order to save the sites of significant events, but also to memorialize the sacrifice that had taken place there.

In September 1861, Confederates of Colonel Francis Bartow's brigade placed a monument on the Bull Run battlefield to mark the site of his death on July 21, 1861. Soldiers of the 8th Georgia erected a white marble obelisk to commemorate the Georgia politician-soldier. Over one thousand people attended the dedication. Unfortunately, the monument is no longer in existence; it disappeared after the Confederates left the area, and its fate was never determined.[6]

Hundreds of miles to the west, soldiers of Colonel William B. Hazen's Union brigade erected a monument on the battlefield of Stones River, near Murfreesboro, Tennessee, in the spring and early summer of 1863. Hazen's brigade had repelled numerous assaults by the Confederates in the Round Forest and had buried their dead where they fought. As the Army of the Cumberland moved southward, Hazen's men remained to garrison the Murfreesboro area. That summer, they built a memorial to their dead on the spot where they had been buried. A burial vault patterned after an Egyptian mastaba, the monument testified to the memory of the fallen with the inscription that spoke of inspiring "to greater deeds." The oldest surviving Civil War monument still stands at Stones River National Battlefield.[7]

During that same summer of 1863, Federals in Vicksburg, Mississippi, marked the "surrender interview" site at which Grant and Pemberton had met to discuss terms of Confederate capitulation. The Federals took from

*Hazen monument at Stones River. In the summer of 1863, members of Hazen's brigade erected what is now the oldest surviving Civil War monument at Stones River to mark not only their position in the battle but also the burial place for their dead.* Battles and Leaders.

a local stonecutter's shop a marble shaft that had originally been intended to memorialize Vicksburg's Mexican War dead. This monument was somewhat different than earlier memorials, however: it marked the site of a significant event only; there was no memorialization of the dead.[8]

As fascinating as such wartime monumentation is, by far the major action of preservation and remembrance during the Civil War was the establishment of national cemeteries. The War Department began the process of burying the dead and enumerating the plots when the war began. Department and army commanders simply buried the dead, particularly battle casualties, on the ground where they had fought. Primarily private land, these battle-sites-turned-burial-grounds then had to be bought or condemned. In order to legitimize national burial sites on private land, the 37th Congress of the United States passed legislation in an omnibus bill that allowed for national cemeteries as deemed necessary by the president, and Abraham Lincoln signed the bill into law on July 17, 1862. Section 18 gave him the "power, whenever in his opinion it is expedient, to purchase cemetery grounds and cause them to be securely enclosed, to be used as a national cemetery for the soldiers who shall die in the service of the country."[9]

*Vicksburg surrender monument. This simple marble shaft marked the site of the surrender interview at Vicksburg between Ulysses S. Grant and John C. Pemberton. No longer standing on the battlefield, the monument has been replaced with an upright cannon.* Battles and Leaders.

As a result of the 1862 legislation, the Lincoln administration created fourteen national cemeteries that year. Most were set up around Washington, DC, and other troop induction and care centers. Alexandria and Soldiers' Home near the capital and cemeteries at Annapolis, Maryland, Camp Butler, Illinois, and Philadelphia, Pennsylvania, held more soldiers who died of disease and accident than of battle wounds.[10]

Several of the fourteen original cemeteries were on battlefields, however, marking the first time actual sites of conflict were preserved to honor the fallen. The War Department erected a small cemetery at the site of the January 1862 battle of Mill Springs in eastern Kentucky and at Chattanooga, Tennessee, and eventually came to govern more famous ones at Sharpsburg, Maryland, and Gettysburg, Pennsylvania.[11]

The Antietam National Cemetery actually began as a nongovernment effort. It was established by the Antietam National Cemetery Association, which was organized under the laws of the State of Maryland in March 1865 and had board members from the various states that had dead in the cemetery, and funding came from appropriations by those various state legislatures. The association bought land, built an encircling wall, and erected a lodge. The corporation soon found itself in debt, however, and the federal government in 1866 and 1867 began to provide funds for the reburial of Union soldiers, which numbered 4,695 from nineteen different states. A third of the dead were disinterred from the Antietam battlefield, but others came from the battlefields at Monocacy, South Mountain, Harpers Ferry, and several hospital sites in the area.[12]

The War Department finished burying bodies at Antietam National Cemetery on September 4, 1867, and a dedication was held later that month. The cemetery itself was a beautiful nine and a half acres situated inside what had been Confederate lines on a tall hill just east of Sharpsburg. A report described the site: "The grounds are handsomely laid off, partly in a semi-circular form, with a twenty-foot avenue surrounding the whole, and numerous smaller paths intersecting the graves." Later, the massive Private Soldier Monument went up in the center of the cemetery.[13]

The Antietam National Cemetery Association was unable to stay out of debt, even with federal money infused into the project. As a result, Congress directed the secretary of war to take control of the cemetery in

*Antietam National Cemetery. An early view of the beautiful and symmetrical Antietam National Cemetery, showing the Private Soldier Monument rising in the center. Clarke,* New York at Antietam.

1870, although it was not until 1877, when Congress appropriated money to pay the debt of the original commission, that the cemetery became a completely federal venture.[14]

Another of the Civil War–era burial sites was the Chattanooga National Cemetery, established by general order of Major General George H. Thomas on December 25, 1863. Demonstrating the era's desire to preserve and honor simultaneously, Thomas wrote that the memorial cemetery be established "in commemoration of the Battles of Chattanooga, November 23–27, 1863."[15]

In his effort to preserve part of the Chattanooga battlefield, Thomas directed that a small knoll near Orchard Knob be used as the burial ground. The knob, rising a few feet above the plain of Chattanooga, would eventually receive the standard stone wall, lodge, avenues, and decorations of most national cemeteries. Comprising some seventy-five acres originally, the cemetery received the dead not only from Chattanooga, but also from Chickamauga, numerous local burial sites in the vicinity, and even the Atlanta Campaign. By 1870, more than 12,000 Union soldiers were interred at Chattanooga National Cemetery.[16]

Perhaps the climax of Civil War preservation and memorialization was the dedication of the Gettysburg National Cemetery in November 1863. After the momentous battle at Gettysburg in July 1863, a corporation similar to the one at Antietam emerged. Led by David Wills, a Gettysburg attorney, the Soldiers National Cemetery Board of Directors, made up of representatives from every state whose dead were there interred, bought some seventeen acres in August 1863 and began the reburial of Union soldiers. Title for the land was placed in the name of the State of Pennsylvania.[17]

By November 1863, some 3,512 Union soldiers from seventeen states rested in a semicircular pattern around a central hub. On November 19, 1863, the entire nation watched as luminaries assembled for the cemetery dedication. The principal speaker was Edward Everett, but President Abraham Lincoln made "a few appropriate remarks," and in doing so defined for the nation not only why they were fighting, but also why this particular section of land on Cemetery Hill had been preserved and why it was so important. "We have come to dedicate a portion of that field as a final resting-place for those who here gave their lives," Lincoln said, and he went on to call for the nation to continue the fight "that these dead shall not have died in vain." Lincoln's Gettysburg Address legitimized preservation even as it made definitive statements about the future course of the nation.[18]

In the years after the dedication, the cemetery took the form of many national cemeteries, complete with a stone wall, keeper's lodge, pathways, and avenues. In 1869, the corporation marked the site of Lincoln's speech, but the board of directors could not oversee the venture properly. In 1872, the State of Pennsylvania transferred the cemetery grounds to the federal government.[19]

The monuments and cemeteries established by and for soldiers during the Civil War reveal much about what the men thought of their actions. The dual emphasis on memorialization and preservation is evident. The early monuments were primarily placed to honor fallen comrades, with a secondary purpose of marking specific and important sites of battle. Likewise, national cemeteries, grander and more impressive than single monuments, performed the same functions. The cemeteries at Gettysburg, Antietam, and Chattanooga all contained dead from those and surrounding battles, thus celebrating sacrifice in general. At the same time, they were the first efforts at preservation on those battlefields. The building of cemeteries was the first concerted involvement of the federal government in preservation and memorialization on a large scale.[20]

Yet these cemeteries offered more than the tangible commemorative and memorial features; they spoke volumes about the American mindset in the mid-nineteenth century toward the dead, particularly military dead. The parklike, landscaped national cemeteries reflected the general emphasis on parks and suburban cemeteries that offered peaceful and serene silence for the dead and mourners alike. One has to look no farther than the carefully manicured avenues, walks, shrubbery, and patterns of early national cemeteries to see the effects of this growing phenomenon.[21]

More importantly, the Civil War–era national cemeteries showed a developing pattern in American military funerary procedures: that of memorializing individual soldiers. Before the Civil War, military dead were generally memorialized as a group, often with a single monument or marker. The national cemeteries of the 1860s, however, utilized individual plots with individual headboards or grave identifications. Perhaps Thomas B. Van Horne, a chaplain in the United States Army in charge of the Chattanooga National Cemetery, best summed up this developing attitude in his report to Major General George H. Thomas, commanding the Military Division of Tennessee immediately after the war. Van Horne noted that extreme care would be taken to "secure a short military history of every officer and soldier interred in the cemetery whose remains have been identified." "It seems eminently fitting that this should be done," he went on. "It accords with our intense individualism as a people, and with the value we attach to individual life; and it is demanded by the eminent worth of those for whom historic notice would thus be secured."[22]

These patterns of memorialization and preservation on Civil War battlefields spread after the war. Most battlefields of the war were situated in the South, most of which was under only light guard by the Union forces. The war thus precluded any burial work at places such as Pittsburg Landing, Tennessee, and Andersonville, Georgia. The primary Union effort was to win the war; care of the dead would have to come later. Thus, while some areas under secure Federal control, such as Chattanooga, received national cemeteries, it was not until after the war that many other burial grounds on Southern battlefields emerged.

One of these postwar cemeteries was at Vicksburg, Mississippi. Established by order of Major General Thomas J. Wood in 1866, a year after the war ended, Vicksburg National Cemetery originally comprised some forty acres. Terraced and landscaped, the cemetery sat on bluffs overlooking the Mississippi River, on which Confederate batteries had sat during the campaign. By 1869, over fifteen thousand Union dead had been removed to the cemetery from nearby battle sites such as Champion Hill and Port Gibson, as well as faraway places such as Meridian and even sites across the river in Louisiana. The cemetery received the customary lodge and encircling wall, as well as the adorning features such as walks and avenues.[23]

Perhaps the most beautiful and unique of the national cemeteries was the ten-acre site established on the banks of the Tennessee River at Pittsburg Landing, Tennessee. Major General George H. Thomas ordered a cemetery built on the battlefield of Shiloh in 1866. It came to contain more than 3,500 dead from that battlefield as well as other areas along the Tennessee River such as Fort Henry. The Pittsburg Landing National Cemetery contained a wide assortment of regimental burial plots, facilitated by their burial as groups originally on the battlefield. The cemetery also contained an encircling stone wall as well as the customary lodge and avenues and paths. Attesting to the cemetery's beauty, one 1867 visitor described the cemetery as "the handsomest cemetery in the South."[24]

The addition of several major national cemeteries after the war highlighted the need for new legislation to legitimize what had already been done. In many cases, such as at Shiloh and Chattanooga, the dead had been placed on private land. As a result, Congress passed and on February 22, 1867, President Andrew Johnson approved "An Act to Establish and Protect National Cemeteries." The act took the 1862 enabling legislation one step further by allowing and mandating certain measures. Specifically, the bill required that each cemetery be enclosed by a wall and have a lodge. Additionally, the legislation required each cemetery to have "a meritorious and trustworthy superintendent, who shall be selected from enlisted men of the army disabled in service," and that each be inspected annually. The bill also required each cemetery to keep rolls of the dead with military information. Perhaps most importantly, the act allowed the secretary of war to "enter upon and appropriate" needed land if the owners were not willing to sell. These measures thus ensured that each cemetery would be protected and that each deceased soldier would be honored and remembered. Practically, the bill took care of the growing problem of private ownership of cemeteries and legitimized condemnation, which would be a major stepping-stone toward future federal control of battlefields. Because of this act, both the Shiloh and Chattanooga cemeteries were condemned.[25]

In building these national cemeteries, the federal government made one great distinction, however, which would affect future thinking about battlefield preservation. By and large, only Union dead were reinterred in the cemeteries; the Confederate dead would be left on the battlefields or moved (by some entity other than the federal government) to local cemeteries. Regulations required that only veterans of the United States military could be buried in national cemeteries. As Confederates were technically not United States personnel, they were traditionally buried elsewhere, although some exceptions existed. This distinction reveals the early attitude of the federal government toward the Confederate dead; the government viewed Confederates as traitors, revolutionaries, and enemies, and made little effort to memorialize or honor the Confederate dead.

In addition to the federal government's creation of national cemeteries, veterans also began to mark the battlefields—slowly at first but steadily gaining momentum as the years passed. The first postwar monuments to go up on a Civil War battlefield were fittingly at Manassas, where in June 1865, only a few days after the majority of the Confederates had surrendered, Federal veterans placed two sandstone obelisks to commemorate the two battles fought on that ground. One placed on Henry House Hill commemorated the first battle, while another placed near the famous railroad cut memorialized the second and larger engagement. Each honored the dead as well as the living and marked the most significant points on each battlefield.[26]

Union veterans of the cemetery association returned to the Antietam battlefield in 1867 to lay a cornerstone in the national cemetery for a soldier's monument made of white granite. Although the cornerstone went down in September 1867, due to a lack of money the monument was not dedicated until 1880. In the meantime, the twenty-one-foot soldier was taken on tour, most notably at Philadelphia's Centennial Exposition in 1876. After the federal government took over the cemetery and paid its bills, the soldier finally went up in 1880. Set in a guard position, the soldier symbolically watched over the dead and was often referred to as the "American Soldier" or "Antietam Sentinel."[27]

Similar activity began on the Gettysburg battlefield, which by far received the most attention in the immediate aftermath of war. Local citizens chartered the Gettysburg Battlefield Memorial Association in 1864, when the Pennsylvania legislature gave it corporation rights. The charter spelled out the exact preservation and memorialization mandate for the association "to commemorate the great deeds of valor, endurance, and noble sacrifice, and to perpetuate the memory of the heroes." After the war, the State of Pennsylvania appropriated the association three thousand dollars in 1867 and then again in 1868, which the group used to buy three small tracts of land—one on Culp's Hill, one on Cemetery Hill, and one on Little Round Top. The state also provided a legal basis for protection and law enforcement and gave the association authority to condemn land if necessary. Despite the valiant efforts of its officers such as Major General John W. Geary and David McConaughy, however, the association soon faded because of the lack of funding. The latter tried to gain financial support from the various Northern states but failed, and the association went dormant until the late 1870s.[28]

Other work also went on at Gettysburg. In 1867, the 1st Minnesota placed a memorial urn/sepulcher in the Gettysburg National Cemetery where their dead were laid. The most impressive monument in the cemetery, however, was the Soldier's National Monument, placed at the spot Lincoln delivered his famous address. Sixty feet tall, the monument used human figures that symbolized America at its best. Crowning the monument was Liberty, holding the laurel wreath of victory. Surrounding the monument at the bottom were an American soldier, a recorder, a mechanic, and a gatherer, symbolizing War, History, Peace, and Plenty, respectively. Perhaps the most important and pathbreaking monument in the cemetery, however, was dedicated on July 1, 1869, to Major General John F. Reynolds, a Federal corps commander killed at Gettysburg.

The use of a human figure, as at the Antietam and Gettysburg cemeteries, ushered in the idea of individualism and humanism. The date of the dedication, the sixth anniversary of the battle and Reynolds's death, began a flood of commemoration on anniversaries in the next four decades, and the dedication exercises, with crowds estimated at as many as fifteen thousand, foreshadowed the great interest the American people would later have in battlefield preservation.[29]

Despite a lack of leadership from the Gettysburg Battlefield Memorial Association, other monuments went up on the battlefield in the 1870s. During the 1878 encampment at Gettysburg by the Pennsylvania Grand Army of the Republic (GAR), for example, the Eire, Pennsylvania, post erected a tablet on Little Round Top to commemorate the spot where Colonel Strong Vincent, a brigade commander, had fallen. At the same encampment, the Philadelphia post placed a tablet to mark the spot where Colonel Fred Taylor, a regimental commander, was killed. A year later, in 1879, veterans of the 2nd Massachusetts Infantry returned to the battlefield and, just as significantly, marked their position at the battle with a tablet that detailed the unit's actions. The GAR and Massachusetts tablets on the battlefield pointed toward the growing idea of marking the exact positions of individual units.[30]

Despite financial setbacks, the Gettysburg Battlefield Memorial Association had begun important work that was the stepping-stone to much larger preservation efforts in the 1880s. The association had hosted reunions at the battlefield in 1866 and 1869, at which many officers marked important positions on the battlefield. They also secured from Congress authority for the War Department to hand over condemned cannonballs and ordnance for marking the field.[31]

In 1878, the Pennsylvania GAR met at Gettysburg, and out of that encampment came a movement for the GAR to take over the fading association. One of the GAR's officers, John Vanderslice, found "scope and possibility," but also "apparent apathy or inactivity of those controlling it." By 1880, local GAR chapters had purchased enough stock in the association to make a majority, and they placed their officers in charge of the association at that year's stockholders' meeting. The result was a major shift toward preservation and monumentation at Gettysburg. The change also placed the foremost Gettysburg authority of the time, John B. Bachelder, in the forefront of Gettysburg preservation. Although not a veteran of the battle, Bachelder had traveled to Gettysburg immediately after the battle and had performed an amazing amount of research, even

*John B. Bachelder. Although not present during the battle, Bachelder traveled to Gettysburg in the following days and spent the remainder of his life building a park there. His first efforts were with the Gettysburg Battlefield Memorial Association, but the last portion of his life was spent as a member of the Gettysburg commission, the only civilian to have a place on any of the commissions. Gettysburg National Military Park.*

interviewing Confederate prisoners still in the area. As a major player in the Gettysburg Battlefield Memorial Association, his ascension to the top would have a marked effect on how Gettysburg developed.[32]

During the 1880s, Gettysburg became the de facto Civil War memorialization and monumentation center. Few other monuments went up on the eastern battlefields, and even less had been done in the western theater at sites such as Shiloh and Vicksburg. Indeed, basic patterns were developing at Gettysburg. Individual commemoration of famous men and of human beings as a whole had become commonplace by 1880. Likewise, the idea of marking specific points on the battlefield down to the regimental level was emerging. Perhaps most important, the effort to commemorate and memorialize was slowly moving out of the cemeteries, which were by definition confined. Veterans began to realize that commemoration of their actions and memorialization of the dead could best be done on the actual battlefield, the place where the history had actually been made. As a result, veterans began to push for battlefield preservation at Gettysburg, in fact pushing so hard that Congress became involved by appropriating money in the 1880s.

Under the GAR's guidance, various groups began to place monuments to remember the dead, honor the living, and mark important points on the battlefield. In 1880, the Norristown GAR post erected a marble shaft to mark the spot where Brigadier General Samuel Zook fell in the Wheat Field. Veterans of the 91st Pennsylvania also placed a monument at their position on Little Round Top, marking the first regimental monument to go up on the battlefield.[33]

The year 1880 was also important in terms of federal involvement at Gettysburg. Perhaps because of the GAR's political clout, Congress passed legislation in that year to appropriate fifty thousand dollars for study of the battlefield, specifically naming Bachelder as the one to do the job. The money would go toward surveying the field as well as compiling information on troop positions and movements during the battle. Congress added further appropriations in 1888 and 1889 to mark the positions of regular army units at Gettysburg as well as various appropriations to house the annual encampments on the site.[34]

The Gettysburg Battlefield Memorial Association became more and more active as the years passed. In 1881, Pennsylvania appropriated ten thousand dollars for Gettysburg, and the association used it to buy land and open roadways. Several new monuments went up that year, including those for the 124th New York, 17th Connecticut, and the 88th and 90th Pennsylvania. The next year, the association bought the famous Wheat Field. By 1883, the association had bought several hundred acres of land, including both round tops, the Peach Orchard, and much of the land around Culp's Hill.[35]

The year 1883 also marked a major first at Gettysburg and thus for the entire country. The State of Massachusetts appropriated five thousand dollars that year to erect monuments to its units at Gettysburg, the first time a state legislature appropriated money specifically to mark a battlefield.[36]

Other notable preservation and commemoration events occurred in the years that followed. In 1884, Pennsylvania appropriated money to mark the spot where John Reynolds had fallen. In 1887, the association bought George Meade's headquarters and also began marking with tablets every division flank on the battlefield. In 1888, the association began the process of marking places such as Zeigler's Grove and the Confederate "High Water Mark" and famous "copse of trees."[37]

The year 1888 was also important in that it was the twenty-fifth anniversary of the battle. Many states that had appropriated money wanted to dedicate their monuments on that important date, making it necessary for the association to supervise and approve all such activity.

The association thus expanded its monumentation approval committee, which passed regulations in an effort to make all the monuments uniform in scope and accuracy. These decisions made in the 1880s were important because they would affect the development of the battlefield for many years.[38]

The work at Gettysburg indeed pointed the direction battlefield preservation would take. The Gettysburg association began the acquisition of battlefield land, which was paramount to any preservation effort. It also ushered in the marking of land with tablets and monuments, even down to the regimental level. The monumentation at Gettysburg also emphasized the human aspect of honoring high-ranking officers killed there and marking the exact spots of their fall. The work further ushered in processes and theories on how to preserve and commemorate; the association endeavored to keep or return the battlefield to the condition it was in at the time of the battle. Tourism was already high and would certainly get higher, and the association recognized future visitation needs by developing plans to turn Meade's headquarters into a museum and welcome station.[39]

The work at Gettysburg also pointed toward future preservation on broader levels. Individual states became involved, thus setting a precedent for future battlefield preservation. The federal government also became involved in the 1880s, ushering in what would become a flood of federal activity in the 1890s.

Another future activity that unfortunately became apparent at Gettysburg revolved around the controversies with which the association had to deal, most of them among the Union veterans, not between Northerners and Southerners. In 1890, the 12th New Jersey and 111th New York fought over the location of their positions in line, but the nastiest controversy was between the association and the 72nd Pennsylvania, which wanted its monument in a prominent location. Unfortunately, that location did not correspond to the association's regulations regarding monumentation in lines of battle. The veterans took their fight to the local county court and eventually to the Pennsylvania Supreme Court, which ruled in favor of the regiment. These controversies would pale in comparison to those that would later occur at Gettysburg and on other battlefields, but they nevertheless foreshadowed what the future would bring. During the 1890s, the determination to be accurate, egos and lack of patience of aging men, and fading memories all combined to cause many disputes over what actually happened where.[40]

*Gettysburg Battlefield Memorial Association cannon. Prior to the Gettysburg park's establishment, the Gettysburg Battlefield Memorial Association worked with limited funds and equally limited success in marking the battlefield. This photo shows one of the less-than-accurate carriages used to mark an artillery position. Gettysburg National Military Park.*

Perhaps the only aspect of the Gettysburg Battlefield Memorial Association's work that did not point to the future, although it was a learning experience that allowed the future work to be done comprehensively, was the lack of Confederate activity at Gettysburg. Just as with the original national cemeteries, Confederates were left out of the process. One association member remembered that in 1882, "arrangements were made for the reception of a delegation of Confederate soldiers, who visited the field for the purpose of locating the position of several commands." It appeared as if the battlefield was "off-limits" to former Confederates. Amid the massive building program at Gettysburg between the battle and 1890, only two small tablets marked anything on the Confederate side of the battlefield. For example, in 1884, veterans of the 2nd Maryland Infantry (Confederate) asked for permission to mark their lines, but the request met some opposition from the association. Nevertheless, the memorial went up in 1886. In 1887, the association itself marked with a tablet the spot of Brigadier General Lewis Armistead's death at the "High Water Mark." Confederate veterans of George Pickett's Division had asked to place a division monument as well as a tablet on the spot of Armistead's death, but the association refused on the grounds that all monuments had to be within the original lines of battle. The result was a compromise on the tablet, which was placed by the association.[41]

By the end of the 1880s, several members of the association had begun to realize that they had been too one-sided in their treatment of the battle. Confederates had only been included to a limited degree, such as allowing the two Confederate markers and involving Southerners in the anniversary festivities. Hardly any of the Confederate troop positions were marked. Since the association "labored under great embarrassment of funds," however, it petitioned Congress to fund purchase of the Confederate lines of battle in 1889, which would then be marked with tablets.[42]

John Bachelder became especially interested in marking the Confederate lines. He understood the necessity of including Confederate positions in a comprehensive study of the battle and also realized that further delay would make that task impossible. He personally was perhaps the most knowledgeable man on Confederate troop positions, having interviewed wounded and captured Confederates immediately after the battle. He argued that his knowledge should not be lost, as it soon would be because of his age. Bachelder sent out a circular letter that implored action on the Confederate side, arguing that visitors would remark, "[W]as there no opposing army at Gettysburg, where was the enemy?" Such a statement, using the term "enemy" in reference to the Confederates, took for granted that all visitors would have Federal sympathies, but it was nevertheless a start in the right direction.[43]

Even with all the activity at Gettysburg, the efforts there before the 1890s were not turning points in battlefield preservation, but rather learning processes. Never before had American battlefields been preserved so extensively, so the Gettysburg Battlefield Memorial Association was learning as it went. Fortunately, it learned important lessons that benefited the various park commissions that would come into being in the 1890s.

As the 1880s faded into history, a new dawn was breaking in American battlefield preservation. Through the years since the Civil War, some efforts had been made to preserve isolated sites on battlefields, most notably through national cemeteries and individual monuments. The most popular battlefield was Gettysburg, which even by 1890 had begun to see federal money involved in its partial conservation. But the stark difference between the preservation efforts prior to 1890 and those that came in that year and beyond provides a fascinating dichotomy that illustrates a massive change in approach to saving Civil War battlefields. In 1890, Congress charted a brand new direction in battlefield preservation that would see five different sites set aside and would set the foundation for decades of additional work, including that which is taking place today.

# 2

## CONGRESS, THE WAR DEPARTMENT, AND THE NATIONAL MILITARY PARKS

### The Context of the 1890s-Era Battlefield Preservation, 1890–1933

THE DECADE OF the 1890s was an amazing time of change for America, setting the stage for a massive preservation program. It was in that decade that the United States broke out of its isolation and forcibly became a world player, fostering patriotism and nationalism and an avid attention to martial exploits. It was also during that decade that America dealt with its race issue through the bonding of the regional sections on the issues of white supremacy and segregation. The nation left Reconstruction behind and healed the sectional wounds caused during the Civil War, linking the two sections together politically and economically. As one tangible piece of evidence of this reunification, it was during that decade that veterans of North and South united to force the federal government into preserving their old scenes of battle.

The growing nationalism, patriotism, and reconciliation seen during the 1890s were very new feelings in America. For decades, the North and South had argued over racial issues and had actually fought one another in the 1860s. The hatred and partisanship that developed during the war was only exacerbated by the decade of Reconstruction that followed. In the South, military rule and martial law caused hostility from white Southerners, who had to deal not only with losing the war but also with Republican and military rule. White Southerners whose pride was hurt by losing the war were only infuriated more by Republican governments that often elected former slaves to high offices. In Mississippi, for example, the Republican government was headed by a Massachusetts Union general, Adelbert Ames, and the state sent blacks to the United States Senate and House of Representatives. White Southerners responded with the Ku Klux Klan and other intimidating organizations.[1]

The Reconstruction years in the North were also marred by racism. Northerners who supported the war, even for moral antislavery reasons, were not prepared to allow former slaves fully into society. It was acceptable and even praiseworthy to push for the end of slavery, as long as the freed slaves remained in the South. But when former slaves, now full citizens, began to compete with poor Northern whites for jobs, the North likewise began to pull back from its wartime morality on the slavery issue.[2]

The result was a retraction of former ideals in the pursuit of peace. By 1876, most Southern states had, in some cases by force, taken their state governments back from Republican control. With religious connotations, this process of reclaiming their state governments was called "redeeming," and those responsible for it "redeemers." The federal government also backed away from Reconstruction in the hastily worked-out deal that would decide the disputed presidential election of 1876. In return for partial Southern support of the Republican candidate, Rutherford B. Hayes promised to withdraw troops from the South. The Compromise of 1877 thus formally ended military Reconstruction and was the first tangible movement toward reuniting the nation. In a compromise in the vein of the antebellum compromises negotiated by Henry Clay, the North and South once again showed they could labor together and make compromise work again, albeit at the expense of the former slaves.[3]

Around the same time, the centennial of the nation's independence also began to bring the sections together. One hundred years after the birth of the nation, Americans of both sections celebrated their common heritage and their shared fight for independence. Both Northern and Southern whites could agree on the dedication and dominance of the American military and thus celebrated together their quest for independence and a republican government. Although Congress appropriated money for a monument at Bunker Hill in 1825, the majority of the Revolutionary War–era commemoration was done after 1876. Congress ultimately funded monuments on eight Revolutionary War battlefields at Yorktown, Bennington, Saratoga, Newburgh, Cowpens, Monmouth, Groton, and Oriskany. The celebrations from 1876 through the centennial of the Constitution in 1887 tended to ease the lingering animosity of the Civil War and remind Americans of all sections that they shared a common heritage and country. In fact, one of the first documented gatherings of both Union and Confederate veterans came in 1875 at festivities to commemorate the Battle of Bunker Hill.[4]

Yet on the racial front, the cultural issues over which the Civil War was fought had still not been settled by the beginning of the 1890s. The large questions of slavery and secession had been decided in 1865, but the lingering issues of how the former slaves and their descendents would fit into American government, culture, and society were still very much in doubt. The gains made during the Civil War had all but been forgotten as the federal government backed away from Reconstruction, and thus its support of blacks in the South, in 1877. In the 1890s, blacks were again abandoned, ushering in decades of segregation that propelled African Americans into a more benign form of slavery. With the rise of government-sanctioned segregation as a result of *Plessy v. Ferguson* in 1896, blacks were once again pushed away from the freedoms that they had gained during the Civil War and Reconstruction.[5]

The rise of Jim Crow segregation was a part of the sectional healing that had begun in the 1870s and continued into the 1890s. By the 1890s, white America, now no longer at odds over Reconstruction and full of patriotism from the centennial, had tired of the racial issues that had divided the sections since the founding of the nation. The lingering effects of this turmoil could still be seen in the 1880s, but by the 1890s, Americans wanted to focus on different issues. Whereas racial issues and problems had caused heated controversy for decades, Americans now sought issues that could reconcile and bring the sections together. Thus the 1890s saw a retreat from issues of race, thus allowing segregation to run rampant in the South as well as in the North.[6]

Rather than fight over race, Americans sought common bonds that would tie them together. What could be more honorable and reconciling than to concentrate on the passing veterans of the Civil War and their courage, bravery, and manliness on Civil War battlefields? The result was an honoring of the veterans, both those who gave their lives and those who still remained. Monuments rose to leaders in Richmond and Washington and on almost every courthouse lawn in both North and South. The primary celebration of the Civil War generation's bravery and courage, however, came to be extolled on the original battlefields, preserved as military parks.[7]

The 1890s was thus a time of cooperation for white America in terms of its common heritage and trials. Although it was a decade of economic, political, and racial conflict, the 1890s saw the nation begin to come together socially, and the veterans of the Civil War led the way. The nationalism of expansion added fuel to the patriotic fire. Annexing Hawaii and other Pacific lands made America a world player, and the short war with Spain in 1898 not only added more territory but also showed the entire world (despite some missteps) that the nation's military prowess, demonstrated domestically during the 1860s, was now a factor on the world stage.[8]

The cumulative effect of this nationalism, reconciliation, and patriotism was a nation consumed with both its heritage and its martial exploits. The result was a fixation on past military actions, namely the Civil War. The Revolutionary War, the War of 1812, and the Mexican War all had their memorials and monuments, but, probably because of the limited numbers involved, the battlefields of none of those conflicts witnessed the extensive preservation and commemoration that Civil War fields garnered.

The decade of the 1890s was thus a critical time for preserving Civil War battlefields. The time was finally right for the North and the South to join together to remember what they had done some thirty years before. It was also critical in terms of practicality; if these battlefields were to be preserved, it had to be done immediately. The veterans were passing away in huge numbers during the 1890s and the pace of their demise would only increase. Similarly, the nation was on the verge of a second industrial revolution that would see towns and cities expand at enormous rates. Because most Civil War battles were fought around towns where transportation routes crossed, that coming expansion in the early 1900s would forever destroy the historic fields. Likewise, the era before the social expansion of the 1900s was a time when the land on which battles had been fought could still be purchased at reasoable cost. Probably most important, the period was a time when Congress had a major representation of veterans within its ranks. When the veteran-lawmakers passed away, newer generations would not be as enthusiastic about battlefield preservation.

All these factors came together at a critical time for battlefield preservation and commemoration. Taking its cue from what had already occurred on an embryonic level at Gettysburg and at nature parks such as Yellowstone, Yosemite, and Sequoia, America was ready and willing to preserve important fields of battle. The result was the establishment of five parks during the 1890s, the Golden Age of battlefield preservation in America.[9]

Beginning in 1890 and continuing throughout the decade, three major groups worked together to preserve these five battlefields. First, the veterans themselves were the key promoters of the parks, and it was veterans who made up the commissions that actually built the parks. Every single battlefield preserved in the 1890s had a veterans' association that began the process of preservation at that specific site. Likewise, when the federal government became involved in preservation, veterans were the workers who poured their lives into the task, not only memorializing their actions in the late war, but more importantly remembering the sacrifices of their friends and comrades who had perished on those fields so many years before. Men such as Henry Boynton and Alexander P. Stewart at Chickamauga, Henry Heth and Ezra Carman at Antietam, John P. Nicholson and E. B. Cope at Gettysburg, Cornelius Cadle and D. W. Reed at Shiloh, and William T. Rigby and Stephen D. Lee at Vicksburg were the leaders of the veteran class that built their respective parks. Such national battlefield experts not only oversaw their own parks, but they also formed an informal set of veterans that advised the secretary of war on matters concerning historic preservation. Most notably, Nicholson, Carman, and particularly Boynton became trusted advisors of many war secretaries making decisions about the parks.

Second, the United States Congress was the body that had to act to create the parks with federal laws and then continue their operation with annual appropriations. Fortunately for the veterans pushing preservation, Congress was still dominated in the 1890s by war veterans who were mostly in tune with the call for action. Congressmen such as Charles Grosvenor, Daniel Sickles, William Bate, and David B. Henderson were all Civil War veterans as well as esteemed members of their respective houses. These soldiers-turned-legislators wielded much power in the halls of Congress and eventually pushed through necessary battlefield legislation.

Third, the War Department and most notably the secretary of war oversaw the work of preservation. Congressional legislation placed each of the five battlefields under the War Department, and the various secretaries of war wielded much power over the battlefields and the veterans they appointed to the various commissions. Working with the veterans on the commissions and with the members of Congress, these secretaries and their trusted advisors such as Assistant Secretary of War Robert Shaw Oliver, chief clerk John C. Scofield, and particularly judge advocate and battlefield expert George B. Davis set the guiding policy for the battlefields.

In mid-August 1890, Congress passed legislation that established the nation's first national military park at Chickamauga and Chattanooga.

An idea of veterans themselves, the park came into being with almost unanimous support from Congress, veterans, and the War Department. Considering all the work already done at Gettysburg and on other battlefields, it seemed that the time was ripe to create a park that would not only honor the dead and the living, but would do so on an intersectional basis: unlike Gettysburg, Chickamauga would be a memorial to both sides. Thus, a major change took place in battlefield preservation, and it fit nicely—indeed drove in part—the reconciliation that was occurring in the United States during that time.[10]

Chickamauga was the first of the battlefield parks established in the 1890s, and it set the standard for the others. At some six thousand acres, the park was intended to preserve the entire battlefield in its original condition. A commission of three men, appointed by Secretary of War Redfield Proctor, oversaw the building of the park and the preservation of the site. Thus emerged the dominant standard of battlefield preservation in the 1890s—that of buying and preserving entire battlefields.[11]

After Chickamauga, however, problems arose as the veteran-dominated Congress realized that it had other pressing matters that demanded money and attention. Veterans were pushing the idea of creating national military parks at Gettysburg and Antietam, but neither effort made much progress. Some fiscal opposition had emerged in the Chickamauga congressional debate, and all that Antietam supporters could get passed was a small appropriation to mark the battle lines—far from a large national military park like the one at Chickamauga. Later attempts to establish a full-fledged park at Antietam failed as well. The Panic of 1893 no doubt concerned legislators as they considered whether to vote for several more expensive national military parks along the lines of Chickamauga.[12]

Nevertheless, Antietam's establishment was important. Passed in late August 1890, the Antietam legislation created a second type of preservation effort. It developed along what was called the "Antietam Plan," where the federal government bought only a minimal area of land to preserve roadways and lines of battle, on which they placed tablets to mark the lines. A two-man board—later increased to three men—worked on the site, but it was obviously at a disadvantage in comparison with the Chickamauga commission.[13]

Gettysburg likewise suffered from the economic troubles of the early 1890s. As much sentiment as there was to preserve battlefields, even the vaunted field of Gettysburg was not immune to a feeling of fiscal responsibility. Gettysburg park supporters tried unsuccessfully to get several establishment bills through Congress in 1890 and 1892. The Gettysburg boosters did, however, get a measure passed that appropriated money for an Antietam-like commission in 1893. That commission went to work marking the lines of both armies, but as in the case of Antietam, it could not match Chickamauga's broader mandate.[14]

During the early 1890s as Chickamauga, Antietam, and Gettysburg benefited from federal dollars, Congress received little guidance from the War Department on how to proceed. Although he did appoint the Chickamauga Commission and the Antietam Board, Secretary of War Proctor, a Civil War veteran, was not in office long enough to exert any real influence, leaving his post on November 5, 1891, to enter the United States Senate. His successor, Civil War veteran Stephen B. Elkins, served until March 5, 1893, and was a supporter of the battlefields, writing in his 1891 official report to Congress that "This work [Chickamauga], when completed, will be of great interest and importance, not only to those who took part on both sides in the memorable events which occurred there, but to the country at large and to future generations." Nevertheless, Elkins never pushed Congress for greater battlefield preservation during his term.[15]

The role of the secretary of war changed in 1893, however, when Daniel S. Lamont came into office on March 5 as President Grover Cleveland began his second term in office. Lamont had served extensively as a state government clerk in New York and had served Cleveland as his private secretary in the first Cleveland term. Lamont would have a historical view in his tenure as secretary of war, making several changes to the army, including an attempt to centralize army archives and helping to modernize the infantry by moving to a three-battalion regiment. Lamont would also turn out to be a chief policy maker concerning military parks, and would wield considerable influence to try to save money for the nation. He would be mostly unsuccessful during his term in office, but in later years his preservation views would ultimately gain momentum and become the dominant battlefield preservation policy in America.[16]

Although Lamont appointed the Gettysburg commission in 1893, he otherwise remained relatively quiet for his first couple of years. During that time, he did promote some preservation efforts such as marking with tablets the historic sites at Appomattox, but in 1895 he realized that the parks needed some organized guidance. The reason Lamont felt he had to become so involved was because of the increase in parks in 1895. Before, the secretary had only the one major commission at Chickamauga to oversee, with the two temporary commissions at Antietam and

*Daniel S. Lamont.
Overseeing the most
rapid growth period
of the military parks,
Secretary of War
Lamont appointed the
Gettysburg commis-
sion, reinstituted the
Antietam Board, and
appointed the Shiloh
commission. Depart-
ment of Defense.*

Gettysburg, both of which did not spend a lot of money and one (Antietam) buried in the bureaucracy of the Quartermaster Department. In
1895, however, Congress passed bills creating Shiloh National Military
Park and Gettysburg National Military Park, both full-sized parks on the
scale of Chickamauga. More detailed opposition arose in Congress to each
park's establishment, reflecting the growing concern about large, money-
consuming parks fashioned after Chickamauga. Nevertheless, Lamont
appointed the Shiloh commission in the early part of the year and ele-
vated the temporary Gettysburg commission, already in existence, later
that year. Congress was also soon debating bills to create more parks. The
time had clearly come to develop an overall plan for the military parks.[17]

Lamont began by formulating policy on an individual park level. He
ordered the Shiloh commission to take a different approach than had
been followed by the other commissions. At all the battlefields, the effort

had been made—indeed the goal was—to restore them to their battle-time configuration. Of course access was also a goal, because thousands of visitors and military officers would certainly visit and seek to learn lessons and locate troop positions. In order to balance the two competing desires, the early commissions had restored woods, fields, and roads on the battlefields. To make the battlefields accessible, however, the various commissions had sometimes opened new roads to provide access to inaccessible portions of the parks. In the case of Antietam, the board wanted to open roadways upon which they could mark lines of battle.[18]

Secretary Lamont wrote to the Shiloh commission that such a plan was not to be followed at Pittsburg Landing. "With a view to make the field assessable, it is desirable that the principal roads crossing the field from East to West should be identified as they existed in April 1862, and should then be improved and made passable. It may be seriously questioned, also, whether the opening of avenues along lines of battle, on other fields of the Civil War, has not contributed to an erroneous understanding of the military appearances by leading the visitor to believe that the avenues and roads on which he passes were in existence during the battle." Road construction at Antietam and Gettysburg had already gone too far to correct, but Lamont was determined that from then on, parks would be as historically accurate as possible.[19]

The Shiloh commission was able to do what Lamont asked. Unlike Chickamauga, Antietam, and Gettysburg, Shiloh had not been fought on primarily stable lines. At each of the other three, the commissions could build a few roads and mark the various major lines of battle. Shiloh, however, had been so fluid that it would take many roads to mark all the major lines of battle. The Shiloh commission was fortunate that an intricate system of small roads and paths already existed in the area at the time of the battle. Whereas the other battlefields had major turnpikes and roadways, Shiloh was so isolated that an intricate web of farm lanes and pathways connected just about every section of the battlefield. The Shiloh commission used those original roads, along with footpaths and open woods, to move the visitor around that battlefield.[20]

Lamont was also interested in a larger national policy concerning the battlefields. With new parks at Shiloh and Gettysburg about to be developed, the secretary of war recommended in his 1895 annual report that Congress make a decision on the issue. He then lobbied for the remaining parks and those in the future to be developed according to the Antietam Plan. "It is important that Congress should early adopt and consistently

*War Department officials at Shiloh. The battlefields were visited from time to time by members of the War Department staff as well as commissioners from their sister parks. This photograph taken at Shiloh shows, from left to right, Shiloh commission members James Ashcraft, Cornelius Cadle, and David W. Reed. To the right of Reed is John C. Scofield of the War Department, followed by Frank G. Smith and Henry V. Boynton of the Chickamauga commission. Next is John P. Nicholson, chairman of the Gettysburg commission, followed by Francis A. Large, the Shiloh range rider. Shiloh National Military Park.*

pursue a fixed policy in regard to the marking of the battlefields of the Civil War," Lamont told Congress. He argued that if the custom in progress at Chickamauga was followed, it would require fifty sites to be developed fully, which would in turn require twenty million dollars initially, with one million dollars appropriated annually for upkeep. Lamont argued that the "policy pursued at Antietam" was the best answer. Such an approach would not only lower costs but could also be accomplished rather quickly. "It is earnestly recommended that Congress authorize the marking of the remaining important battlefields in the same manner adopted at Antietam, which can be completed in a few years at moderate cost," Lamont advised.[21]

Although Secretary Lamont had little success with his plan to create a military park policy, Congress continued to turn out legislation pertaining to it. In December 1895, Lamont sent a bill to Congress that allowed the secretary of war to use the Chickamauga park as camping and training grounds for the military. The House Committee on Military Affairs amended the bill to include all the parks, present and future. The Senate military committee went along with the amendments, but the bill still faced debate on the floor. Members of Congress in both houses were concerned over language in the bill such as whether the state militias could utilize the parks because the bill stated only the regular army and "national guard" could use them. By far, the major concerns regarded expenses. In a Congress concerned about spending, several members voiced anxiety about increased expenses. Representative Joseph Cannon of Illinois (Appropriations Committee chairman and a future Speaker of the House) asked bluntly, "Is this a real necessity, for the benefit of the Army, or is it a power granted which will result in much expense and something of pleasure, without resulting in profit to the Army?" Ultimately, all fears were allayed with assurances that no new expenses would be incurred, one member pointing out that the secretary could send the troops anywhere he wanted already. The bill became law on May 15, 1896, and the parks, particularly Chickamauga and Gettysburg, were regularly used afterwards, especially during times of war.[22]

Congress also passed legislation on March 3, 1897, for the protection of the military parks. The statute lumped many of the protection clauses found in the various parks' enabling legislation bills into one act that protected the parks and set rigorous punishments for anyone committing acts of destruction. It is noteworthy, however, that this bill also did not cost the federal government any money. It seemed that Congress was willing to pass laws regarding policy and protection of the parks, but was unwilling to spend any money to create new parks or organize an overarching bureaucracy that would oversee them.[23]

The case of Vicksburg was illustrative of this desire to save money. Vicksburg locals and veterans developed the idea of creating a park in 1895 and began to lobby Congress to do so. Several bills failed. Even staunch battlefield supporters were disillusioned. When one Vicksburg veteran talked to the powerful Representative David B. Henderson of Iowa, all he heard was: "That simply can't be done. The boys have declared they didn't intend spending another dollar on military park appropriations. You ought to have put this bill before Congress two years ago. It's too late now." Indeed, efforts to get a Vicksburg bill through Congress failed in 1896, 1897, and 1898. The Vicksburg supporters did not give up, however, and barely got their bill passed in 1899. Unfortunately, Vicksburg was the final battlefield preserved by Congress in the 1890s and indeed for the next twenty-five years.[24]

Vicksburg was the exception rather than the rule in the late 1890s. Speaker of the House Thomas B. Reed, known as "Czar" Reed, simply would not allow many bills to come to the floor. Many other park bills, some fourteen in all by 1902, were written in the 1890s but never made it to the floor. The House Committee on Military Affairs held several hearings on proposed parks at Bull Run, Petersburg, Atlanta, and Fredericksburg. When the secretary of war in 1899 called for the "Fredericksburg and Adjacent National Battlefields Memorial Park" to provide a military camping facility near the capital, a significant opposition developed. "It is not possible to report favorably all the many parks that are proposed," the Military Affairs Committee insisted.[25]

Ironically, it was not Congress that made the most salient decision on national battlefield policy in the late 1890s; it was the United States Supreme Court. The Gettysburg commission had, since its original appointment in 1893, faced the prospect of a railroad company building a line right through the battlefield. Efforts to deal with the company failed, and the United States condemned the land for national military park use. The various sides appealed lower court rulings, and the Supreme Court finally decided the issue in January 1896. In a landmark decision, the Court decided that the federal government could indeed condemn land for preservation purposes. The way was clear for battlefield construction by condemnation if need be. By then, however, congressional action creating battlefields in the 1890s had almost concluded, but the ruling did make it easier for the existing parks to obtain land and proved to have a lasting effect in the decades to come.[26]

Secretary Lamont left office with President Cleveland on March 4, 1897, to be replaced by William McKinley's secretary of war, Russell A. Alger. Entering office on March 5, 1897, Civil War veteran and former governor of Michigan Alger proved to be a military park supporter. In his 1897 annual report to Congress, he wrote, "[T]hese battlefields marked and to be marked, as they have been and will be, are an object lesson of patriotism, wherein heroic deeds are enshrined for the contemplation of the youth of the country. The monuments bear a brief historical legend, compiled without praise and without censure. Like an official seal, they import absolute verity." Unfortunately, Alger was not in office long enough to be a major factor in park development. Most of his attention was on what became the Spanish-American War in 1898, and complaints about his handling of that war brought a request for his resignation on August 1, 1899. Alger's replacement, however, would

*Elihu Root. As secretary of war, Root instituted various reforms in the War Department, including cut backs for the military parks. Root fought for limited additional establishments, a combined national commission, and streamlined disbursements. His policies affected the Vicksburg commission most of all, as it was the only commission still in the process of making major budgetary decisions during his term. Department of Defense.*

have a dramatic effect on the military parks at a critical time in their history.[27]

A native of New York, Elihu Root had been too young to fight in the Civil War. After a solid career as a lawyer, he came into office as secretary of war on August 1, 1899, advocating sweeping changes that revolutionized the military in the days after its less than stellar performance in the Spanish-American War. Root ushered in changes such as creating a General Staff College patterned after that of the Germans, alternating officers between staff and line duties, and increasing the size of the military overall. He also touted joint operations between the army and navy, conserved fiscal appropriations, and reformed and strengthened the National Guard. In all, the "Root Reforms" created a modern military that in a few years had to wage one of history's most deadly wars. In the midst of all the change, Root also took aim at the military parks and the lack of a central policy to govern them.[28]

Root began to streamline various aspects of the commissions' work in order to save money. Several lower positions were cut as he streamlined the bureaucracy. The largest piece of purging, however, was his response to increased calls for more parks. By 1902, some fourteen different military park bills were before Congress, including Civil War parks for

Petersburg, Atlanta, Perryville, Stones River, Wilson's Creek, Franklin, Fredericksburg, and Fort Stevens and Revolutionary War parks for York-town and Valley Forge. Root realized that if a three-man commission was established for each park, the cost would be astronomical. Something had to be done.[29]

At the request of the House Committee on Military Affairs in 1902, Root presented his views on the conduct of battlefield preservation. He listed the amount of money already spent on the four national military parks at Chickamauga, Shiloh, Gettysburg, and Vicksburg, which totaled more than two million dollars. On the other hand, he slyly noted that all the federal government had spent on Antietam was about one hundred thousand dollars. Although he was not vocal about it in 1902, it was not difficult to see what type of battlefield preservation policy Root desired.[30]

More vocal was battlefield specialist George B. Davis, a Civil War veteran who had risen through the ranks and become one of America's foremost authorities on military law. As a brigadier general, judge advocate general for the army, and a leading preservationist, Davis was a man people listened to. He was chairman of the board publishing the *Official Records*, so he was deeply involved in the battles and battlefields. Numerous secretaries of war used him to scout and mark battlefields, and he had been president of the temporary board that marked the Antietam battlefield. His round, balding head and short cropped mustache did not exactly personify a fierce warrior, but his looks did betray his intense intelligence. Although not blessed with the physique of a traditional warrior and mostly encumbered with administrative jobs throughout his career, Davis nevertheless had the personality of a fighter: he would tangle with anyone or anything that got in his way. His intense makeup fit well with his administrative duties, however, whether it was in compiling the *Official Records* or building the Antietam battlefield. He was an effective leader and got the job done.[31]

In April 1902, when it was dealing with commission policy, the House Committee on Military Affairs called on the veteran battlefield expert Davis to testify. Davis's original idea was to preserve intact one eastern and one western battlefield for visitors and military study alike. "There the acquisition of large areas should cease," Davis told the committee. He envisioned a day when many unacceptable scenarios would come about: he shuddered to think that in the future, a budget-strapped Congress might cut off funding to maintain all the parks. They would then become "a refuge for tramps and all sorts of people." He also dreaded to

*George B. Davis. A stalwart in the War Department, George B. Davis served several secretaries of war as a chief policy advisor on battlefield parks. When the Antietam Board was in need of steady leadership, it was Davis as temporary president who put it on the right track. Unlike Henry Boynton, another policy advisor, Davis espoused a limited version of preservation based on the Antietam Plan. Library of Congress.*

think what would happen if "people of competence in the matter of land-scape work fall into control, and they make it a park like Central Park."[32]

Davis rather desired to see the battlefields preserved on the Antietam Plan, which he had originally suggested to the secretary of war. "I think the experiment at Antietam was entirely successful," Davis argued. Most battlefields should have "tablets and cannon-ball monuments in the roads," he argued, and small areas for "monuments for special purposes." He reminded the committee that this had been done at Appomattox, despite a bill pending for a twenty-five hundred acre park. Stating that most of the major events occurred within a 150-acre site, Davis argued that a large park "would commemorate nothing, it would perpetuate the memory of nothing."[33]

When asked about the idea of a central commission instead of a different one for each battlefield, Davis agreed with the chairman of the committee that "it needs some general scheme." Davis reminded his hearers that the time was fast approaching when the commissions would die away anyway. He did, however, seek to look after the commission members who would be displaced, asking that the committee see to the welfare of these aged men.[34]

In response to Root's letter, Davis's testimony, and the need to determine a coherent but cost-effective policy of preservation, Congress began to debate a bill that would revolutionize the military park commissions. H.R. 14351 contained nine sections that first abolished each of the four battlefield commissions then in place. The commissions would have two years to complete their work, at which time a national commission would be formed. One member of the four original commissions, as well as an army officer, would be selected for the presidentially appointed commission. They would then oversee battlefield preservation on the lines of the Antietam Plan. With "general power to restore, preserve, mark, and maintain," the commission would report to Congress which battlefields needed work and what that work should encompass. Other sections of the act read much like the original park bills, with authority for states to erect monuments, penalties for vandals, and allowance for condemnation and tenancy. In all, two hundred thousand dollars would be appropriated for the new commission, a sum, the committee reminded the House, that each individual military park commission had requested for that year.[35]

This was not a new idea. It had first surfaced around the time of the Spanish-American War when Assistant Secretary of War Henry Breckinridge had broached the subject. Later, Colonel Charles H. Heyl in the Inspector General's Office of the War Department had supported the effort. Congress became involved when Representative Joseph Cannon included language in a sundry civil bill calling on the secretary of war to look into the idea. In what Henry Boynton called "rather a tangled affair," Secretary Root also became a prime mover of the idea behind the scenes, though he would not publicly push for the change.[36]

In 1902, the House Committee on Military Affairs wholeheartedly endorsed the effort, except for calling for at least two of the five new commissioners to be Confederate veterans. Offering a commentary on the process, the committee acknowledged that "separate commissions were necessary to prepare these great parks," but the "system is too cumbrous to be continued beyond the time necessary." The members decided it was not necessary to have a new park on each battlefield, but to mark each site with "plain cannon-ball monuments" and to acquire narrow strips along roadways or lines of battle. In essence, they endorsed the Antietam

*David B. Henderson. As a veteran of Shiloh, Henderson was instrumental in getting funding for that park. He was very involved in Vicksburg's establishment as well, and as Speaker of the House was a supporter of the commission system of running the parks, even killing a measure to combine the commissions. House of Representatives.*

Plan. In sending the bill to the full House, the committee reminded the members that "[p]atriotism demands the preservation of these spots. But it is plain that they will not be preserved if a salaried commission has to be created for every spot."[37]

The effort to consolidate the park commissions was not successful. The military park commissioners themselves opposed the idea vehemently, and Secretary Root, although supportive of the measure, did not make it a major priority. There also was a turf war between the House Committee on Appropriations and the Committee on Military Affairs. The military committee refused to report the money-saving bill in order to blackmail the money-conscious appropriations committee to deal with monetary concerns. Most important, however, were the commissions' friends in Congress. Shiloh commission chairman Cornelius Cadle wrote one of his fellow commissioners that he had been "advised by one of the powers that be that it will not be permitted to pass." Cadle was even more blunt in writing another member of his commission, saying, "'Our Friend' said he would simply put a 'spike' in this." By "Our Friend," Cadle was referring to Representative David B. Henderson, who had supported many of the park bills. In 1902, Henderson just happened to be Speaker of the House of Representatives.[38]

Yet the idea refused to die. A second round of hearings on essentially the same bill occurred in 1904. This time, a new secretary used his considerable influence to support the idea. William Howard Taft had become Theodore Roosevelt's new secretary of war when Root resigned (ultimately to become Roosevelt's secretary of state). In his annual report to Congress, Taft wrote, "The development of the plans contemplated in the establishment of the different national military parks . . . has reached a point where, with a view to economy and uniformity of administration, the four different commissions . . . might well be consolidated into a single commission consisting of three members, or possibly five." Taft then explained the lack of War Department support in 1902: "The conditions heretofore have been such that the Department has not felt called upon to suggest bringing this work into the hands of a general commission, a step against which no valid objection can lie if only public interests are to be considered." Taft was beginning his patterned approach of little support for the commissions. Indeed, in almost every decision regarding them, he would rule against the commission members.[39]

In 1904, H.R. 14748, another bill similar to the 1902 effort was before the House of Representatives. The House Committee on Military Affairs noted that the number of park bills before Congress had grown to seventeen, with the additions of Appomattox, Balls Bluff, and the "Valley of Virginia Memorial Park." Taft and the revisionists got no further in 1904 than they had in 1902, however. The bill again languished in Congress.[40]

Still undeterred, the House Committee on Military Affairs again took up a new but similar bill, H.R. 7046, in 1906. Once again, this bill did not gain momentum. Secretary Taft had no luck moving the bill forward, despite suggesting to Congress that "with a view to more economical administration . . . the conditions that now prevail result in salary rolls out of all proportion to the total expenditures for improvement [at the parks]." Taft's suggestion failed again, however, and the idea of a centralized commission was to be brought up no more.[41]

Although no new bills to centralize the commissions came forward, no new parks were established either. And while the consolidation idea languished, Congress did ultimately address the issue; a small provision was inserted into an appropriations bill in 1912 that stopped the appointment of new commissioners to fill vacancies. The bill read: "Hereafter vacancies occurring by death or resignation in the membership of the several commissions in charge of national military parks shall not be filled, and the duties of the offices thus vacated shall devolve upon the remaining commissioners or commissioner for each of said parks." When a vacancy occurred, the secretary of war would become an ex-officio member of the commissions. The president who signed the bill was William Howard Taft. It is not known whether President Taft laughed aloud as he had the proverbial last laugh regarding streamlining the commissions.[42]

A variety of secretaries of war oversaw the parks through 1933, men such as Luke Wright, Jacob Dickinson, Henry L. Stimson, Lindley Garrison, Newton Baker, John Weeks, Dwight Davis, James Good, Patrick Hurley, and George Dern. As time passed, however, they made fewer and fewer decisions regarding the parks. As the army grew larger in the early 1900s with the "Root Reforms," the clout carried by the parks and their commissions proportionately lessened. And with the coming of World War I, the parks became almost a bother to very busy secretaries and their staffs. Once the pride of the War Department in the 1890s, the national military parks by the 1920s were relegated to inferior status by events beyond their control taking place half a world away.

In fact, the parks began to be shuffled about various bureaus of the War Department. By the 1920s, the parks' annual reports did not even appear in the War Department's published report to Congress. In 1923, Secretary of War John W. Weeks transferred the five Civil War parks to the Office of the Quartermaster General. In 1930, the parks were transferred again, this time by Secretary of War Patrick Hurley, to the "commanding generals of the corps areas in which they are severally located." It seemed the parks had gone from big fish in a small pond to tiny fish in a very big pond.[43]

But in the 1890s, during the Golden Age of battlefield preservation, and in the first decade of the 1900s, the five military parks were indeed considered important, the queens of American remembrance and memorialization. Their amazing stories tell loud and clear what the veteran generation was thinking, how they viewed their war, and what they intended to do about it. And it all began one fine summer day when two Union veterans tramped their old fighting ground. Hardly anyone knew what would ultimately develop when Henry Boynton first dreamed the dream of a national military park along the banks of the river of death.

# 3

## "A WESTERN GETTYSBURG"
### Chickamauga and Chattanooga
### National Military Park, 1890–1933

WHILE PRESERVATION EFFORTS at Gettysburg were growing in the 1880s, other battlefields of the Civil War faced neglect. Soldiers returning to those fields remarked on how much the battlegrounds had changed and how they had problems finding their old positions. Such was the case at Chickamauga. One veteran had returned to the battlefield in the early 1870s and described it as already being "all overgrown with trees and underwood." In 1881, the Society of the Army of the Cumberland held its annual reunion in Chattanooga, purportedly the first time a Union organization held a reunion in the South. One group of veterans returned to the Chickamauga battlefield intent on finding their old positions and landmarks. "When we got there," one remembered, "there wasn't a man in the whole crowd that could tell a thing about it." Another veteran told of returning to the field and finding an old position in battle, only to be corrected by a local farmer who had been on the battlefield during the time and remembered where the veteran's specific unit had been located.[1]

Some tourism-minded marking had taken place during and in the years after the war. When Confederate president Jefferson Davis visited in late 1863, Confederates placed small markers to designate particular points and then took him on a tour. Later, one observer remembered "little wooden tablets driven into the ground and . . . shingles nailed to the trees." But unlike Gettysburg, the idea of making Chickamauga a park did not surface until the early 1880s. Members of a Chicago post of the Grand Army of the Republic (GAR) attempted to raise money to buy the battlefield at that time, even taking options on the land for twenty-five dollars an acre. The attempt failed when the group could not raise the necessary money. The next major attempt to save the battlefield came on a Sunday in the summer of 1888, when two Union veterans returned

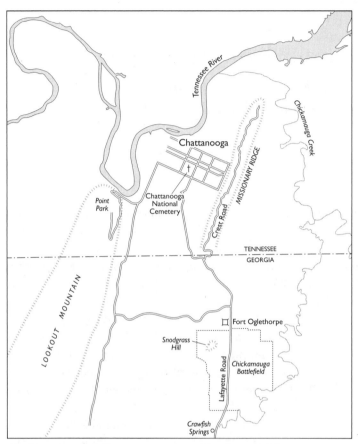

*Chickamauga and Chattanooga National Military Park*

to Chickamauga to tour their old scenes of conflict. Henry Van Ness Boynton had fought at Chickamauga as a lieutenant colonel in the 35th Ohio Infantry, later going on to win the medal of honor at Chattanooga. Chickamauga veteran Ferdinand Van Derveer, who as a colonel had led Boynton's brigade during the battle, accompanied Boynton. As the two old soldiers toured the battlefield, they compared the different atmosphere they felt then to the circumstances the last time they had been on the battlefield in 1863. Hearing "the voice of solemn song" from a nearby country church, the two remembered "the thunder of that hell of battle which had loaded the air with horror through all that earlier and well-remembered Sabbath." It was in the midst of such a serene atmosphere that they struck upon a novel idea. They would work to make Chicka-mauga into "a western Gettysburg."[2]

Boynton and Van Derveer floated the idea that September at the annual meeting of the Society of the Army of the Cumberland, which met in 1888 in Chicago. The idea received so much support that the society organized a committee of five to look into the idea and report at the following year's Chattanooga meeting. As a member of the committee, Boynton had definite ideas about how the venture should be run, and he became the major player in the effort. Although a rather diminutive man,

*Henry V. Boynton. The "Father of the National Military Park," Henry Boynton not only served as historian and chairman of the Chickamauga commission from 1890 until his death in 1905, but he also instituted the idea of the national military park. He also served as one of the War Department's roving experts on battlefield preservation, getting into heated arguments with both the Shiloh and Vicksburg commissions. Here he can be seen in his uniform as brigadier general, a rank he held during the Spanish-American War in 1898. Chickamauga and Chattanooga National Military Park.*

the heavily gray-bearded veteran was not the type to let anything get in his way. Perhaps his long, drooping face and beard reflected the many controversies in which he had become involved, even taking on William T. Sherman over the truthfulness of his memories. And the disagreements would not end anytime soon. A passionate and volatile person, Boynton often had arguments and controversies with other veterans and politicians alike, and usually won. When he backed an idea, he did it with all his might.[3]

A Washington correspondent for the *Cincinnati Commercial Gazette*, Henry Boynton proselytized to the veterans as well as the general public by writing several articles on the proposed park. He envisioned something very similar to Gettysburg's memorial association, but with one major change: Chickamauga would be a intersectional effort of both North and South. "Those who have thus far considered the matter have in mind an organization formed after the general plan of the Gettysburg Memorial Association," Boynton wrote, "only differing from it in any essential feature in its being a joint association of both Union and Confederate veterans." Whereas Gettysburg at this time was still primarily a Union memorial and was only beginning to talk about marking and memorializing the Confederate positions, Boynton wanted Southern inclusion from the beginning at Chickamauga. "The Chickamauga Association would be a much more comprehensive organization," he argued.[4]

"There is no other great battlefield of the war where Northern and Southern veterans could meet harmoniously and with equal satisfaction to preserve the field of their magnificent fighting," Boynton wrote. He described how each side would have a victory to honor, the Federals at Chattanooga and the Confederates at Chickamauga. "Its preservation as one of the great historical fields of the war would signify for both sides, more than anything else, the indelible marking of the theater upon which each of the two armies engaged performed as stubborn, brilliant, and bloody fighting as was done upon any of the great battlefields of the war," Boynton argued.[5]

Appointed by former general William S. Rosecrans, then president of the society, Boynton and the committee met in Washington, DC, on February 13, 1889, with Rosecrans and War Department official Sanford C. Kellogg, who was a famous Chickamauga veteran himself. (Kellogg had been involved in the famous misunderstanding that caused Rosecrans to remove a division out of line just as the enemy attacked.) Desiring Southern support, the group decided to meet the next day, February 14, after invitations had been sent to former Confederates who had been at Chickamauga. The next day, an intersectional group of seven Union officers and eight Confederate officers met in the committee room of the Senate Committee on Military Affairs and discussed plans to memorialize and preserve the battlefield. The group formed a memorial association organizational committee to obtain a charter. They also prepared a list of influential veterans who should be part of the association. The formation committee met the next day, February 15, and finalized plans for creating the association.[6]

The Chickamauga Memorial Association held its first official meeting on September 19, 1889, the anniversary of the Battle of Chickamauga, during the Society of the Army of the Cumberland's annual reunion in Chattanooga. Meeting in a large tent set up for the reunion, the group of some twelve thousand veterans heard speeches by such luminaries as Rosecrans and Boynton. The latter told the veterans exactly what was in the works: to ask Congress for an appropriation to make a national military park out of the Chickamauga and Chattanooga battlefields. The next day, September 20, the veterans met at Crawfish Springs for "one of the largest barbeques ever held in the South." After the meal, the men met formally at "the Baptist Church on the battle field of Chickamauga" and organized the Chickamauga Memorial Association. The group elected officers nominated by the various veterans' groups: former Northern general John T. Wilder as president, former Southern general Joseph Wheeler as vice president, former Confederate Marcus Wright as secretary, and former Federal Joseph S. Fullerton as treasurer. Twenty-eight former Confederate and Union officers made up the board of directors. The Chickamauga venture was a joint effort from the beginning.[7]

During the speeches made on September 19 and 20, the orators placed heavy emphasis on unity. Rosecrans declared: "It is very difficult to find in history an instance where contending parties in after years meet together in perfect amity. It took great men to win that battle, but it takes greater men still, I will say morally greater, to wipe away all the ill feeling which naturally grows out of such a contest." Georgia governor John B. Gordon also spoke of reconciliation, calling on the veterans: "Let us bury the foul spirit of discord so deep that no blast of partisan political trumpet, however wide sounding and penetrating, can ever wake it to service again."[8]

The association drew up a twenty-year charter, which was approved in the court system of Walker County, Georgia, on December 4, 1889. Unlike Gettysburg's association, the Chickamauga corporation did not sell stock, implicitly indicating that it was a nonprofit organization. By the time the charter became effective, however, efforts were in full swing to get federal government support in preserving the battlefield, and with some success. The War Department had already become involved, with Sanford Kellogg's presence at the original meeting in Washington. He had also been involved in mapping the battlefield to make department maps of the battle as accurate as possible. Kellogg had even met with veterans on the battlefield in November 1888 to resolve slight discrepancies in the maps, which the department published in 1889.[9]

It was crucial to get Congress involved, however, and that created problems. Perhaps knowing of that body's slowness, one member of the organization remarked, "the project is a good one, if it don't die a-bornin." Henry Boynton, however, was the prime mover, drafting a bill in consultation with members of Congress, the press, local supporters such as Chattanoogan Adolph S. Ochs, and the Society of the Army of the Cumberland. Many congressmen fortunately had personal ties to the battle; eleven senators and thirteen representatives had fought there. Ultimately, Boynton delivered the bill to Congressman Charles H. Grosvenor, an Ohio Republican who had been a lieutenant colonel at Chickamauga in the 18th Ohio Infantry.[10]

The bill Boynton wrote and Grosvenor introduced had eleven sections. From the beginning, Boynton clearly stated why the park would be established: the twofold purpose that had developed shortly after the Civil War—preservation and commemoration. Boynton went further than justifying the fields for historical study and memorialization, however; he included language that allowed for "professional military study." He also delineated the boundaries in the enabling legislation, which comprised some "7,600 acres, more or less," and cited an 1888 act that allowed for condemnation.[11]

The bulk of the bill placed the park in the bureaucratic organization of the federal government and detailed the duties of the park officials. It placed the park under the secretary of war and allowed for interagency cooperation to mark the boundaries. The bill also allowed persons living on park land to remain as long as they cared for the property and "all tablets, monuments, or such other artificial works" that might be placed on the battlefield. Everyday administration would be in the hands of three commissioners appointed by the secretary of war. Two would be "appointed from civil life" while the third would be active military and detailed from the War Department. The duties of the commission were to open and repair roads on the two battlefields and to mark the lines of battle. To aid the commission in this duty, the secretary of war was allowed to hire "some person recognized as well informed in regard to the details of the battle of Chickamauga and Chattanooga" to serve as historian. Congress also mandated that the commission mark the lines of battle of United States Regular Army troops engaged at Chickamauga.[12]

The last part of the bill dealt with monumentation and regulations. Various states, as well as the Chickamauga Memorial Association, were allowed to enter the park and place monuments and markers to locate troop positions. However, these objects had to be in compliance with park regulations and approved by the secretary of war. The secretary of war was to make regulations "for the care of the park and for the establishment and marking of the lines of battle and other historical features of the park." He also was to provide law enforcement at the park.[13]

Finally, $250,000 was to be provided to create, construct, and maintain the park. The secretary of war had to give approval for disbursements, and he had to make an annual report on the park to Congress.[14]

Grosvenor introduced Boynton's bill in the House of Representatives on January 13, 1890, but he soon realized the bill was flawed and needed additional wording. Correcting the minor problems, Grosvenor then introduced a new but very similar bill on February 6, 1890, telling the House, "by omission of the drafter of that bill and by an error in printing[,] the [original] bill has been rendered practically valueless." The new bill was offered as a substitute, assigned the number H.R. 6454, and referred to the Committee on Military Affairs.[15]

The House Committee on Military Affairs reported to the House on March 5, 1890, but made its own argument about the need to establish the park. Noting that eastern armies had a semipreserved battlefield at Gettysburg, the committee argued for the conservation of a western battlefield. In arguing for Chickamauga and Chattanooga's preservation, the committee reminded the House how vicious the fighting had been in terms of casualties and how dramatic the battles there had been. Here occurred, the committee argued, "some of the most remarkable tactical movements and the deadliest fighting of the war of the rebellion." But the committee went further than just preserving the battlefields as memorials to the armies and men that had fought there; it added a practical aspect to the preservation. "The preservation for national study of the lines of decisive battles," the committee lectured, "may properly be regarded as a matter of national importance." Later in their report,

the committee continued that the battlefields would be "an object lesson of what is possible in American fighting, and the national value of
the preservation of such lines for historical and professional study must
be apparent to all reflecting minds." In order to make the fields useful to
historians and the military, the committee proposed the "restoration of
the entire field to its condition at the time of the battle."[16]

The committee also had definite ideas of what was not important in
the work at Chickamauga and Chattanooga. "The political questions which
were involved in the contest do not enter into this view of the subject,
nor do they belong to it. The proposition for establishing the park is in
all its aspects a purely military project," the committee counseled. It also
reminded the House that the battlefields were in such pristine condition
that little work would be required to preserve them. The "cutting away of
underbrush over a very limited area" was all that was needed, the committee continued. Attempting to cut off any opposition on the grounds
of fiscal responsibility, the committee maintained that "once established,
the cost of the care of the park and its approaches will be very small."[17]

Noting that this park would honor both sides, the committee warned
the House that the bill enjoyed great support from the people and had
been endorsed by the various veterans' organizations. With one small
amendment regarding expediting work, the committee sent the bill to
the House with unanimous approval.[18]

On Wednesday May 28, 1890, Representative Grosvenor brought H.R.
6454 to the floor of the House of Representatives. The bill faced challenges
from the start. Only through the efforts of Speaker of the House Thomas B.
Reed was it ever brought up, because the House was in "the rushing days
of the session." Appropriations bills had the right of way, but Boynton
wrote that Reed "earned a debt of gratitude from all soldiers" by allowing
the bill to come up. If Reed had not done so, it would have had to wait
until the next session of Congress. Thus Grosvenor was given the time,
and after the bill was read, he asked for passage by unanimous consent.
Texas representative and Confederate veteran Constantine B. Kilgore (D)
objected, saying, "I am very much inclined to object." Continuing, Kilgore
stated, "I am opposed to this character of legislation. I do not believe Congress ought to indulge in legislation of this kind and appropriating the
people's money to buy lands to make parks all over the country." Asking
what the appropriation was, Kilgore persuaded Grosvenor, apparently
in an on-the-spot decision, to cut the amount of money from $250,000
to $125,000. Kilgore then softened to the idea, but still wanted a debate

on the subject, "to consider it now in the proper way, and not rush it through without discussion or consideration." Others agreed, saying the bill needed to be referred to the committee of the whole. Illinois congressman and former colonel of the 112th Illinois Thomas Jefferson Henderson threatened to object to the bill if it was going to take a long time to debate. The chair asked for objection to the present manner of consideration, and hearing none continued the process.[19]

Grosvenor then went through several amendments, mostly concerning wording and syntax. As he droned on, the impatient members of the chamber cried, "Vote!, Vote!" Hearing the desire of the House to move on, Grosvenor finished with his amendments and told the House he would not address the body on the bill. He did request that anyone desiring to speak be given room for comments in the record, which was granted with unanimous consent. The clerk read the bill a third time, and the vote was taken: 120 yes to 8 no. With unanimous consent that the motion to reconsider be laid upon the table, the House passed the bill and sent it to the Senate. The debate had taken all of twenty-three minutes.[20]

The next day, the Senate referred the bill to its Committee on Military Affairs, which accepted the House committee report with a few amendments. The committee reported on the bill on June 5, 1890, but the full Senate did not take up consideration until mid July. On July 16, Committee on Military Affairs chairman Joseph R. Hawley, a Connecticut Republican and former Union general, brought the bill to the floor during debate on an appropriations bill. Having yielded for other matters, the appropriations chairman did so again so that the bill could be passed. Hawley spoke briefly on the battle and the proposed park, reminding the senators that seven of them had fought in the battles. He then brought forward the amendments the committee recommended, most of which dealt with wording and spelling errors. The only substantial change was an amendment that required the commissioners to be veterans of the battles. Each amendment passed, whereupon Senator Randall Gibson, a former Confederate general, rose to support the bill: "I think it may be proper as one of the soldiers on the Confederate side in that battle that I should rise and say that for one I cordially endorse the bill." The bill was then passed by unanimous consent, but since it differed from the House version, Hawley requested that the "Senate insist upon its amendments to this bill and ask for a conference with the House of Representatives thereon." The president pro tempore authorized Hawley and former Confederate generals Francis M. Cockrell of Missouri and Edward C. Walthall of Mississippi to represent the Senate in conference. The entire process had taken less time than in the House, a mere twenty minutes.[21]

The House took up the conference request, but could not get a consensus on whether to accept the Senate amendments. Finally, on August 12, the House granted the conference, the speaker appointing Grosvenor, Union veteran of the 65th Ohio Samuel P. Snider of Minnesota, and former Confederate general Joseph Wheeler of Alabama. By August 16, both the House and Senate passed the conference report in which the House receded its nonconcurrence with the Senate's amendments. In addition, both houses agreed to more amendments, chiefly changes in wording. Immediately upon passage of the conference report, Representative H. Clay Evans of Chattanooga took the bill to the White House, where President Benjamin Harrison signed it on August 20, 1890. Fortunately for battlefield preservation, Congress was in a spending mood; this Congress would later be termed the "Billion Dollar Congress" because it was the first in United States history to appropriate that amount of money. With part of that staggering amount, the Federal government created America's first national military park.[22]

The movement to establish the park and the congressional process that did so were important for America and for the preservation and commemoration movement that had begun during the Civil War. The legislation not only established the nation's first national military park, but it also set the parameters for such preservation. The legislation created the park to commemorate the battles there and to preserve the battlefields, but Congress placed another wrinkle in the preservation mentality: to provide professional military officers a battlefield to study. The creation of Chickamauga and Chattanooga as a park was also pathbreaking in that it mandated inclusion of both sides in the Civil War. Gettysburg was moving in that direction, but Chickamauga and Chattanooga was the first park so created. Other lessons learned and decisions made would also affect the coming wave of preservation. The minor opposition in Congress, the manner in which the parks were developed with monuments and tablets, and the restoration of the fields to their Civil War appearance would all become hallmarks of 1890s preservation activity. Thus the legislation of this first effort at battlefield conservation on a national level would directly affect how other parks coming along in the 1890s would be developed.

This first attempt at battlefield preservation had not gone without opposition, however. Representative Kilgore's lecture against building parks was echoed by others. When the Chickamauga Memorial Association began to talk about buying the battlefield, Brevet Major General Samuel H.Hurst opposed the venture at a GAR meeting. He feared that the land transactions would require "middlemen" and "speculators" who would make money off the venture. One veteran stated, "[Hurst] has gotten into his head that some of the parties connected with the project are working up land schemes, and are attempting to make a large amount of money out of the Government, while they are furthering the project itself." Apparently, Hurst had Boynton in mind, and quite a controversy between the two erupted in the papers. Ultimately, Hurst realized the effort was ethical and dropped his opposition. The resistance to the Chickamauga park, however, foreshadowed opposition to the entire battlefield preservation movement.[23]

In accordance with the enabling legislation, Secretary of War Redfield Proctor, a firm supporter of the military park idea, appointed the Chickamauga and Chattanooga National Military Park Commission. The legislation called for the commission to be made up of two civilian veterans of the battle, one from each side, and one veteran still on active duty with the army. Proctor nominated Joseph S. Fullerton of Missouri, Alexander P. Stewart of Tennessee, and Captain Sanford C. Kellogg of the 4th United States Cavalry. Union veteran Fullerton had been on Major General Gordon Granger's staff at Chickamauga and Chattanooga. Stewart had been a major general in command of a Confederate division at both battles, and had made dramatic assaults on the Union lines on both days at Chickamauga. Kellogg had been an aide on Major General George H. Thomas's staff during the battles and had recently been involved in War Department work at Chickamauga, such as the 1888 examination of the battlefield with former officers to correct department maps. As historian and secretary to the commission, Proctor appointed Chickamauga's most ardent supporter and originator of the idea of creating the park— Henry V. Boynton. The secretary also named Edward E. Betts and Atwell Thompson as engineers and Hugh B. Rowland as commission clerk.[24]

The commission soon met at the battlefields to plan their work. A simple organization was soon established in which Fullerton would act as chairman and maintain the office in Washington. Stewart would be in charge of construction on the battlefields and would actually reside there as the resident commissioner. Kellogg, on active duty, would serve as commission secretary. Boynton and the engineers would also be present on the battlefields to do the work and guide historical efforts.[25]

*Alexander P. Stewart. A division commander in the Army of Tennessee at Chickamauga and Chattanooga, Stewart served as the Confederate commissioner at that park for eighteen years. As resident commissioner for most of those years, he represented the Southern veterans and also oversaw construction on the park.* Battles and Leaders.

The first order of business in creating the park was land acquisition, and that proved to be a problem. In rural north Georgia, where the Chickamauga battlefield lay, farmers and locals had not always registered land deeds. Some deed transactions had been lost in a fire at the local courthouse. The government insisted on clear chains of title before acquisition, so land agent Judson C. Clements thus had a difficult job dealing with the more than two hundred landowners.[26]

Many landowners asked exorbitant prices for their land, which had recently increased in value due to a railroad on the western edge of the proposed park and coal and iron discoveries nearby. Some landowners boosted the price when they realized the government wanted it, Fullerton remembering that the enabling legislation was "a notice to all land-owners to be on guard." A few landowners within the authorized boundary did not wish to sell their land, forcing Congress to amend the legislation to implement major condemnation proceedings. That process in itself was very complicated, necessitating appraisals and court action. Fortunately, there was no problem with the state governments involved, which ceded rights to the roadways and lands under their jurisdiction.[27]

The work of land acquisition continued for several years, the commission condemning the majority of the Chickamauga land in three bulk actions. The first took place on July 9, 1891, bringing 1,258.66 acres under government ownership. The second condemnation took place on November 10, 1891, netting 2,567.75 acres. The third took place on January 5, 1892, bringing in 1,485 acres. By the end of the 1892 fiscal year, therefore, the commission was able to report "the greater part of the land has been acquired." By 1893, the commission reported it had bought some ten square miles at Chickamauga, in addition to several "detached reservations" such as Orchard Knob in Chattanooga and Braxton Bragg's headquarters, the DeLong Place, and portions of the Tunnel Hill area on Missionary Ridge. Except for a few hundred scattered acres, the commission reported, the park was nearing completion by the end of 1893. The next year, the commission reported 5,521 acres in the park, with an additional 1,006 scheduled for acquisition. Some of the landowners, particularly on Missionary Ridge, were asking such exorbitant prices that the commission recommended no further action on them. Despite such setbacks, the commission had moved exceedingly quickly in gathering the land needed for the park.[28]

Work immediately began to restore the land to its battle condition. The commission and its engineers, Betts and Thompson, worked feverishly to re-create the 1863 setting. Year after year, the commission reported its work in "the restoration of the field to the condition in which it was at the time of the battle in 1863." Representative Charles Grosvenor and Senator John Palmer, both veterans of the battles, reported the progress to their respective houses: "The park is not in any sense a pleasure ground, and no work of beautifying it is in progress or contemplated. The central idea is the restoration of these battlefields to the condition which existed at the time of the engagements."[29]

The engineers first made a thorough survey of the entire battlefield, with the land laid out meticulously into various plots. Laborers under road engineer Atwell Thompson closed postbattle avenues and opened those that had been in existence at the time of the battle. By 1895, some forty-one miles of roads had been opened and improved. Likewise, the laborers tried to restore the wooded areas of the park by clearing out the dense undergrowth that had appeared since the war. Over 3,500 acres of underbrush had been cleared by 1896, leaving only trees, which resembled the open range used by the farmers at the time of the battles. One member of the commission recorded that "carriages can now drive in all directions through the great forests and along the various lines of battle."[30]

As more of the battlefields came under government control and the laborers restored the land to its 1863 appearance, the work of marking the battlefield went on under the direction of Henry Boynton, the park's first historian. He and the commission performed the massive job of collecting reports, maps, and veterans' oral histories to determine exactly where units had fought. Fortunately, the War Department was then in the process of publishing battle reports in the *Official Records*, but many of the units' reports were missing from those volumes. Chairman Fullerton publicly called for those reports still in private hands. The commission also enlisted the help of Chattanooga Confederate veteran J. P. Smartt, who had studied the Confederate lines and reports extensively and was, in Boynton's words, "an excellent authority, and a most enthusiastic and impartial student." After compiling the necessary data, the commission began to mark the battlefields. The commission placed 212 unit tablets, 286 location and distance tablets, and 51 battery tablets by September 1895 to mark unit positions and headquarters, while nine pyramids of cannonballs marked mortuary sites where general officers fell. The individual states also became involved, with many making appropriations for monuments to honor their units. Congress also appropriated money to honor the regular army units engaged during the battles. To further facilitate the study of the battles, the commission placed five observation towers at various locations at Chickamauga and Missionary Ridge to offer, they said, "comprehensive views of the field of conflict." The commission also produced highly detailed topographical maps, although these often led to disagreements over troop positions.[31]

By the end of the 1894 fiscal year, therefore, the commission had created a park that was nearing completion. Most of the land had been acquired, many of the states were nearing completion of their monuments, iron tablets marked corps and division unit positions, and newly opened roadways offered access. Brigade tablets and the four hundred artillery tubes the commission obtained from the Ordnance Department still needed to be placed, but by and large the park, which Boynton called "a most complete object lesson in war," was almost ready. In all, the commission spent $581,056.05 in its first three years.[32]

The commission had performed a massive job well, even working around a change in personnel when the secretary of war detailed regular army representative Sanford Kellogg to France as the "Military Attaché of the American Legation in Paris." In the first of many such controversies, Kellogg had become isolated from Commissioners Fullerton and

Stewart. These two commissioners did not agree with the interpretations on Kellogg's 1889 maps showing troops positions, or with Kellogg's views about the positioning of regular army monuments. More importantly, Kellogg had been very critical of his counterparts in their work, fiscal responsibility, and personal actions. He even wrote Secretary Lamont advising that a central authority be placed in charge of the commission, with of course himself as that officer. Stewart and Fullerton responded in defense, Stewart writing a scathing letter in which he disputed every charge and stated the accomplishments he and Fullerton had achieved. Furthermore, Stewart made his position clear regarding Kellogg as leader of the commission. "For myself," Stewart wrote, "I respectfully decline to be a subordinate of his, or to submit in any way to be reprimanded or disciplined by him." Secretary of War Lamont ended the matter by transferring Kellogg from the commission. Major Frank G. Smith, commander of Battery I, 4th United States Artillery at Chickamauga, replaced Kellogg as secretary. Boynton praised Smith's appointment, reporting that "he had the distinction [during the battle] of losing a greater percentage of men than any battery on the field, of remaining through the battle, and losing neither positions nor guns."[33]

With the park nearly constructed, greater attention went to interpretation. The commission wanted the ever-increasing number of visitors to be given a general history of the battles. They set up a visitor center at the Crawfish Springs Hotel, from which assistant superintendent William Tillman ran the park and where the commission held its meetings. There visitors could register, spend the night, and hire guides to tour the park. They might even visit with the park's aged resident commissioner, former Confederate general A. P. Stewart. Visitors arriving on the railroad or trolley cars that served the park area could also hire horses and carriages and take advantage of the interpretation set forth by troop position markers and monuments as well as the towers that offered sweeping views.[34]

By the end of 1894, the commission had completed the park to a degree that plans for a dedication could go forward. Congress became involved in December 1894, appropriating money and setting the date for the dedication around September 18–20, 1895, the anniversary of the battle. Congress envisioned three days of speeches, parades, gun salutes, and reunions. Secretary of War Daniel S. Lamont became the chief facilitator of the event and named commission chairman Joseph S. Fullerton to act as grand marshal.[35]

Led by Mayor George W. Ochs, the city of Chattanooga displayed "practical enthusiasm." The city and county officers upgraded the road system around Chattanooga and leading to Chickamauga. They also provided "an abundant supply of ice water" along the major thoroughfares. With large crowds expected, lodging became a concern, but quarters for fifteen thousand people were established among the city's population, with others staying at hotels and many in campgrounds on the Chickamauga battlefield itself. To provide transportation, city and county officials called for wagons and carriages from as far away as Nashville, Birmingham, and Knoxville. The three major railroads in the area also cooperated, connecting their tracks and making a loop so that all trains ran the same direction from Chattanooga down to Chickamauga and back to the city. In order to direct visitors, the city also printed an "Official Souvenir Program."[36]

The pre-dedication planning paid off, because an immense crowd estimated at fifty thousand people invaded the battlefields on September 18, and no major problems emerged. One participant remembered that no one charged exorbitant prices for lodging or transportation. Even the rail road system worked to perfection, he remembered. "The result was that the immense crowd was handled without a single accident and with dispatch," he wrote. Even security was not a problem, despite the fact that Vice President Adlai E. Stevenson, four members of the cabinet, nine senators, fifteen governors, and twenty-three representatives were in attendance.[37]

The first day of the celebration, September 18, 1895, was set aside for state monument dedications. All through the day at various points on the battlefields, eight different states dedicated their regimental and state monuments that had been erected "where the representatives of the regiments think the organizations made the most notable record." The Michigan and Missouri commissions dedicated their monuments in the morning, while Ohio and Wisconsin held their ceremonies at noon. Illinois, Minnesota, and Indiana held dedication services at 2:00 p.m., and Massachusetts finished the day at 4:00 p.m. At each dedication, several prominent veterans and officials spoke to the large crowds. Many governors spoke of their state's achievements at the battles, and state commission members likewise detailed their actions. Famous veterans and politicians also spoke, including, for example, Lew Wallace at the Indiana dedication and Governor William McKinley at the Ohio dedication.[38]

The night of September 18 was reserved for the annual reunion of the Society of the Army of the Cumberland. The planners had built large tents in Chattanooga and that night over ten-thousand veterans arrived. At the meeting, O. O. Howard offered an opening prayer, followed by speeches by such veterans as John Schofield, Grenville Dodge, Daniel Butterfield, and Horace Porter. Veteran Union general James D. Morgan made a special welcome to the Confederates in attendance, and Boynton also addressed the crowd.[39]

The dedication of the Chickamauga portion of the park was held at noon the next day in "an extensive natural amphitheater at the foot of Snodgrass Hill." Estimates ranged from forty to fifty thousand in attendance. The crowd had been witness to a modern battery and infantry drill that morning, and a noon salute of forty-four guns called the dedication services to order. Chairman Fullerton introduced the keynote speaker, Vice President Stevenson. Veterans themselves spoke, one from each side during the battle. Union veteran John N. Palmer and Confederate veteran John B. Gordon, both generals during the war, represented their differing sides. Generals John Schofield and James Longstreet also made brief addresses, as did various governors. The service ended with patriotic music.[40]

The night of September 19 saw a reunion in Chattanooga, this time a combined meeting for the Army of the Tennessee (Union) and Army of Tennessee (Confederate). Former generals on both sides again spoke, O. O. Howard and Willard Warner for the Union and Joseph Wheeler for the Confederates.[41]

On September 20, the crowds moved into Chattanooga for the dedication of that portion of the park. After a parade of regular army units composed of the 6th and 17th Infantry and the 3rd Artillery as well as Civil War veterans, another forty-four gun salute brought the meeting to order. Once again, speeches from veterans of both sides dedicated the park. Former generals William Bate (Confederate) and Charles Grosvenor (Union) gave the featured addresses, and many of the various governors also spoke briefly. That night, veterans of the Army of Northern Virginia (Confederate) and Army of the Potomac (Union) held their reunion in the large tent in Chattanooga. Veterans such as Edward Walthall, William C. Oates, and James Williamson spoke to the large crowds.[42]

The three-day dedication at Chickamauga and Chattanooga was a vivid portrayal of the reunion and reconciliation occurring during the 1890s. In each of the sessions, the organizers were very careful to include both sides in the orations and speeches. Those speeches themselves were filled with references to reunion and reconciliation. Vice President Stevenson spoke to the crowd about the veterans: "They meet, not in deadly conflict, but as brothers, under one flag—fellow citizens of a common country." Former Union general John M. Palmer said: "We are here to-day 'with malice toward none and charity for all;' we meet as citizens of a common country, devoted to its interests and alike ready to maintain its honor, wherever or however assailed." Former Confederate general John B. Gordon spoke of "the heroic remnants of the once hostile and now historic armies of the sixties [that] meet as brothers." Senator William Bate, former Confederate general, spoke of the change over time: "With sheathless swords in sinewy hands we, Confederate and Federal, fought that great battle of duty, and now, thirty-two years after, we again obey the assemble call, we respond to the long roll and fall in line, not to renew the battle nor to rekindle the strife, nor even to argue as to which won the victory, but to gather up the rich fruits of both the victory and defeat as treasures of inestimable value to our common country." Representative Grosvenor, former Union general and sponsor of the park bill in Congress, spoke for the Union and reminded his audience of what had taken place: "This is the achievement of which we are proudest. This is the result which makes us happy to-day. It is that we are no longer enemies, but brothers."[43]

The reconciliatory festivities soon ended, but the work of park establishment continued. For the next few years, the park commission added to the acreage, continued the process of building monuments and markers, and began positioning artillery in the park. The process was slowed in March 1897 when Chairman Fullerton was killed in a train wreck at the Youghiogheny River on the Baltimore and Ohio Railroad in western Maryland. Writing for the commission, Boynton described Fullerton's death as "a severe loss to the public service." In his place, Secretary of War Russell A. Alger appointed the fiery Boynton to head the comission, a logical decision in that he had been the chief figure in park affairs all along. It was Boynton who began the idea of creating a park at Chickamauga, it was he who pushed until it was done, and it was he who directed the historical work at the park. Boynton's elevation to chairman, although because of tragic circumstances, benefited the park in the long run. To fill the position of historian, the secretary of war appointed Colonel Henry M. Duffield, but Boynton remained the chief historian of the battle.[44]

The process of park building went on under the new leadership. The major activity after the dedication was the addition of land at Chattanooga, most notably on Lookout Mountain. In 1897, the park bought the battlefield on the mountain, a shelf about midway up the slope, for $22,065, and immediately began to fashion it into a part of the park. Now in control of the area around the Cravens' House where the Federals drove a small contingent of Confederates from the mountain on November 24, 1863, the commission cleared the undergrowth, prepared paths and trails to reach "every difficult point of its rugged topography," and placed historical tablets detailing the action. Two years later, the commission succeeded in acquiring sixteen additional acres at the top of the mountain, the area that became known as "Point Park." Tablets and monuments to brigades and batteries soon went up, as did fourteen historical tablets that described the complete action around Chattanooga from a point at which the visitor could view the entire battlefield.[45]

The commission also finished the newly christened park at Chickamauga. The work of clearing the lands of undergrowth was completed by 1896, while the engineering crews persistently worked on keeping the roads in order, opening new roads, building foundations for the many state monuments, and increasing the water supply in the park. Even the locals living around the area pitched in to help build the park. Citizens in the area donated land to the park in order to widen the roads. One strip of land along the Lafayette Road in the Chickamauga park was donated by more than three hundred landowners. Citizens living along the Crest Road on Missionary Ridge also donated land to the park. Boynton described the citizens' generosity as "evidencing the interest taken in the park project." The major effort of the commission after the dedication, however, was in placing the remaining tablets, monuments, and guns. By 1899, the commission was able to report 228 monuments and 341 markers, along with 554 historical unit tablets, 237 artillery pieces "mounted upon cast iron carriages painted so as to be an exact representation of the carriage of 1861," and 448 distance and locality tablets. In all, the commission had marked every brigade line of both sides at both major battlefields of Chickamauga and Chattanooga, plus other markers at nearby Wauhatchie, Tunnel Hill, and Ringgold.[46]

The states were just as active during the postdedication period. Numerous state monuments were dedicated in the five years after the 1895 festivities, and these dedications continued to exemplify the reconciliation and reunion of the decade so vividly demonstrated at the dedication services. These monuments "of imposing design" illustrated the honor and bravery of the troops while at the same time portraying a united nation. For instance, Georgia dedicated a state monument and fifty-five

*Georgia monument at Chickamauga. Illustrating the reconciliation prevalent during the Golden Age of preservation and in the years afterward, this 1899 photo shows the Georgia state monument at Chickamauga immediately before its dedication. The bronze portion of this Confederate monument is veiled in a United States flag. Chickamauga and Chattanooga National Military Park.*

regimental monuments on May 4, 1899. Their monument was unveiled by removing a large United States flag. Divided Kentucky dedicated monuments to her sons of both North and South on the same day. Illinois and Indiana also placed monuments at Chickamauga and Chattanooga.[47]

The post-1895 monument dedications continued the feelings of reconciliation and harmony between the North and South. At Pennsylvania's dedication in 1897, for example, that state's governor, Daniel H. Hastings, reminded his audience that "time has cooled the ardor; has tempered the judgment; has healed the wounds and has mellowed—aye, obliterated all sectional animosities." At Iowa's dedication ceremonies in 1906, Governor Albert B. Cummings told the crowd, "We [North and South] are now a mighty instrument of advance and progress. We are now fighting shoulder to shoulder for all the blessings of good government. We are now, side by side, grappling with the problems of peace in a united country, with a common heart filled with love for the old flag, filled with hope for the glory of the human race."[48]

Even as the park became more complete while the 1890s waned, the practical aspects of the site became clearer. The park was foremost created to commemorate the battles and those who fought there, but practical application by the military in both professional learning and use were also important. In 1896, Congress had passed legislation that added to the professional study clause in Chickamauga's legislation. The 1896 act declared that every military park would not only be used for professional study by officers but would also be training grounds where entire units conducted exercises. One congressman remarked that study of the actual fields, marked as they were with tablets and monuments, "would be worth an entire course in textbooks on the strategy of a campaign and battle tactics."[49]

With the original legislation and the 1896 law, Chickamauga soon became a haven of army activity. As early as 1890, the park had hosted Georgia State Militia units, and in 1897 it hosted various garrisons from the deep south in times of "yellow fever visitation." With the advent of war with Spain in 1898, however, Chickamauga became busy as a staging area for army units heading for the war zone. Chairman Boynton enthusiastically backed the idea, and he and historian Duffield received brigadier generals' commissions. In order to handle the influx of soldiers while still maintaining the park as a historical artifact, the army set up Camp George H. Thomas in one section of the park.[50]

The army began moving into the park in April 1898 after the declaration of war against Spain. Colonel J. G. C. Lee, assistant quartermaster general of the army, arrived to set up subsistence stores for the troops that would soon be coming. By mid May, some 2,700,000 rations were in transit to the area in order to keep three months' supply on hand. Major General John R. Brooke also arrived in April to command the post, but he soon turned over control to Major General James F. Wade in order to lead troops to Puerto Rico. In June, the army set up a hospital in a new hotel in Crawfish Springs, immediately south of the park. The hospital could accommodate 285 patients and had a staff of 14 medical officers, 38 stewards, and 34 female nurses. In the short time the park was used a base, 70,734 officers and men, 8,366 horses, and 6,673 mules passed through Camp Thomas.[51]

The months of active army operations were extremely hard on the park resources. The commission's annual report in 1899 discussed the myriad problems caused by the army's presence, ranging from damaged roads to mass sickness among the troops. Assuming command of the reserve after the majority of the troops had left, chairman Boynton reported that the use of the park was of "great practical use to the War Department," but that "the park was left in a most filthy and deplorable condition by the outgoing troops, so far as unfilled sinks in many camps and unburned refuse of various kinds could defile it." Despite specific orders, Boynton reported that the soldiers had left 3,175 unfilled sinks. The filth required the park commission to do cleanup work, which Boynton noted was "an immense amount of most disagreeable work which did not fall within the sphere of their duties."[52]

Perhaps most troubling was the fact that the commission had to pay for the cleanup. Boynton informed the secretary of war that "the work of restoration has also called for the expenditure of a considerable portion of our appropriation." The commission paid $14,224.86 for cleanup and to repair roads, which saw a great deal of "continuous and very heavy" traffic. Boynton asked that the park be reimbursed for this amount, and also itemized other future expenses such as cutting some three thousand trees killed by animals, refilling and leveling some two thousand sinks, and removing some six thousand yards of manure from Vittetoe Field, which the army had used as a dumping ground for its stables and corrals.[53]

The army's presence at Chickamauga was a trying time. In fact, seven battalions of the 6th and 8th United States Volunteer Infantry regiments remained at Chickamauga immediately after the war, and others came and went in the years ahead. All the while, however, Chickamauga continued fulfilling its legislated purposes. Although not exactly within the commemorative aspects of the park and despite its annoyance, Boynton was able to issue positive statements on the episode. The presence of the army, he said, had left no permanent damage, and the support for the war the park provided was "a source of satisfaction to the commission." In addition, the buildings built for the army could be used in the future, and the sickness that attended such a large concentration of men was falling. All in all, Boynton could report a positive experience.[54]

The influx of military personnel during the Spanish-American War not only distracted the commission from its work, but it also opened a new chapter in Chickamauga's history. Although most of the troops left after the war, there remained a military presence at the park. The buildings erected for the war were later used as a "field-supply station." Troops returning from the war zone, such as the 7th United States Cavalry and the 3rd United States Artillery, were temporarily housed there. Established in

*Spanish-American War camp at Chickamauga. The Sternberg Hospital served the medical needs of soldiers stationed at Camp George H. Thomas, which was located on the Chickamauga battlefield. This 1898 view shows the incomplete Wilder Tower in background. Chickamauga and Chattanooga National Military Park.*

1904, Fort Ogelthorpe also ensured army activity in the area. Many units of the regular army as well as state National Guard units used the park for camping and maneuver exercises in the years that followed the war. During World War I, several army entities were established at Chickamauga, including Camp Warden McLean, an officer candidate school; Camp Greenleaf, a medical camp; and Camp Forrest, a reserve officers' training camp. During that war, the troops damaged the park again, even constructing trenches on Snodgrass Hill and polo fields and golf courses elsewhere. In all, over sixty thousand troops passed through the area during World War I. Most of the troops left after "the signing of the armistice," and the commission again had to remove the buildings and restore the area to its original state.[55]

Despite the distraction of the military's presence, the park commissioners at Chickamauga and Chattanooga continued their work of park building. The park itself continued to grow in size and road mileage. Each year, small plots and new roads were added, so that by 1908 the commission was able to report some 6,876 acres in the park, serviced by "a trifle over 105 miles" of roadway. The most significant construction project after the initial building of the park was the Point Park improvements, which were completed by 1905. The commission constructed a "monumental

*Point Park arch construction at Chattanooga. This 1905-era photograph shows the major construction needed to build the Point Park arch atop Lookout Mountain. Chickamauga and Chattanooga National Military Park.*

entrance to the park" by erecting a stone wall across Lookout Mountain. The entrance gates were made of "two battlemented observation towers" connected with a "cordeled and crenelated wall, to which is built the buttress portal, and containing an arch entrance." The structure resembled the Corps of Engineers logo. Portions of the wall were temporarily left unbuilt so that the massive New York monument, then under construction, could be moved to its place on the park.[56]

The commission also worked to maintain and preserve that which had already been built. One problem facing the commission was erosion and unsightly washes, which they controlled by planting trees and establishing grass-planting programs. Even Secretary of Agriculture James Wilson and the superintendent of the United States Botanic Garden, William R. Smith, became involved after their visits to the park. Secretary Wilson donated a "generous supply of those seeds which he deemed best fitted for the soil and climate of the park." Superintendent Smith worked to reforest 150 acres of cleared land that were originally timbered during the battle. Commission chairman Boynton reported that the experiments "produced excellent results."[57]

Another problem the commission battled less successfully was the massive influx of roaming animals such as horses, cattle, mules, and hogs. The animals, particularly hogs, caused significant damage, the commission reporting that "large areas of fine turf have been rooted up and many tablets smeared, and some tablets were rooted off of their stands." The commission first tried issuing regulations which stated that it would drive offending livestock off the park and would "prevent its return." The regulations also stipulated that the owners of the livestock would face "penalties of fine and imprisonment." The regulations helped only for a time. Commission chairman Boynton reported 3,969 livestock driven off the park in 1901. Unable to solve the problem, the commission decided to fence the entire park grounds. By October 1900, the park had enclosed the Missionary Ridge and Lookout Mountain tracts in wire fencing. By October 1902, the Chickamauga battlefield had thirteen miles of fencing.[58]

The task of marking the field went on despite the fact that the majority of the work had been accomplished in the 1890s. By 1908, the commission reported 278 artillery tubes in place on replica carriages. Most were at Chickamauga, but others lined Missionary Ridge and Lookout Mountain. The commission did not foresee much more artillery monumentation and thus turned over forty-nine guns to Gettysburg's commission and traded other cannon with Shiloh. Sixty-eight pieces remained at Chickamauga, however, for future marking. The number of tablets and markers in the park likewise grew through the years. The commission reported 643 historical tablets and 368 distance and locality tablets in 1902, and that number grew by small additions as more land was added to the park.[59]

In the years after the park's dedication, many more states placed monuments on the battlefields: Iowa, Ohio, Maryland, Pennsylvania, Indiana, Connecticut, New York, Alabama, and Florida. Many of the monuments were large and cost impressive amounts of money, such as the grand New York monument in Point Park and the Illinois monument on Missionary Ridge. Veterans of John Wilder's Union brigade built a stone observation tower at Chickamauga, where the brigade fought on the second day of the battle. Begun in 1892 and completed in 1903, the tower was dedicated during a reunion on the battlefield. The commission also placed cannonball pyramid monuments designed by Betts to mark headquarters sites of general officers. One of the most interesting monuments was acquired through Tennessee senator H. Newell Sanders. A six-inch gun mount from the battleship *Maine* was recovered from Havana harbor and donated to the park in 1913.[60]

As the park's monumentation and historical markers became complete, the commission began a process of ensuring accuracy in their work. They acted with a feeling that they were not only preserving an important site where they had fought and comrades had died, but also that they were preserving and writing history, and they wanted that history to be totally accurate and complete. To ensure accuracy, the commission in 1900 implemented an inspection process, which was open to anyone interested in the project but mostly aimed at veterans of the battles. A commission circular designated October 9–11, 1900, as a time of "general inspection of the work of the commission." Thus, Boynton and the commission invited veterans to return and inspect the hundreds of markers, monuments, and tablets on the battlefields.[61]

The event received the support of all the prominent veterans' organizations, and each state that had monuments on the fields appointed commissions to check their accuracy. The Society of the Army of the Cumberland held its annual reunion in Chattanooga during the time of the inspection so that veterans could participate in it. Numerous state monument commissions sent representatives to the battlefields, and local railroads offered special half-off rates for veterans who wished to attend. In the end, "a very large attendance of veterans from all sections" arrived in Chattanooga and took part in the work.[62]

The veterans were given forms on which to list specific tablets, monuments, or markers that contained errors. The results showed just how accurately the battlefield had been marked. Regarding the 228 existing monuments, only two questions emerged, one on a monument that had been argued over for years. Only 2 of the 341 state markers were questioned, and one of those was a marker placed by the commission in an approximate location. The veterans questioned only 6 of the 680 historical tablets, mostly concerning times of engagement. Several misspellings and name changes were pointed out, but by and large, the veterans approved the work. After the grand inspection, the commission placed blank forms in local hotels and transportation businesses to continue the process.[63]

The park commission also printed the official history of the battles themselves. Boynton, the chief historian of the battles, led these efforts first as park historian and then as commission chairman. He produced two slim volumes that detailed each unit's action at both Chickamauga and Chattanooga. *Battle of Chickamauga, GA., September 19–20, 1863: Organization of the Army of the Cumberland and of the Army of Tennessee* (1895) and *Battles About Chattanooga, Tenn., November 23–25, 1863:*

*Orchard Knob, Lookout Mountain, Missionary Ridge: Organization of the Union Forces and of the Confederate Forces* (1895) later became standards for future park commissions to emulate. Boynton also compiled and wrote *Dedication of the Chickamauga and Chattanooga National Military Park, September 18–20, 1895: Report of the Joint Committee to Represent the Congress at the Dedication of the Chickamauga and Chattanooga National Military Park*, in which he accumulated the speeches and programs that took place at the dedication. Boynton privately produced *The National Military Park: Chickamauga-Chattanooga. An Historical Guide, With Maps and Illustrations*, which gave an overview of the campaigns and took the reader on a tour of the park. To replace Kellogg's deficient maps, Congress appropriated money in 1897 for the printing of *Atlas of the Battlefields of Chickamauga, Chattanooga, and Vicinity*, drawn by Betts and marked by Boynton, with a second printing including expanded maps in 1901. The commission was also involved in visual aids, including a large display at the 1904 Louisiana Purchase Exposition in St. Louis. Perhaps the most unusual production was a "model in relief of the battlefield region around Chattanooga." The nine-and-a-half-by-fourteen-foot terrain model detailed 171 square miles and included all the battlefields. The commission had three maps produced from the original in hopes, Boynton argued, of carrying out Congress's mandate of professional military study. One such model went to the United States Military Academy, one to the "Army Military School" at Fort Leavenworth, and one to a war college in Chattanooga. "The copy sent to West Point," Boynton happily reported, "has excited much interest and favorable comment."[64]

Numerous dignitaries visited the park in these years. Prince Henry of Prussia toured the park in 1902, as did President Theodore Roosevelt in 1903. President William Howard Taft visited the park on October 10, 1911, and toured in the company of the park officials. Veterans' societies also held reunions at Chickamauga, including the GAR encampment September 15–20, 1913, and the United Confederates Veterans (UCV) reunion May 27–29, 1913.[65]

The October 1900 veterans' approval, the pomp and circumstance of visiting dignitaries, and the success of the commission's publications, however, did not mean the commission worked without controversy. In fact, the commission era of the park's history is fraught with controversies ranging from problems with local landowners over boundaries to quibbles with veterans over troop positions and outright animosity and resignations within the commission itself. In a time of strong emotions, aged veterans on both sides wanted their stories told accurately and thus fought vigorously and passionately when anyone opposed their remembrance.

The local population was sometimes an important part of park's problems, with the condemnation cases being a major controversy. Problems with the grazing herds on the park and the commission's fencing in response also drew outcries from the locals. Even after the park was firmly established, boundary disputes erupted often, including squabbles over fencing, drainage, and rights of way. One incident involved the aged General Stewart. A local resident, L. Coleman, fought Stewart over Coleman's alleged encroachment on government property. Stewart told Coleman by letter to have a fence removed from the park's property "by the end of this week." Coleman immediately wrote back, blaming Stewart for the mix-up. "I call your attention to the fact that you, yourself, drew that deed," Coleman responded. The locals also complained of the filthy nature of the military camps in the park during the Spanish-American War, prompting Boynton to defend himself and the commission against "the wild charges with which the country was filled, that Chickamauga Park was a pest hole and unsuited for a camp."[66]

Controversy also erupted between the national commission and the veterans. With so many monuments and tablets, there were bound to be differences in forty-year-old memories. Some were minor and resolved peacefully, such as those that arose from the 1900 call for inspections. Other differences were not handled so well. In 1901, the explosive Boynton charged the Indiana state commission with "perpetuating erroneous history" in its printed report, which, he asserted, had misrepresented the national commission's findings through various changes, omissions, and interpolations. Regimental veterans also had problems with the commission. The 96th Illinois veterans argued with Boynton over their monument positions, and the 9th Indiana Infantry regiment's veterans also charged the commission with misplacing their monuments and with inappropriately emphasizing the role of Ohio troops over that of Indiana troops. Both were hard pressed to get anything changed that the powerful Boynton had decided on, however.[67]

Another controversy involved the son of Confederate general Archibald Gracie. The son visited the park in 1904 and quickly realized that the monumentation on Snodgrass Hill did not match what his father had told him. In an effort to tell the correct story of the battle, Gracie published *The Truth About Chickamauga* in 1911. In his book, Gracie charged

*Snodgrass Hill at Chickamauga. One of the most famous events at Chickamauga, the story of Snodgrass Hill was somewhat distorted by Henry Boynton, making the actions of his regiment more glorious than they actually were. His misrepresentation was discovered and made known by the son of a former Confederate officer,* Titanic *survivor Archibald Gracie. Photo from Boynton,* Dedication of the Chickamauga and Chattanooga National Military Park.

Boynton had erroneously marked Snodgrass Hill in order to make his own unit, the 35th Ohio, more important than any other. Boynton had actually shuffled the Union positions and placed his own Ohio regiment on the most prominent point on the series of hills, when in actuality they fought farther west. According to Chickamauga historian Jim Ogden, Boynton's incorrect positioning would have gone unnoticed if he had also shuffled the Confederate positions corresponding to the Union line. It is not known how flagrantly, if indeed at all, Boynton *willingly* changed the story, but it is evident that Boynton wanted to emphasize the Snodgrass Hill action (where his unit served), and that is one of the reasons the area is so well known today.[68]

By far, the most heated controversies regarding troop positions involved former Federal general John B. Turchin, who argued that the place where he and his brigade attacked on Missionary Ride was marked as the position of another brigade. Boynton and the commission examined the available records and decided against Turchin's allegations, Boynton saying, "I stake my reputation as the historian of the National Commission on the assertion that no claim more nearly approaching utter nonsense has been made since work on this park began." Never one to back away from a controversy, Boynton was regularly involved in controversies, such as one with William T. Sherman, and later another with the Shiloh Commission over its placement of tablets for the Army of the Ohio (the forerunner of the Boynton's Army of the Cumberland) at Shiloh.[69]

Foreshadowed by the Kellogg affair, there were also major controversies within the park's leadership, and Stewart, the Confederate representative, was often in the middle of them. Frequent quibbles erupted regarding land acquisition, such as a motion to buy the land on which Sherman fought on Missionary Ridge. Stewart said the land would be useless unless the Crest Road, which ran along Missionary Ridge, became part of the park. Stewart, however, acquiesced to the majority and wrote that if they gained authorization and the "price [was] not too high, I consent." The former Confederate general also vehemently objected to Minnesota's using a paraphrase of the famous Andrew Jackson quote "The Union, it must and shall be preserved" on one of its regimental monuments. More than just disagreement emerged later, however. Several park laborers, including the bookkeeper, leveled accusations against Engineer Betts, and they caught the ear of Commissioner Stewart. The accusations centered on Betts's waste of government funds in digging wells for the park's dedication. "Under a misapprehension of the facts, or in order to exonerate Mr. Betts," Stewart took the matter to the full commission. "I have no wish, certainly, to injure Mr. Betts," Stewart wrote, "nor do him an injustice. Neither am I willing to go on as matters stand." Ultimately, the secretary of war dismissed the charges against Betts, and the commission fired the bookkeeper and his accomplices.[70]

There were also problems of criminality. In one overblown incident, Commissioner Smith wrote Engineer Betts regarding a pair of stolen scissors. "If the *scissors* reported as having been taken from the office by unknown party are regarded as lost beyond recovery," Smith bureaucratically counseled, "a certificate or an affidavit to this effect should be made as a voucher to Abstract I, and the scissors so dropped from the return." As more monuments and relics went up on the field, however, the park began to experience real criminal activity. In July 1900, three vandals stole several bronze mountain howitzers from the headquarters area of the park near Dyer Field. The Chattanooga police department quickly apprehended the three thieves, who were sentenced to prison at hard labor. Warrants were issued for the "firm of junk dealers" who supposedly bought and disposed of the guns, but nothing ever resulted. In April 1913, a vandal "mutilated" the statue of a soldier on the 37th Indiana

Infantry monument near Brotherton Cabin. The criminal broke the soldier's gun and cap, and "badly battered" the nose, eyes, and ears, but the commission was never able to find the culprit. In 1922, vandals damaged the Illinois monument on Missionary Ridge. Other acts of lawlessness occurred through the years, including horses being stolen from the park corral, soldiers shooting livestock on the park, and even prostitution.[71]

A far more damaging event occurred on April 24, 1908, when, as the commission chairman reported, "the park was visited by a cyclone storm." The tornado destroyed many outbuildings at the park office at the Dyer Farm, including the park's barn, stable, carriage house, wagon shed, and storehouse. The storm also did severe damage to the park's roads and monumentation; several roads were washed out and many tablets were broken or displaced. The storm destroyed thousands of trees, necessitating a large workforce to repair the roads and clear an area used by the military. The destroyed buildings were also replaced, but the damage forced Congress to make an emergency appropriation of twenty-six thousand dollars. Other acts of nature, such as when lightening struck the Wilder Tower on August 21, 1914, forced the commission to make emergency repairs.[72]

The lawlessness and natural damage could be repaired, but the major difficulty the commission faced was the aging of its members. As the veterans began to die away, nonveterans began taking over control of the park. This later generation of park managers could not be expected to have the same love, pride, and devotion to the battlefields that the veteran generation had displayed. The veterans could not live forever, but by preserving the battlefields, later generations, whether military or civilian, could continue learning what had happened in America's past.

The commission remained fairly stable through 1905. Most of the changes in the early years came in the engineering department. With new parks coming along, the secretary of war tapped Chickamauga's seasoned engineers for help at the new parks. Atwell Thompson left Chickamauga in 1895 to become Shiloh's chief engineer when that park was established. E. E. Betts had become the assistant superintendent at Chickamauga in addition to his engineering duties in 1898 when William Tillman vacated the position. Betts was likewise away from the park for a couple of years after April 1901. With Vicksburg's new park under construction, Secretary Root detailed him to that park to oversee its development. Betts would remain on the Chickamauga payroll, however, and would later return to supervise the work there until 1911 when he retired.[73]

On June 3, 1905, a major change occurred. Henry V. Boynton died, his death marking for Chickamauga and Chattanooga the passing of the father of that park, the man who so fervently and faithfully had pushed the idea and then worked tirelessly and made it happen. One commission member wrote of Boynton's passing as "a distinct loss to the public service, and particularly to the park, to the development of which he had given unremitting study and constant work."[74]

Secretary of War Taft appointed, in accordance with Boynton's deathbed request, Antietam Board member Ezra A. Carman to become the new chairman. Carman had been a member of the board that had built the Antietam park, and as a clerk in the War Department, he was still very much involved with that effort. Unfortunately, Carman did not mesh well with some veterans. He began a process of editing and revising many of the old tablets and monuments that Boynton and Fullerton had approved and moving them to different locations, and of course that did not sit well with some. One veteran, in fact, wrote of Carman's decisions at Chattanooga as being based "on a false hypothesis which would have been noticed by thousands of Union veterans who participated in the battle had his conclusions and findings been made public." Many monuments and tablets were indeed moved, with the support of the secretary of war, but Carman lived only until December 1909, when he died on Christmas Day. To replace Carman, the secretary of war appointed lifelong Chickamauga supporter Charles Grosvenor. Like Boynton, Grosvenor had poured the latter part of his life into the venture. It was he, as an Ohio congressman, who had sponsored the legislation to create the park.[75]

The position of Confederate representative also saw changes in the early part of the 1900s. A. P. Stewart, after long and faithful service, died on August 30, 1908. The secretary of war replaced him with Major Joseph B. Cumming of Georgia. Another Confederate, commission secretary Baxter Smith, died on June 25, 1919, after nine years of service.[76]

The third commission position also began to see vast changes in the first decade of the 1900s. Commissioner Frank Smith retired on July 31, 1908, to be replaced by Colonel John Tweedale, who himself retired on May 20, 1910. In his stead, after an amendment in the enabling legislation that discontinued the regular army officer's presence on the commission, the secretary of war appointed Major Webster J. Colburn. Unfortunately for Colburn, he ran afoul of Grosvenor and Cumming, who outvoted him on the rekindled controversy over Carmen's replacing of monuments.

Colburn also clashed with Grosvenor and Cumming when he complained that the two were making decisions without his knowledge and holding meetings at various places other than Chattanooga. When Colburn issued a minority opinion concerning monument changes, he received a curt note from the War Department requesting his resignation. Colburn unsuccessfully fought the process, even appealing unsuccessfully to President Taft. John T. Wilder, then secretary and historian on the Shiloh commission, replaced him.[77]

The death of so many commission members brought a change in War Department policy. In an effort to save money, the War Department began recommending as early as 1902 that the five park commissions be integrated into one central commission. The idea had not gone over well, and the various commissions had successfully parried the threat then and in the following years. By 1912, however, the nature of the commissions had changed, and most parks were opting for civilian and nonveteran superintendents to oversee everyday operations. Congress thus phased out the commission system. Rather than firing the aged veterans, however, Congress determined in 1912 to let nature run its course. At Chickamauga, the retirement of E. E. Betts as resident engineer in 1911 forced the hiring of a superintendent. The secretary of war appointed former clerk Richard B. Randolph to the position on July 1, 1911. The present commissioners would be retained until their resignation or death, but the positions would not be filled.[78]

The idea of an eventual central commission and then superintendents marked a practical change for the War Department. As the department began to get bigger, the national military parks became less important than they once were. During the 1890s, the parks had been the talk of the War Department, but they took a secondary role with the advent of the Spanish-American War and the mushrooming of the bureaucracy in World War I. For Chickamauga, the official office was transferred from Washington to Chattanooga in 1910. The department no longer needed or desired direct everyday control over the park. Thus, the entire park operation was administered from Chattanooga's Custom House, where the headquarters had been for many years after it was moved from Crawfish Springs.[79]

Chickamauga park's last commission-era historian, J. P. Smartt, died on September 9, 1914, and the position was not filled. The first commissioner to die after the 1912 legislation was John Wilder, who died on October 20, 1917. Commission Chairman Grosvenor died just ten days later on October 30, 1917. Neither position was filled, and the secretary of war appointed the Confederate representative, Joseph Cumming, the only remaining commissioner, as chairman. Cumming remained very involved, even holding commission meetings periodically and keeping immaculate records; on December 11, 1918, for example, he reported, "The Chickamauga and Chattanooga National Park Commission met this day at its office in Chatt., Major Jos. B. Cumming, Chairman, being present." Cumming died on May 15, 1922, leaving sole responsibility of the park to Superintendent Randolph.[80]

In the postcommission era, there was greater emphasis on interpretation. While the original intentions had been to preserve and memorialize veterans' actions, the passing of that generation demanded new ideas. In order to bring the feeling of battle to a generation that had not witnessed the war, the park hosted a reenactment for Chickamauga's anniversary in September 1923. On September 18, sixty years after the battle, local army units as well as nearby Reserve Officer Training Corps cadets tried to reenact the Confederate assaults up Snodgrass Hill. Nearly ten thousand people attended the event, with about half taking part in "a barbecue luncheon." The War Department also made plans to interpret the battles on more individual terms when it implemented guide services and instructed its superintendents to be extremely knowledgeable about all aspects of the battles and park. At Chickamauga, Superintendent Randolph guided the park workforce as it interacted with an ever-growing population of visitors. To help interpret the park, the War Department re-published Boynton's pamphlets, such as *The Battle of Chickamauga, Georgia* (1932), *Battles About Chattanooga, Tennessee* (1932), and *The Campaign for Chattanooga* (1932). Finally in 1933, the War Department gave up the military parks in an executive branch reorganization. Although not without opposition, President Franklin D. Roosevelt transferred the battlefields to the National Park Service of the Department of the Interior, an organization with a much firmer grasp on preservation and interpretation. Randolph became the first National Park Service superintendent at Chickamauga.[81]

As Chickamauga and Chattanooga continually developed in the War Department era, a pattern of methodology emerged that places the park into the context of the federal 1890s-era battlefield preservation efforts. By 1900, the park had actually developed into two different parks. The Chickamauga and Chattanooga portions were entirely different entities, although part of the same parent park. Chickamauga was a massive area of land that encompassed the vast majority of the battlefield. As such, much of the park's appropriated money had gone to land acquisition. At Chattanooga, however, only a small percentage of the battlefield was actually in government hands. Rather than buying the entire area, which by that time had become engulfed in the city's urbanization and industrialization, the commission opted to buy roadways and only small "reservations" at which important events happened. The plan at Chattanooga, as opposed to Chickamauga, where the tactical movements were traced in vivid detail, was to interpret and describe the events from the main roads and points of high elevation that offered a panoramic view, such as Lookout Mountain and Missionary Ridge.

The dual paradigm at Chickamauga and Chattanooga National Military Park exemplified what was occurring at other parks established in the 1890s and in the thought processes of preservationists in Washington. By 1895, Congress had established parks not only at Chickamauga and Chattanooga but also at Antietam, Shiloh, and Gettysburg. With the new parks emerging and doubtless others to follow, the War Department recommended that Congress establish a "fixed policy" concerning the nature of the parks. Two methods had developed by that year of 1895, one of which was the Chickamauga method devised by Henry Boynton, in which the entire battlefield was bought and developed into a park. The other was the means used at Chattanooga, but more famously at Antietam. By 1895, the Chattanooga battlefield was so urbanized that acquisition of the entire battlefield was unrealistic, and thus it was preserved in pieces. Five hundred miles to the northeast, the battlefield of Antietam was going through a similar process but for different reasons.[82]

# 4

## "THE EXPERIMENT AT ANTIETAM"
### Antietam National Battlefield, 1890–1933

AFTER THE PRESERVATION success at Chickamauga with which the decade of the 1890s began, the next battlefield to be preserved was at Antietam. But whereas Chickamauga was a full-blown national military park with huge acreage and massive monumentation, Antietam would turn out to be much different. The Maryland battlefield would, in fact, be more akin to the Chattanooga unit of the Chickamauga park. "The experiment at Antietam" looked favorable in 1890, but it is unfortunate that such an important battle did not receive the same treatment as did the other battlefields in the 1890s.[1]

Antietam had beginnings similar to Chickamauga's. As early as October 1887, the 51st Pennsylvania placed a monument on the end of the Burnside Bridge across Antietam Creek. Others began to discuss the idea of a monumented park, and an Antietam Memorial Association emerged in 1890 to create a park at the battlefield. Maryland congressman Louis E. McComas and Rev. C. L. Keedy began the work of the association, obtaining assistance from the Gettysburg association then in the process of directing monumentation on that battlefield. The stated objective was to "make of the Antietam battle-field what was made of the scene of the conflict at Gettysburg." An observer noted that the association even "laid out some avenues along battle lines on that field and encouraged organizations to erect monuments," which, he said, was "done to some extent." The association further intended to purchase the battlefield and ask more states to erect monuments in order to "perpetuate in lasting and worthy tributes the historic features of that memorable battle."[2]

The association thought it could garner "the same amount of interest" as at Gettysburg, but that hope failed to materialize. There is no evidence the Antietam Memorial Association made much headway toward its stated goals. Perhaps it was because it had no need to, for the chief backer of the association, Louis E. McComas, was then in Congress, ready to leap past

*Antietam National Battlefield*

private preservation to federal conservation. McComas offered a park establishment bill in the House of Representatives on June 7, 1890. It became H.R. 10830. Unfortunately, McComas received little support for his bill, but he did not give up. A local newspaper, the *Keedysville Antietam Wavelet*, reported later that year that McComas, "by a short cut," included a portion of the bill in that year's sundry civil bill. Not getting all he wanted, McComas nevertheless got one paragraph in the civil bill, which read:

> For the purpose of surveying, locating, and preserving the lines of battle of the Army of the Potomac and of the Army of Northern Virginia at Antietam, and for marking the same, and for locating and

marking the position of each of the forty-three different commands of the Regular Army engaged in the battle of Antietam, and for the purchase of sites for tablets for the marking of such positions, fifteen thousand dollars. And all lands acquired by the United States for this purpose, whether by purchase, gift, or otherwise, shall be under the care and supervision of the Secretary of War.

The massive spending bill became law on August 30, 1890, with the Antietam paragraph intact. McComas did not get everything he wanted in 1890, but it was a start.[3]

The congressman kept up pressure to get his full park bill through Congress. He reintroduced a full establishment bill on September 5, 1890, which became H.R. 11966. This time the bill at least made it to the Committee on Military Affairs. Its hearing on February 27, 1891, provided support for the effort. In its report, the committee gave a historical lecture on Antietam's importance as the bloodiest day in American history. It also put Antietam into the context of what was happening at Gettysburg and Chickamauga. The committee argued that the preservation effort at Antietam was "absolutely necessary." "A nation should preserve the landmarks of its history," the committee concluded.[4]

Unfortunately, the House of Representatives did not heed the committee's recommendation, and the matter was never brought up again largely because chief sponsor McComas lost his bid for reelection in 1890. Thereafter, without McComas to push for a park, Congress passed only sustaining appropriations in the years to come. Thus Congress somewhat inadvertently made an important policy decision concerning battlefield preservation: not all battlefields would be preserved along the massive Chickamauga Plan. A different type of battlefield park would be established, one that would save money and acquire only small amounts of the original fields of battle. A crucial decision had been made with little thought to the repercussions.[5]

Still, the War Department now had a second park to construct, albeit a smaller one than Chickamauga. Many tasks had to be performed. The department had to start the flow of money, equipment had to be bought, and relations with landowners had to be established. Most importantly, the secretary of war had to appoint another commission like that at Chickamauga. The legislation did not call for a commission, but Secretary Proctor felt it was the obvious thing to do. In a subtle difference, however, the veterans building Antietam would be referred to as the "Antietam

Board" rather than the Antietam commission. Here was another sign that Antietam would not be considered one of the first-rate national military parks that would come into being in the 1890s.[6]

A spirited fight emerged just as the board appointments were about to be made. Ezra A. Carman, a veteran of Antietam, desperately sought a position on the board and had very influential friends lobby for his appointment. Antietam originator Louis McComas wrote the secretary of war asking that Carman be appointed, as did Representative William Cogswell of Massachusetts. Even the army's quartermaster general supported Carman. Secretary of War Redfield Proctor ultimately did not appoint Carman, however, due apparently to some question regarding an unfulfilled contract he had once held. After being turned down, Carman wrote McComas about the "gross injustice" of it all. Carman would not have his day until later.[7]

Meanwhile, Secretary Proctor delayed organizing the work at Antietam. It was not until July 1891 that the secretary made the appointments. And when they were made, the result clearly showed Antietam's status as a second-rate effort in the War Department. The secretary appointed only two men to serve as "agents" on the Antietam Board for one year. Proctor chose as the Federal representative Colonel John C. Stearns of the 9th Vermont Infantry and as the Confederate representative Major General Henry Heth. Showing how differently Congress and the War Department viewed the work at Antietam, neither board member was even a veteran of the battle. Similarly, they reported to the quartermaster general in the War Department, not the secretary of war himself, as did Chickamauga's commission and those to come later. Nevertheless, the members would be paid $250 a month salary, out of which came office rent and travel expenses. Although a precious year had passed since congressional authorization, by August 1891, the board members were on site in Sharpsburg, ready to begin their work.[8]

Stearns and Heth accomplished very little in the next three years. Both men were reappointed after their year of service was up, but by that time each had realized exactly what kind of troubles faced them. A major problem was that the battlefield had changed over the years. Even more problematic, both men were aged, with debilitating sickness taking much of their time. Still, the two managed to perform some work at Antietam. They contacted veterans of the battle such as James Longstreet and William Franklin and accompanied them on visits to the battlefield to locate troop positions. Heth and Stearns also placed ads in newspapers asking for information on other positions. Many veterans responded, including Francis Barlow and Lafayette McLaws. By October 1891, the two veterans had located all the regular army positions at Antietam, marking them with temporary wooden markers, which lasted only a short time. The local farmers and tourists regularly moved or destroyed these stakes. Heth and Stearns then replaced these temporary markers with more substantial wooden signs, hoping to place stone markers in the future. The two veterans also worked out a plan for mapping and marking the battlefield. They had located the line of battle for the Army of Northern Virginia by June 1892 and the line of the Army of the Potomac by June 1893. They also plotted the opening battle lines on a map and planned more detailed troop position maps in the future, showing the farthest Union advance on a second map and the lines at the close of the day on a third map. Additional congressional appropriations on August 5, 1892, and March 3, 1893, provided the board with funds to acquire and ship troop position tablets to Antietam in the future.[9]

Yet at times work was nonexistent. The board members found that reports and evidence from the battle were so skimpy that it was hard to determine even individual brigade movements, let alone regimental actions, and they settled on divisional positions as the best they could locate. Likewise, problems emerged with getting veterans to the battlefield to help mark troop positions. The board made the point in 1894 that the Gettysburg commission (appointed in 1893) had the luxury of a lifelong student of the battle on its commission (Bachelder) and the Chickamauga commission had funding to bring veterans to that battlefield. "Had we been placed on the same footing with the Chickamauga Commission," Stearns and Heth wrote, "we would have been able to report greater progress." Even the local *Keedysville Antietam Valley Record* editorialized that "compared with Gettysburg it is but a barren field. The citizens of Sharpsburg should awake and push matters." The age of the board members also caused many delays, most notably as a result of the summer heat. Heth and Stearns openly admitted the work had not progressed as they had hoped.[10]

Still, the two veterans were able to report some additional progress as time passed. By January 1894 they had nailed some two hundred wooden signs to trees around the battlefield to mark troop positions. They also worked out a plan by which the artillery positions would be marked with cannon and the infantry brigades would be marked with monuments or tablets. They had also begun the process of dealing with landowners about the possibility of acquiring land. Even that issue caused problems, how-ever. The board reported to the War Department that some of the land-owners would not sell directly to the government, but apparently think-ing they would get a fairer price, wanted their land condemned. They soon found that was not the case. The landowners also balked at the idea of selling only small parcels of their land; they wanted to sell all or nothing. Looking out for the landowners in this regard, the board recommended opening avenues along the lines of battle, with the strips of land to be owned by the government in order to keep the visitors already beginning to come to Antietam from trampling through the farmers' fields.[11]

Despite some progress, major changes were on the way. By the sum-mer of 1894, Secretary of War Daniel S. Lamont was in office and asking serious questions concerning the work at Antietam. He bluntly wrote the quartermaster general, who supervised the work at the battlefield:

> While fully aware of the difficulties that attend upon undertakings of this kind, at Antietam and elsewhere, I cannot resist the conclusion that the Board as organized under the order of June 17, 1891, is less expeditious in its operations than Congress and the Department have a reasonable right to expect. Over three years have passed since the scheme was undertaken, and the Board has so little to show in the way of accomplished results as to lead to the belief that difficulties have been encountered which are either insurmountable, or cannot be overcome by the Board as at present constituted.

Lamont asked that the board respond with a report by August 1. The War Department also ordered Stearns to return to Washington to "resume [his] duties." "You will report by what authority you are absent from your duties," the order concluded.[12]

Lamont's blunt talk caused a flurry of activity. Stearns resigned as a member of the board, leaving only Heth. Rumors began to fly that the entire effort would be discontinued. Even Senator Henry Cabot Lodge, worrying that Massachusetts's appropriation for monuments at Antietam might be wasted, wrote the War Department asking if such rumors were true. Obvi-ously taken aback, Heth pointed out in his August 1 report that the lines of battle had been located and maps were being prepared. He noted that he had cannon on site to mark artillery positions once land became available. He also reported on the land acquisition effort, stating that the landowners wanted to sell all their land, not merely chunks. He also added that to buy

*Ezra A. Carman. A War Depart-
ment clerk while not serving at
the battlefields, Carman was a
member of the Antietam Board
in the mid-1890s and then, at
Henry Boynton's request, was
made chairman of the Chickamauga commission upon
Boynton's death. Antietam
National Battlefield.*

mere spots in a certain field "would cost as much, or more than the entire field." In closing the report, Heth defended his colleague Stearns, saying that his health had been very bad for the past eighteen months and that "finally it gave way altogether." He closed by stating that "it is hardly necessary to add that in consequence of Col. Stearns' bad health, the work has not progressed as rapidly as it would otherwise have done."[13]

With Stearns gone and Heth on the defensive, old Antietam friend Ezra Carman not only renewed his request to be appointed to the Antietam Board, but he also asked that he be allowed to take charge of the work. Carman had fought at Antietam as colonel of the 13th New Jersey Infantry and was brevetted a brigadier general after the war. A clerk in the War Department, Carman was a combative veteran who wore a snow-white goatee that made him look handsome even in his advanced age. His competence was just as inspiring; he was able to work with people easily although firmly. Not as brash as his counterparts Boynton and George B. Davis, Carman was nevertheless able to remain focused on what he wanted, as exemplified by his renewed application to lead the board. Lamont, perhaps irritated by Carman's boldness, did nothing about the letter for a few months, but then he made a major decision in Antietam's history. Whether he ever contemplated discontinuing the work is not known, but Lamont completely reorganized the board in October 1894. Heth remained the Confederate representative, and Carman finally received his appointment as the Union representative and "historical expert," but not as the president of the board. That duty went to War Department official Major George B. Davis, an extremely competent administrator who had become a trusted advisor on battlefield preservation and had studied and reported on the problems at Antietam. Davis had served in the 1st Massachusetts Cavalry during the Civil War and had risen in the ranks after the war, becoming a noted authority on military law. He was also president of the board publishing the *Official Records*. But he was not a veteran of Antietam, which again showed the difference between Antietam and her sister battlefields, which had commissions composed of veterans of the battles at those sites. Nevertheless, Lamont hoped Davis would be able to accomplish something in the near future. The secretary also authorized the hiring of an "Expert Topographer" to aid in the board's mapmaking efforts. Former "Stonewall" Jackson cartographer Jed Hotchkiss joined the board in October 1894.[14]

Lamont also made major changes in the supervision of the Antietam Board. To keep a better eye on the members and their work, which had been under the administrative oversight of the quartermaster general, Lamont took oversight responsibility himself. He sent a flurry of orders for the quartermaster general to turn over all papers and the balance of funds to the secretary of war himself. Lamont was obviously serious about getting the work done at Antietam.[15]

Not only did Lamont change the logistics and oversight of the board, but he also began to wield a vast amount of power on how the board would handle its duties and what type of work would be done at Antietam. Much of that power was wielded through his choice of Davis as president of the board. Lamont also took a more hands-on approach to Antietam than he or any other secretary of war would with the other parks, perhaps because of the lack of progress in the previous three years or perhaps because of the lack of a formal commission like those at the other parks.

In his report to Congress in 1894, Lamont laid out his plan for Antietam. He admitted that work had indeed been going on at Antietam but added that "no idea of the work done is to be obtained by an inspection of the battlefield." He warned that little would be noticeable in the future until land was acquired and markers went up. He envisioned some eight hundred acres in total, which would cost around fifty thousand more dollars. He also envisioned over two hundred tablets to mark infantry brigades and artillery positions. To mark the latter, he said, the Ordnance Department had already sent condemned cannon to Sharpsburg. Lamont also lectured Congress on the best way to preserve this and no doubt other battlefields. The duty of preserving the field was best accomplished by letting the landowners remain in control of the vast majority of the battlefield and letting them continue to cultivate the land. If the government took over control of the land, it would have to begin "operations of agriculture," which Lamont argued would be costly and "outside the ordinary and usual scope of governmental endeavor." The secretary thus planned to buy parcels of land when he could, marking troop positions there, and tell the story of the battle primarily from that land.[16]

Thus in October 1894 Lamont set into motion his plan for Antietam and his board to do the work. The result was a flurry of activity by men passionate about the project. Davis in Washington, DC, Carman on site at Antietam, and Hotchkiss, occasionally at Antietam but mostly at his home in Staunton, Virginia, put their hearts into the work and produced more results in eleven months than the original board had produced in three years. Davis took care of all the contracts from his Washington office. He saw his responsibility as keeping the entire operation on time and moving forward. After writing a letter about hurrying the work, Davis confided to Carman, "It is only by constantly pushing in these small ways that we can keep the whole project in motion." Carman was the man on the scene and dealt with landowners and locals as well as the historical portion of the work. Hotchkiss also frequently stayed on what he termed "one of the most unique battle-fields of the war," mapping the area and offering many suggestions that Davis did not always heed. Nevertheless, the board began to make preparations for mapping the battlefield, casting tablets to mark troop positions, buying what land they needed along roadways and lines of battle, and opening and fencing roadways. Everything occurred in one simultaneous process, resulting in eleven months (October 1894–August 1895) of brisk work that saw the battlefield of Antietam transformed.[17]

The inhabitants of Sharpsburg were amazed at the feverish activity. "When I am asked, as I am a half a dozen times daily, what the govt. proposes doing, I invariably answer that that depends nearly altogether upon the people, that we merely propose to mark the field and make it of interest and value to the country," Carman wrote Davis in October 1895. Carman also noted that the inhabitants believed that the government "should first consider what is best for this place."[18]

The first order of business was creating an accurate map of the battlefield and the lines of battle on September 17, 1862. By using the map, the board could then determine what land was needed, what roads were usable and where new ones were wanted, and where to place the tablets and monuments to mark those troop positions. In fact, Davis wrote Carman just days after the reorganization, stating that "we must get our [map] plates into the hands of the lithographer at the earliest possible date—certainly within two months, and must make up for lost time generally."[19]

Davis also wrote to the board's topographical engineer, Jed Hotchkiss, and put him to work. The main plan was to take war-era maps of Antietam, most notably the 1867 Nathaniel Michler map, and enlarge them. Ultimately the resulting map proved of little use in placing units on the battlefield. Hotchkiss recommended enlarging the map four times, making one grand map from which the various series of troop position maps could be adapted. Davis spurred Hotchkiss on: "All now depends upon dispatch."[20]

By November, Hotchkiss had done some work on the map, but he took his time sending it to Heth for his approval. Apparently, Hotchkiss felt the Confederates needed to stick together. Heth never seemed to carry much weight, particularly after the debacle of the first three years of the board's existence. But Hotchkiss came aboard with heightened passion for the job. His old loyalties to the South still existed, and he made a point to include Heth in all that he did. Perhaps, too, Hotchkiss did not believe Heth was representing the Confederacy strongly enough and was determined to make sure the Old South was heard from on the Antietam Board. Hotchkiss slowed in his work to the point that he had still not turned in a map by February of the next year. When asked by Davis where the map was so that Carman could begin to place troops on it, Hotchkiss told him he would soon deliver it so that *he* and Carman could mark the troop positions.[21]

By the end of March 1895, Davis had had enough. He informed Hotchkiss that since the board had gone five hundred dollars over budget for maps, "our existing arrangement will have to come to an end on April 30. I regret exceedingly, but the limited appropriation leaves no other course open." Perhaps reading between the lines, Hotchkiss responded that he would continue his work without pay, which left the situation in the same place:

with Hotchkiss holding the reins on the map. By June, Davis had still not received Hotchkiss's map and turned to a different topographer, Julius Bien, to enlarge the Michler map to twice its original size. Davis wrote that his relations with Hotchkiss had "well nigh proved a failure." Carman was not so amicable: "It is a burning shame that Hotchkiss acts as he does. I did think that finally he would place his map in your hands, but now I have lost all faith in his promises or in his honest intentions." While Bien was working on the new map, Carman began to place the troop positions on "photolithographic" copies of the Michler map. By July, he had recorded most of the troop positions on the maps while Bien was still in the process of making some topographical changes recommended earlier by Hotchkiss and Carman.[22]

The problems with Hotchkiss and the maps did not greatly stall the board's work in other areas. They continued to buy land, build roads, and place tablets on the field. The next major effort went into land acquisition, which was minimal at best but still substantial enough of a concern to cause some tense moments. After all, the board needed the land and roads before it could open new roads or place tablets and artillery.

A similar concern of the board was to open new roads to offer access to the somewhat inaccessible battlefield. Upon initial observation, Davis found that a few roads had been moved from their wartime route, which caused some disagreement concerning where certain actions had taken place. Upon further study, Davis and Heth reported to Lamont that three roads ran from the little town of Sharpsburg out to various points on the battlefield. Without lateral roads, visitors had to return to town and take another route to see a different section of the field. "Communication should be opened between the turnpikes," Davis wrote, which would incidentally follow the lines of battle, which ran perpendicular to the three major routes. By opening four roads, Davis argued, the field would be almost entirely accessible.[23]

The board decided to begin with the famous Bloody Lane but soon ran into trouble with many landowners. After initial observations, Carman reported that the main source of trouble would be S. D. Piper. The board had also been somewhat concerned about William Roulette, but after talking with him, Carman decided he was "a very strong Union man, very public spirited." Later, Carman chanced to meet Piper on the street, and the latter assured him of easy dealing. Still, other landowners spoke their mind concerning road-building activity. Carman reported to Davis in early November 1894 that "the citizens are now agitating the improvement of

*Bloody Lane at Antietam. One of the most famous of all Civil War sites, the Bloody Lane was the first of the relatively few sites bought by the Antietam Board under its new and radical plan named for the battlefield.* Antietam: Report of the Ohio Antietam Battlefield Commission.

the [Burnside Bridge] road." There was also some debate about whether to surface the bed of the Bloody Lane or build a road outside the lane to preserve its integrity. Showing his concern for preserving the battlefield's features, Carman wrote in reference to building another road near the Miller homestead that "no historic point would be lost by the change of route."[24]

By early November 1894, enough road planning and land acquisition talk had taken place to make offers to the landowners. Davis informed Carman on November 6 that he was coming to the battlefield "chiefly to have a showdown about land." He planned to get an offer from the landowners. Davis had already made up his mind he would like to start negotiations at around fifty dollars an acre, but he would go up to one hundred an acre. "If they accept, well and good. If not, we stop; for further discussion would be idle," Davis informed Carman. Then he would implement condemnation proceedings for the land. "The United States has to make a stand, somewhere or another, and this is as good an occasion as is likely to present itself," Davis wrote. He also intended to begin with a farmer who would sell for less that one hundred dollars an acre, thereby putting pressure on the remainder of the locals. "We must bring the matter to a head, however," Davis told Carman and remarked on the absurdity of paying more than one hundred dollars an acre for land that would not sell for half that if nothing significant had taken place there. "If any of the land on the field has value, it is historical . . . and cannot be expressed in dollars and cents," Davis wrote.[25]

Davis's trip to Antietam resulted in verbal land-purchase agreements. He wrote Boynton at Chattanooga that he had "been more successful there than I had hoped in the matter of acquiring land. It looks now as if we would get the land for the avenues that we need to have there at a reasonable price, and within a short time, without a resort to condemnation proceedings." But the real test would come when the actual sales took place. Davis wanted to begin with a small road and picked George Poffenberger's land: "What we want now is a lane for a starter, and the Poffenberger lane seems to be the one to begin with," he wrote Carman. Carman approached Poffenberger, who quoted a price of four hundred dollars an acre. Davis responded that he would pay only one hundred and asked for a quick reply so that he could "make other arrangements, immediately, if you decline to sell." All Davis had to do was threaten condemnation and Poffenberger agreed to one hundred dollars an acre.[26]

Davis then turned his attention to other landowners, who agreed more readily than Poffenberger. In particular, Piper became a very trusted ally because the board agreed to hire his son, Elmer E. Piper, as the engineer in charge of road construction. Assisted by Fillmore Smith, Piper began the road construction process, which was actually done by contractor James Snyder, who had completed some work for the national cemetery before 1890 and had won several contracts for road construction elsewhere. Poffenberger came back to the board asking one hundred more dollars because the roadway "cuts his farm badly." The Union man Roulette also created problems, but in the end Poffenberger gave in when Davis offered him fifty dollars in damages so they could settle for seventy-five. In the midst of all the headaches, Davis wrote Carman, "I sometimes feel that it would be the part of wisdom to do such marking as we can on the turnpikes, and let the whole thing go at that." Fortunately, Davis never gave in.[27]

By January, there was a flurry of transactions. Getting an agreeable price was only the beginning of the action, however; abstracts of titles followed. The board used a local attorney, Charles G. Biggs, to take care of the legal paperwork. The process was rough and rocky at times. The spring 1895 board correspondence is full of references to landowners causing minor problems, such as "Mr. Fisher kicked a little on the right of way," "old friend Roulette has recently been acting like a spoiled child," or "I had to read the riot act to the aforesaid Poffenberger this morning." Poffenberger would not allow the contractor on his land, at which time Carman notified him he would implement condemnation proceedings that afternoon. Poffenberger gave in again. At other times, the board agreed to pay for damages to wheat, fruit trees, and stone fences. Davis often became quite frustrated with the locals, writing Carman, "It is simply exasperating to deal with those people up there." When told that word of a secret deal with Piper on his wheat damages had gotten out, Davis wrote Carman asking, "Has George Poffenberger any wheat? I sincerely trust not."[28]

Fortunately for him, Davis always had the condemnation card to play, even though he did not have to use it, as most owners readily agreed to sell. Still, Davis and Carman kept a close eye on a case then in federal court over condemnation at Gettysburg. Davis informed Carman that "the Circuit Court in Philadelphia decided adversely to the power of the United States to condemn lands for battlefield parks. The case will be appealed, however." Because land acquisition was going so well at Antietam, Carman wrote back on April 27, "Thank God we are nearly through our real estate deals and we can snap our fingers at the court decision . . . I can see clearly the beginning of the end."[29]

Heavy snows slowed the road-building process through the winter of 1895, but the board and its contactors continued to build as fast as they could. Davis later appointed M. F. Smith as inspector of road construction, overseeing Snyder as he continued to work on his contract as well as the James March and Company, which the board also hired to macadamize roads. As spring passed into summer, the board had to extend Snyder's contract again due to slow land acquisition. A minor controversy emerged with the March company, which had little experience in macadamizing roads and took the job at no profit margin. Davis recommended that Carman not cause a scene but let March finish the work and "get rid of him at the earliest moment." March finished his job by July 1895, and by year's end the board was able to report some five miles of roadways built and "metalled" at Antietam, allowing "the visitor to reach, by public highways, the points of greatest military interests."[30]

Davis also began the process of erecting wire fences along the avenues. By August 1895, the board had spent much time on the fence issue. Davis first mentioned the idea in December 1894 while dealing with landowners about where he would place gates so that the farmers could get from the roads to their land. Carman began researching the difference between wood and metal posts to support the wire. Davis was also looking into the post issue, telling Carman, "I am told, here, that no iron post has yet established its claim to permanence, or has proven a serious competitor to wooden posts." The board thus went with wood posts, contracting Adam H. Baer in February 1895 to erect the posts and "Jones Locked Wire Fencing."[31]

Baer began his work in early March but soon ran into difficulties. The plan was to place a cap and a cannonball on each fence post, so Davis wanted the posts cut off squarely. More ominously, the board had to extend Baer's contract several times because of bad weather (the ground being frozen too hard to dig postholes) and slow land acquisition. By late March, however, the fence project began to come together. Carman praised Baer's fences to Davis: "I am pleased that Baer continues the fence work; he is putting up a good fence and it gives general satisfaction." The board also let a contract for cast-iron ornaments for fence post caps and guide boards to E. N. Gray and Company in late March. By April, Davis was ready to begin painting the fence. "If you can find a Democrat it would be well," Davis wrote Carman, "as about all our men have hitherto been Republicans, and we may well change the medicine a little." Later Carman reported, "I have organized my painting gang; four of the five are Democrats and three of the five are Union soldiers, so no one can complain." Baer and Gray finished around three thousand fence posts and ball ornament caps over the summer. Thereafter, only minor additions took place as new roads were opened. The fences turned out to be extremely well made, standing up to much use. The only problem came in May 1896 when Carman reported "no breaks, except two or three places where a runaway team and a couple of bull fights have bent some wire."[32]

The main goal of the board, of course, was to mark the battlefield with tablets funded by Congress. As the preparations for buying land and building roadways went on, always with the chief goal of erecting markers that would be accessible, the board also went about the process of writing text for, casting, and erecting the tablets. Davis and Carman would be the chief writers of the tablets, and they began their task as soon as the new board was constituted in October 1894. Davis began to inquire of other park builders to find the best foundry from which to buy the tablets. He wrote John P. Nicholson at Gettysburg as well as the commission at Chickamauga. Nicholson responded that it appeared the Chattanooga firm that was providing Chickamauga's tablets provided the best-quality goods at the lowest price.[33]

Meanwhile, Carman and Davis both wrote the text for the tablets, checking each other for accuracy and grammar. Each would write the text for a military unit and ship it to the other, often a corps' tablets at a time. The two veterans poured through reports and letters and often visited with veterans on the field itself. Davis sent the first drafts for tablets for the 12th Corps, Army of the Potomac, on November 5, 1894, and continued to churn them out as the days passed. The men quickly realized they would need more than the two hundred tablets they had envisioned at first. By mid-November, when they had text for some eighty tablets written, Davis and Carman could see at least three hundred would be needed.[34]

Davis and Carman also envisioned a more unusual interpretation method, different from that of the other commissions at work. Davis broached the idea of placing thirty-foot-tall poles along the various lines of battle, with color-coded balls (blue for Union and Red for Confederate) atop each pole. Set at intervals of around five hundred feet, these poles would vividly "give a visitor an idea of the length of operation of the lines of battle." This unorthodox scheme never materialized, however. The board settled for the standard position tablets for brigade level and up, placed "on the public highways and on lanes purchased by the United States for that purpose." The board left it to the states themselves or veterans to place monuments to individual regiments.[35]

As the planning continued, the board settled on the Chattanooga Car and Foundry Company to cast the tablets, although they continued to shop around for lower bids. The veterans envisioned a long process but wanted to place the tablets quickly, given the amount of time that had already passed since Congress's creation of the park. Davis even wrote Boynton at Chickamauga asking him to get the foundry president to hire extra workers so they could create Antietam's tablets as well as those Chickamauga had ordered earlier. Later, in December, Davis wrote directly to the foundry and asked the managers to expedite the process. "Please hurry forward the work. . . . We are ready to set them up and I am anxious to do so at the earliest day possible, in order to keep our force employed," Davis wrote.[36]

During the casting process, the board ran into further trouble. They began to find small errors of spelling and fact in some of the texts, which they called to the foundry's attention. For those tablets not already cast, these changes presented no problems. But for those already finished, repair was expensive. The board also realized that for all the roads they did not own, they would need permission from the road owners, whether they be government or private, to place the tablets on the battlefield. Davis contacted several turnpike companies as well as the county government for permission. All readily allowed the board to place the tablets— one stipulating the provision that "they will not skeer horses, traveling along the pike." Despite the problems, the board's success was clear when Gettysburg's chairman wrote and asked for a sample of the Antietam tablets. Davis sent back a description of their scheme of marking only brigade units and above. No doubt the Antietam Board felt pleased when the vaunted Gettysburg commission asked for their assistance.[37]

By early April 1895, the board had received all the necessary permissions and was ready with a force on hand to erect the tablets. Davis wrote to the foundry in Chattanooga asking it to furnish at least fifty tablets so the workers could begin. The same day, J. E. Evans wrote (the letters crossed paths en route) to tell Davis that he would have the tablets ready by the end of the month. "I had an idea that you might want them on the grounds on the occasion of the Anniversary services of May 30," Evans kindly wrote. In the meantime, Davis and the board worked on aesthetic factors, asking for the specific sizes of the tablets so that they could place them in relation to the fences going up on the roadways; Davis wanted the top of the tablet to be parallel with the top of the fence. Evans wrote again later in the month stating that the tablets would be ready by April 20 and that he would send them all by one railcar, so that they would not have to be unloaded and reloaded.[38]

The tablets finally shipped in early May, and Carman hired several men to place them on the battlefield. Carman already knew one man he wanted to hire: "I have a good man in view," he wrote, "a Union soldier, wounded at Gettysburg, a Democrat, and not a whiskey guzzler." Finally, the Antietam battleground began to resemble the other parks at Chickamauga and Gettysburg. Over the summer, Carman and Davis wrote more texts, although Carman was at times very sick because of the heat and "the limestone water which I am compelled to drink in the absence of cistern water." By July all the tablets had been written, and Davis began to put more pressure on Evans at the Chattanooga foundry. Davis explained that their yearly appropriation ran out in August and that he was "exceedingly anxious" that the tablets arrive before then so they could pay laborers to place them on the battlefield. Evans responded that he would try to cast them but reminded the board that "the commissioners for the Park here [Chickamauga] are very anxious to get everything in readiness for the Dedication," which would take place in September 1895. Evans was not able to cast all the tablets, but he sent what he could by mid-August, the rest arriving in early October. Later in December, the board also placed tablets in the South Mountain gaps as well as at Shepherdstown.[39]

Several other projects also went forward in the eleven months between October 1894 and August 1895. The board wanted to place two observation towers on the field, one at Bloody Lane and the other on the southern portion of the field. Snyder built the one at Bloody Lane up to sixteen feet before money ran out. When more funds became available, Snyder demolished the wooden structure he had started and built a stone tower, finishing it by December 1896. The board also hired a stonemason and several laborers to build small bridges, culverts, and retaining walls on the battlefield. Snyder was placed in charge of that work too. Roadwork also continued, with some new construction as well as the thickening of existing roads to bear heavy traffic. In the process, the laborers unearthed six Confederate bodies near the Dunker Church. The board shipped the remains to Henry Kyd Douglas for burial in the Washington Confederate Cemetery near Hagerstown, Maryland. Perhaps most important in terms of marking the field, the board placed "simple monuments marking the places where general officers were killed." Cannon barrels turned upside down and mounted in stone bases marked each position.[40]

The board did not make a priority of placing large numbers of artillery pieces on the battlefield. Although Davis had thirty-six guns on site, he simply did not have the money to buy carriages. By September 1896, the board only had a few guns mounted on the battlefield, but nevertheless termed them the "most striking features" of the area. Secretary of War Lamont reported that the board had marked "the more important artillery positions." Davis knew getting money for carriages would be difficult, writing that "appropriation committees are harder to appeal to than ever before." Since tablets marked battery sites, it was not as if the artillery was shunned by the board. Still, in the years ahead, the board sought and received small yearly appropriations to continue the work, and more guns were added in later years.[41]

Even before the sprint to build the park began after October 1894, the board was in contact with several state commissions and regimental associations desiring to place monuments on the battlefield. When the reconstituted board began to make headway, other states caught the fever and sent delegations. By March 1895, veterans from New York, Connecticut, Maryland, Ohio, Maine, and Rhode Island had either sent delegations or inquired about placing monuments at Antietam. Some were under the impression that the board would place the monuments, while others thought the government owned the land. Unfortunately, thinking their monuments would not be cared for, some veteran groups were frightened away from Antietam because it was not a national military park. Davis had to deal with each group, explaining that the veterans themselves would have to buy land from the local owners for the monuments. Davis and Carman met with each commission and helped determine where the monuments would go. As historical expert, Carman was not always impressed with the state commissions. In December 1894 he wrote Davis, "I have just gotten rid of the Ohio commission. . . . I don't know any more now than I did before they came, but they knew more than the Pennsylvanians did."[42]

Only a small number of veterans' groups and states placed monuments at Antietam during the first half of the 1890s. Connecticut led with several regimental monuments in October 1894. The most novel idea was a monument and small park honoring the Philadelphia Brigade, which members dedicated on September 17, 1896. The veterans purchased eleven acres of land for their little "park." The dedication day was a festive occasion as the Marine Band played and speakers sang the praises of the brigade. Veteran Jacob I. Peterson spoke at the dedication and continued the reconciliation themes so prevalent at other dedications of the decade, saying, "Let no angry thoughts against those whom we fought mar the solemnity of this scene."[43]

Federal money was fast dwindling by August 1895, and Davis could see the end coming. He could rightly be proud of his board's work, which was "practically begun and finished this year." In all, the board had acquired seventeen acres of land, built five miles of macadamized roads, placed more than two hundred tablets, and accomplished it all in time for the anniversary of the battle in September. Surprisingly, little fanfare occurred at Antietam that September, however, because of the Chickamauga dedication as well as a large reunion in Louisville, Kentucky, both of which took place around the same time in September.[44]

The work was nevertheless done. Davis laid off all his workers except those needed to finish the tower and erect a few more tablets still outstanding. Having been reassigned to West Point to teach law, Davis himself resigned on August 1, 1895, saying that he was at "too great a distance to direct the work to advantage." As he left, he wrote the secretary of war to report on the significant progress. "The work on this field, save for a little in the way of embellishment, is practically finished," he wrote. The only major remaining item was the map. Davis took a moment to praise his coworker Carman, whose work he said was "of the highest character." In fact, knowing the board would be dissolved, Davis recommended Carman for the Gettysburg commission. Indeed, the board was dissolved, with Carman and Heth receiving letters dated August 17 informing them that their services were no longer required. Carman, however, received another letter from Secretary Lamont, stating that he could remain at work without pay. The passionate Carman thus stayed on.[45]

To replace George B. Davis as president of the board, Secretary Lamont appointed Antietam veteran George W. Davis (no kin to George B. Davis). George W. Davis was another powerhouse in the War Department. He had served in the 11th Connecticut Infantry during the war and risen to major in the following years. During his tenure at Antietam, Davis finished some of the lingering work that needed to be done. When asked about the future, Davis predicted that the park would go to the Quartermaster Department and be supervised by the Antietam National Cemetery superintendent. There was some hope for Antietam to become a national military park, but Davis did not see this idea coming to fruition. "So far as I know, there is no measure pending in Congress" to make Antietam a national military park, he stated, adding, "It is not considered by the Department that any public good would be attained by changing the status of Antietam to a park."[46]

The board system was not entirely done at Antietam, however, which caused some problems. Hotchkiss grumbled about the lack of a Confederate representative. "I feel sure that the pressure to have a Confederate associate in this work will be irresistible," Davis wrote Carman. When the secretary of war reconstituted the board for a short time between July 1 and December 31, 1896, Hotchkiss unsuccessfully began writing letters to get himself appointed. Hotchkiss remarked that he did not want Heth's position if Heth was to have it back. All he wanted was his due: "I have done more work in this matter of permanent value than any one that has been connected with it except Gen. Carman and all that I want is to have opportunity to complete my work and have proper credit for it and not let someone else and especially some one on the other side come in and get the credit of my labors," he said. Obviously Hotchkiss was unreconstructed, and Carman and Heth resumed their old positions.[47]

By the latter days of 1896, George W. Davis was the only remaining member of the board, Heth and Carman's second appointment having expired at the end of December. Most of the work was done, except for

Hotchkiss's original responsibility: the maps. Still operating on the obviously inaccurate Michler map, Davis now wanted to tie up that loose end. He had one last idea. He wrote to John P. Nicholson, chairman of the commission at Gettysburg: "I want to ask a favor," he said. "Will you not lend to the Antietam Board the services of Colonel [Emmor B.] Cope," who was serving as Gettysburg's engineer. Davis promised the work would only take a week, and Nicholson agreed, saying that he had work planned for several days but could spare the engineer the next week. In early December, Cope, his assistant engineer Hays W. Mattern, and rodman Edgar M. Hewitt traveled to Antietam and began their work. Carman reported that Cope had completed the transit work by December 18 and that "many errors have been found in addition to those I had noted."[48]

The problem came during the next several months as Davis continually asked Nicholson for Cope or Mattern to work on the maps. Nicholson balked, saying that every minute they were away from Gettysburg delayed their own work. Davis kept pushing, and Nicholson kept balking. On New Year's Eve, Nicholson irritatingly wrote that "we hope to have an interview with you upon this subject." In February, as his own laborers were "standing idle" while the Gettysburg engineers were at work for Antietam, he wrote: "Cannot some arrangements be made with your own Engineers to do this?" All along, Davis had been asking and receiving permission from the secretary of war to extend Mattern's time at Antietam, first by ninety days and then for another month. By June 1897, Nicholson had had enough: "Little by little I have yielded to request after request. . . . If I had had the slightest idea that Mr. Mattern or Colonel Cope's services would continue to July 1, 1897, other arrangements would have been made." Taken aback by Nicholson's letter, Davis recommended that he and Nicholson meet "before our common superior, the Secretary of War, for his orders in the case." Ultimately, Davis gave up. He informed Carman to "retain every scrap of data we own" and added that "I shall make no request for further help."[49]

Davis did not adhere to his promise, however. He was soon asking the secretary of war to detail Mattern again. Tiring of it all, Nicholson acquiesced but asked Davis to wait until the fall, when he was not so much needed and when the harvest would be in. "The corn will then be cut and nothing to interfere," Cope wrote Davis. Cope and Mattern returned to Antietam in October and worked on the map. Davis informed the engineers that money would run out in December and he needed the first two maps before then. Cope was able to provide them by February 1898, when Davis realized that getting the third map prepared was out of the question. Davis managed with what he had and thoroughly thanked the Gettysburg engineers and commission. He knew he had been a bother, but he got most of what he wanted.[50]

While the maps were being created, Davis also took care of a few other loose ends. He acquired five thousand dollars to place tablets at Harpers Ferry, the South Mountain gaps, Shepherdstown, and the newly completed tower at Bloody Lane. Heth, whom the secretary of war reappointed for a five-month period beginning August 1, 1897, was very helpful. His principal duty was to work with Carman, who was not reappointed but remained a member of the War Records Office and was marking Union and Confederate troop positions on the map. A few tablets also went up during this time.[51]

By December 31, 1897, Davis was thus able to report to Secretary of War Alger that the park was all but completed, with a total expenditure since 1890 of $78,031. With 408 tablets set at Antietam and in the surrounding areas, mortuary monuments, and some eight cannon erected on carriages, the only remaining task was to place troop positions on the new maps, which Carman volunteered to do in his off time at night at his home. Heth was reappointed for a two-month stint in 1898 to deal with Confederate troop positions on the map, but he also returned to his War Department job after that time. The two placed the lines of battle on the third of three maps that had been produced over the years, one being a map of the theater of operations, another of the battlefield as it existed in 1897, and the third the battlefield as it existed in 1862. Davis himself was relieved of duty as the board's president on May 31, 1898, and assigned to duty "with troops in the field."[52]

Thus ended the board period in Antietam's history, the formative era of the battlefield. Now established, Antietam reverted back to the administrative control of the quartermaster general, who placed the roads, property, and tablets under the supervision of the Antietam National Cemetery superintendent. The board was no longer a factor. George B. Davis became a noted lawyer and judge advocate general in 1901 with the rank of brigadier general. George W. Davis also became a brigadier general and was active in the Spanish-American War, becoming military governor of Puerto Rico. General Heth died in 1899. Only Carman spent any further time on Antietam, which placed him as the supreme authority on the battle and battlefield. As a clerk in the War Department before being appointed chairman of the Chickamauga commission, Carman continued to exercise an important amount of power over Antietam's development.[53]

But Carman's official association with Antietam was over. He returned to his office job in the War Department and left the battlefield in the hands of the quartermaster general. The nearest local official in the Quartermaster Department was the depot quartermaster in Washington, who received word in March 1898 that he would be held responsible for Antietam. The quartermaster requested permission to hire a watchman and laborer for fifty dollars a month, but that was turned down. The only option was to place the battlefield under the Antietam National Cemetery superintendent.[54]

All involved quickly realized that turning the battlefield over to the cemetery superintendent was not working. The depot quartermaster reported that this was "much more than the Superintendent can properly attend to," and recommended the battlefield have its own superintendent. The quartermaster general turned this idea down due to a lack of funds, but took the idea to the secretary of war, writing that "complaint is made that there is no supervision and no responsible authority who may guard the tablets erected by the government and the monuments erected by states and regimental organizations." He called for a superintendent for Antietam.[55]

Secretary Root was able to get something done. He pushed an appropriation through Congress that afforded Antietam $1,500 a year, with $1,200 of that for a superintendent's salary. On June 14, 1900, Root appointed Charles W. Adams as superintendent, the appointment to take effect on July 1.[56]

Adams's administration of the battlefield was uneventful, at least in the first few years. As time passed, however, a few minor controversies emerged. Stock owners allowed their animals to graze at will on the battlefield roads. Ultimately, the department placed warning signs on the roadways advising farmers to keep their cattle off the roads or face their impressment into government service. A major problem later occurred when one of the cows ate weed killer. The owner complained, but the War Department refused to take responsibility, although it stopped using the weed killer in the future.[57]

Although Adams was the superintendent, Carman still retained and wielded most of the power concerning building and marking the battlefield. From his Washington, DC, office, Carman worked with Adams, veterans, and state and regimental commissions to place monuments and mark maps of the battle. He also continued to make land acquisitions.

Finally, Carman had success with his maps. As the climax of the map-making process that had been such a headache through the years, the War Department in 1904, with a revised edition in 1908, published an atlas of fourteen Antietam maps. Significantly, Carman also became superintendent for a day. In May 1905, Quartermaster General C. F. Humphrey asked the secretary of war to remove Adams due to his "inability . . . to take charge of this work" and appoint Carman as superintendent. With recommendations from George B. Davis, Boynton at Chickamauga, and Nicholson at Gettysburg, Secretary Taft did so on May 27, with the appointment to take effect on May 31. The secretary of war retracted his action on May 31, however, when local congressman George A. Pearre complained. Adams remained as superintendent, and Carman was later tapped to chair the Chickamauga commission. Even in Chattanooga, Carman still remained involved with Antietam. He left some Antietam correspondence unwritten the day he died.[58]

Monuments continued going up even after the major building phase was over. The states of Ohio, New York, Indiana, and Pennsylvania funded such projects. The 20th New York Infantry caused a minor controversy when it wanted to place an owl on its monument. The issue was whether a nonmilitary emblem could be used. Realizing that Vicksburg and Gettysburg both had monuments with nonmilitary emblems on them, the War Department acquiesced.[59]

These new monument dedications, most of which occurred after the turn of the century, continued the themes of reconciliation and memorialization. At the dedication of several individual Pennsylvania regimental monuments on "Pennsylvania Day," September 17, 1904, one veteran remarked, "we the boys in blue contended for the maintenance of the Union, and glorious was the victory, now, to the gratification of both the blue and the gray." Confederate general Stephen D. Lee, a commissioner at Vicksburg, echoed such remarks in a letter regretting he could not accept Pennsylvania's invitation to join them. "Men who fought so bravely on both sides, certainly feel they were right and patriotic, and the record is an honorable one for the American Soldier, on either side."[60]

At the dedication of Ohio monuments on October 13, 1903, Union veterans continued the same theme of reconciliation and remembrance. General Robert P. Kennedy said

It is a matter of deepest concern to us all that we are again reunited and that these battlefields are now the meeting places of one com-

*New York monument dedication at Antietam. New York dedicated its monument with elaborate ceremonies in 1920. Many of the veterans had passed away by then, but several were still able to attend, including one Antietam veteran who later became a lieutenant general in the United States Army, Nelson A. Miles. Clarke, New York at Antietam.*

mon people, instead of contending factions battling for the mastery. . . . No longer is there division and strife; no longer a divided and broken country. With one single purpose the sons of the men who fought on these battlefields and contended so bitterly for the mastery are joining hands in the upbuilding of this marvelous Republic, and day by day are adding to its wealth supremacy and power. No longer is the blood of the North and the blood of the South hot with the rivalry of hate and contention, but joining hearts and striking hands, we saw them moving up the smoking sides of San Juan, and fighting shoulder to shoulder at El Caney.

Another orator said: "looking into your faces today, I believe you are all in happy accord with us, and rejoice as heartily as we do that the war terminated as it did, and that you rejoice with us that we are again a united, happy, prosperous and strong nation; that we have but one eternal emblem 'old glory.'"[61]

New York dedicated its large monument near the Dunker Church on September 17, 1920. The reconciliation spirit had not ebbed even by that time. Lieutenant General Nelson A. Miles, a veteran of Antietam much earlier in his career, spoke at the dedication, telling his hearers, "If the same sublime patriotism manifested by you on this battlefield and in your lives since is maintained and perpetuated by the citizens of this country, then our Republic will be forever safe and will ascend to even a higher and more exalted civilization and a purer destiny." A New York state senator echoed such patriotic thoughts, saying, "One happy result of those four years of internecine strife—what is rarely recorded in the annals of the nations—is that for the vanquished, no less than the victors, the outcome of it was a boon and a blessing. This every true American is now ready to corroborate unqualifiedly."[62]

Ironically, one of those monuments helped lead to the assassination of Superintendent Adams. There had been quite a bit of complaint about the William McKinley monument. One visitor spoke of its "scandalous and disgraceful condition," whereupon the local quartermaster officer responded that Ohio had not turned the monument over to the War Department and that it was so new that no landscaping work had been done yet. The Bemer family owned the plot of ground on which the monument stood and claimed that the State of Ohio had never paid for the land, despite having promised to do so. More importantly, Adams had apparently testified against one of the Bemer sons, John, in earlier years. The family thus had a history of problems with the park and its superintendent and took their frustration out on Adams. On June 6, 1912, young John Bemer encountered Adams on his way to the battlefield and shot him nine times. The local authorities followed Bemer to his house, whereupon Bemer killed himself. The local quartermaster in charge of overseeing the park and its superintendent notified the quartermaster general: "I have the honor to report the death, June 6, of Supt. Charles W. Adams." He enclosed a letter from the national cemetery superintendent that described how Adams was "foully murdered." The cemetery superintendent temporarily took charge of the battlefield again.[63]

There was then a lively scramble for the superintendent's position. Even former board nemesis George Poffenberger wanted the job, but the War Department, having "serious doubts as to his ability to handle the work to the satisfaction of the Department," knew better than to give it to him. Instead, George W. Graham took the oath of office on August 5, 1912, and trouble immediately began again.[64]

Graham lived in Harpers Ferry, was an honorably discharged Union Civil War veteran, and had the recommendation of various elected officials and veterans' organizations. Very quickly, however, he turned out to be a major problem. He suffered from alcoholism and was often drunk on the battlefield. He also had a fondness for guns and scaring people with them. Locals testified that he often shot his guns at night and even once aimed a shotgun at a visitor who had climbed the observation tower. Locals testified that Graham was never able to handle money and often borrowed funds from employees by threats of taking their jobs. He also would make locals sign notes for him. On top of all that, he apparently liked vulgar women, one local telling that he kept the company of "a strange woman." Graham's wife testified that "my husband . . . was living in adultery on the Battlefield of Antietam." She went there and found the woman at his house, but "he put me by force out of his house and yard." One visitor even wrote President Woodrow Wilson, saying he was "insulted by the Superintendent who was drunk."[65]

The deciding factor came in April 1913 when Graham's house burned down with many government tools and supplies in it. Locals testified that Graham kept "a quantity of whiskey in bottles in his house on Bloody Lane," which might have fed the blaze. When a War Department inspector arrived at Antietam, he found Graham "absent without leave." He took several convincing statements, ultimately preferring charges of absence without leave, drunkenness, borrowing money from employees, misappropriation of funds, and "conduct to the prejudice of good order." He concluded that Graham was "whiskey crazy and that he is a dangerous man to have as superintendent of the Battlefield."[66]

Of course, Graham denied all the charges, writing his congressman: "That gang that formerly used to drill under C. W. Adams deceased Supt. [t]hat I succeeded are now fighting me very bitterly." Although Civil Service rules required a delay in order for an investigation and trial, even Graham's congressman could not help the superintendent. The War Department discharged him on August 1, 1913, and made him pay for the government losses incurred in the house fire.[67]

None of the superintendents afterwards came close to providing the fireworks that Adams and Graham had. Indeed, the history of Antietam battlefield settled into a pattern of ordinary maintenance under four different superintendents from 1913 to 1933, when Antietam became part of the National Park Service. John L. Cook, the cemetery superintendent, oversaw both entities until June 1915, when Jacob Manath became the park superintendent. He died in June 1925, causing a problem for the War Department, still operating under legislation that required the superintendent to be a Union veteran. As no more such men of stable health could be found, Congress had to amend the language to allow C. H. Bender to

*Dunker Church at Antietam. This view of the Dunker Church shows the original*
*structure, which was unfortunately destroyed by a wind storm in 1921.* Antietam:
Report of the Ohio Antietam Battlefield Commission.

become superintendent from June 1925 to February 1928. After his term, George B. Alexander became superintendent, holding the position until the park became part of the National Park Service. For unknown reasons, he was not kept on when the park came under the jurisdiction of the Department of the Interior. Little of major interest occurred during this time, except the loss of a major historical structure; the original Dunker Church was blown down on May 21, 1921, during a high wind.[68]

The history of Antietam was so different from that of Chickamauga that it is hard to recognize the similarities. Policy, procedure, people, and result were all different, but the overarching idea of memorialization was the cornerstone of both. The approach at Antietam was simply a more cost-effective and less complicated way to commemorate. Antietam's emergence in 1890 offered a second and more simple plan by which battlefields could be marked and memorialized, and much debate on style attended the creation of future parks. Indeed, this type of battlefield, first developed at Chattanooga and Antietam, would see wide use in the decades to come. Yet by the mid-1890s, with Chickamauga and Antietam mostly finished, a strong foundation for the Golden Age of battlefield preservation had been laid, and Congress was more than willing to build on it. The next move came at an isolated and almost forgotten river landing in Tennessee.

# 5

## "THIS GREAT BATTLEFIELD"
### *Shiloh National Military Park, 1894–1933*

BY THE MID-1890S, Civil War battlefield preservation was reaching a climax. Chickamauga and Chattanooga, the nation's first battlefield park, had been established in 1890, with Antietam following the same year. Gettysburg was already in the process of becoming a park, having its own commission, though Congress had not officially authorized it. As the battlefield preservation movement reached a fevered pitch, Congress then branched out on a different path. The parks preserved thus far were near large cities and were capable of handling large numbers of people—civilian and military alike. Gettysburg was of course already a tourist attraction. Chattanooga could accommodate many visitors, with Chickamauga having railroad access. Antietam was on the eastern seaboard and easily accessible. The next park, Shiloh, did not fit the mold. Far from any big city, any significant accommodations, and any major transportation route except the Tennessee River, the battlefield site did not offer the kind of amenities the others did. Nevertheless, Congress saw fit to preserve this battlefield too, and not just partially as at Antietam. Shiloh became a full blown park like that at Chickamauga, illustrating the fact that 1890s era preservationists were not singly tourism minded or even access minded. The desire to honor and preserve was foremost in their minds when they established the isolated and less-visited battlefield of Shiloh.

As at the first parks, the desire for both reconciliation and preservation drove Shiloh's conservation, but other, more emotional issues also emerged. Veterans returning to the battlefield over the years were appalled to hear stories of farmers plowing up soldiers' remains. Roadwork also unearthed bodies. Growing more and more sentimental by the year, aging veterans hated to think that their comrades of the 1860s still lay buried in undiscovered common battlefield graves. Realizing that all such graves could never be found, these veterans agreed that the next best option was to preserve the entire battlefield. Unit pride also played

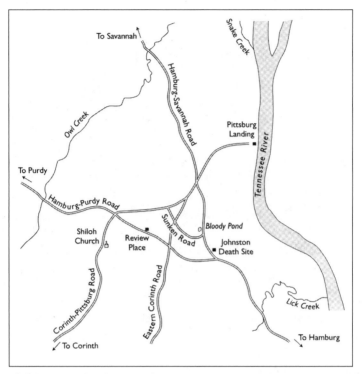

*Shiloh National Military Park*

a role in the grassroots movement to establish a national park at Shiloh. Since Congress had already appropriated money for battlefield parks for the Army of the Potomac at Gettysburg and Antietam and for the Army of the Cumberland at Chickamauga and Chattanooga, Army of the Tennessee veterans desired a park to commemorate their actions in the war.[1]

The thought of establishing a park at Shiloh first emerged in 1893 when several Union veterans returned to the battlefield in April of that year. They heard farmers' and workers' stories of unearthing skeletons of soldiers. The outraged and saddened veterans determined to ensure that such horrors would not continue. Returning north on the steamer *W. P. Nesbit*, these aging soldiers discussed the idea of establishing a marked battlefield like those already being developed at Chickamauga and Antietam. By the time they had reached their destination, the veterans had formed an organization with temporary officers called the Shiloh Battlefield Association. As had been done at Chickamauga, Antietam, and Gettysburg, this organization actively sought the cooperation of former Confederates.[2]

Members of the association held a more formal meeting later in 1893 at Indianapolis, Indiana. The veterans elected a permanent group of officers and appointed committees to work on various aspects of the project, including lobbying Congress for funds. To gain veteran assistance, the organization appointed a special committee to gather the support of the major veterans' organizations such as the Society of the Army of the Tennessee and the GAR. To generate support for the project, the association called for annual reunions on April 6 and 7 to be held at the battlefield.[3]

By 1894, the association had gathered the support of many prominent men. At the Indianapolis meeting, the veterans elected as the organization's first permanent president a former division commander in the Army of the Tennessee at Shiloh, Major General John A. McClernand. The members also elected a private of the 41st Illinois Infantry, Eliel T. Lee, as secretary and Dr. John W. Coleman, a former surgeon in the 41st Illinois, as the association's treasurer. The members also elected honorary vice presidents from a vast array of famous officers who had served at Shiloh, including Union division commanders Benjamin Prentiss and Lew Wallace and Army of the Ohio commander Don Carlos Buell. Demonstrating the reconciliation of the times, the group also named prominent Confederates to the list, including former generals Basil Duke and Joseph Wheeler, and former Tennessee governor and staff officer Isham G. Harris, now a Democrat in the United States Senate. By 1894, the association had assembled an impressive array of veterans to lobby for Shiloh's establishment as a park.[4]

The association immediately began working on convincing the federal government to preserve the battlefield. Since the mass of veterans themselves would have to lend their influence to the idea, the association sent delegations to the GAR and Society of the Army of the Tennessee, both of which readily lent their assistance. They also called on Southern congressional leaders such as Senator Harris and Representative Wheeler to help. These former Confederates supported the idea; after all, the battlefield still contained the remains of some two thousand Confederate dead.[5]

The Shiloh Battlefield Association mostly needed the support of the United States Congress. Along with the prominent veterans in that body, the association's Congressional Committee lobbied for a park and impressed many congressmen, gaining a "promise of assistance" from them. David B. Henderson of Iowa and Joseph Wheeler of Alabama, both

*Shiloh veteran reunion. Veterans met in April 1894 on the battlefield of Shiloh to remember what had taken place there over thirty years before. This photo shows a gathering of veterans at Shiloh Spring, near Shiloh Church. Shiloh National Military Park.*

Shiloh veterans, lent their support in the House, while in the Senate, Senator Harris and John Sherman of Ohio, brother of Shiloh general William T. Sherman, led the effort.[6]

The Shiloh Battlefield Association advertised its goal and requested donations. Each member of the twelve-thousand-man association, almost all from the enlisted ranks, paid small dues to help fund the venture. The association held reunions at the battlefield and encouraged battle survivors to write their senators and representatives to support the bill. The group took concrete action in the spring of 1895 by taking out options on thirty-four plots of land (some twenty-six hundred acres) for a dollar a plot. They intended to donate the options to the government once it began operating at Shiloh. E. T. Lee filed the options in the Hardin County courthouse on March 26, 1895, thus reserving the land at a total cost of $32,830.50. The options ran out on March 4, 1896, only a year later.[7]

The Shiloh Battlefield Association had called attention to the need for a national military park at Pittsburg Landing, but they could only do so much. Their main goal was to persuade Congress to fund the venture. To get the process moving, the association's congressmen met in early 1894 to write a bill.[8]

Iowa representative David B. Henderson seemed to be a good choice to author the legislation. He was a Shiloh veteran and by the 1890s had become a powerful member of the House, serving as Judiciary Committee chairman and later as Speaker of the House. Henderson's service in the war and his ranking authority in Congress both made him an obvious choice to write the bill and to push for a park at Shiloh. Personal interests also played a role; Henderson's brother Thomas, killed at Shiloh, lay buried in the Shiloh National Cemetery.[9]

Henderson quickly realized he needed help. Although Congress had preserved several battlefields, it had established no formalized process to oversee them. As a result, the different battlefields had their own sponsors and supporters, creating a disjointed group that would eventually be a forerunner of a national park system. In that context, Henderson asked for assistance from those who understood more about the subject of battlefield preservation than he did, particularly from Henry V. Boynton.[10]

With Boynton's help, Henderson soon crafted a bill creating a Shiloh National Military Park. Containing only eight sections, the legislation recommended a military park similar to that already established at Chickamauga. The bill listed reasons for the action, explained the legal process of acquiring land, and specified a geographical boundary for the park, comprising some three thousand acres. The secretary of war would have authority over the park, and that authority included the right to acquire land by condemnation if necessary. Although the bill authorized condemnation procedures, its framers saw no need to uproot the families and thus allowed for tenancy on the field. A three-man commission would carry on the day-to-day governmental affairs at Shiloh, but the bill stipulated that each commissioner should be a veteran of the Civil War and a veteran of the armies that fought at Shiloh, and one commissioner would be named from each army. Such an arrangement would maintain the ratio of two Union commissioners and one Confederate, as established at Chickamauga. The bill also authorized the secretary of war to employ "some person recognized as well informed concerning the history of the several armies engaged at Shiloh" to act as historian. Lines of battle were to be determined and marked with tablets or other monuments, while states that had troops at Shiloh could locate and mark with monuments the positions of their volunteer units. Tampering with

monuments or markers, destroying fences or buildings, cutting or damaging trees, removing battle relics, hunting within the park boundaries,
or destroying earthworks brought fines, while the last section of the bill
provided an appropriation of $150,000 "to begin to carry out the purpose
of this act." All in all, it would be very similar to Chickamauga.[11]

Henderson introduced the bill on March 30, 1894, in the House of
Representatives. The House assigned the bill a number, H.R. 6499, placed
it on the calendar, and referred it to the Committee on Military Affairs.
The committee returned unanimous approval in June. Representative
Joseph H. Outhwaite of Ohio, chairman of the committee, submitted his
report to the entire House on June 22, 1894. He and the committee recommended that the "unsightly tract of land" be made a national military
park along the lines of the other parks. Since the bill did not totally place
the work in its historical context, the committee added its own historical
perspective. The representatives wanted the battlefield preserved for the
reasons stated in the bill as well as other factors, including the desire to
mark the field before the veteran generation passed on—a "monument
to them" before they "left this world." The committee also called on Congress to expand the idea and establish other national military parks.[12]

Outhwaite placed the legislation in its most favorable light—perhaps
thinking the bill would face opposition because of differences concerning battlefield preservation and its costs. The congressman argued that
the historical knowledge gained from establishment of the park would
"put at rest once and for all time to come the uncertainties and misrepre-
sentations surrounding the battle." He said the roads leading to the field
made the battlefield "easily accessible." He continued that the only work
required to preserve the field in battle condition was to remove underbrush and timber. Concerning costs, the chairman argued that the price
would be small once the initial appropriation acquired the land, which
could be done for only twelve dollars an acre.[13]

Outhwaite's arguments were inaccurate about the cost, amount of
work needed, accessibility, and historical advantage to be gained. Still, the
committee unanimously passed the bill with only seven minor spelling or
grammatical amendments.[14]

Once the committee reported the bill to the House, Henderson shep-
herded it through the political process. Because 1894 was an election
year, he anticipated trouble ahead in the 2nd session of the 53rd Congress. Henderson had only two or three months to get his legislation
passed before Congress adjourned. "Appropriations are unpopular before

Congressional elections," he admitted, and championed the bill as best he could in late summer. Henderson ultimately worked out a deal by which he would delay the bill until the 3rd session of the 53rd Congress, which began after the elections, when it would be passed. Several key congressmen, including Appropriations Committee chairman Joseph D. Sayers of Texas, promised he would give "generous cooperation" to H.R. 6499 in the coming session. Confident of victory, Henderson delayed his bill for several months but continued to lobby for it in the meantime.[15]

A reelected Henderson arrived in Washington after the elections and immediately began preparations to get H.R. 6499 to the floor. He brought the legislation to the House on December 4, 1894, the day after Congress reassembled. Committee on Military Affairs chairman Outhwaite acted as floor manager of the bill, yielding to Henderson after calling the legislation to the House's attention.[16]

The Shiloh veteran spoke briefly on "this great battlefield of Shiloh," reminding the members that both the powerful GAR and the Society of the Army of the Tennessee supported the bill. He also said that options were already being taken for tracts of land and that time limitations required a swift passage. Henderson also promised that the land could be attained for approximately ten dollars an acre, a figure that Charles Grosvenor of Ohio, author of the earlier Chickamauga-Chattanooga National Military Park legislation and future Chickamauga commission chairman, agreed was "a wonderfully low one." Grosvenor compared that figure to the twenty-eight dollars an acre the government had paid for land at Chickamauga.[17]

Because of the hour limit on debate, Henderson ended his speech and allowed questioning on the bill. Representative Alexander M. Dockery of Missouri took the floor and asked if Henderson would be content with half the requested appropriation—seventy-five thousand dollars. The Iowan responded that he would like to have the full amount, but that he would consent to a lower appropriation if the House so desired. Grosvenor once again spoke up, stating that experience told him that the park would need less money at the beginning because "controversies about titles and matters of that sort" would delay work. Henderson agreed to a lower appropriation.[18]

House members then began asking hard questions, which Henderson seemed unable to answer. Nelson Dingley of Maine inquired about an estimated figure of total appropriations, and Henderson was not able to provide one. Dingley pressed for figures on costs of improvements, monuments, and tablets, and once more Henderson had no answers. He could only respond that "there will be the usual monuments and other things of the kind that these battlefield parks usually contain." Dingley pressed the matter. Speaking of all parks, he asked if the Committee on Military Affairs had "formulated any plan with reference to [all of] them." Henderson again had to admit ignorance but added somewhat foolishly that he was "meet[ing] the wishes of the Western armies." This statement only highlighted the lack of battlefield preservation coordination at the highest levels.[19]

Grosvenor asked about the wording requiring commissioners to be members of the armies but not requiring that they actually be Shiloh veterans. Henderson responded that there would be no trouble finding veterans of the battle to serve as commissioners. Thomas R. Stockdale of Mississippi offered a successful amendment that "no discrimination shall be made against any State." Outhwaite saw he needed to take over from the rattled Henderson and unsuccessfully tried several times to cut off debate. Finally, Outhwaite moved that the appropriation be cut to seventy-five thousand dollars, which the members accepted. The House then agreed to the committee amendments and passed the bill.[20]

On December 6, the bill moved to the Senate, where it was referred to its Committee on Military Affairs. Committee chairman William Bate of Tennessee, a Shiloh veteran himself, reported the bill out of committee on December 13. Very little debate occurred in the committee hearing, although some opposition emerged regarding the need to create additional military parks.[21]

The Senate took up debate shortly thereafter. Isham G. Harris of Tennessee, yet another Shiloh veteran, took the floor on December 18 and gave notice that he or Senator Bate would call up H.R. 6499 the next morning, having been unable to do so that day during the morning hour. He ended with a plea that "I hope to get the consent of the Senate to pass it."[22]

On December 19, Bate called the bill to the floor of the Senate. He asked unanimous consent to consider the legislation, but former lawyer and Indian fighter Joseph N. Dolph of Oregon immediately objected, apparently over the issue of creating too many military parks. A surprised Bate asked that the bill be acted on at once due to its importance. He added that the House had passed it and "are very anxious that it should be passed at an early date." The Oregon senator agreed "out of personal regard for the Senator from Tennessee," and the Senate moved on. Bate presented the bill without amendment and secured the members' approval. Although he did not vote against the bill, Confederate veteran Francis M. Cockrell of Missouri gained the floor after passage and curiously offered his opposition to the idea of establishing military parks. Although he had been a Conference participant on the Chickamauga bill, Cockrell informed the Senate that he had not supported the Shiloh bill in committee. "I think it is an entering wedge to an immense mass of business which will entail upon the country an annual expenditure of thousands and hundreds of thousands of dollars. This is only the entering wedge for making every battlefield a national park," Cockrell argued.[23]

The bill passed both houses of Congress despite such minor opposition and needed only the signature of the president. Chief executive Grover Cleveland signed the bill into law on December 27, 1894. Shiloh National Military Park was a reality.[24]

Secretary of War Daniel S. Lamont appointed the commission and workers soon after Congress established the park. Many veterans were available, such as members of the Shiloh Battlefield Association like John A. McClernand and E. T. Lee, who expected an appointment. Retired general Don Carlos Buell, Confederate colonels Robert F. Looney and William Preston Johnston, and Confederate generals Alexander P. Stewart, Basil W. Duke, and Joseph Wheeler were also possibilities. Ultimately, Lamont named Colonel Cornelius Cadle of the 11th Iowa Infantry to head the commission and Don Carlos Buell and Robert F. Looney, former colonel of the 38th Tennessee Infantry, to round out the body. The secretary of war appointed Shiloh historian and veteran of the 12th Iowa David W. Reed as historian. The road engineer at Chickamauga, Atwell Thompson, became chief engineer. Captain James W. Irwin, James M. Riddell, and Francis A. Large also gained appointments to positions as land agent, commission secretary, and range rider.[25]

Analysis of Lamont's choices leads to the conclusion that he made his appointments carefully. He named no members of the Shiloh Battlefield Association to the new commission, notably E. T. Lee, who had put so much effort into the venture. Lee's ego and demands turned Lamont against him. Instead, the commission consisted of an aged Buell and Looney, both of whom held very definite ideas about the battle's history but had very little political clout. Buell's war record was not that of a hero such as Grant or Sherman, and he had no power base in Congress. Looney also had little influence. Indeed, Looney never played a significant role in any of the decisions concerning the park. His primary assignment, it appears, was as liaison with the State of Tennessee.

*Shiloh commission. The park commission and laborers gathered for this photograph in front of the commission's tents, situated in the cemetery near Pittsburg Landing. From left to right are: Will Pride, laborer; Francis A. Large, range rider; James W. Irwin, land agent; Cornelius Cadle, chairman; David W. Reed, secretary and historian; J. R. Duncan, laborer; Robert F. Looney, commissioner; J. T. Curtis, laborer; Atwell Thompson, chief engineer; and M. A. Kirby, laborer. Note J. T. Curtis's peg leg. Shiloh National Military Park.*

The real power behind the Shiloh National Military Park was evident: Cornelius Cadle, who oversaw the work with his trusted associates, historian Reed and engineer Thompson. Cadle was a small man with a bushy mustache but made up for his petiteness with a strong will that he exercised freely but delicately. Second in authority was the slightly rotund Reed, who dominated the historical work with no such diplomacy. The strong-willed historian wore a slight mustache and resisted anyone who challenged his interpretation of Shiloh's history, but always did so with an extremely careful and lengthy analysis of the sources. The fiery English-born Thompson actually ran the affairs of the park on a day-to-day basis at Pittsburg Landing.[26]

The commission also had a strong political force behind it. Congressman David B. Henderson did not end his association with Shiloh once he pushed the bill through the House. He continued to be actively involved, especially in appointments to the park's roster of leaders. Henderson was heavily involved in defeating E. T. Lee's bid to become a member of the commission. He also successfully petitioned Lamont for Cadle's and Reed's appointments, as he did for others such as Range Rider F. A. Large.[27]

Secretary of War Lamont ordered his new commission to assemble at Pittsburg Landing on April 2, 1895, to organize themselves and celebrate Shiloh's thirty-third anniversary. Major George B. Davis of the War Department had already inspected the area in March, when he had toured the site to get an idea of the task ahead. The first official act of park development, however, came with the arrival of the commissioners in April.[28]

The Shiloh National Military Park Commission thus met on that historic ground to transform the battlefield into a memorial and to honor those who had fought there some thirty-three years before. As the commission began its work the next day, April 3, they inaugurated the long process of shaping the isolated land into a national park.

Unfortunately, the commission found very little infrastructure to support its needs once it arrived at Pittsburg Landing. Major Davis had warned the commission that the "present outlook for offices and quarters at Pittsburg Landing is not promising." When Cadle and the other commissioners arrived, they found that to be the case, although several buildings stood at the landing itself, most importantly the national cemetery lodge and outbuildings. There they met cemetery superintendent Clayton Hart and his staff. The commission also met many veterans and visitors who were at the battlefield to celebrate the anniversary.[29]

With only meager resources, Cadle realized the commission would have a difficult task building a park. The commission needed offices, living spaces, furniture, and sundry smaller items to help it operate. The War Department successfully requested that the Post Office Department increase mail service to Pittsburg Landing to six days a week. War Department officials also began the flow of money. Cadle immediately began the paperwork for payrolls and bought needed items such as stationary, furniture, and horses. The commission also bought a typewriter for correspondence.[30]

Unfortunately, the commission did not have a building to house its headquarters. Cadle erected tents for housing but had to do so in the cemetery. The Quartermaster Department gave the necessary permission and the commission erected its tents along the western edge. For comfort, Cadle had these tents equipped with wooden roofs and floors. Reed made his quarters seem more homey by nurturing a large rose bush that grew up his roof. The War Department also provided wooden bins full of sawdust in which to keep ice. The tents did not solve the problem of a headquarters office, but Cadle found temporary office space in the cemetery lodge.[31]

The lack of adequate facilities created an awkward system of administration very similar to that at the other parks. It also fostered the growth of Cadle's, Reed's, and Thompson's authority. Like so many other commissioners at the time, Cadle established commission headquarters in his hometown (Cincinnati, Ohio), where he and clerk J. M. Riddell tended to the park's official business. D. W. Reed maintained his home in Illinois and later Iowa, working on the historical accounts of the battle. Atwell Thompson controlled the everyday work of park building at Pittsburg Landing itself. Cadle and Reed visited the park often, as did Buell and Looney. Correspondence was even more frequent. But the commanding figures were Cadle, Reed, and Thompson, and their three-way communication dominated Shiloh's establishment.

Many problems emerged when the commission began purchasing land. It as yet had no maps of the area showing landownership or topography. Numerous landowners were not happy about losing their property, some of which had been in their families for generations. Owners who were willing to sell sometimes asked exorbitant prices, which the initial appropriation could not cover. Worst of all, E. T. Lee and the Shiloh Battlefield Association still held land options on much of the battlefield.

Lee and his group proved to be the major obstacle. As the association's secretary, Lee began to create problems within the organization. Viewing himself as the father of the park idea, he became angry when he did not receive a commission appointment. Holding the options, Lee severely hampered the commission and ironically delayed his original goal of establishing the park.[32]

The War Department and the commission refused to be beaten. They looked at various ways to get around the association's land options, inquiring about the association's status of incorporation, the legality of its options, and even appealing to the members' patriotism. All attempts were unsuccessful.[33]

Lee held on to his options despite expulsions from almost every veterans' organization to which he belonged. Major George B. Davis of the War Department called Lee "that blackmailing humbug . . . who should be disposed of in some way." He called the entire episode the "nearest nonsense" and advised the commission that all would turn out in the end because

Lee would find it "difficult to compete with the government." The War Department decided to wait until the land options ran out and then buy the land; it advised Cadle and the commission to concentrate on gathering the remainder of the land until the options ran out on March 4, 1896.[34]

Land acquisition and the work of the commission went forward slowly with almost half the land designated in the enabling legislation under option until March 1896. Cadle and the commission thus decided to turn their attention to other work. Cadle hired workers to draw maps, locate battle lines, and purchase land not optioned to Lee. In this manner, the commission produced results even while a majority of the most important land tracts remained un-purchased.[35]

Cadle had his engineer Thompson work on the most basic need—an accurate map showing topography, boundaries, and landowner tracts. With such a map, the commission could begin "the work of converting mere land into a park." The secretary of war had originally advised employing the county surveyor, but Cadle soon realized that the task required a full-time engineering staff. Secretary of War Lamont then authorized hiring an engineer and several supporting personnel.[36]

Thompson began work on the site on May 1, 1895, dividing his laborers into two separate transit teams. Each team began surveying the field, establishing east-west and north-south lines that provided a grid system for marking the field. Thompson surveyed an east-west line at the southern boundary of the park, taking special care in surveying this line to check the distances and measurements "both by chain and transit." Every two hundred feet along this line, he had workers drive stakes into the ground, and then he and his transit parties surveyed north-south lines from this standard line. These lines lay two hundred feet apart, corresponding with the stakes set in the original line. The north-south lines were as long as three and a half miles in length, depending on the boundaries of the park. Workers also placed stakes every two hundred feet on these north-south lines, from which they surveyed east-west lines. Thompson and his workers cleared sight paths along all these transit lines so that each stake, two hundred feet apart, could be clearly seen from neighboring stakes.[37]

Thompson then turned his attention to creating maps of the battlefield, producing a large blueprint showing the topography, water courses, and roads. He placed on the map sites of buildings, natural features, and the boundaries of the park. The commission thus by December 1895 had an accurate topographical map that showed landownership. Thompson also printed individual maps of each resident's property. Buell also created an April 1862 map, while historian Reed laid out troop positions on Thompson's battlefield map.[38]

Land agent J. W. Irwin also used Thompson's map for land acquisition. The task was not easy, but Irwin waded through the difficult process. At one point, he admitted that "we find it very tedious work getting up abstracts." Many disputes over boundaries emerged, prompting Cadle to complain about titles "being found very imperfect." Thompson had to take time out of his mapmaking and land-clearing duties to resurvey and clear up disputes.[39]

The work of acquiring land progressed slowly but surely, particularly after March 4, 1896. The commission purchased five tracts of land (797.25 acres, at ten dollars an acre) in the first four months of 1897, the landowners eager to sell. One was not so amiable, however. W. C. Meeks owned 180.9 acres at Pittsburg Landing on the Tennessee River and asked twenty-five thousand dollars for it. The commission refused and condemned the land. On April 27, 1897, in *The United States v. W. C. and O. C. Meeks*, the district court of the United States awarded the park title to the land for $6,000, thus bringing the price down from $138 per acre to $33 per acre.[40]

Cadle believed the condemnation proceedings as well as the precedents set by purchasing inland tracts for around ten dollars an acre gave the government leverage in future land deals. Most owners readily sold their land for around ten dollars an acre. They realized that they could not fight the government in court and win. In Cadle's view, they also believed that the government was not trying to cheat them, but rather was paying a fair price.[41]

By February 1897, Cadle and Irwin had spent $18,675 of the $20,000 limit for land on 1,390 acres. With the appropriated money almost gone, however, more money was needed. Cadle reported to Representative Joseph G. Cannon of Illinois, chairman of the House Appropriations Committee, and received a new limit of fifty thousand dollars in the sundry civil bill of 1897. Between 1897 and 1903, Irwin and the commission bought twenty-four more tracts with no threats of court action.[42]

The vast majority of the battlefield was thus in the United States government's possession by 1903. Irwin had secured 3,313.76 acres at a total price of $48,318 (just under fifteen dollars an acre), Lee's earlier options apparently not raising prices. The commission later acquired isolated and small pieces of property, usually those surrounded by the earlier purchased park lands. Ironically, Irwin's success resulted in the

*Road packer at Shiloh. War Department secretary Daniel S. Lamont cautioned the Shiloh commission to utilize historic roads, not build new ones. This photo shows some of the roadworking tools used at Shiloh. Shiloh National Military Park.*

elimination of the position of land agent as Secretary Root cut costs in the War Department.[43]

The commission, with so much land coming into the park, soon turned its attention to marking the battlefield. The first order of business, however, was to establish rules covering a variety of matters from monument placement to commission conduct. Cadle, Looney, and Buell met often to work out these guidelines, but controversy soon developed between them. Buell complained directly to the War Department that he was being left out and shunned by the Iowa contingent on the commission (Cadle and Reed). He offered "slight but polite exception" to Cadle making decisions without a commission vote. Cadle "confidentially" admitted to Reed that he had done so, but insisted that he had the War Department's approval. Buell more forcefully questioned the practice of keeping all commission records closed to the public and even to Buell himself. He correctly argued that private records prevented necessary supervision. Buell called for a meeting of the commission to work out procedures and then successfully challenged a set of earlier rules written by Cadle and Reed. He offered a substitute set of regulations that included open files. The War Department lectured Cadle on the need for "entire unanimity in the Commission," so Buell had made his point.[44]

On July 20, 1896, the commission unanimously accepted most of Buell's suggested regulations, including a majority commission vote for any action—a move clearly aimed at diluting Cadle's power. The new regulations also stipulated that any two commissioners could call a meeting, and they would constitute a quorum. The critical regulation concerned keeping the files open to public view, which limited Cadle's ability to make decisions in sole consultation with Reed. At least two commissioners now had to approve any action, and Buell apparently believed that the Southern member would side with him more often than not. The new regulations did not bother Cadle, however. He wrote to Reed, saying, "There is nothing that will limit our work or make any trouble."[45]

The commission also passed "Rules to be Observed in Preparing the Battle Map," which would be used as the basis for marking the battlefield. It instructed Reed to locate the lines of battle on Thompson's topographical map, indicating all geographical features present during the battle. Reed was also to locate houses, roads, and fences as they were in April 1862.[46]

The commissioners approved the sources Reed might use in making the map: the "Thom" map, made by Colonel George Thom of Major General Henry W. Halleck's staff, and the "Michler" map, made by Captain Nathaniel Michler of Buell's staff. The commission also authorized the use of the *Official Records*, oral histories from participants, and physical evidence remaining on the field. Finally, it prohibited any marking of the field until the map was completed.[47]

A third set of regulations specified the process of marking the field, authorizing the marking of general lines of battle "as described in the official reports," as well as other points "worthy of identification." The commission advised marking successive Union and Confederate positions on both days of battle. Lastly, it ruled that before any monument went up, it had to first be approved by the commission.[48]

Volume 10 of the *Official Records* became Reed's most helpful source as he waded through the history of the battle. Large veteran turnouts at reunions also provided him with oral evidence to clarify any confusion in battle reports. Veterans of all ranks returned on the anniversary of the battle and frequently found their old positions, reminiscing about their exploits. Most of these veterans were of lower rank and could describe only a small portion of the battle, but these remembrances were invaluable to Reed.[49]

Former higher-ranking officers were also helpful in locating positions and clearing up misunderstandings in the reports. Reed visited generals when they could not travel to Shiloh. He met with John McClernand in Illinois and A. P. Stewart and James R. Chalmers in Chattanooga. Well-known figures also came to the battlefield to mark specific points, such as Lew Wallace, who returned to mark his route of march, and Isham G.

Harris, who returned to locate the death site of Albert Sidney Johnston. The return of well-known men brought excitement to the area, particularly when a veteran had become a political celebrity, such as Tennessee senators William Bate or Isham Harris. On one occasion, a crowd of veterans asked to hear a speech from former Confederate general and current Chickamauga commissioner A. P. Stewart, but he could not be found because he was "off locating places in the battle." Buell, of course, was especially active in this effort.[50]

Isham G. Harris's visit in April 1896 provided several important results. The official place of Johnston's death was located. Northerner Reed also saw the depths of Confederate emotion regarding Shiloh; Harris had asked Reed not to speak of Shiloh because it was such a bitter memory to him. Most importantly, Harris had a change of heart. The senator had remarked to Reed on the way to the battlefield that, despite his support in the Senate, he had very little sympathy with those preserving battlefields. He preferred to forget about all that had happened. After his experience at Johnston's death site, however, Harris congratulated Reed and said, "I have changed my mind about your work here, and say that I am pleased with your plans and will take pleasure in doing anything I can, in Congress or out, to assist you in the work."[51]

After the troop positions were marked on Thompson's maps, Reed began marking the field itself. As at Chickamauga, Antietam, and Gettysburg, tablets would "mark, in letters of iron, the history of the battle." Cannon would mark artillery positions, and monuments would add to the scene. Realizing that this process would take years, the commission first marked the field with temporary wooden signs, providing some interpretation while the park was being developed. Reed placed more than one hundred wooden signs at prominent points on the field in the spring of 1896. Poplar boards painted white with red letters, these signs located prominent natural features such as fields, springs, and houses and also locations of prominent battle sites such as Bloody Pond, the Peach Orchard, the Sunken Road, and the Johnston oak tree. The commission had visitors in mind when its staff placed the boards, desiring them to go up "before the spring excursion parties begin to arrive."[52]

Controversy erupted within the commission concerning the type of permanent tablets to be used, with Buell once again finding himself at odds with Reed and Cadle. Buell wanted a distinct coloring scheme, but Reed and Cadle disagreed, and their view prevailed. The position tablets were to be painted white and trimmed in red for the Confederates, in yellow for the Army of the Ohio, and in blue for the Army of the Tennessee, with camp tablets trimmed in black. Cadle, Reed, and Thompson later changed the background color from white to silver, which Thompson viewed as "the prettiest we have: my old university colors." The shape of the tablet also mattered. The first-day tablets were square with ornamental corners, while the second-day tablets were oval. Camp tablets were pyramidal, signifying a cross section of a wall tent. Larger rectangular signs described the movements of large organizations of men such as armies, corps, and divisions, while smaller signs denoted roads or historical points.[53]

Cadle contracted with an "expert iron master" to cast the tablets: the well-known Chattanooga Car and Foundry Company. Atwell Thompson traveled to his old hometown to oversee the casting process. He remained on hand to answer questions about letter size, capitalization, and spacing on each tablet.[54]

D. W. Reed concentrated on the camp tablets first and Thompson had all eighty-three placed on the field by November 1900. Many permanent road signs also went up. Reed then turned to the more complicated process of erecting troop position tablets. He needed 199 square tablets with ornamental corners to mark the first day's action. Thompson immediately placed them on the field when they arrived from the Chattanooga foundry on May 23, 1901. The second day's tablets, as well as division, corps, army, and law tablets, went up in the next two years. Cadle was able to report that the work of erecting tablets on the battlefield had been completed by 1908. There were 651 tablets in all: 226 Union, 171 Confederate, and 254 road signs and explanatory markers, costing $11,726.14. An example of the work was put on display at the St. Louis Louisiana Purchase Exposition in 1904.[55]

Reed dominated the decisions on the design and placement of the tablets. He decided the colors, wrote the inscriptions, and marked the positions. He made the foundry correct several errors, and once the tablets arrived at Pittsburg Landing and Thompson's crews placed them according to Reed's notes, he often returned to inspect them. He sometimes found tablets facing in the wrong direction and had the laborers correct such mistakes. In all his pickiness, however, Reed established the first permanent interpretive scheme at the park, wording the text in such a way that a visitor could "follow easily the movements of each organization from the morning of April 6, 1862, to the close of the battle."[56]

The commission also placed artillery pieces on the field. On November 14, 1896, Cadle ordered 215 cannon tubes from the War Department.

*David W. Reed. The "Father of Shiloh National Military Park," D. W. Reed served first as historian and then as chairman of the commission. He literally wrote the history of Shiloh, and his lasting influence has been immense. Shiloh National Military Park.*

The secretary of war had already turned over hundreds of obsolete pieces to Chickamauga, Antietam, and Gettysburg, so he readily approved guns for Shiloh. The steamer *City of Paducah* arrived at Pittsburg Landing on March 3, 1897, with 188 cannon tubes. Others arrived in following days, ultimately totaling 250 cannon tubes from five different arsenals. Reed and the commission were not yet ready to place them on the battlefield, however. They needed carriages, which would have to be bought through a bid process. Cadle and Reed opted for "a platform of crib work" to hold the guns until their placement. Cadle had these stacks built atop the bluff overlooking the landing.[57]

With the guns in hand by early 1897, Cadle began investigating where to get the carriages built. He obtained sample carriages from two firms, one in Gettysburg and another in Chattanooga. The two foundries had earlier made carriages for Gettysburg and Chickamauga, but the commissioners had not been satisfied with their work. Gettysburg commission chairman John P. Nicholson told Cadle not to buy anything from the Gettysburg foundry.[58]

In late 1900, Cadle began the process of letting bids for the carriages, placing advertisements in several newspapers around the nation. Five foundries responded with final bids ranging from $65 to $250 per carriage. Eventually, the contract went to the lowest bidder, the Ross-Meehan Foundry Company of Chattanooga, Tennessee.[59]

By November 1902, Thompson had received and painted the first group of carriages with primer and olive green paint, trimmed with black.

The commission had to request seventy-seven more carriages, and these began arriving on December 27, 1902, filtering in as late as August 1, 1903. By September 1903, Thompson and his crews had finished placing the additional seventy-seven cannon.[60]

In addition to marking the field, Reed also produced two documents that still stand as basic sources for understanding the Battle of Shiloh: the Reed maps of the battle and the official commission history. Like his historian-comrades at Chickamauga and Antietam, Reed completed two large troop-position maps in 1900, one for each day. He produced these accurate maps by combining Thompson's topography map and his own knowledge of troop movements. The diagrams showed the action as it unfolded, demonstrating to the viewer the successive positions of the armies. Reed's prose was even more descriptive than the maps. Having long been involved in historical scholarship, Reed had written pamphlets for veterans' organizations and would later publish a history of his regiment, the 12th Iowa. Reed published his crowning achievement in 1902 under the auspices of the Shiloh National Military Park Commission and through the Government Printing Office: *The Battle of Shiloh and the Organizations Engaged.* The book, much like the earlier Chickamauga and Chattanooga histories, quickly became the standard treatment of the battle and would remain so for seven decades, creating the dominant historical interpretation of the battle of Shiloh.[61]

In some of his historical work, Reed, like Boynton, may have inadvertently let his pride guide his memory. He downplayed the significance of the Army of the Ohio's arrival on April 6 in response to arguments by Army of the Ohio veterans that they had saved Grant's army from destruction. He also refused to admit that the Army of the Tennessee had been surprised on the first day. Most importantly, Reed probably overstated the importance of the Hornet's Nest, the area of the battlefield where Reed's unit had fought.[62]

Reed also oversaw state monument placement on the battlefield. Within general government regulations, the states acted on their own accord and created monuments of differing shapes and sizes, adding personality to the battlefield. Some states, such as Wisconsin, Minnesota, and Michigan, placed large central monuments; others such as Indiana and Ohio opted for individual memorials to commemorate each unit, while some, such as Illinois and Iowa, erected large central monuments as well as individual unit memorials.

*Shiloh battlefield. This view of the battlefield shows the area around the Cross-roads, looking north toward a Methodist Church on the battlefield, but not the famous Shiloh Church. Note the cow at right. Shiloh National Military Park.*

As on the other battlefields, the Northern states erected the most monuments at Shiloh. The North won both the battle and the war, and many veterans desired to honor that victory. While Northern states had ample money to spend on these memorials, Southern states were still reeling economically from the war that Shiloh had played such an integral part of. The Southern states had little unencumbered money to spend on memorializing Confederate defeat, which was not in the forefront of Southern minds in the first place, as Senator Isham G. Harris so aptly expressed it.

Not a single Southern state legislature appropriated any money for a memorial during the War Department administrative period, while eight Northern state legislatures erected varying forms of monuments at Shiloh. Arkansas and Alabama eventually built monuments, but the United Daughters of the Confederacy (UDC) oversaw this work, also placing a large Confederate memorial on the field. Two wealthy Confederate veterans also paid for regimental monuments themselves, one for the 2nd Tennessee and another for the Crescent Louisiana Regiment. Proud

Northern states, dominated politically by veterans, preserved the memory of Shiloh, while Southern legislatures, also made up of veterans and sons of veterans, seemingly wanted to forget the battlefield.

As at the other battlefields, the dedication ceremonies for these monuments exuded reconciliation and harmony. Cadle spoke at the Ohio dedication in June 1902, describing the Confederate and Union veterans in attendance "as more than friends now—they are blood brothers." Josiah Patterson, formerly a congressman and one of a series of Confederate representatives on the commission, also spoke of reconciliation, asking "with common traditions, a common language and a common origin, where is the citizen of the Republic who does not rejoice we have a common flag and a common country?" "Sectional animosities have been swallowed up in the patriotism and magnanimity of a common country," he concluded. Finally, a former Confederate colonel representing the governor of Tennessee stated, "It is a matter of rejoicing that we now have a common flag that represents a common country."[63]

At the Indiana dedication in April 1903, Josiah Patterson admitted that the way to heal animosity was not to forget. Forgiveness was "to be found in mutual respect and forbearance." He further claimed that "it was fitting that the work of reconciliation and rehabilitation should begin with the old soldiers." Cadle spoke of the battle and the war that "convinced the Nation, both North and South, that it was a war between Americans that could only be ended by courage, blood and time." Confederate General Basil W. Duke, another in the series of Confederate representatives on the commission, spoke at the Illinois dedication in May 1904 and stated, "[W]e, who once confronted each other on this field in 'stubborn opposition,' now meet with friendly intercourse—meet with no thought of the past conflict, save to wish to honor its heroes on both sides." Duke spoke to the crowd with similar words at the dedication of the Wisconsin monument in April 1906. He argued that the South had been constitutionally right in its efforts but morally wrong to secede and fight; a Confederate victory, he said, would have divided a strong nation, and he thought the Confederacy would not have stood due to the precedent of secession. Duke admitted in the end that he was glad that the two sides were now one. Many Confederate veterans attended the dedication, and a feeling of camaraderie was evident. Duke also spoke at the Iowa dedication in November 1906, stating, "In that terrible ordeal we learned that we were truly the same people, and must remain the same nation."[64]

The same patriotism and reconciliation prevailed at the Confederate dedications. Duke spoke at the 2nd Tennessee monument dedication in 1905, stating that "the dead who lie here, Federal and Confederate, all distinction between them forgotten, all enmity buried in the grave, shall be held in equal honor as American soldiers." He also spoke at the Alabama dedication in May 1907, returning to his theme of reconciliation. "But out of all that ordeal [war] we have come a stronger and a wiser people," he thundered amid the pouring rain. In applauding the establishment of the park, Duke spoke of a place "where citizens of a common and reunited country, all former enmity forgotten, may meet in amity to recall with proud remembrance the deeds of a sad but glorious past and witness equal honors paid to all the dead." Thomas F. Gailor, Episcopal bishop of Tennessee from 1898 to 1935, spoke at the UDC monument dedication in May 1917 and said that "the time has long since passed when a gathering like this in honor of the Confederate soldier could be in any way or degree construed as an occasion to revive outworn political controversies or reargue the questions that were at issue among our people fifty years ago." In dedicating the monument, he sent a message "to all our young men, not only in the South, but throughout the United States, to rejoice that they are Americans."[65]

Despite such sectional reconciliation at dedication ceremonies, Reed did face opposition from some veterans who did not agree with his interpretations. Veterans of the 4th Tennessee, 32nd Illinois, 81st Ohio, and 15th and 16th Iowa all carried on long and exhaustive controversies with Reed, as did Lew Wallace and other officers such as Allen Waterhouse. Most complaints were about Reed's placement of monuments or the inscriptions on them. Wallace, however, was trying to rescue his tarnished name. In each of the quibbles, Reed stood firm, even when the matter was ultimately appealed to the secretary of war. In most cases, he won the appeals, proving just how historically sound he was.[66]

The nastiest commission controversy concerned Don Carlos Buell and his representation on the commission. Buell and Looney realized early in the history of the commission that Reed and Cadle, and to a lesser degree Thompson, ran the park. Buell and his Confederate counterpart felt left out. The Southerners on the Shiloh commission, as well as on other military park commissions, had very little bargaining power with the federal government, but Buell felt he did. His resulting actions, as well as those of that army's defenders, soon created a controversy of immense proportions that shook the commission to its foundation—not unlike the other commissions of the time.[67]

Buell and the defenders of the Army of the Ohio, namely the Society of the Army of the Cumberland, alleged errors in many of Reed's conclusions on the army's monuments and tablets at Shiloh. Influential men soon arrayed themselves against what they believed was an Army of the Tennessee cabal running Shiloh National Military Park. Old commission friend Henry V. Boynton, now commission chairman at Chickamauga, soon became involved. As a former member of the Army of the Cumberland, Boynton felt it his duty to defend that army's precursor, the Army of the Ohio. Given Boynton's zeal for controversy, he soon had Cadle and Reed squarely in his sights.[68]

Boynton first took issue with Reed's book, stating that it contained gross inaccuracies regarding the Army of the Ohio. Boynton took issue with Reed's claims that the Army of the Tennessee had not been surprised on the morning of April 6, with his failure to recognize the positive effect of Buell's arrival on the evening of April 6 and his failure to state truthfully when the Army of the Ohio engaged the enemy on April 7, and even with Reed's small stylistic lapses. In what had by this time become a custom, Reed produced a lengthy rebuttal to every allegation.[69]

Boynton would not let the matter fade, however, and he soon leveled an even more sustained attack against the commission, complaining to the secretary of war that the Shiloh commission was conspiring to discredit the actions of Buell's army during the battle and had ignored Buell as a commission member. In a scathing letter to Secretary of War Taft, Boynton asserted that Buell was "constantly ignored by the Chairman of that Commission, acting with its Historian." He further argued that Cadle and Reed had purposely destroyed Buell's maps and notes on the battle's second day and had even denied their existence. Boynton further stated that although a majority of the commission (Buell and Looney) voted that the question of surprise was outside the commission's realm of activity and thus should not be treated, Cadle and Reed had nevertheless defended Grant's army against accusations of surprise. Finally, Boynton argued that Cadle ignored correspondence and protests from Buell and Looney. Buell's stepdaughter, Nannie Mason, also offered damaging testimony against Cadle and Reed, citing inaccessible park files and allegations of the destruction of Buell's maps. Given Boynton's high standing with the War Department, his accusations carried a lot of weight.[70]

The controversy grew messier later in 1905. Boynton penned another harsh letter to Secretary Taft, this time with the sole purpose of "further discredit[ing] the historical work of the National Shiloh Commission, and its Historian, Major Reed." Boynton once again attacked Cadle's and Reed's insistence that Grant's Army of the Tennessee had not been surprised on the morning of April 6, 1862. In an effort to support a thesis that Reed had done shabby historical work, Boynton and the Society of the Army of the Cumberland argued that the nonsurprise position "tends to cast serious doubt upon the historical methods adopted, and the historical accuracy of the rest of the work." Following Reed's example, Boynton compiled a very lengthy argument that Grant's army was indeed surprised but that Reed had "wholly ignored" the issue and that Reed's book and his positioning of tablets and inscriptions "have been used to keep that controlling fact out of sight."[71]

Boynton's accusations were more than the commission could ignore. A stunned Reed responded to what he called Boynton's "very discourteous" attacks. "I see no need of argument or explanation over this matter," he fumed. Nevertheless, he responded at length and again refuted Boynton's entire thesis. While the affair did not elicit a critical response from the War Department, Assistant Secretary of War Robert Shaw Oliver, a Boynton friend, reminded Reed that he had invited criticism in his 1902 publication and requested that he submit a revised edition encompassing pertinent corrections. Reed obliged and, exhibiting animosity toward Boynton, remarked on his "well known proclivity to attack everything that is not the product of his own brain and ready pen." The new edition of Reed's book appeared in 1909, but incorporated few changes brought to light by Boynton.[72]

Boynton also alleged that the commission underrepresented the Army of the Ohio in placing tablets. Reed had erected almost two hundred tablets for the Army of the Tennessee and more than one-hundred and sixty for the Confederate army. By contrast, the Army of the Ohio had only forty-one. Finally tiring of the dispute, Assistant Secretary of War Robert Shaw Oliver submitted the entire matter to a "specially constituted Committee of the War College for consideration and report." The special committee made no formal report but did recommend that "the changes suggested by the National Military Park Commission be adopted." Even the vaunted Boynton could not dislodge Reed.[73]

Reed's marking of the battlefield and the publication of his history created the dominant historical interpretation of the battle of Shiloh. As a member of the 12th Iowa, which fought squarely in the midst of the Hornet's Nest, Reed tended to emphasize that portion of the field. Historians are beginning to examine several pieces of evidence that point to the fact that the Hornet's Nest was not quite the most important position on the battlefield, but, like Boynton, they are finding Reed's interpretation extremely hard to dislodge.[74]

Like the other parks, the Shiloh commission changed over time as veterans died and others replaced them. Don Carlos Buell became the first commission member to die. At eighty years of age and after a lengthy illness, he died on November 19, 1898, at his home in Kentucky. Cadle and Reed did not miss Buell, who would continue to cause the commission problems through the efforts of Henry Boynton. Letters between Cadle and Reed discussed Buell's death matter-of-factly and quickly moved on to other park affairs. No commission representative attended the funeral, something that was routinely done for other members during Cadle's tenure.[75]

After Buell's death, Cadle remarked to Reed that "there will be a lively scramble for his place [on the commission]." The secretary of war soon filled the void by appointing James H. Ashcraft of Kentucky as the representative of the Army of the Ohio. Ashcraft had served at Shiloh as a first lieutenant in the 26th Kentucky Infantry, and his appointment was dated January 12, 1899.[76]

After several months of failing health, the seventy-five-year-old Robert F. Looney died of heart failure at his home in Memphis on November 19, 1899, a year to the day after Buell died. Despite Cadle's support of Land Agent J. W. Irwin, the secretary of war appointed Tennessee politician Josiah Patterson to replace Looney on January 1, 1900. After serving as a first lieutenant in the 1st Alabama Cavalry at Shiloh, Patterson had served in the Tennessee state legislature and three terms in the United States House of Representatives. Cadle and Reed welcomed the appointment, Cadle even writing Reed that he "will be in accord with us." After a short and uneventful term, however, Patterson himself died on February 10, 1904.[77]

On February 20, 1904, the secretary of war appointed General Basil W. Duke to replace Patterson as the Confederate representative. Duke had served at Shiloh as acting adjutant for his brother-in-law, John Hunt Morgan. He later was colonel of what became the 2nd Kentucky Cavalry. Duke served a long but uneventful term. He had no startling effect on the commission, although he became known as quite an orator.[78]

One more departure directly affected the leadership organization at Shiloh. With the park all but built, Atwell Thompson resigned in October 1905 to find "private work in his profession." He did return periodically, however, to perform skilled engineering work. Thompson ultimately became city engineer at Jackson, Tennessee, before dying in 1912.

*Tornado damage at Shiloh National Cemetery. The 1909 tornado devastated the Shiloh National Cemetery as well as adjacent areas of the park, including the impressive Iowa monument. Seven people lost their lives in this storm near Pittsburg Landing. Shiloh National Military Park.*

Thompson's departure caused a vacuum of leadership, prompting Reed to move from Illinois to Shiloh in 1905.[79]

Even more destructive than the commission controversies, a "cyclone" hit the Pittsburg Landing area on the evening of October 14, 1909, destroying much of the cemetery as well as much of the park's building infrastructure. In addition to toppling the massive Iowa monument, the storm killed seven and injured thirty-three at Pittsburg Landing alone. Work began immediately to repair the damage, but the destruction at Pittsburg Landing was more severe than the workforce or the annual appropriation could handle. The War Department told Cadle to submit a list of needs, and Congress responded with an emergency appropriation of $19,500 for the park, $8,000 for the cemetery, and $15,000 for repair of the Iowa monument. Congress delegated the money for the Iowa monument with the understanding that the state would reimburse the federal government.[80]

The storm also produced major changes to the commission. In January 1910, Cadle received notice from Secretary of War Jacob M. Dickinson that "for some time past the Department has been thoroughly dissatisfied with your method of conducting business. . . . It is therefore requested that you immediately forward to me your resignation as a member of said commission." Without even giving notice to Reed, Cadle resigned as commission chairman, effective January 31, 1910. Very little is known about the causes of the War Department's action. The only direct evidence is that Cadle, suffering some type of health problems due to "exposure" resulting from the tornado, "became disabled." This makes little sense, however. Adding to the mystery is the secrecy with which Cadle offered his resignation; he did not even tell his trusted friend Reed.[81]

The best possible guess is that the seventy-three-year-old Cadle's health had deteriorated drastically because of the increased activity of rebuilding the park, and he realized that such stress was something that his feeble health could not endure. Supporting this supposition is the fact that Cadle died after an extended illness at his home in Cincinnati on January 13, 1913, only two years later. After a solemn funeral led by Union general Grenville Dodge and Rev. George A. Thayer, Cadle was cremated and buried in his hometown of Muscatine, Iowa. Apparently, there is more to the story than that, however. Reed and Cadle had always been close friends and confidants, yet there is no record of Reed ever making any mention of Cadle's 1913 death. More importantly, there was some correspondence between Reed and the War Department over Cadle's failure to respond to Reed's requests and inquiries. Although Cadle recommended that Reed replace him as commission chairman, Reed and Cadle's relationship apparently ended, indicating that some animosity had developed between the two men. No postresignation correspondence between the two has been found.[82]

The War Department thus had to fill Cadle's position and reorganize the commission. Cadle had recommended Reed for the job, and the secretary of war complied. An added problem was the location of the official commission office and files in Cincinnati. Reed, as new chairman, began to deal with each problem systematically. While his appointment kept the park's affairs in the hands of its most knowledgeable individual, it also consolidated jurisdiction. The original leadership of three had dwindled to Cadle and Reed with Thompson's resignation and now consisted of Reed alone. He became the supreme park authority at Shiloh. Moreover, he now lived in the park, thus further consolidating his control.[83]

Personnel changes continued to take place on a regular basis. To replace Reed as secretary and historian, the War Department on February 4, 1910, appointed Colonel John T. Wilder, a veteran of the 17th Indiana, but it quickly transferred him on September 30, 1911, to a position as a full commissioner at Chickamauga. General Gates P. Thurston then became secretary at Shiloh on October 4, 1911, but he remained only until his death on December 10, 1912. In his place, the War Department appointed DeLong Rice of Nashville, Tennessee.[84]

The aging Reed could no longer see to the day-to-day activities of the park, and Ashcraft and Duke, both older men, did not even live in the park. Thus the need for a superintendent became acute. Fortunately, Rice was available and on the scene and impressed Reed so much that the chairman supported his promotion to head the park. Rice officially took control in 1914, with the title "Secretary and Superintendent."[85]

As time passed, Reed and the other commissioners slowly faded away. Duke died on September 16, 1916, leaving only Ashcraft and Reed. By this time, however, Reed was also very sick, having suffered for several years from deteriorating health. When called to Washington to testify concerning appropriations in 1912, he sent Duke because he was not "just now in very robust health." In May 1913, Reed was thrown from his carriage and "suffered a broken thigh." This event ended his mobility, and he was soon forced to hand over his on-site duties to Rice and return to Iowa. He died in Iowa on September 22, 1916. J. H. Ashcraft was now the only remaining commissioner, but he too died on January 19, 1920.[86]

The War Department promoted Rice to park director just two months later, although he would use the title "superintendent" for the remainder of his service at Shiloh. And that service would have a profound effect; DeLong Rice's legacy is clear. He took the park from an ailing Reed and modernized it in the midst of the second American industrial revolution, seeking ways to bring a greater number of people to the site. Rice was also the first person to interpret the park to visitors not of the veteran generation. In so doing, he blazed a new trail, creating tour routes and interpretive pamphlets. He never let go of his roots, however, and the interpretation of his mentor, D. W. Reed. Even amid the physical and interpretive modernization, Rice always advanced the traditional Reed thesis centering on the primary importance of the Hornet's Nest.[87]

Unfortunately, Rice died as a result of a massive accidental explosion in his home on September 29, 1929. With Rice gone, the reins of control over Shiloh National Military Park were transferred to another dedicated individual. Clerk Robert A. Livingston, born and raised on the park, had served faithfully for nearly thirteen years. He knew the park and the duties of the superintendent, so he was the logical choice to replace Rice.[88]

Livingston's first four years ran into 1933, when the park was transferred to the National Park Service. His major duties were to maintain the site and facilitate visitors who flocked to its grounds. Little unusual activity took place during Livingston's first four years as superintendent; he basically continued what he had learned from Rice—the Hornet's Nest thesis. Reed had trained Rice, and Rice trained Livingston. The Reed interpretation lived on.

The establishment of Shiloh National Military Park showed not only the extent to which Congress and veterans would go to preserve such an out of the way battlefield, but also the passion with which they did it. And it also continued established patterns from all the 1890s era battlefields. As at Chickamauga-Chattanooga and Antietam, the growing reconciliatory attitude was evident at Shiloh. Likewise, even in Shiloh's woods, H. V. Boynton again appeared as a force in battlefield preservation.

But Shiloh was not the last park assembled. Even as Shiloh developed, a fourth and much more famous sister park in Pennsylvania was moving along the same lines.

# 6

## "A SPLENDID MONUMENT TO AMERICAN VALOR"
### Gettysburg National Military Park, 1895–1933

DESPITE GETTYSBURG'S PRIZED position and the hard work put into it for years prior to the 1890s, the Pennsylvania battlefield was ironically the fourth of five reservations preserved by the federal government in the Golden Age of battlefield preservation. Although Congress began even in the 1880s making appropriations dealing with certain aspects of preservation at Gettysburg and would even provide for a three-man commission like other battlefields in 1893, Congress would not officially make Gettysburg a national park until 1895, after Chickamauga, Antietam, and Shiloh had already been preserved. Such a late start does not diminish Gettysburg's historical position, but it does show that Gettysburg was not the foundation upon which all federal battlefield preservation was built. If there was a turning point in federal preservation, it was with Chickamauga-Chattanooga's establishment in 1890.

Still, Gettysburg is important; it was the only battlefield that saw any federal preservation efforts prior to 1890. It was also the only battlefield to receive major federal funding prior to 1890. And it was the only extensively marked battlefield Americans could visit for more than twenty years after the war.[1]

The legislative history of Gettysburg is complicated at best. In 1890, the same year that Chickamauga and Antietam were preserved, backers of the Gettysburg park idea asked Congress to establish a park there. Representative Henry H. Bingham of Pennsylvania brought a bill, H.R. 4972, to the floor of the House on January 14, 1890. Bingham's bill called for a one-man governor of the park—John B. Bachelder. Committee on Military Affairs chairman Byron M. Cutcheon of Michigan reported to the full House that the committee "has not considered it best to intrust so great a discretion to a single individual, however competent." The commitee

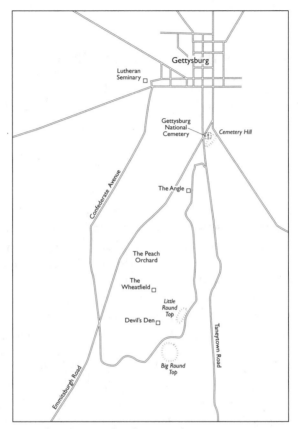

*Gettysburg National Military Park*

thus replaced H.R. 4972 with H.R. 11868, which followed Henry Boynton's lead in the Chickamauga bill and instituted a three-man commission. The new bill continued the reconciliatory rhetoric of 1890, stating that "no American need ever blush for the record of either side. It was a great battle, so grandly fought that it compelled each combatant to respect the other forever after" and asking, "[W]hat grander evidence of magnanimity and strength could the nation give than thus to preserve the historical data of the great turning battle of the war[?]" The committee also continued the emphasis on marking the Confederate troop positions. Although the committee argued that the work needed to be done before the veterans passed away, it unfortunately also drastically cut the appropriation. Finally, the committee also recognized that the work needed to be done by the federal government: "It must be done by the National Government or remain undone," the members argued. The full House did not heed the committee's warning, however, and took no action on the measure.[2]

A parallel effort was also under way in the Senate; Senator Joseph R. Hawley of Connecticut introduced a similar bill, S. 2188, on January 14, 1890. He was not able to bring the bill to the floor until September 16, 1890. Senator Hawley admitted that the bill was "modeled upon the bill that has become a law for establishing Chickamauga Park," complete with authorization for buying land and placing markers and monuments. Hawley reminded his colleagues that the government had spent relatively little money on the Gettysburg battlefield, the cemetery being the exception. He reminded the Senate of the fifty thousand dollars they had spent in 1880 to survey the field and the additional fifteen thousand dollars they had spent almost a decade later to erect monuments for the United States Regular Army troops there. In comparison, he noted that Northern states had spent over one million dollars on monuments at Gettysburg. Unfortunately, he went on, "nothing has been done to mark the positions of the Confederate troops, and if done it must be by the National Government." Hawley concluded that, if passed, the bill would create a park that would "offer the grandest study in the world for students of the military art and for lovers of patriotism and admirers of magnificent valor." The Senate passed the bill that day, but with the lack of success in the House, the effort died.[3]

Supporters of the Gettysburg park idea did not give up, however; they again sought to create the park in late 1892. On December 21, Representative Oscar Lapham of Rhode Island led another effort in the House Committee on Military Affairs. The committee cited the common arguments for the park, that "the history, so far as practical, of this momentous battle may be written upon the ground itself." It also argued that the land was in jeopardy from "an association . . . devoted to building lots, and that an electric railroad is to encircle the whole." The need was to preserve the field now, before the battlefield was damaged and before the veteran generation passed. The committee thus argued for a phased course of action in which the first appropriation would allow for surveys to preserve the threatened land. Later, Congress could establish the park itself. The committee thus called for a commission to begin the work. Unfortunately, the full House never saw the bill, and it died like all the others.[4]

The Gettysburg supporters in Congress finally made some headway in 1893. On January 21, 1893, Representative Joseph H. Outhwaite brought up S. 2914, which again proposed to establish a park at Gettysburg. Unfortunately, the bill met opposition in the House. Representative Marriott Brosius of Pennsylvania objected to different shapes of tablets for different branches of service. Representative Outhwaite put out that fire by explaining that various service branches needed various shaped tablets to differentiate them and also to mark various "evolutions and movements of the troops." Brosius dropped his opposition, but others succeeded in killing the bill for a time. Opposing members demanded each individual amendment to the bill be voted on, instead of as a group. Time soon ran out in the agreed-upon period for debate, and Outhwaite was never able to bring the bill back to the House in its original form.[5]

Supporters of the bill, like those for a park at Antietam, did manage to attach a smaller version of the legislation to the year's sundry civil bill, which became law on May 25, 1893. The section reserved for Gettysburg quietly appropriated twenty-five thousand dollars for marking the battlefield with tablets, opening and improving roads, and fencing those roads. The work was to be done "without praise and without censure," the legislation read, and stipulated that both side's lines would be marked. Part of the act also stipulated the appointment of three commissioners to do the work.[6]

The federal government had finally become involved with the work, although not in the way many veterans had hoped. Most wanted a full park like that at Chickamauga, but instead they received a limited establishment much like that at Antietam and Chattanooga. Yet, there was still a glimmer of hope. Considering all the work done by the Gettysburg Battlefield Memorial Association, many veterans envisioned land being presented to the government, making for a Chickamauga-like park in the future.

For now, however, the veterans had to settle for the three-man commission with limited powers at Gettysburg. Secretary of War Lamont quickly appointed the commission on May 25, 1893, the same day the bill passed. In accordance with the custom at Chickamauga, two members were Federals and one Confederate. The secretary appointed Lieutenant Colonel John P. Nicholson of the 28th Pennsylvania Infantry, a veteran of Gettysburg and a member of the battlefield association, and he would become the dominant figure in Gettysburg's history. In fact, his stature in the War Department parks system would rise almost to that of Boynton at Chickamauga. Partly because of Gettysburg's place in history and partly because of Nicholson's competence, he would be a major figure in all War Depart-

*John P. Nicholson. As chairman of the Gettysburg commission, John P. Nicholson was a paramount figure in battlefield preservation. He led the Gettysburg efforts for nearly thirty years. Gettysburg National Military Park.*

ment work on the parks. Even his stature was imposing; Nicholson was a rather large man with a thick white beard that made him look very dignified. Gettysburg scholar John B. Bachelder, although not a veteran himself, also received an appointment. Bachelder had arrived on the battlefield just days after the fight ended and had been studying its history ever since, serving as a major player in the Gettysburg Battlefield Memorial Association. Finally, the secretary of war appointed Brigadier General William H. Forney as the Confederate representative. A member of the 10th Alabama Infantry, Forney had been severely wounded and captured at Gettysburg, only to recover and attain a brigadier general's commission by the end of the war. The newly appointed commission met six days after its appointment, but unfortunately, General Forney was ill and could not attend. Nicholson and Bachelder thus began the work of the commission by themselves.[7]

Secretary of War Lamont gave explicit instructions to the commission: to elect a chairman, to keep an office in Gettysburg, to mark permanently the lines of battle, to stay within budget, and to follow the Antietam Plan (and Gettysburg Battlefield Memorial Association plan) of "purchasing strips and small parcels of land rather than large areas." With instructions in hand, the commission met again on July 1, 1893, and formally began its work. Forney was able to attend this second meeting, and the commission thus began to appoint second-tier workers. The most important of the selections was military engineer Colonel Emmor B. Cope as the topographical engineer and his assistant, S. A. Hammond. Cope had served at Gettysburg as an engineering staff officer, and army commander George Meade had detailed him immediately after the battle to map the battlefield. Cope's profession and long association with the battle made him an obvious choice. The commission also voted to rent a room in Gettysburg and to allow Cope to begin a survey of the battlefield.[8]

The commission found many obstacles at Gettysburg, chief of which was the threat of a new "electric railway" that was to run across the battlefield. Incorporated in 1891, the Gettysburg Electric Railway Company had begun construction of the railway as early as April 1893. The commission, as had the association before, began efforts to fight it. One commissioner noted that the officers even "found important lines of battle occupied by an electric railway," including a spur to Little Round Top and the main line over the area of the famous July 3 Confederate charge. Yet the commission had very little power to act.[9]

The commission at one time thought that the case might be settled in 1893 when negotiations led to "a suspension of the work upon the electric railroad." The commission also stated that it felt that the road would "eventually be removed from historic localities, at a small expense to the Government." By June 1894, however, the commission had given up all hope of a peaceful settlement with the railway and asked Secretary Lamont to begin condemnation proceedings. Congress passed a joint resolution supporting condemnation if necessary, while the attorney general of the United States began the proceedings in Philadelphia on June 8, 1894. The case went to court in August. The railway requested a postponement, so the "trolley case" did not begin until September 11, 1894. The Gettysburg court heard the case for five days before it adjourned to hear more argument in Philadelphia. Ultimately, the court ruled in favor of the railway, awarding it thirty thousand dollars for damages. Each side appealed, the railway saying the sum was too low and the government saying it was too high. The railway's attorneys argued that marking a battlefield did not constitute the requisite public use importance to allow for condemnation. Thus, the case became bogged down in the judicial system.[10]

While the legal wrangling continued, Cope and his engineering team surveyed the battlefield and found important positions on the grounds.

The commission reported that "the first work was to establish a meridian," which they would use to mark other features of the battlefield. "Using this meridian as a base of operations, there has been run many miles of back-sight transit lines on various parts of the field," noted one commissioner. In their work, the commission located "many traces of the Confederate breastworks" and many locations of stone walls used as defenses. Cope and his workers "surveyed and computed" these positions. At the same time, the engineer corps of the army also surveyed portions of the field.[11]

The surveying and inspecting led quickly to a map of the Gettysburg battlefield. Bachelder's knowledge also came into play, and troop positions were placed on the map. Veterans also returned to locate lines of battle. Members of the "Stonewall" Brigade returned in August 1893, and Antietam Board member Henry Heth visited in August 1894. The commission reported that the Confederates "seemed deeply impressed with the importance of this work and enthusiastic in the assurance of cooperation from the Confederate veterans."[12]

The commission also proceeded to buy land and build roads. The first purchased land was 5.26 acres on September 18, 1893. Thereafter, the commission purchased several more tracts, but it encountered locals who wanted more money. "The work of the commission has been hampered by the expectations of numerous people representing various interests, in their demands for high prices for land," the commission reported. The locals were ultimately unsuccessful, however, and the commission was able to purchase more land. The Gettysburg Battlefield Memorial Association also voted to begin the process of donating its considerable landholdings to the commission.[13]

Cope and his engineering team worked closely with the commission in rectifying contested boundary lines, mapping the battlefield, and surveying the area. They also began the process of drawing and planning roadways. Cope and the commission laid out a roadway along the Confederate lines, very reminiscent of the lanes at Antietam. The commission deemed it necessary to make its landholdings wide enough to include (and thus preserve) the principal earthworks on the battlefield. A 500-foot-wide avenue would include all the Confederate earthworks in most areas. At other points, a road 150 feet wide would encompass the works.[14]

The commission's principal effort, however, was to mark troop positions. The marking of United States Regular Army positions had already been authorized by three acts of Congress in the 1880s. A major portion of the land acquired by the commission had been United States Regular Army sites, where they had placed by 1894 some forty cast-iron tablets and twenty-five guns on iron carriages. For the volunteer units, the commission also wanted to mark each regiment's flank with a marker and each battery's position with a single gun mounted on a carriage.[15]

Although some problems emerged, the Gettysburg commission could be proud of its work during 1893 and 1894, but the electric railway was always a threat. Inclement weather and "the beginning of snow" also forced the commission to postpone some work. The death of Confederate representative William H. Forney on January 16, 1894, also slowed the commission until Secretary of War Lamont replaced him in March with Major William M. Robbins, a veteran of the 4th Alabama, then living in Statesville, North Carolina. Despite the postponement of work and perhaps learning of the disfavor the Antietam Board was in for its slowness, the commission was determined to make its annual reports "one[s] of progress." Secretary of War Lamont was evidently pleased, even making a trip to the battlefield with his wife on November 3, 1893. He noted in his report to the House of Representatives that "the work of preserving the lines of battle at Gettysburg and of permanently marking the positions of the commands of both armies there engaged is making satisfactory progress under the direction of the commission appointed for its supervision."[16]

Despite the praise, the Antietam-type commission faced too many problems that their colleagues to the south did not. The Gettysburg commission had too little power against a myriad of problems, chief of which was the electric railway. Secretary of War Lamont recognized the problems and lobbied Congress for more forceful legislation. Citing the major work of the Gettysburg Battlefield Memorial Association, Lamont reported in 1893 that "in the absence of any other provision for the permanent care and maintenance of this completed work[,] it has been suggested that the General Government might well accept that charge and assume its control."[17]

Having not been successful in getting Congress to fund a major park at Gettysburg in 1893, Lamont lobbied again in late 1894. In December 1894, in the midst of the Shiloh establishment debate, Gettysburg veteran Daniel Sickles of New York introduced a bill into the House of Representatives, having won his seat on the sole issue of getting a park at Gettysburg. On December 6, his bill became H.R. 8096 and was referred to the Committee on Military Affairs. Sickles, however, was not satisfied with the bill and the committee reported a substitute out on December 18, 1894, which became H.R. 8252.[18]

When the House returned to work in January 1895, that body took up debate on H.R. 8252. On January 16, Committee on Military Affairs chairman Outhwaite brought the bill to the floor in a timed period for dealing with appropriations bills. With only a few minutes of the allotted block of time left, Representative Joseph D. Sayers of Texas suggested that Outhwaite wait until the next day to give more time and also a thorough understanding of what the bill authorized. The Speaker agreed, reminding Outhwaite, "In the few minutes remaining there would scarcely be more than time to read the bill." Sickles then spoke up and agreed to delaying the bill to the next day if the full rights of the committee to bring up the bill be extended to the morning hour the next day. The House agreed to treat the bill as pending.[19]

In reviewing the revised bill, however, Sickles and War Department officials found several flaws. As a result, the Committee on Military Affairs did not bring the bill up again until January 22, at which time Sickles asked that a third version be substituted. "The changes are merely technical," he assured the House, and consisted of only boundary adjustments and an idea to open a soldier's home at Gettysburg. The clerk read the new bill and the House accepted the substitute as well as one other amendment dealing with a clerical error. The standard House operating procedure then went into effect, with a second and third reading, after which the bill passed with no opposition.[20]

The bill then went to the Senate, which disposed of the work in short manner. The legislation was referred to the Senate Committee on Military Affairs, which reported it out on February 1, 1895. The Senate took the bill up for debate on February 4, and it was passed with no opposition. President Cleveland signed it on February 11, 1895. The Gettysburg National Military Park became a reality.[21]

The bill contained nine sections, most of which were similar to the other park bills passed in the 1890s. The major difference came in the first two sections. Since Congress had to deal with the transfer of an already semipreserved battlefield, an issue with no other park preserved in the 1890s, the first sections authorized the federal government to accept "about eight hundred acres" of land owned by the Gettysburg Battlefield Memorial Association. In return, the government would pay the association's debts, amounting to around two thousand dollars. Once the association's land was taken under federal control, the site would become the

Gettysburg National Military Park. Likewise, since Gettysburg already had a commission at work locating lines of battle, the legislation allowed for the same commissioners to be placed in charge of the national park under the secretary of war's jurisdiction.[22]

Other than appropriating money for "a suitable bronze tablet" to commemorate President Abraham Lincoln's Gettysburg Address in the national cemetery, the bill was similar to earlier ones. It authorized the government to obtain new tracts apart from the association's donated land through either purchase or condemnation. It set a rough boundary of the park by citing a map drawn by Daniel Sickles, the representative ushering the bill through Congress. Laws and regulations, in very similar wordage and consequences to the other park bills, protected the park, while the last section appropriated seventy-five thousand dollars for the park and required the secretary of war to report to Congress every year.[23]

Gettysburg finally had a park much like those at Chickamauga and Shiloh. Given the preservation work that had taken place beforehand, however, perhaps the most important development was that Gettysburg now had what historian Ed Bearss described as "a commission with teeth in it." The already-established commission now had authority along the lines of the commissions at Chickamauga and Shiloh and worked closely with War Department officials such as the various secretaries of war, Robert Shaw Oliver, and particularly George B. Davis, in the effort to preserve the battlefield. To show their newfound power, in 1895 the commission immediately issued a set of regulations governing the battlefield.[24]

The Gettysburg commission still faced numerous problems, leading it to proceed in a much different way than the other parks. Land acquisition, the first priority for other commissions, was not the first order of business at Gettysburg. Because the Gettysburg Battlefield Memorial Association already held a large parcel of land, the commission would not have to move quickly to secure property before preservation work could be done. More importantly, the pending Gettysburg Electric Railway court case caused further acquisition delay.[25]

The commission thus began its work by building and restoring avenues and roads on the lands already under government or association control. In a pattern similar to that at Antietam, the commission built twenty- to twenty-five-foot wide roads along the fairly static lines of battle for both armies. The commission named these roads after army commanders, local landmarks, or national organizations. Thus roads such as United States Avenue, Seminary Avenue, and Confederate Avenue became common

*Road construction at Gettysburg. The Gettysburg commission used the Telford system of building roads, which included laying a firm base of large rock as a foundation. Gettysburg National Military Park.*

names, as did roads named for individuals such as Hancock Avenue, Slocum Avenue, and Meade Avenue.[26]

"After full consideration and study," the commission chose to build these roads scientifically. The Telford system used a conglomeration of syenitic granite and ironstone that was "very hard and of excellent quality." As a base, workers placed eight-inch flat stones on edge. On top of that, the workers placed small one-and-a-half-inch stones four inches deep. Atop the twelve inches of rock was placed a layer of clay "as a binder," which held a top layer of small pebbles some quarter inch in diameter. The commission used a fourteen-ton steamroller to roll the roads, which when finished produced "roadways smooth and solid and which will last for generations."[27]

As time went on and more land began to come into the park, more roadways were constructed using the Telford system. But one section of road still bothered the commission. It complained for several years about a major portion of Confederate Avenue along Seminary Ridge being outside government hands and therefore delaying the work. Comprising the area from which the third day's attack was launched, the area was of particular interest to the commission: "There is no part of this battlefield so inaccessible as this. Encumbered by bushes and briars and cross fences, with not even an open footpath over it, visitors here never see this ground because they can not reach it." The landowners asked such exorbitant prices that the commission had to condemn the land, which took years to do. Finally, by 1901 the commission had the land, and the last sections of Confederate Avenue were opened.[28]

The commission also built the attending features to the roadways, such as bridges across several creeks, drains to allow water to flow without eroding the roads, and fences along the sides of the avenues. Fortunately, there was an abundance of rock in the area, particularly on Big Round Top and Devil's Den, to facilitate construction. The bridges over Plum Run were "massively built of Gettysburg granite," while the drains were laid with flat rock. Fences and stone walls were also built or restored using local stones. Barriers to prevent "careless driving off the roadway" were prepared by placing granite boulders topped with thirteen-inch cannon-balls. Grass was set out all along the roadways to keep erosion down and to create a beautiful setting.[29]

The commission was pleased with its road-building—even taking over the care of the local roads, such as the Emmitsburg and Taneytown roads, when Congress passed additional legislation allowing the State of Pennsylvania to cede jurisdiction of the roadways to the federal government in 1899. Such work was necessary, for thousands of visitors were already coming to Gettysburg every year, and that number would only grow. In 1899, the engineering department reported that nine thousand vehicles, carrying thirty-six thousand people, traveled the roads in one month alone.[30]

By 1904, the commission had built some twenty miles of roadways in the park, and road-building was carefully weighed against the possibility of destroying the battlefield's topography and terrain. The commission reported that "particular care is . . . taken to avoid cutting away and changing the natural surface of the ground when constructing the avenues. Fortunately the lines of both armies mainly occupied ridges, slopes, and valleys of such character that avenues can be constructed so as to follow those lines closely without seriously disfiguring the ground with cuts and fills in grading." The commission also chose to build narrower roads in certain areas: "to widen them would seriously mar the face of the ground which the Commission have taken great care to preserve as nearly as possible as it was at the time of the battle."[31]

While the commission concentrated on the roads and avenues at Gettysburg and fretted over land acquisition, the courts were handling the larger issues of land condemnation. The entire operation at Gettysburg hinged on the electric railway case, which made it all the way to the Supreme Court of the United States. Judges of other pending cases logically awaited the high court's ruling on the constitutionality of condemnation before making their own decisions. Thus the land acquisition work at Gettysburg was temporarily put on hold while the two sides fought it out in the judicial system.[32]

The electric railroad was not the only source of land disputes at Gettysburg. Even before the secretary of war appointed the commissioners, local parties had formed the Gettysburg Land and Improvement Company, also known as the Land Syndicate. The company bought up large chunks of land and took options on the rest. They "at once placed exorbitant prices on these lands—prices several times greater than what they paid or agreed to pay for them." (The ire in the commissioners' voices can well be imagined.) The commissioners had no way to pay such high prices and thus they resorted to condemnation, which dragged the process out for years. The land along Confederate Avenue that took so long to acquire was one example of such delay.[33]

The major issue on which all other cases hung, however, was the railroad case. Despite opposition from the Gettysburg Battlefield Memorial Association and later the Gettysburg commission, the railroad company had bought up land in the Devil's Den and Plum Run area and had begun to construct its right of way. The commissioners complained that the company built the road "so as to deface and change the topographical features of the Battlefield where important military operations took place." The jury had earlier awarded thirty thousand dollars to the railroad company, which both sides appealed. Such was the situation as the newly established park took form after the legislation passed Congress in early 1895.[34]

The lawyer for the railway company soon appealed on the grounds that condemning land for preservation purposes was unconstitutional. After the railroad position was upheld by a district court, an appeal went to the Supreme Court and was argued on January 8–9, 1896. Despite some early concern that the government might lose, the high court ruled in its favor on January 27, 1896. In a landmark decision, the court ruled that the United States could indeed condemn land for preservation purposes.

Justice Rufus W. Peckham wrote in the opinion that "there can be no well founded doubt" that preserving a battlefield was in the public interest. It also put the federal government's stamp of approval on what had taken place earlier in the 1890s and all that would come in the future.[35]

When the Supreme Court opened the door for condemnation, the commission took on the Land Syndicate with the full power of the federal government behind it. Case after case went forward with the opposition hiring "Attorneys and Counsel of eminence and reputation from Washington DC and a large number of the members of the Bar of Adams County, [Pennsylvania]." The juries lowered the price of land from the hundreds to $80.62 an acre on average, but the Land Syndicate appealed, which delayed the work even more. In its annual report in 1898, the commission lectured the secretary of war, as did other parks' commissioners, that the reason the Confederate lines and positions had not been marked was that the government did not own the land. "Prompt action by the courts in condemning the needed lands when held at exorbitant prices, and liberal appropriations by Congress for the purchase of lands which can be bought at reasonable rates, are the two main requisites for the realization of the patriotic purposes of the Government with reference to this battlefield," the commission argued. Ultimately, the syndicate lost its appeals, and the commission went forward with its work of land acquisition. Nicholson and his commission wrote that "it is apparent what were the motives of this Syndicate in purchasing so suddenly the lands which they judge the Secretary of War was obliged to acquire."[36]

Despite the go-ahead from the courts for large-scale land acquisition, the commission did not deem it necessary to buy large tracts. It was operating under instructions from Secretary Lamont to buy only small areas of land for monuments and roads and not "great areas [that] would not only cost heavily, but would also entail a continuous useless expense to maintain them." In response, the commission reported it had "at all times entertained the opinion that the acquisition of any lands beyond what were owned by the Gettysburg Battlefield Memorial Association (The State Corporation) was dependent upon the judgment of the Secretary of War as to what he would 'deem best calculated to serve the public interest.'" The commission thus did not push for large-scale acquisitions like those at Shiloh and Chickamauga but opted for something between the Antietam Plan and the strategy of other parks. But the park grew slowly as it acquired roughly a hundred acres each year. By 1904, when the

*Emmor B. Cope. One of the most important engineers in battlefield preservation, Cope not only oversaw work at Gettysburg but also mapped the battlefield of Antietam at that board's request. Cope would go on to become Gettysburg's first postcommission superintendent upon Nicholson's death. Gettysburg National Military Park.*

development of the park was initially declared as semicomplete, the park contained around 1,380 acres.[37]

Other major engineering work went on during the first years of the park, although it was not as visible or noteworthy as land acquisition and road construction. Engineer Cope led a large force of workers who toiled on the battlefield eight hours a day five days a week. In addition, the park owned several draft animals that pulled wagons and carts hauling rock, lumber, and dirt. When not at Antietam, Cope kept a watchful eye on his workers, making them keep the park in spotless condition even during their work. "The field shall always appear as nearly as possible neat and finished, while in fact there is always a large amount of important work in progress," wrote the commissioners. In addition, five guards roamed the battlefield to prevent damage caused by "mischievous visitors and foolish relic hunters."[38]

On the battlefield itself, the workers built the roads, cleared new tracts of heavy underbrush, and surveyed the field. Fencing was a major concern, with the laborers rebuilding battle-era fences and stone walls. By 1904, more than thirteen miles of pipe fencing, eleven miles of post fencing, and nearly five miles of stone fencing adorned the battlefield. Almost thirteen miles of guttering ran along the Telford roads in the park. In order to restore the battlefield to its original configuration, the commission also had its laborers plant new trees to reforest the areas on which timber grew in 1863. In 1904 alone, the commission planted 8,100 trees under the supervision of Samuel B. Detwiler of the United States Bureau of Forestry. In order to make the battlefield more visible to the visiting public, the commission also built five large steel towers in 1895 and one in 1896 on such high ground as Culp's Hill, Seminary Ridge, Big Round Top, Oak Hill, and Ziegler's Grove. To mark the battlefield sufficiently in terms of natural features as well as troop positions, Cope also produced a series of highly detailed maps of the battlefield. Cope also built a storage building for his tools and equipment.[39]

The engineering component of the work at Gettysburg was only an infrastructural support for the major reason to preserve the Gettysburg battlefield: that of marking the troop positions and battle lines for all to study and to commemorate what happened there. The historical work at Gettysburg went on much like that in the other parks at Chickamauga, Antietam, and Shiloh. The commission used primarily veteran testimony, along with the *Official Records*, to determine unit placement and troop positions. There was one major difference in the case of Gettysburg, however, that made the commission's job much easier: Gettysburg had already been studied in great detail and the history of the battle was well known. So much, in fact, was known about the battle and battlefield that states had already placed large numbers of monuments and markers at Gettysburg to locate troop positions. In the years before the 1895 establishment of the park, Congress had seen fit to pass appropriations to locate battle lines of groups that had previously been left out, such as the United States Regular Army and the Confederates. When the commission began its major historical work, therefore, much of its job had already been done. Moreover, one of the main workers in that effort was fortunately on the commission itself: John B. Bachelder. He would continue to provide historical oversight to the commission until his death on December 22, 1894. Bachelder provided so much historical information, in fact, that quite a scare emerged after his death when the commission erroneously feared it had lost his papers containing years of research on the battle. Secretary of War Lamont appointed Major Charles Richardson of the 126th New York Infantry to replace Bachelder.[40]

The Gettysburg commission saw the wisdom of producing a major series of maps that would guide historical efforts on the battlefield. Engineer Cope was extremely busy producing maps not only to mark troop positions, but also to aid in land acquisition and engineering work. The commission had Cope mark troop positions on a map as early as 1897, but by 1900, the commission had turned its full attention to a series of maps that would become the basis of the commission's historical work. Colonel Cope and his engineering staff produced a base map that covered some seventeen square miles of territory. The map was twenty-nine inches by forty-five inches, "with every detail of topography accurately represented." One base map was marked with present 1900-era trees, roads, fences, buildings, and monuments, while the other was made to represent 1863-era conditions. Troop positions for every hour of the day were placed on the 1863 base map, and the commission concluded that it would need nine different maps for the first day positions, twelve for the second, and fourteen maps for the last day of the battle. The base maps were completed by the winter of 1900, but it took years of study to place accurately all the troop positions. The first day's maps were completed by 1902, with the other two days' maps done by 1904.[41]

Meanwhile, the commission continued the already established process (both at Gettysburg and on the other parks) of marking the battlefield with tablets denoting troop positions. It fully realized that most of its work would concentrate on the Confederate lines, since most of the federal positions had already been determined and marked by the states under the supervision of the Gettysburg Battlefield Memorial Association. The commission invited former Confederates to the battlefield and even asked that commissions be appointed to represent various groups. Nicholson and the commission did its work with optimism, stating at the outset that they felt "sure that they will be able within a reasonable period of time to determine and mark with very great accuracy the positions and evolutions of all the various commands of the Confederate army on this field."[42]

The commission soon needed additional land to mark the Confederate lines. While they waited on the court cases to be decided, the commissioners thought about how best to tackle the problem of locating Confederate commands. Of course, the commission would use "handsome tablets of iron." The commissioners noted, "Much thought has been given to the preparation of these tablets and their inscriptions for the Confederate commands, so as to arrive at the utmost possible historic accuracy with regard to each one as well as perfect consistency and fairness among them as a whole. This is a work requiring great deliberation and painstaking [work], but we hope to accomplish it satisfactorily." Ultimately, they decided to place a "principal tablet" at the position each command held in the main line of battle, with "subordinate and ancillary tablets" to mark subsequent positions held by each unit. Each tablet would have a short inscription detailing the hour of engagement and a description of the fighting.[43]

The commission began placing iron tablets on the field in 1898 but ran into trouble regarding regulations for bidding on government projects. Nicholson and the commission complained to the secretary of war that they wanted the same treatment given to the Chickamauga commission— the ability to buy tablets on the open market. In the next few years, the commission was thus able to erect numerous tablets and signs to acquaint the visitor with the battlefield. Tablets for several United States regular regiments went up in 1900, but the commission mainly concentrated on placing tablets denoting Confederate commands. The commission first placed tablets to mark brigade positions and then branched out to place some regimental and many division, corps, and army tablets. These tablets were created with the same dimensions as those already on the battlefield denoting federal positions, measuring three and three quarters by two and a half feet, "with carefully prepared inscriptions cast in raised letters describing the part taken in the battle" by the units. In addition, road signs also went up, as well as directional markers "to give useful hints and directions to persons driving over the field." The commission also branched out and placed several orientation and historical tablets in neighboring towns that were along the paths of advance of the two armies that met at Gettysburg. In all, by July 1904 the commission placed 461 metal tablets of all shapes, sizes, and kinds on the battlefield.[44]

Another major objective was to place artillery pieces wherever that branch of the army was located during the battle. The original Gettysburg Battlefield Memorial Association had begun the process of marking Union battery positions, but it had done so on wooden carriages from the Navy Department and very inaccurate iron carriages. By the time the commission took over the battlefield and the association's cannon, their main concern was replacing many of the old deteriorated carriages. The commission soon contracted for "gun carriages admirably resembling the usual wooden ones, but made of iron." They were almost identical to those used at the other parks.[45]

Once the older carriages had been replaced, the commission established new artillery positions on newly purchased land. They marked each artillery position with at least two guns. At every point, the commissioners attempted to mark the batteries "with the kind of gun used by each battery, respectively, in the battle." They also placed an iron tablet to give a detailed description of the action in which the battery participated, its losses, and number of rounds fired. By 1904, the commission had placed 322 guns on the battlefield.[46]

The commission also continued the association's work of erecting monuments. As before, these stone pieces of art and remembrance were primarily placed by the respective states. After the commission took control of the field in 1895, a slow down in monumentation took place. (By far, the major period of monumentation at Gettysburg was during the Gettysburg Battlefield Memorial Association's governance, between 1884 and 1893.) By 1897, however, the states were again active, with New York, Minnesota, West Virginia, Maine, Pennsylvania, and Vermont regimental monuments going up. Other states such as Virginia and North Carolina followed suit in later years, with state, regimental, and individual monuments going up all over the battlefield. Equestrian statues were especially popular, with those of Major General John F. Reynolds and Henry W. Slocum erected at their particular points of service or death. A monument also marked the position where park supporter Daniel Sickles had been wounded. Repair work also took place, such as to repair damage from lightning striking the Major General Winfield S. Hancock equestrian statue. All the monumental work was done with state-appropriated funds. Pennsylvania even placed a monument to an elderly citizen of Gettysburg, John Burns, who took musket in hand to fight the enemy. As at the other parks, the monumentation was heavily weighted toward the Union side, with very few Confederate states willing to fund such projects. In fact, only one more Confederate monument went up around the turn of the century, a monument placed in 1904 to honor the 4th Alabama Infantry—the unit in which Commissioner William M. Robbins had served. He paid all the costs for the commemoration.[47]

As the states placed their monuments at Gettysburg, their dedication speeches were very similar to those on the other battlefields, displaying a vivid sense of reunification and reconciliation. Major General Daniel

Sickles spoke at the dedication of the New York monument on "New York Day," July 2, 1893, reminding his hearers, "There is no thought suggested by this occasion, that we should give pain to any of our countrymen to-day. We rejoice, yes, as all of our countrymen may rejoice, in a Union success-fully defended; in a government whose authority was here maintained; in a Constitution firmly established; in Republican institutions made im-perishable. In these results, to which the victory of the Union arms at Gettysburg contributed so much, every American, and every well-wisher in America, may find satisfaction." At the dedication of the Pennsylva-nia memorial on September 27, 1910, Pennsylvania governor Edwin S. Stuart said, "None can doubt but that our country is being more firmly welded together day by day and year by year, and that the men of the South and the men of the North are evincing a more considerate regard and a warmer appreciation of each other's interests." Later he reminded his audience that "every memorial placed here in love and gratitude becomes at once, not only a tribute to the valor of the American soldier, but is also an inspiration to increased patriotic devotion to our common country."[48]

Even the Southerners got in on the reconciliation. At the North Carolina monument dedication in July 1929, North Carolina governor O. M. Gardner spoke of the spirit the monument typified, "not a spirit of partisanship, nor of envy of another section, but a spirit of supreme devotion to our common country, its traditions, and its aspirations. We no longer think in terms of physical combat, but in terms of peaceful progress. . . . To defend the flag of our country we would give our all." The UCV even lent its support and praise to the effort of reconciliation. At its annual reunion in May 1899, its commander John B. Gordon issued a statement in which the veterans voted to support the efforts at Gettysburg and the other parks to make "permanent memorials of the prowess of American soldiers with-out respect of section." They also called on the Southern states to build monuments at the parks "in honor of our glorious heroes in gray who fought and died for what they believed to be right."[49]

In all the monumentation and reunion activity, one of the chief goals of the commission was to "restore and preserve the features of the battle-field as they existed at the time of the battle." The commission spent much time restoring original and rebuilding broken down stone fences and walls, restoring forests and stands of timber, and refurbishing his-toric buildings on the battlefield. Even its road building activity was done with an eye toward keeping the natural terrain the way it was in 1863.

Like the other park commissions, Gettysburg's was profoundly convinced of the need to keep the battlefield a revered land rather than a landscaped and beautified commercial attraction.[50]

Other types of memorialization occurred outside the park. Gettysburg and the other parks endured Secretary of War Elihu Root's obsession with displaying park items at the St. Louis Exposition in 1904. Engineer Cope packed up a sampling of its work and shipped it to St. Louis in April 1904, where it was placed in "the excellent position allotted to the Commission." Of course, Shiloh and Chickamauga also sent a sampling of their work. Gettysburg's exhibit included mostly maps and blueprints, particularly the large maps drawn by Cope displaying both the 1863- and the 1890s-era topography. Framed photographs added beauty to the exhibit. Cope also sent a large framed map of the battlefield of Antietam that he had made. Apparently, the commission was no more excited about shipping their priceless maps to St. Louis that any of the other battlefield commissions were. In its 1904 report, the commission noted that the large fourteen-by-ten-and-a-half-foot map of the battlefield was "put in position with great care, fortunately without injury."[51]

In the midst of the memorialization and commemoration, the Gettysburg commission helped produce and strengthen some of the most basic interpretations of the battle that are still taken as the truth today, although they might not be correct and are beginning to be challenged by historians. Bachelder had long been involved in making the "High Water Mark" the central position on the battlefield, and many monuments went up to mark that location. Little Round Top was also becoming very famous. During and immediately after the war, neither was considered as important as it is today, but in the nation's mind both have come to be perceived as places where the battle was won and lost. Indeed the entire battle rapidly came to be seen as the engagement where the Civil War was decided. Historians today are beginning to take a second look at the contemporary sources, finding out that the beloved sites may not have played such a critical role in the fighting but were rather the creations of battlefield aficionados who promoted their own memory of the battle.[52]

More tangible than the interpretive and memory issues, Gettysburg, like the other parks, endured its disputes as aged veterans' memories began to fail and their pugnaciousness increased. These disputes, although passionate, were fortunately never on the scale of those at Shiloh, Chickamauga, and later at Vicksburg and never threatened the makeup and integrity of the commission.

The locals of course provided regular contention. Many small disputes occurred over land when the owners would not sell and the commission felt forced to use condemnation proceedings. The locals also complained that once the park had possession of the land, the commission would not allow them to place mailboxes along the roads on park land. The commission's presence in town also caused some trouble. Residents complained of the commission's stable in town, and the Gettysburg town counsel petitioned for the commission to open gates in the park's fences to allow for travel off the roads.[53]

Gettysburg also had its quota of ruffians and looters. The commission reported a problem with "thoughtless or mischievous visitors, and particularly the mutilation of monuments by the sacrilegious relic hunters that sometimes infest the grounds with the sense of reverence wholly undeveloped." One such vandal damaged nine monuments and "seemed to have no other motive but pure maliciousness." The five guards under employment also reported "petty pilfering" from the gun carriages as vandals stole the small and intricate parts for souvenirs and even chipped some of the granite monuments. The park also had to place strict speed limits of six miles per hour to keep visitors safe.[54]

Like the other parks, the commission also at times had trouble with the War Department. When the department's disbursing clerk, W. S. Yeatman, performed clerical work for the commission and turned in what the commission thought was an exorbitant bill, the commission refused to pay. Ultimately, the case went to the judge advocate, who ruled in Yeatman's favor and forced the commission to pay. Veterans frequently asked permission to camp on the battlefield, and the commission had to turn them down, fearing such camping would damage the park. At other times, the commission stopped women from camping with the veterans who had received permission.[55]

As was the case with the other parks, the commission particularly sparred with the veterans, who thought certain actions were wrong or should be done another way. One such controversy involved road names. In 1913, a group of veterans led by John Bigelow wanted United States Avenue to be changed to Hunt Avenue to honor the artillery chief of the Army of the Potomac, Henry Hunt. Even Oliver Wendell Holmes supported this idea, but the commission would not budge. Chairman Nicholson reminded the War Department that Secretary of War Daniel S. Lamont had named that particular road during a visit to the field in 1895, the first road named by the government. Nicholson protested that if one person was able "by letters, or the employment of attorneys," to undermine a decision of a secretary of war, "it is impossible to say how far the agitation for change may go." The name remained.[56]

A more powerful veteran also became a problem for the commission: Daniel Sickles. Although he had authored the legislation that had established the park, Sickles's reputation for corruption would affect the park and the commission. Sickles evidently thought he was entitled to special treatment, but he found out otherwise when he wanted to camp on the battlefield during the Slocum monument dedication. The commission refused permission. Sickles also complained when local guides informed visitors that he had made mistakes during the battle. The major problem with Sickles, however, came in 1912 when some twenty-eight thousand dollars was found missing from the New York Monuments Commission, of which Sickles served as president. The state issued an arrest warrant for embezzlement, but the sly old one-legged politician, now ninety-three, avoided jail time once more, just as he had done as a congressman before the Civil War when he had killed Francis Scott Key's son in Washington, DC. Sickles was able to stay out of jail when friends raised enough funds to pay the money back. Upon Sickles's last visit to Gettysburg for the 1913 reunion, someone asked him if he was irritated that he had no major monument on the field, to which he replied, "Hell, the whole damned battlefield is my memorial."[57]

The major controversy between veterans in Gettysburg's history came in 1902 when former Alabama representative and governor William C. Oates petitioned to place a monument to his regiment, the 15th Alabama, on Little Round Top. The commission would not allow such a placement because it believed Oates's men never reached the point where the politician desired to place the monument. The commission responded that the regulations demanded that monuments be placed in the particular line of battle to show "battle array." Oates responded that he "felt indignant." He then lectured the commission on how he had supported the commission in Congress and had gotten Forney and Robbins placed on the commission. The commissioners did not budge, and Joshua Lawrence Chamberlain's testimony that Oates's positioning was incorrect helped their case. To Nicholson's horror, however, Oates then took the matter to Congress, where he lobbied successfully for a Senate joint resolution, SJR 530, which called for the monument and asked the secretary of war why it had been disapproved up to this time. The commission maintained its stance, however, even though it placed the commissioners in a ticklish position—especially Robbins, the Confederate representative, who had fought in the same brigade as Oates at the battle. He wrote Nicholson, "I hope you will try to avoid placing me in the front of this controversy with General Oates." Ultimately, the secretary of war sided with the commission and its regulations and the argument that to place monuments where particular veterans wanted them would "so encumber the Gettysburg National Park as to mar its significance." Oates could not even get the support of Commissioner Robbins, who in the past had endured disparaging remarks from Oates. Robbins's lack of support effectively killed the notion. Oates was never able to place the monument, despite the bad press the commission received over the issue. One writer even recommended taking the word "national" out of the park's title, because, he said, it was only sectional in scope.[58]

Many other Confederates took their cue from Oates and did not respond to invitations from the commission, especially Confederate representative Robbins, to place monuments on the battlefield. They wanted to place monuments where they had actually fought, not where they had stood in line awaiting orders to advance. Since Federal veterans had already placed monuments all over the battlefield before the park was established and before the commission posted regulations, the Confederates wanted the same opportunity. This never happened.[59]

The vast majority of the population was pleased with the efforts of the Gettysburg commission, however, whether they were veterans of the battle or descendents of veterans or just curious and patriotic Americans. As early as 1896, the commission reported "visitors in great numbers from all sections of our country, as well as some from abroad." In its 1900 report, the commission claimed "multitudes of visitors . . . , including thousands of veterans of both armies." They also reported that the veterans and visitors were "unanimous in approving the Government's design to make this battlefield a splendid monument to American valor." On occasion, famous figures toured the battlefield, including many military officers from the American and British armies, various secretaries of war, and in 1904 President Theodore Roosevelt.[60]

By 1904, the Gettysburg commission had all but concluded its initial phase of park-building. The majority of the land had been acquired, most of the roads had been constructed, and a majority of the initial tablets and artillery pieces had been positioned. The commission wrote in its 1904 report that there were only a few small parcels of land that still needed to be bought, a few short avenues to construct, and a small number of tablets to be placed before "the object of the Government in establishing the Gettysburg National Park will have been substantially accomplished." In fact, the commission reported, "In our opinion the acquisition of any further extensive tracts of land here by the United States would be a waste of public funds."[61]

Work continued after 1904 but not on a grand scale. The commission continued to be the major jurisdictional body at Gettysburg, but its membership changed over the years. After William M. Robbins of the 4th Alabama Infantry took General Forney's place and Major Charles A. Richardson of the 126th New York Infantry took Bachelder's place, the commission remained constant for several years. But then Major Robbins died on May 3, 1905, and was replaced by Major General Lunsford L. Lomax, who had served in the 11th Virginia Cavalry at Gettysburg before attaining higher rank. Both Major Richardson and General Lomax died after the 1912 legislation that precluded any more appointments, General Lomax on May 28, 1913, and Major Richardson on January 24, 1917. Thereafter, Colonel Nicholson remained the only commissioner.[62]

The commission, even as it dwindled, continued to oversee the large group of laborers and workers on the park. The mowing crew continually kept the grass cut around the park and on the roads and also provided hay for the commission's use. "Trimmers and axemen" kept the timbered areas of the battlefield clear of undergrowth and small trees, while others used the park's steamrollers to maintain the miles and miles of roads. A carpenter and his assistant made needed repairs to historic structures on the park, while the painting crew made continual cycles around the park painting the buildings as well as the many tablets and artillery carriages. Others kept the bronze on the tablets and monuments in good shape. Other workers made rounds cleaning gutters and picking up trash, limbs, and leaves, and generally "keeping everything in complete order."[63]

A major portion of the laborers' work dealt with the park's numerous historic buildings. Old houses and barns that stood on the field during the battle were preserved, and the workers also maintained a few modern structures to house the commission and its equipment. The commission of course had an office in Gettysburg and also a stable to keep the horses. The commission rented office space until 1914, when the government built a new "United States Public Building," a two-story structure that housed the post office on the bottom floor and the commission on the second floor. "These new rooms are very much more convenient and satisfactory in every way than the old quarters," Nicholson reported.[64]

In addition to the park structures, the park workforce also became involved for several years in opening up land for "pupils of the Gettysburg schools" to work gardens. In an effort to provide food that was needed during World War I, these schoolchildren worked the gardens and provided potatoes, corn, and other foods for the war effort. As far back as 1898, when Congress had passed legislation enabling the practice, the park also allowed tenants to live in the park's farmhouses and work the land. Under the general leadership of William C. Storrick, some nineteen farms totaling around 1,400 acres were under lease by 1920.[65]

The commission and laborers also spent a lot of time with the ever-growing number of visitors to the park. As time passed and the automobile made travel easier, the park saw increasing numbers of tourists. Dignitaries also visited on numerous occasions in this later period, such as various secretaries of war and army officials. President William Howard Taft visited in 1909 to dedicate the United States Regular Army monuments, with Vice President James S. Sherman visiting in 1911. Throngs of veterans also returned and toured the battlefield, with the GAR of Pennsylvania holding its encampment in June 1913 on the battlefield.[66]

All the while, the commission continued to build and refine the infrastructure of the park under its efficient engineer, Colonel Cope. He assumed more and more responsibility as the commissioners died. His assistant Augustine Hammond's resignation in 1908 left him as the sole engineer. Under Cope's leadership, most of the initial building had taken place before 1904, however. Small bits of land continued to come into the park as more land became available or was condemned by the government. Likewise, more roads emerged as new parts of the park were opened to visitors. When the automobile became the chosen method of travel, the commission turned to piking and oiling the roadways to keep them thoroughly smooth.[67]

The historical arm of the park's work also went forward in later years, although most of that work had also been completed during the initial construction phase. The work of restoring the battlefield continued as more property came into the park. "The Commission . . . has kept in view the purpose of preserving the features of the battlefield as they were during the battle," the 1908 annual report read. As more roads were built, the commission endeavored to follow contour lines without cutting large parts of the ridge down, thus altering the battlefield as little as possible.[68]

Of course, the dominant historical work dealt with the monuments and tablets at Gettysburg. The major work regarding tablets in this later period was an effort by the commission to replace iron corps, division, brigade, and itinerary tablets with more substantial and beautiful bronze tablets set atop granite foundations. Once approval from the War Department came, the commission acted immediately. First to go up in 1907 were large granite-based bronze tablets to each corps in the opposing armies. Workers placed bronze army tablets and replaced the itinerary tablets in 1908, with division tablets up by 1910. The more numerous brigade tablets for both armies also went up: sixty-four Confederate bronze tablets by 1911 and seventy-four Federal bronze tablets by 1912. In 1914, the commission marked the site of each corps hospital with bronze tablets on granite bases.[69]

As monuments continued to go up on the battlefield, some controversy emerged, prompting action by the commission to further organize the effort. So many tablets and state and federal monuments were appearing that the War Department formally ruled in January 1910 that all future monuments, markers, and tablets had to be placed on the already established lines of battle, with no deviation to mark subsequent or prior positions held by the units. (This declaration merely formalized the accepted commission method.) The rules did allow the monuments and tablets placed on the line of battle to indicate prior and subsequent positions held by the units, but that position in the actual main line had to be sufficient to memorialize the specific unit. The rules also required approval of the secretary of war to place a monument to an individual, and the secretary had to deem the individual "entitled to special commemoration."[70]

The rules allowed the states to continue to erect monuments, which they did. Pennsylvania dedicated its large and elaborate memorial in September 1910, with as many as ten thousand visitors on hand for the ceremonies. Connecticut dedicated a monument in June 1913, with Virginia dedicating its impressive state memorial featuring an equestrian statue of Robert E. Lee in June 1917. The commission also erected its own monuments to Federal commands. Working through committees of United States Regular Army veterans, the commission dedicated forty-five small monuments to the regulars on May 31, 1909, with President Taft attending. The commission also placed large granite bases with upright cannon shafts and bronze plates at the site of each army and corps headquarters.[71]

Even as more monumentation went up, the commission worked to take the story of the park to more people, both on the battlefield and off. The park had already sent an exhibit to the St. Louis exposition in 1904, and portions of the exhibit were displayed at the Lewis and Clark Exposition in Portland, Oregon, in 1905. Gettysburg also sent an exhibit to the Alaska-Yukon-Pacific Exposition at Seattle, Washington, in 1909. By far, the vast amount of instructional effort went on at the park, however. The commission implemented a licensed guide service in 1915. Before, the park had allowed locals to take visitors on tours, but the War Department ordered that the guides be tested and also established regulations to govern their conduct. The commission began the process in 1915, and the first guides were licensed in February 1916. In order to enforce the rule that only the new licensed guides could give tours, the commission arrested some nonlicensed guides in October 1915. The commission also created a relief map of the battlefield, made out of pine boards shaped to conform to the battlefield's contours. The eight-by-eleven-foot relief map was formed to represent every inch of the battlefield, and Nicholson reported the map was "a perfect miniature of the ground it represents." To better help visitors locate monuments and markers on the battlefield, the commission also published a short booklet entitled *The Location of the Monuments, Markers, and Tablets on the Battlefield of Gettysburg*. First printed around the turn of the century, the commission reprinted and revised the booklet on numerous occasions in order to keep up with the growing number of monuments and tablets on the field.[72]

The growing park also hosted or hoped to host historical commemorations. Remembering the Chickamauga dedication in 1895, members of the House of Representatives and Senate, led by Congressman Daniel F. Lafean and Senator Boies Penrose, both of Pennsylvania, authored bills to dedicate formally the Gettysburg park. Unfortunately, nothing ever came of the idea. A "Lincoln Memorial Way" was also contemplated to connect Washington, DC, to Gettysburg—"a national tribute of affection toward Abraham Lincoln." Several congressmen authored other bills involving Gettysburg commemoration but failed to obtain funding.[73]

One venture that did materialize and was a huge success was the 1913 fiftieth anniversary commemoration of the battle. Chairman Nicholson had called a town meeting to discuss the issue as far back as 1908. Over the next couple of years, the State of Pennsylvania became involved, as did other states, and even Congress appropriated money for the event. Nicholson argued that such a move was of "national importance," and the nation agreed. On October 13–14, 1910, the commission met in Gettysburg with representative committees from the various states as well as congressional committees that would oversee the project.[74]

*Veterans reunion at Gettysburg. The year 1913 saw the fiftieth anniversary of the battle at Gettysburg. National observances were held, with President Woodrow Wilson giving the keynote address at the reunion. Here, several veterans of blue and gray meet at the famous "High Water Mark" of the Confederacy.* Pennsylvania at Gettysburg.

The State of Pennsylvania led the way, forming a "Fiftieth Anniversary Commission of the Battle of Gettysburg." Nicholson met regularly with the Pennsylvania commission. Cope also surveyed the land to provide camping areas for the throngs of veterans that would return to the battlefield. Throughout 1911 and 1912, plans went forward, with Congress appropriating $150,000 for the anniversary, to be spent by the Pennsylvania commission heading up the work. The ruling commission from Pennsylvania incorporated other states' representatives as well as a congressional committee. The entire national committee then went forward with the plans, with much of the work being done by the Quartermaster Department of the army, which leased two tracts on which to camp the expected fifty thousand veterans. Nicholson said the anticipated celebration would be "one of the grandest events in the history of the country."[75]

July 1–4, 1913, arrived, and the commemorations were all that everyone had expected. A feeling of reconciliation was once more in the air, with Confederate veterans at the reunion passing several resolutions thanking various entities for making it possible that former enemies could "meet in friendship here today." Other resolutions included thanks not only to the State of Pennsylvania and her commission that spearheaded the event but also to the United States government and United States Army for overseeing the logistics. The veterans also thanked the Confederate armies for, in their words, proving that the United States could not be broken apart. The festivities were just as moving. July 1 was Veterans Day, with prayers, music, and addresses by the respective commanders of the GAR and the UCV, Pennsylvania governor John K. Tener, and Secretary of War Lindley M. Garrison. Day two, July 2, was Military Day, with the same types of prayers, music, and speeches by representatives of each army. July 3 was Governor's Day, with speeches by several governors and a reenactment of Pickett's Charge. A very moving and poignant moment occurred when the veterans of the Confederate attack reached the angle and eagerly greeted their former enemies with handshakes. Fireworks concluded day three.[76]

Day four was the climax of the event, with President Woodrow Wilson giving the keynote speech. The president was on a tight schedule, and his visit had to occur on the strictest timetable. He arrived in Gettysburg at 11:00 a.m. and was taken directly to the great tent where the celebrations were being held. Entering through a line of Boy Scouts and being introduced by Governor Tener, the president was greeted with "Hail to the Chief" from a Pennsylvania National Guard band. He spoke for a short time and then departed immediately to catch a train back to the capital. "How wholesome and healing the peace has been!" the president spoke. "We have found one another again as brothers and comrades, in arms, enemies no longer, generous friends rather, our battles long past, the quarrel forgotten—except we shall not forget the splendid valor, the manly devotion of the men then arrayed against one another, now grasping hands and smiling into each other's eyes."[77]

Once the president departed and the veterans returned to their homes, Gettysburg went back to normal, except for one great difference: the military was there to stay. The vast military presence during the anniversary events was only a precursor to what would come to Gettysburg later. Through the years prior to World War I, Gettysburg saw an increasing amount of military activity. Unlike Chickamauga, it missed the major operations during the time of the Spanish-American War because it was relatively new as a federal park and because of its location far away from the gulf staging area. Gettysburg did not miss the intervening years, however, or the World War I activity, where it played a major role in training, organizing, and shipping off several regiments for the war in Europe. The idea of using national military parks as training grounds for the modern military was very much evident at Gettysburg.

Such military activity had begun in earnest in 1902 when the graduating class of cadets at West Point visited the field. The next decade and a half saw the cadets attend staff rides at Gettysburg almost every year. The Pennsylvania National Guard also held summer encampments at the battlefield, actually beginning as far back as 1884. In July 1910, the War Department established an army camp at Gettysburg, complete with portions of the 15th United States Cavalry, 3rd United States Field Artillery, 2nd and 29th United States Infantry, engineers, signal corps, and hospitals. Other state national guards joined in, with units from Maryland, Virginia, New Jersey, Pennsylvania, West Virginia, and the District of Columbia taking part. Of course, there was also a heavy presence of United States troops on the battlefield during the anniversary commemorations in 1913. Even United States Marines visited the park in 1916, but a visit by the Army War College that year had to be postponed "on account of the trouble on the Mexican border." All along, other students and dignitaries regularly visited the field. Most left with a firm sense of passion for the history of the battle. Tragedy struck during one military encampment, however. In July 1908, the Pennsylvania National Guard as well as officers from Fort Leavenworth were on the battlefield when "severe electric storms" developed, killing three soldiers and injuring many more.[78]

The major military activity at Gettysburg came as the United States became embroiled in a world war. Many units that normally visited the park had to change their plans. The secretary of war notified Chairman Nicholson on May 22, 1917, that the Gettysburg park would be the recruiting station for four new infantry regiments and the campsite for two already established regiments then "en route from the Texas border." The 4th and 7th United States Infantry arrived in Gettysburg in early June.[79]

In his 1918 report, Chairman Nicholson described the activity in the park. "The camp extended over many acres," he told the secretary of war, and "the troops were constantly drilling." No doubt Nicholson remembered back to his own combat in 1863. The two regiments were augmented by recruits, making a total of six regiments: the 4th, 7th, 58th, 59th, 60th, and 61st United States Infantry. The soldiers drilled and became fit for duty before they departed in October and November 1917. Almost all had left by November 26, 1917.[80]

*World War I army camps at Gettysburg. This view shows the massive army mobilization camps at Gettysburg. Note the monuments in the foreground. Gettysburg National Military Park.*

After the first influx of troops had passed, the War Department established another camp at Gettysburg in March 1918, naming this one Camp Colt. In charge of this camp was a young captain who would forever be tied to Gettysburg, Dwight D. Eisenhower. The new facility used the old buildings, water systems, and parade grounds of the former camp. A unit of the "Tank Corps" was housed at Camp Colt, but nearly all these troops had likewise departed by July 1919. By then, only a small detachment of the Quartermaster Corps remained to see to the buildings and equipment.[81]

The park commission was heavily involved in all the work. As there were no engineers among the troops and no equipment, the commission's engineer, Cope, had to help with much of the work. Likewise, the cleanup went no better at Gettysburg than it had at Chickamauga. The company hired to come in and dismantle the camp and the buildings and restore the park managed to carry away everything of use but did little to restore the battlefield to its former state. Likewise, the Quartermaster Department did not fulfill its promise to restore the roads damaged by the troops and heavy equipment. Chairman Nicholson noted that the troops worked "until the armistice was signed," but the commission was never able to get the work completed by the army. Nicholson had to pay for the restoration out of the commission's funding.[82]

After the war, the military continued to use the battlefield for train-ing and study. In a dramatic event, United States Marines from Quantico, Virginia, reenacted Pickett's Charge on July 3, 1922, using Civil War–era tactics and formations. Then the marines assaulted the Union line again the next day using modern military tactics. The difference was stark. On hand to witness the event were President Warren G. Harding and General John J. Pershing.[83]

The decade of the 1920s brought much change in the governance of the park. Like most of the other parks established in the 1890s, the commis-sion ceased to exist when its last remaining member died. In Gettysburg's case, this was Chairman Nicholson, who had been the only member for several years. With his passing on March 8, 1922, the commission ceased to exist. Yet, the original commission had done much work. By the time the park passed into the hands of a superintendent, Gettysburg had more than 2,530 acres with some fifty-nine miles of roads, thirty-four miles of them of the Telford system. Fifty-three miles of fencing was on the park, with twenty-five stone bridges and twelve culverts. The six observation towers still gave visitors a panoramic view. Still, the monumentation was the core of the park, with 839 monuments erected by the states, 81 bronze statues (5 of them equestrian), 946 bronze tablets on monuments and granite pedestals, 454 iron tablets, and 417 artillery pieces, caissons, and

*Gettysburg observation tower. As a site for military study as well as a preserved battlefield, the Gettysburg park contained several observation towers to allow visi-tors sweeping views of the battlefield. This tower on Hancock Avenue gave visitors a good view of the center of the battlefield. Gettysburg National Military Park.*

limbers. By far the most monumented, Gettysburg was then and still is the most famous and elaborate of all American battlefields.[84]

While the direction of the park passed from the commission to a superintendent, that did not mean that veterans were out of the picture. Fortunately, Engineer Cope was still around and, although eighty years old, was able to take the reins and become superintendent upon Nicholson's death. Unlike other parks, the veterans still had a say in how the park was governed. Cope would lead the park until his death in 1927, at which time Colonel E. E. Davis, a veteran of World War I, took charge as the first superintendent who was veteran of a conflict other than the Civil War. Colonel J. F. Barber and James R. McConaghie would follow Davis as superintendents. Like the other parks, Gettysburg would be shuffled around within the War Department until 1933, at which time it would be transferred to the National Park Service of the Department of the Interior.[85]

Gettysburg's position in postwar monumentation and preservation history is clear. There is no doubt that the battlefield was the focal point of preservation activity after the war or that it was the best known of all the Civil War sites. Indeed, the word *mecca* was often used in reference to Gettysburg. But while Gettysburg's position as the chief battlefield in the decades immediately following the war and up until the 1890s is clear, that does not seem to be the case after 1890. Although the battlefield was still hailed as the major Civil War site in America, it was the fourth of five battlefields preserved by the federal government in the 1890s. Gettysburg did not receive proper attention until after work had begun at Chickamauga, Antietam, and Shiloh and long after War Department policy, with the dual Antietam and Chickamauga systems, had been set concerning battlefields. The modern Gettysburg, it seems, was a result of preset policy rather than pioneering federal preservation activity.

But it was not the last. There was one more great battlefield to follow— hundreds of miles to the southwest at Gettysburg's sister July 1863 battlefield at Vicksburg, Mississippi.

# 7

## "A VALUABLE CONTRIBUTION TO MILITARY SCIENCE"
### Vicksburg National Military Park, 1899–1933

THE LAST OF the Golden Age battlefields to be preserved was Vicksburg, where the Union Army of the Tennessee had split the Confederacy by opening the Mississippi River in 1863. Like the other Civil War battlefields, few had paid any attention to Vicksburg before the late 1880s. Even Ulysses S. Grant, passing through the city in 1880, did not stop to see the battlefield, although he did visit the national cemetery. Louisiana veterans erected a monument in Vicksburg to their state's troops in 1887, but little evidence of reconciliation or broad memorialization occurred in the years prior to the 1890s.[1]

The first efforts to preserve Vicksburg came, as did all such efforts, from the veterans themselves. Ironically, the movement behind establishing this last 1890s-era park began as early as the others, if not before. By the dawning of the 1890s, reconciliation was becoming evident even in Mississippi. A major Blue-Gray reunion like those at Gettysburg and Chattanooga took place in Vicksburg on May 25–30, 1890. With so many veterans in town and visiting the battlefield, thoughts of preservation emerged into open discussions. Vicksburg, the veterans thought, should join the fledgling preservation efforts like those at Chickamauga, Gettysburg, and Antietam. A joint visit of veterans from both sides to each other's respective cemeteries brought a feeling of embryonic reconciliation. The foundational feelings for establishing the park had been laid.[2]

Yet matters at Vicksburg moved slowly as other parks took veterans' attention. A local Vicksburg man, Thomas Lewis, began to speak on the need to create a park, but he carried little weight. A Vicksburg park historian writing in the 1930s remembered, "Prior to 1895 . . . all efforts looking toward the creation of a military park were sporadic, lacking in organization and the coordinated support necessary to insure success."

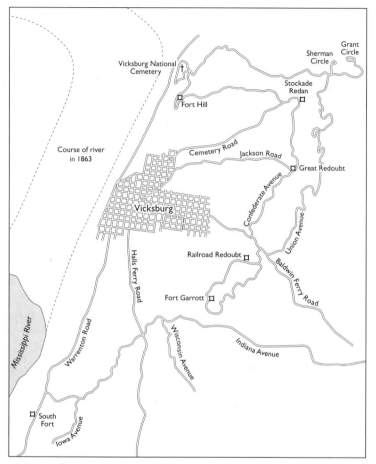

*Vicksburg National Military Park*

Still, many veterans remembered their Vicksburg days and desired to memorialize them. On April 26, 1893, former Confederates acted when they dedicated a monument to their dead in the city cemetery, where the majority of the Confederate dead rested. A Vicksburg newspaper reported that the parade was the largest on Vicksburg streets since the war, presumably meaning since the Union army marched in and took possession of the city.[3]

Just one year later, the specific idea of establishing a park emerged as Union veterans from Iowa visited the battlefield. Captain John F. Merry, a veteran of the 21st Iowa and then an agent with the Illinois Central Railroad, led the group, and out of his visit came plans for an organizational meeting of both sides in Vicksburg. Merry envisioned creating some type of association much like the ones at Chickamauga, Antietam, Gettysburg, and Shiloh, exclusively created to push Congress to establish a park at Vicksburg. Meeting on October 22, 1895, the group elected officers and established the Vicksburg National Military Park Association. The veterans elected as its president Stephen D. Lee, former Confederate lieutenant general and current president of the Mississippi Agricultural and Mechanical School in Starkville (present-day Mississippi State University), with Charles L. Davidson of Iowa as vice president, William T. Rigby of Iowa as secretary, and Charles C. Floweree of Mississippi as treasurer. An executive committee and board of directors were also named, with such luminaries as Edmund W. Pettus, Fred Grant, Mortimer Leggett, and John M. Stone.[4]

The association soon began its work in earnest. They received a charter of incorporation from the State of Mississippi in mid-November 1895, around the time of the association's first formal meeting. The directors also made many decisions concerning what they wanted the future park to look like in terms of size and what type of engineering work on which to concentrate. The association also gathered options for much of the land in question. With many of the fundamental questions answered, the officers went to work writing a bill to establish the park. Secretary William T. Rigby was the main author, and the officers presented the legislation to the executive board, which met on January 10, 1896. From then on, the association concentrated on getting Congress to pass the bill.[5]

Association members fanned out over the nation to whip up support for the project. Captain Rigby himself traveled to various GAR meetings to gain assistance. The Society of the Army of the Tennessee was especially active in the endeavor. Not satisfied with preserving only Shiloh, veterans of the western theater also wanted their most notable achievement preserved and memorialized. Thus at their 1896 reunion held in St. Louis, Captain James G. Everest offered a resolution that called upon Congress "for the purpose of promoting legislation looking to the establishment of a national military park to fittingly commemorate the campaign and siege of Vicksburg." Everest argued that "Gettysburg and the surrender of Vicksburg were the two greatest events of the Civil War, and that the valor which attained these results should be equally commemorated." The resolution was to be transmitted to the Speaker of the House as well as the Committee on Military Affairs chairman. The society also appointed a committee to take the matter directly to Congress. The president of the society appointed Captain James G. Everest as chairman and Major Hoyt Sherman, Colonel Nelson Cole, Colonel Fred D. Grant, and Captain William T. Rigby as members.[6]

The association delivered its bill to Representative Thomas C. Catchings, Vicksburg's representative in the House. He submitted the legislation, H.R. 4339, on January 20, 1896, and it was referred to the Committee on Military Affairs, where it was approved and placed on the House calendar. Unfortunately, the bill was never brought to the floor, apparently because the Speaker and Rules Committee never called it up. As a result, nothing happened for some time, despite their efforts to get individual members of the veterans' societies to "labor with [their] member[s] of Congress to have that matter called up." The association's officers made several trips to Washington during this period to meet with key legislators, including Speaker of the House Thomas B. Reed, who proved to be the main impediment. Captain Everest reported to the Society of the Army of the Tennessee, "I suppose the Speaker had good reason for not calling it up" and that the effort had "expired with that Congress." Speaker Reed, who wielded an amazing amount of power, let his fiscal conservatism block any idea of bringing the expensive park bill to the floor. Indeed, park supporter David B. Henderson, who was so influential in getting Shiloh's bill passed, told Merry on one of his visits to Washington: "This simply can't be done. . . . The boys have declared they didn't intend spending another dollar on military park appropriations."[7]

Not to be dismayed, supporters got the same bill submitted the next year in the 55th Congress, on December 7, 1897. The bill became H.R. 4382, and was again referred to the House Committee on Military Affairs, which reported the bill out on March 1, 1898, with a strong recommendation that the park be established. In its report, the committee continued the preservation, memorialization, and reconciliation theories and themes established during the 1890s. The committee responded positively to the idea of surveying the lines of battle, clearing the area, and "restoring the various forts, redoubts, and intrenchments connected with that memorable siege and defense." Putting the campaign and siege into the context of the war, the committee further argued that Vicksburg was a fitting addition to the other four "great battlefields of the war." "The importance of the campaign and siege of Vicksburg is not inferior to any of the fields now thus dedicated," the representatives argued. In fact, they said, Vicksburg and Gettysburg were inseparable in the war. "It would be impossible to justly weigh the significance of Gettysburg without associating Vicksburg with it," the committee continued, and if Gettysburg was "an accomplished fact," why then should the other be neglected? "Your committee is of the opinion that equal justice can only be extended by preserving both as historic fields," they told the House.[8]

Preservation and commemoration were not the only reasons for creating the park, however. The committee cited the need for military study at Vicksburg: "It has been said that 'it [Grant's campaign] destroyed all military maxims and precedents,' and owing to the ultimate success of the campaign it may be properly prized as a valuable contribution to military science." The hope of reconciliation was also in the committee's minds. In honoring the bravery and courage of the soldiers who had fought in the campaign, the committee remarked, "It is but just, however, to say that persistent and energetic as were the besiegers, the besieged were not wanting in any of that heroic devotion and valor which characterized their entire faith in the prowess of their arms." A listing of the veterans' organizations, North and South, that supported the idea firmly illustrated the joint support for the park's creation.[9]

The committee sent the bill back to the House with a favorable recommendation that the park could be created in a manner similar to that at Chickamauga, "except that the entire expense of the proposed park will not be much more than a tithe of the cost of the former." Finally, a list of nine amendments was included, mostly dealing with wordage. The committee did, however, cut the appropriation from $75,000 to $65,000.[10]

The bill sat in the House almost a year before any action took place, unfortunately competing with larger issues of national importance. The free silver issue was raging in the latter part of the 1890s, and the war with Spain that erupted in 1898 consumed lawmakers' attention that year. Yet a growing body of support was gathering, with thirteen state legislatures calling for passage along with numerous veterans' organizations such as the GAR and the Loyal Legion.[11]

Oddly enough, when the Vicksburg bill finally came to the floor of the House and Senate, the legislation moved very quickly. On February 6, 1899, with William T. Rigby in the gallery, Chairman John A. T. Hull of Iowa asked that the rules regularly governing the passage of bills be dispensed with, including the reading of the entire bill. Representative Joseph W. Bailey of Texas objected to such quick work, saying, "I think it is a bad practice to pass bills without being read." A native Mississippian, Bailey

had for some reason "opposed the passage of the bill with much earnest-
ness at all previous times," a Vicksburg newspaper declared. Hull thus
withdrew his request, and the clerk read the eight-section-long bill. The
Speaker then ordered a voice vote and, determining that two-thirds had
voted in the affirmative, declared the bill passed.[12]

With passage in the House, the bill then went to the Senate the next
day. Referred to the Senate Committee on Military Affairs that day, the
bill gained approval from that body two days later, on February 9. Chairman Edmund W. Pettus of Alabama, himself a Vicksburg veteran and a
member of the board of directors for the Vicksburg National Military
Park Association, sent the bill back to the full Senate, which took the matter up on February 10, 1899. Mississippi Senator Henry D. Money brought
the bill up and reminded his colleagues that the effort had firm support
from many veterans' organizations, from the GAR to the UCV. "I presume
that no objection will be made to it," Money said, and he was right. The
Senate, after the formalities of ordering and hearing a third reading,
passed the bill. Action in the Senate had been every bit as fast as in the
House.[13]

The executive branch was just as quick to support the bill. President
William McKinley signed the legislation on February 21, 1899. The entire
action took so little time that it makes the nearly year-long wait in the
House seem a shame, not to mention the years it took for the bill to garner enough support to be brought to the floor.[14]

The bill itself had eight different sections and was patterned very
closely after the legislation creating the other parks in the 1890s. Like
the others, it spoke of preserving the history of the campaign and siege
"on the ground where they were fought." The bill established the name
and also determined the boundaries of the proposed park. The boundaries created a park in the Gettysburg fashion—a kind of hybrid between
the Antietam Plan of buying only strips of lands and the Boynton style of
buying entire battlefields. Most of the core park would contain the entire
battlefield as at Chickamauga and Shiloh, while other portions of the park
along the extended siege lines would be preserved in strips in the Antie-
tam/Chattanooga manner. In all, the Vicksburg park would encompass
some 1,200 acres. Like the others, the secretary of war would have control of the park and could use condemnation proceedings to gather the
needed land. The familiar three-man commission would oversee building
the site, with the three commissioners to be veterans of the campaign—
two Union and one Confederate. Like Gettysburg and Chickamauga,

the legislation did not specify who would be chairman but allowed the commission itself to "elect one of their number chairman." The bill also provided for a secretary/historian similar to the other parks' positions but specifically stated the holder of that position had to meet the same requirements as the commissioners. Later sections of the bill tasked the commission with restoring the battlefield and opening roads and with placing markers and monuments to locate the various lines of battle and providing a means by which the various states could commemorate their troops at Vicksburg. Lastly, the bill provided law enforcement and punishment for crimes and appropriated sixty-five thousand dollars to build the park.[15]

The congressional career of the Vicksburg enabling legislation brought new faces to the preservation movement as well as highlighting others already firmly engrained in the process. House Committee on Military Affairs Committee chairman J. A. T. Hull became an avid supporter of the bill, as did Representative Hugh Reid Belknap of Illinois. Mississippian Thomas C. Catchings, in whose district the park was located, was a tireless lobbyist for the park, as was old preservationist David B. Henderson, who had been so prominent in Shiloh's legislation. In the Senate, Committee on Military Affairs Committee chairman Edmund W. Pettus worked hard for the bill, as did Missouri senator Francis M. Cockrell, who apparently had a change in heart from his earlier opposition to park building, perhaps because Cockrell had served at Vicksburg and not at Shiloh, which he had opposed.[16]

With the bill's passage, Secretary of War Alger had another park commission to appoint, but deciding who to place on the commission was difficult. The two Union representatives eventually appointed had been involved in the effort to establish a park at Vicksburg for years, and both had served on the special committee appointed by the Society of the Army of the Tennessee to lobby Congress for the park. Captain William T. Rigby of Iowa and Captain James G. Everest of Illinois, the chairman of the Society's committee, both became commissioners, although some opposition developed to Rigby's appointment over the matter of state representation. Given the number of troops it sent, Illinois had to be represented; Captain Everest lived in Chicago and had served in the 13th Illinois Infantry. But plenty of Iowans served on commissions already, especially at Shiloh. By far, however, the two major figures on the commission were Captain Rigby and the Confederate representative, Stephen D. Lee. The heavily bearded Rigby lived in Mount Vernon, Iowa, and was a veteran of the 24th Iowa Infantry. His administrative ability would prove beneficial to the upcoming work, and his fiery personality when challenged would be very akin to Boynton, Davis, and other battlefield preservationists of the era. To fill the Confederate representative's position, Secretary Alger appointed Mississippi Agricultural and Mechanical College president Stephen D. Lee, who had also been actively engaged in the park idea. Lee had served in the Vicksburg campaign as a brigadier general, later rising to the rank of lieutenant general, the youngest in the Confederate army. Like Rigby, Lee was rather combative when challenged. The dignified college president, who wore a close-cropped white beard, was familiar with administration and would carry those talents into the commission's work.[17]

The three commissioners met on March 1, 1899, in Washington, DC, to organize themselves and begin the massive job before them. The first order of business was to elect from among themselves a chairman. Rigby and Everest agreed that Lee should be chairman, which in itself was a major action. No other Confederate at the other parks had carried much weight on their respective commissions, much less served as chairman of a commission in the building phase (Joseph B. Cumming became chairman at Chickamauga in 1917, but by then he was the only living commissioner). It seemed that reconciliation was indeed becoming reality in the 1890s.[18]

Lee led the commission in choosing its second-tier appointments, such as secretary and historian, engineers, and other supporting positions. As secretary and historian, the secretary of war appointed, at the commission's request, John S. Kountz of Toledo, Ohio. A Medal of Honor recipient, Kountz had served as a drummer in the 37th Ohio Infantry, losing a leg at Missionary Ridge. He was later an Ohio GAR commander. To aid Kountz, the commission asked and the secretary of war approved that Charles L. Longley, a former quartermaster in the 24th Iowa, serve as an assistant to the secretary and historian. More appointments came in May 1899, including former Confederate Richard C. Weightman, also as an assistant to the secretary and historian. Secretary of War Alger also appointed the engineering team, consisting of Major Joseph H. Willard of the Corps of Engineers as chief engineer and G. C. Haydon as assistant engineer.[19]

Being new at the task of park building, the veterans regularly sought help from the other parks. The commission contacted Chickamauga and Shiloh on most occasions, they being the nearest and most similar parks. The commissioners also realized that they needed to make friends of

*Vicksburg commission. By far, Vicksburg's commission was the most stable, with only one position change. From left to right, James G. Everest (seated), John S. Kountz (standing), Stephen D. Lee (standing center), William T. Rigby (standing), and Charles L. Longley (seated). Vicksburg National Military Park.*

powerful men in the preservation community. For example, when Henry Boynton proposed a visit to Vicksburg in 1899, Lee recommended to the commission that no expense be spared, even if the commissioners had to split some of the costs among themselves.[20]

The park commission held its first formal meeting on March 15, 1899, at Vicksburg. There, they eventually set up an office in a rented house in the city and began their work, some of which resulted in the additional appointments. The major effort, "immediately thereafter begun" according to Lee, was to begin the difficult process of land acquisition. Working within the authorized boundary of the park, the commission soon determined what land should be acquired. They agreed on the plan adopted when they had been association members, of creating what they termed a "main park," with two "Confederate wings" and two "Federal wings" projecting from the main park and running along the lines of the siege works.[21]

The commission and its engineers delved into the work. Lee reported successful negotiations for the vast majority of the main park by July 7, 1899, and had by September 30, 1899, gathered "voluntary conveyances in carefully prepared options" from all the landowners in the main park and two Confederate wings. There were only a few problems. Most landowners readily signed the options at an average of around forty dollars an acre, but some owners would not consent to that price. Lee and the commission, governed as they were by the limited appropriation for land, had to agree "to give said owners use and possession, rent free, for a term of years after the land was conveyed by them to the Government." In three cases, the owners would not even budge that far. Henry L. Meyer and Sallie Strong owned small plots the commission wanted, five and a half and two acres respectively, and Lee reported to the secretary of war that negotiations were continuing. In the case of Mrs. W. A. Thomas, who owned thirty-five acres the commission wanted, Lee reported the probable need for condemnation. In order to get as much support as possible, Lee and the commission met with the Vicksburg Board of Trade and the Cotton Exchange, both of which readily lent their support. Everest reported in October 1899 that the park had gained the support of "nearly every business man in the city."[22]

Limited as they were to forty thousand dollars for land, the commission had to halt its work on the Federal wings. "The commissioners are restricted by the limited appropriation for the purchase of land, and may not be able to acquire all the land that, in their opinion, is needed to adequately illustrate the positions during the siege of all the Federal organizations, thus fully completing the park," Lee reported to the secretary of war. Nevertheless, they continued dealing with the landowners of the Federal wings in the hope a new appropriation would be made.[23]

Situated as it was around Vicksburg, the park had few of the deed problems confronted at more rural parks such as Shiloh and Chickamauga. On August 30, 1899, the park employed the Vicksburg law firm of Catchings, Hudson, and Catchings to "draw deeds and prepare the necessary abstracts of title." The process went so well that Lee reported he would have the deeds to the main park and Confederate wings, some 950 acres in all, to the secretary of war by December. The commission again warned the secretary, however, that the park lands could not be completed without an additional appropriation for the Federal wings.[24]

Amid the land buying process, the park's engineers went to work on surveying and mapmaking. The commission tasked Assistant Engineer Haydon with surveying the boundaries of the park. Haydon began his work on June 1, 1899, and was finished by April 30, 1900. The veterans also wanted plats of the various landowners' holdings. Haydon began this task when he finished the field maps, which kept the engineer and his laborers busy until August 31. After the deed work, the commission ordered Haydon to begin a topographical survey of the entire park, but again, Lee warned that the meager appropriation would not cover the completion of the project and asked again for additional funding. Lee reminded the secretary of war that nothing could be done in terms of estimating roads and bridges and the restoration of earthworks until Haydon completed the topographical survey, which itself hinged on the appropriation.[25]

By the end of 1899, Lee and the commission had only scraped the surface of the work that needed to be done. But little more could be done until more money became available. Nevertheless, while waiting on an additional appropriation and while the engineers did their work, the commission began to plan for the future. The veterans envisioned a road that would follow the Confederate earthworks, running some eight miles in length. They also contemplated a secondary road that would branch off the Confederate road, entering the Federal earthworks and following those for several miles. The commissioners also wanted roads to connect the various headquarters sites of general officers. In all, they estimated some twenty-five miles of roads when completed. These roads would require several large bridges, the commission warned, estimating at least twelve, including four large steel bridges. Lee and the commission also contemplated restoring the earthworks "as they were during the siege."[26]

The park commission also had problems with the enabling legislation. Lee notified the secretary of war that the Vicksburg bill had not allowed them to mount guns. He said that the idea was to mount cannon in all the artillery positions in the park, and even a few outside the park at important locations, contingent of course upon the landowners' approval. The commission also complained that "the act establishing the park only contemplates restoring the exterior lines of defense and attack of the two armies. No provision is made to restore the water batteries on the river front, or to commemorate the part taken by Admiral Porter's fleet during the siege of forty-seven days and nights." Lee recommended that the commemoration of the navy as well as the Confederate river batteries be made law.[27]

Ultimately, Congress came through with an additional appropriation for the park. With such leeway, the commission was then able to continue its work of buying land, building roads and bridges, and mapping the field. All this work, of course, was preparatory to the actual marking of the field.[28]

By October 1900, Lee was able to report that the entire main park and Confederate wings had been bought. With additional funding, the commission had also been able to determine the sizes of the Federal wings. The southern Federal wing consisted of almost 59.68 acres in thirty-three different tracts, which the engineers estimated would cost $2,700. It included a portion of land that Lee reported would have to be condemned, and two tracts that required friendly condemnation due to minor heirs who had inherited the land. The northern Federal wing contained 46.6 acres, which the engineers determined would cost $1,096. In addition, the commission asked for and received permission to buy and mark Grant's and Sherman's headquarters sites, a total of 14.5 acres for $365, and to build a road along the Federal earthworks on 19.2 acres, costing $380 for the land. Finally, the veterans desired to complete the Fort Hill road, which required some 2.065 acres for $350. Most of these land acquisitions took place, and by October 1900, the commission reported the entire park contained 1,231.08 acres in 111 tracts, costing a total of $50,488.48.[29]

Throughout the following years, minor additions took place as more land became available, as more earthworks were discovered, and as surveying work determined the need for additional land. By 1908, the commission reported that the total park acreage had risen to 1,282.89, having cost $58,879.18, or $46 an acre. The governor of Mississippi ceded jurisdiction over the majority of the land on June 28, 1901, and in subsequent smaller actions as later parcels came into the park.[30]

With the park land secured, Lee and the commissioners began in 1900 to turn their attention to projects that ranged from clearing underbrush to marking boundaries to fence building. In 1900, they placed 637 oolitic limestone posts thirty inches long and six inches square. The posts were labeled VNMP, and all were set by the summer of 1901 at a cost of $709. Similarly, they placed an iron and brick fence along the boundary between the park and the "Hebrew cemetery" west of the park. The fence, iron with a brick base, was also completed by the summer of 1901, costing a little over one thousand dollars. Likewise, the commission began clearing underbrush from the park, hiring several laborers for a dollar a day to clean the land and plant Bermuda grass. The work began on September 1, 1900, the laborers first cleaning the Confederate works. Over the years, the work expanded to the entire battlefield and continued for several years in order to thoroughly clear all unwanted trees and plants. Eventually, the commission decided to allow cattle grazing in the park, which in large part took care of the undergrowth. In direct opposition to Chickamauga's policy, Vicksburg's commission openly welcomed cattle.[31]

The park commission also restored the only surviving wartime structure on the park, the Shirley House, also known as the "White House." They asked for money to restore the house as early as 1900, but failed to get permission until 1902. At a cost of three thousand dollars, the house was refurbished by July 1903. The commission reported "its restoration to the condition and appearance existing at the beginning of the siege," noting that the reconstruction "preserves a notable landmark of the battlefield, and is gratifying to the veterans of both armies." The park later rented the house out to contractors building monuments on the park.[32]

The major engineering work during the early years at Vicksburg was road building, but the commission found this expensive project was hard to get going and difficult to sustain. As early as 1900, Lee and the commission requested authority for the topographical survey of the park grounds to facilitate the engineering roadwork. Of course, that authority rested on the ability to get a new appropriation, which was not forthcoming. Thus, Secretary of War Root would not allow the survey. Then the veterans requested permission for a much cheaper topographical survey of the area through which the Confederate road would travel, a distance of a little over eight miles. This authority was also denied for fiscal reasons.[33]

The commission was displeased with the lack of monetary support from Congress. Lee appealed to Secretary Root: "We respectfully invite your attention to the necessity of beginning at an early date the making of a survey preliminary to and necessary for the work of road making. The commissioners are of opinion that the construction of the inside park roadway should be the first work undertaken, and should be commenced at the earliest possible date." Then Lee further explained to the secretary the importance of the road: "When this roadway is completed, the important and historically interesting parts of the park area will be accessible, and it will begin to realize your expectations and the expectations of the commissioners as to the visitors it will attract." Lee further noted that, with land acquisition almost complete, "it would seem that the work of establishing the park must of necessity come to a standstill until authority is given by you for either a topographical survey of the park or for such a survey as may be necessary to locate the inside park roadway." Thinking the secretary of war might be hesitant, the commission also used its political influence to gather support from important Washington figures such as J. A. T. Hull (Committee on Military Affairs chairman), D. B. Henderson (Speaker of the House), and even the president to try and persuade Secretary Root to the commission's views.[34]

The commission's curt explanation of progress at Vicksburg either got the secretary of war's attention or aggravated him to a point of agreement, for he gave permission to conduct the inside Confederate road survey. Assistant Engineer Haydon began the work on November 1, 1900, and finished some seven months later. In accordance with the commission's instructions to place the road inside the Confederate works and as near to them as possible without destroying the earthworks or historic ground, Haydon laid out a twenty-eight-foot-wide roadway that ran for eight miles. In the process, Haydon found the road would have to cross two major watersheds, one major road, and a railroad.[35]

Problems began with the initial road survey. Haydon's total cost, including the bridges, was far more than Secretary Root would approve. Perhaps untrusting of this engineering newcomer, the secretary of war tapped an old and trusted engineer for his advice on the matter, hoping he could save the department some money. On April 24, 1901, Root ordered Edward E. Betts from Chickamauga to confer with the Vicksburg commission and try to save money.[36]

Betts made several recommendations that sharply cut costs. He recommended narrowing the width of the road from twenty-eight feet to twenty-two feet, reducing the span of the bridges "as much as possible," and using cheaper viaduct bridges rather than the elaborate steel and stone bridges recommended by Haydon. Betts's recommendations saved eighty-eight thousand dollars, and the secretary of war was pleased. The commission was not. Lee wrote Rigby in July 1901 that "we are virtually in Mr. Betts hands." Making the situation worse, the secretary approved Betts's short-term appointment to Vicksburg for six months to build the road he had recommended in his report.[37]

Evidently perturbed, Haydon took Betts's arrival as a demonstration of a lack of confidence in his work. He even wrote Rigby complaining that "he [Betts] is either an ass or fully determined to discredit my work."

He also disputed Betts's claim that Haydon had destroyed government records. Haydon requested "an indefinite furlough without pay," beginning on July 31, 1901. The commission granted the request, but spoke only positive words of their association with him. "The commissioners regret that he had withdrawn from the park work, and they have a high appreciation of the conscientious and faithful service which he has rendered." They also remarked that much of Haydon's original survey could be used by Betts as he built the road.[38]

The entire commission took exception to what the members viewed as the secretary of war's unwanted tampering in its business. Lee wrote Rigby in July 1901 that, due to the secretary's actions, "we are mere figure heads." Making the situation worse, Secretary Root also asked another veteran park builder to survey the Vicksburg situation and advise him. The secretary asked Chickamauga Chairman H. V. Boynton to get involved, and Betts was Boynton's chief engineer. Boynton and other commissioners such as John Nicholson from Gettysburg had visited Vicksburg in May 1901, along with War Department official John C. Scofield. Apparently the secretary of war thought Boynton was familiar enough with the engineer and the battlefield that he could offer good advice. The Vicksburg commission was not so sure. Lee continued his gloomy synopsis of the problem, telling Rigby, "the actions of Gen. B. and Betts with the secretary, destroys our individuality as Park Commissioners." Lee also complained that with so much Chickamauga influence, Vicksburg National Military Park would not be unique. "So it looks now to me," Lee complained, "we are to follow in almost every detail, in steps of Chickamauga Park, regardless of physical and other conditions surrounding our park." Later, he wrote to Rigby, "It looks to me, we are not to have a Park to compare favorably with the others—with the constant restrictions imposed by the secretary" and "our park will be a small affair and not what its friends hoped it to be and not what the survivors of the great armies desire."[39]

The major problem the commission had with Betts's plan, however, was not in the tampering in internal affairs by the secretary and Boynton but in the effect the new road, as Betts laid it out, would have on the historic battlefield. The commission argued that Haydon's original road had run behind Confederate lines, essentially out of the battle area. Betts's line, on the other hand, ran in and out of the Confederate works, crossing them at several points and in places actually running between the Union and Confederate lines—onto the historic field itself. The commission's chief concern of preserving and restoring the battlefield to its original configuration would thus be permanently thwarted. Rigby heatedly argued in May 1902 that the commission "believe[d] that the park is established to restore and preserve historic conditions on this battle-field." Unfortunately, Rigby's complaints were not heeded. In the end, Secretary Root upheld most of Betts's survey, saving some $80,000 out of the full $88,000 worth of changes the engineer had recommended.[40]

Betts also saved the War Department money on the comprehensive topographical survey of the entire park but again opened a major controversy between himself and the commission. The commission had asked authority to survey the entire park in November 1900, with chief engineer Major Thomas L. Casey estimating the cost at ten thousand dollars. The secretary of war was not willing to pay that much. Again depending on the veteran engineer Betts, the War Department asked him to go to Vicksburg and make an estimate. In a report dated May 15, 1901, Betts's cost was some four thousand dollars cheaper, which the secretary of war approved. On June 15, he also directed Betts to return to Vicksburg and make the survey. The commission could only complain of the "Scofield-Betts-Boynton" trio running Vicksburg National Military Park.[41]

Betts spent much time at Vicksburg undertaking the topographical survey, and his original six months was soon extended much longer. Betts's work at Vicksburg saved the department money but at the expense of controversy with the Vicksburg commission. It also caused some concern at Chickamauga. Boynton, chairman of that commission, wrote in September 1901 of the work of his commission being "somewhat retarded" by Betts's absence. Nevertheless, Betts remained at Vicksburg throughout the latter half of 1901 and into 1902. The secretary of war approved his survey on March 22, 1902. After all the surveying, Betts made a "topographical map of the park and the land adjacent thereto."[42]

This topographical work led to more friction between Betts and the commission. Commissioners complained bitterly to the secretary of war about Betts's survey and his use of maps as sources, but the secretary again sided with his veteran engineer and Betts's ultimate boss, Henry Boynton, who again became involved at Vicksburg. Having all of Boynton that he could stand, Lee railed against the Chickamauga chairman, writing Rigby that "it would not be wise for us to lay down our self respect, and willingly accept Gen. Boynton as our mentor and advisor. . . . He is not our friend but Mr. Betts' friend." Lee even got the commission into some trouble by going over the secretary's head and appealing to friends in Congress. Realizing the serious position the commission was in, Lee counseled, "[W]e owe it to ourselves to try and get right with the secretary, but not through Gen. B." Commissioner Everest and others counseled caution: "The Secretary of War depends largely upon General Boynton for every thing connected with Military Parks in general and . . . his word and his judgment goes a long way with the Secretary."[43]

The controversies became so heated that many well-known veterans joined in. Historian Kountz counseled moderation in responding to a scathing letter Rigby was contemplating sending about Betts. "I think that some of the language used against him is unnecessarily severe and shows too much feeling," Kountz wrote, and he reminded Rigby that such a letter would not "only make him more intense in his opposition to the plans of our commission, but also arouse the animosity of Gen. Boynton and Mr. Scofield, who are his friends, which would be unfortunate." Kountz also admitted, "I consider our situation now far more serious than at any other time since the organization of the commission." Veteran Andrew Hickenlooper also became involved in correspondence with the powerful David B. Henderson, then Speaker of the House. Supporting the commission wholeheartedly, Hickenlooper wrote, "I cannot understand why such a spirited opposition to the views of the commission should have been worked up, especially by persons who were not participants in that campaign, and are not supported in their views by those who were." Hickenlooper was obviously aiming his scalding pen at Boynton. Taking the other side of the issue, Gettysburg commission chairman John P. Nicholson supported Betts, stating that his plan "disfigures the field to a minimum," and argued that the "controversy results from a misunderstanding of the relative views of those concerned." Iowan David B. Henderson himself even sent a letter to the secretary of war, asking, "Is it not possible to get Harmony in regard to the Vicksburgh park between your Department and Commission so that work may be commenced?" Henderson then betrayed his own personal stake in the matter by reminding the secretary, "We are losing important time. Iowa has made large appropriations to build monuments for that state, but . . . it is impossible to go ahead."[44]

The controversy eased over time, with Betts and his supporters in Chattanooga and Washington more in control than the Vicksburg commission. Ousted engineer G. C. Haydon wrote Rigby, "It is simply a ridiculous state of affairs into which the Secretary of War has allowed the Park progress and administration to assume." Nevertheless, Haydon was out and Betts was in, and the Chickamauga engineer soon became involved in road building at Vicksburg. Betts and the commission, realizing they had to work together, thus began making decisions based on his survey and the amount of money available at any given time. The first decision was how much of the Confederate road to build, and Betts and the commission decided on one section and let out a contract on May 1, 1901, to a local construction company owned by Robert Nicholson. The commission estimated the work taking a little over a year to complete. Meanwhile, bids for a second section of the road were let, but only two contractors bid, and both were too high for the commission. They then asked for bids on the second and a third section of the road together. The commission also began looking at the feasibility of constructing the road around the Union earthworks. Of course, Betts had to lay out that avenue as well before work could begin.[45]

The Vicksburg commission received great news in August 1902, but such good news soon turned into more problems. E. E. Betts resigned his position at Vicksburg effective July 31, 1902, in order to return to Chickamauga. The commission's glee no doubt turned to gloom when the members learned that their new engineer would be E. E. Betts's brother Raymond D. Betts, who had worked for his brother at Vicksburg. R. D. Betts picked up where his brother left off and continued the stormy relationship while building the park's roads.[46]

Once the problems were worked out, the "brothers Betts" and the commission began to make quick work of the roads. By July 1902, Nicholson had finished the grading and culvert work on the Confederate avenue, a total of eight miles. The Union avenue work was also 80 percent complete by July 1902. Work also began on covering the roads with rock, for which the park bought a road roller and a road machine in 1902. Attending the roadwork were the necessary processes of building bridges, gutters, and viaducts. By July 1904, the commission was able to report it had completely graded and drained both the Confederate and Union avenues, some sixteen and a half miles, at a total cost of $56,191.76. They also reported that work on the secondary roads would be done as time permitted.[47]

Over the years, additions were made to the park road system, such as an extension of the Confederate avenue in 1905 and some twenty "short avenues or circles," mostly around the monuments that were going up in the park. By 1908, the commission reported "about 31 miles" of roads in the park, with sixteen bridges of varying types. The park hired J. T. Crass of Vicksburg "for metaling the park roadways." Eventually, Crass would surface more and more roads in the park. An important product of all this road building was the recovery of artifacts, which kept the commission and workers reminded of their original duties of commemoration and memorialization. Workers found numerous cannonballs, bullets, and buttons and even unearthed two skeletons of Union soldiers in 1904.[48]

Many other smaller yet significant controversies erupted over the years. Some locals did not like the threat of the park taking their land through condemnation, and others complained about new drainage schemes that adversely affected their property. The commission continually faced money shortfalls and opposition from the War Department, such as when they ordered 250 copies of the Vicksburg volumes of the *Official Records*. The secretary of war grudgingly approved. Limited by small budgets, the commission sought to convert funds from one account to another, trying in June 1903 to pay for a topographical map out of funds to be used for an exhibit at the Louisiana Purchase Exposition in 1904. War Department official John C. Scofield scolded the commission for its lack of budgetary responsibility, which apparently had little effect. The next year, in April 1904, Acting Secretary of War Robert Shaw Oliver sent the commission's old nemesis Henry Boynton to Vicksburg "for the purpose of advising [it] in regard to certain park matters under your jurisdiction." No doubt, Lee, Rigby, and Everest were in no mood to hear Oliver's glowing letter telling of Boynton's "wide experience in this line of work and particularly in view of his exact information of the conditions which surround [the] park appropriations." It was a slap in the face.[49]

Despite the controversies, the work of establishing the infrastructure of the park had by the summer of 1901 progressed to the point that the commission and veterans could begin to think about placing monuments and markers in the park. As had become customary at the other parks, many states that had troops at Vicksburg began to organize monument commissions. These commissions researched their troops' roles in the battles and siege and soon visited the fledgling park to find troop positions and appropriate positions for their monuments. These veteran commissions worked in the memorial climate of the 1890s and early 1900s, seeking to preserve and mark the battlefields as well as memorialize the dead who had given their lives forty years earlier. The Vicksburg commission itself was of like mind, reporting to the secretary of war that the intention was to "permanently mark the positions thus ascertained and worthily commemorate the valor and services of their soldiers in the campaign, siege, and defense of Vicksburg." Such a statement speaks volumes of the contemporary mindset, from the inclusion of both sides by referring to both the "siege" and the "defense" of Vicksburg to the now customary emphasis not on divisive issues but on reconciliatory values such as valor and devotion. From the beginning, Vicksburg was a worthy addition to the 1890s-era battlefield preservation movement.[50]

The historical work at Vicksburg progressed under the steady eye of the very involved commission. Lee poured all his energy into the effort. Rigby and Everest were likewise dedicated to the park. The major historical work, however, was done by the commission historian, John S. Kountz. His assistant in historical work, Charles L. Longley, also worked to determine troop positions and organizations, as did former Confederate Richard C. Weightman. The commission used the now familiar sources such as volume 24 of the *Official Records*, and the vast number of veterans who returned to Vicksburg, some even having their expenses paid by the secretary of war. These veterans ranged from the lowest-ranking men all the way to generals, including Major General Peter J. Osterhaus, who arrived on May 22, 1904, the forty-first anniversary of the major assault on the Confederate works. But the battlefield itself was the major source of information, more so than any of the other parks created during the 1890s. At Vicksburg, fairly pristine remnants of the siege lines guided the historical work in a way not seen at any other battlefield. The result of the historical work was a detailed positioning of the units at Vicksburg through tablets and markers. The commission also produced in 1901 an official history written by Kountz, entitled *Record of the Organizations Engaged in the Campaign, Siege, and Defense of Vicksburg*. The small book was along the lines of Reed's book on Shiloh and Boynton's on Chickamauga and Chattanooga. Rigby also wrote a small, non-government-sanctioned volume entitled *Historic Vicksburg, An Epitome of the Campaign, Siege, and Defense of Vicksburg, March 29–July 4, 1863* (1906). Others also published various volumes, such as those by the state monument commissions and Illinois Central Railroad's *Vicksburg for the Tourist* (1911).[51]

The historical work at Vicksburg also caused some difference of opinion among the commissioners themselves. Lee and Rigby, although close friends, often disputed each others' historical facts. Never one to back down, even from the secretary of war, Lee saw himself as the sole defender of the Confederate army on the Vicksburg commission and thus mainly disputed facts concerning the Confederates at Vicksburg. His correspondence with Rigby included many phrases such as "facts as I understand them," "made a little more accurate," and "improved a little."

There were certain matters that the two never agreed on. Despite the friendly disagreements, however, the two remained close friends and colleagues.[52]

The differences of opinion between Lee and Rigby were probably not among the many reasons that Lee decided to resign as chairman of the commission on November 21, 1901 (the resignation was not accepted until April 15, 1902). Though Lee disagreed with Rigby over historical facts, their disagreements were never personal like those they both had with Secretary of War Root, Betts, and Boynton. In fact, the tiring controversies over engineering at the park probably had more to do with Lee's resignation than did any disputes with Rigby. Also, Lee's wife was ill, which caused the general to need more time for her care. Finally, Lee himself was experiencing bad health. The cumulative effects of all these problems caused Lee to resign. He had temporarily handed the chairmanship off to Rigby in December 1899, and Rigby in fact had always acted as de facto chairman. At the commission meeting on April 15, 1902, however, Lee resigned his chairmanship for good, with Rigby being appointed to replace him. Lee, however, continued to serve on the commission.[53]

When it came time to begin monumenting the park, the commission queried the planners of the other military parks for information on how they had managed the erection of monuments and markers. Based on what they learned, the commission produced in 1904 a document entitled "Regulations for the Government of the Vicksburg National Military Park," patterned most closely after Gettysburg's document. With regulations in hand, states appropriated liberal amounts of money for large monuments and the federal government placed a large number of markers and tablets. Though Vicksburg was the last of the 1890s-era parks, the novelty had not worn off and the park was not neglected. Lee wrote in 1901 that the commission "expect[ed] that the state monuments and tablets that will be erected on the Vicksburg Park will be equal, in cost, beauty, and appropriateness, to those erected on any of the national military parks." Indeed, Vicksburg soon became more of "a western Gettysburg" than Chickamauga. The monuments and markers at Vicksburg far surpassed those at Shiloh, Antietam, and even Chickamauga.[54]

The commission itself began the process of placing tablets and markers on the park in 1903. Observing that the tablets would be "of a permanent character," they recommended the possibility of having them cast in bronze instead of iron as in the other parks. They went so far as to get bids for both iron and bronze tablets. The fiscally minded Secretary of War

Elihu Root would not allow bronze tablets, however, so the commission signed a contract with George P. Tilton of Newburyport, Massachusetts, for 151 cast-iron tablets. Unfortunately, Tilton was not able to produce the tablets in the allotted time, and the contract became void. The commission then gave the contract to William F. Runnells, also of Newburyport, for the 151 tablets plus 304 more. The commission also gave a contract to the Chattanooga Car and Foundry Company, no stranger to dealing with the parks, for an additional fifty-eight "guideboard tablets." The commission asked for and received permission to place bronze plaques at important locations in Vicksburg itself.[55]

By July 1906, the park had received all but four of its tablets and had placed the original 151 tablets and 58 guideboards. The commission placed the additional 305 tablets by July 1907, and thereafter began working to place 381 trench position markers and 40 more guideboards, all from the Chattanooga foundry. These went up by the summer of 1908. By that year, the War Department and other entities had placed 979 tablets, all cast iron except twenty-nine bronze markers. Total cost for the government's 874 (out of 979) markers was $15,418.57.[56]

The commission also worked to place artillery on the battlefield. The original intention of placing all guns that were in action in 1863 was not feasible, but the commission did receive permission from the War Department to emplace 125 cannon. In 1904, the commission signed a contract with the Chattanooga Car and Foundry Company for the carriages, at a cost of eighty-seven dollars per carriage—up from the sixty-five dollars per carriage Shiloh was able to broker. Ten of the carriages would be larger in order to emplace siege guns. By July 1905, the park had received its 125 guns from the War Department and had mounted 110 of the 114 field guns. Two more were to go at the Illinois state monument, then under construction.[57]

The park engineer placed the gun carriages on temporary wooden foundations in the original earthworks. The plan was to remove the guns when the restoration of the siege lines began, and then place the gun carriages on concrete foundations. Fourteen siege guns were also mounted in 1908. By that year, the park had placed 128 guns (66 Union and 62 Confederate) at a total cost of $17, 278.52.[58]

As at the other parks, the major effort to commemorate the soldiers who fought at Vicksburg was through monumentation, which in itself was very impressive. Vicksburg's monumentation was quite extraordinary and exhibited a prevailing desire on the part of veteran-dominated state legislatures to commemorate and memorialize the soldiers of the Civil War. Between 1903 and 1908, Massachusetts, Ohio, Pennsylvania, New Hampshire, Illinois, Iowa, and Minnesota all dedicated their impressive monuments, with work progressing on monuments for Rhode Island, New York, Wisconsin, Indiana, and Mississippi. By 1908, the commission reported 422 "memorials, monuments, and markers" placed by the states and expected some 260 more in the near future. Among them were impressive equestrian statues of Ulysses S. Grant and John A. McClernand as well as statues of other notable commanders such as Jefferson Davis. The Vicksburg monumentation continued the pattern of Union domination, however. The federal government did not have a Union preference, but the Northern states showed much more willingness to remember the Civil War than did the Southern states. Of the 422 monuments up by 1908, only 24 were Confederate.[59]

Massachusetts had the honor of dedicating the first state monument at Vicksburg on November 14, 1903. Other states soon followed with much larger commemorations. Ohio for example dedicated thirty-nine unit monuments and twenty troops position monuments on May 22, 1905. Iowa dedicated a state memorial, thirteen monuments, and fifty-nine bronze tablets on November 15, 1906; Major General Grenville Dodge accepted them on behalf of the government. Other notables received monuments also, such as Chickamauga commission chairman Ezra Carman, who accepted the Minnesota monument for the government. By far, the most exquisite effort at memorialization came from Illinois. That state dedicated a large "memorial temple," costing upwards of two hundred thousand dollars, along with seventy-nine monuments and eighty-five markers on October 26, 1906. John C. Scofield, a prominent member of the War Department, accepted the Illinois monuments on behalf of the government. The elaborate temple itself showed the emphasis of honoring the soldiers themselves by listing every Illinois soldier who had fought at Vicksburg.[60]

The dedication ceremonies at Vicksburg also continued the feelings of nationalism and reconciliation so prevalent in the other 1890s-era parks. In dedicating the massive Illinois monument in 1906, for example, War Department official John C. Scofield reminded his hearers,

> It was a war not of aliens, but of brothers—not of enemies, but of friends; a war of principles and not of aggrandizement or conquest; and when the awful struggle was ended the men who fought on either

side, accepting the results and facing the conditions that surrounded them like true Americans, wrought sincerely and effectively to heal the wounds and remove the scars that war had made, to revive and strengthen those natural ties of affection and interest between the North and the South, and to restore the harmonious and cordial relations that make for their mutual well-being.

At the same dedication, Mississippi governor James K. Vardaman told the crowd, "I want you, my friends from Illinois, to understand that the Confederate soldier and the sons of the Confederate soldiers join with you in words of commendation and words of praise of your brave men." The governor of Ohio, Myron T. Herrick, spoke of "we of the north and south who meet here today as men and brothers, vying with each other in love of our

*Illinois monument construction at Vicksburg. Dedicated in 1906, the Illinois monument at Vicksburg was the most impressive memorial on any of the five 1890s-era battlefields. This photo shows the major task of constructing the monument. Vicksburg National Military Park.*

*Indiana monument dedication at Vicksburg. Indiana dedicated her monuments at Vicksburg in December 1908. This photo shows the elaborate preparations needed for such an observance. Adams,* Indiana at Vicksburg.

common country" at his state's dedication in 1905. He also thanked the governor of Mississippi for allowing him to bring "armed Ohio troops" through his state and noted that relations between the two states were somewhat better than the last time Ohio troops had visited Mississippi. At the Indiana dedication in 1908, Indiana governor J. Frank Hanly spoke of the hardships of war but reminded his hearers that "there was a nobility about it all, that, seen through the intervening years, silences discord, softens hate and makes forgiveness easy. Today, we laugh and weep together. Wounds are healed; asperities are forgotten; the past is remembered without bitter ness." Mississippi governor Edmond F. Noel responded in like fashion, stating, "Our common country seeks to blot out and to forget all that might excite or perpetuate bitterness on account of the late unpleasantness." Similarly, Governor Albert B. Cummings of Iowa spoke at that state's dedication, saying, "I remember I am speaking to chivalrous southern men, whose hearts beat with loyalty to the Union and love for the old flag." Governor Vardaman responded, "You are right, sir, when you say that the people of the south are loyal to the stars and stripes." At the Mississippi monument dedication in 1909, former Confederate general Benjamin Humphreys spoke: "However went the battle, however keen the anguish that marked the hour of defeat, no man today can read the story of that conflict and note how men died and women tasted worse than death without catching from it all an inspiration to patriotism, and that is the only lesson worth while that any soldier ever taught on any battlefield." The dedication speeches at Vicksburg mirrored those at other parks, illustrating in vivid prose the reconciliation that was even then taking place right before their eyes.[61]

The park commission also became involved in another type of monumentation prevalent on the national military parks—the observation tower. Antietam, Chickamauga, Chattanooga, and Gettysburg all had towers, and Shiloh had tried to get funding for one but was unable to do so. The Vicksburg commission began an eighty-foot concrete tower, "circular in form with four landings," in 1907 on Logan Circle, and had it completed by 1908. Later, the commission built another of similar form on the Confederate side.[62]

By 1908, much of the park had been completed, and that year marked a transition in the park's history. The major engineering work of surveying the land and laying out roads had been accomplished by then. Likewise, most of the commission's monumentation with tablets and artillery was done. Many of the states had already dedicated their elaborate monuments, and most of the others were nearing completion and would dedicate them shortly. Thus the establishment phase came to an end by 1908, marking a watershed in the park's history.

The commission had done a remarkable job. The park had come together much faster than the others, probably because the commission remained quite structured through its early days. Lee, Rigby, and Everest seemed to get along rather well, with few of the controversies between commissioners that marred other parks. Likewise, comparatively few controversies over troop positions emerged, showing that the commission did its work clearly and accurately for all. Although Vicksburg was smaller and involved more static troop positions than the other parks, thereby decreasing the amount of time needed for land acquisition and allowing less chance of debate over troop positions, the park commission could be proud of its work.

The year 1908 also marked a watershed for Vicksburg in the passing of Stephen D. Lee, the Confederate commissioner and the commission's first chairman. Lee died on May 28, 1908. He had been commander of the UCV and an important Confederate advocate in the War Department. While other Southern commissioners played only minor roles on their commissions, Lee was a major force at Vicksburg. Rigby said it best when he wrote the secretary of war, "[T]he country lost a good and great citizen, the commission an efficient worker, and each of its remaining members a dear and personal friend." Showing the esteem others had for Lee, the mayor of Vicksburg, Benjamin W. Griffith, requested that the president order United States flags to be flown at half-staff on the day of Lee's funeral. Secretary of War William Howard Taft announced that flags in Vicksburg, Jackson, and Columbus would be flown at half-staff for one hour during Lee's funeral. To replace Lee on the commission, the secretary of war (upon the advice of Rigby) appointed former Confederate captain Lewis Guion of New Orleans, a member of the 26th Louisiana Infantry.[63]

If 1908 marked a watershed in Vicksburg National Military Park's history, the phase following that date can best be described as a time of maintaining what had been earlier established. By 1909, the commission turned its attention to maintenance rather than construction. That is not to say that no more new work took place, because the commission continued to buy land, to perform roadwork, to restore the battlefield, and to clear the park of reoccurring underbrush, but at no time was the work done on the same scale as before. The commission, for example, continued to buy small bits of land through the years, mostly in one- to five-acre increments. By 1920, the commission reported owning 1,322.63 acres, which it boasted contained "nearly all the fighting ground of the siege and defense operations from May 18 to July 4 [1863]." Similarly, the commission continued to maintain the roadways and build newer connecting roads where needed, such as circles at the various state and national monuments. By 1920, the park boasted 31.86 miles of roads in the park. All major roadways were thoroughly "metaled" with local gravel and contained gutters to keep erosion down. Some major work had to be done in 1913 to stop serious erosion in "the heads of deep gulches that were getting dangerously close to Confederate Avenue." In order to restore the battlefield to its original look, the commission continued to clear the area, even using a "horse mower" to keep smooth areas from growing up. The commission was unable, however, to fulfill its goal of restoring the earthworks. Such massive work would not come until the 1930s.[64]

The commemorative work also continued in the post-1908 era. The veterans placed only a few more guns, which totaled 128 by 1920. That year, the commission also reported a total of 1,020 tablets and guideboards in the park. More monumentation, however, went on during this maintaining phase. Rhode Island and Indiana dedicated monuments in 1908, Mississippi in 1909, Wisconsin in 1911, New York and Missouri in 1917, and Louisiana in 1920. Other states continued to erect memorials, as did the commission, which constructed two more observation towers in 1910 and 1911. The commission also pushed the effort to place monuments, busts, or relief portraits of officers engaged at Vicksburg, contacting friends, family, and other organizations that might have photos of the commanders. The commissioners joyously accepted a statue of their former colleague Stephen D. Lee in 1909, "the gift of his son and friends in 27 states." Unfortunately, the War Department in 1911 ruled that recent regulations for Gettysburg National Military Park prohibiting honoring individuals except for "conspicuous and exceptional acts of heroism" would be used in the entire park system. Having already begun the process, the Vicksburg commission appealed, and the secretary of war "modified" the regulations for Vicksburg. By 1920, the commission reported having 168 portraits, which was all but six of the original commanders. One monument the commission was not able to place, however, was a Confederate naval monument to correspond with the Union naval monument. Although asking for an appropriation year after year and even getting a site approved by the War Department, the commission was never able to get money from Congress. Likewise, the secretary of war denied United States Colored Troops veterans permission to erect at Vicksburg a monument to black soldiers in the Civil War. The secretary argued that the park only commemorated the siege itself, in which no African Americans had fought, and that their role in the campaign was "properly commemorate[d]" in campaign tablets near the site of the large equestrian statue of Grant.[65]

The Vicksburg commission also continued its work of commemoration and memorialization by hosting veteran reunions and observances. The Society of the Army of the Tennessee held its annual meeting in Vicksburg in November 1907, and the UCV met there on November 11–12, 1909. Even as the veteran numbers dwindled, the old soldiers still returned in later years. The Mississippi UCV held a reunion at Vicksburg on October 12, 1927, while the Mississippi National Guard encamped on the park at various times. Perhaps the most novel event on the park came in 1916 when the Selig Polyscope Company asked permission to use the park in its "proposed photo play, 'The Crisis.'" The War Department gave its approval for this early movie, only requiring that no damage be done to the park.[66]

By far, the largest commemorative event was the joint reunion on October 16–19, 1917. During the "National Peace Jubilee," as many as seven to nine thousand old soldiers made their way to the park to encamp for several days. Under Colonel William D. Newbill, the army used a $150,000 congressional appropriation to provide a camp for the veterans, complete

*1917 National Peace Jubilee at Vicksburg. A veterans reunion of the grandest scale, the 1917 National Peace Jubilee saw several thousand veterans of both blue and gray come together. This photo shows the large logistical effort made for the reunion. In the center is the large meeting tent, with the long rows of picnic tables used for meals in the foreground. Vicksburg National Military Park.*

with large tents to sleep in and running water and electric lights. The old veterans exhibited a kindred spirit, with major speeches by governors echoing the reconciliation then in process. Governor William L. Harding of Iowa spoke of the world war then going on, remarking that "the sons of Confed-erate soldiers and the sons of Union soldiers will continue their march to Berlin." Press accounts of the event emphasized the reunification theme, printing reports that "the magnificent hills of Vicksburg have again felt the tread of the blue and the gray, this time in fraternal association." The old soldiers celebrated "their first meeting since the war by affectionate demonstrations when recalling the circumstances of first acquaintance." Leftover monies from the event went to construct a mammoth memorial arch at the entrance to the park, dedicated on October 18, 1920.[67]

*William T. Rigby. Serving later than any of his fellow commissioners, William T. Rigby lived until 1929. Although a native of Iowa, Rigby desired to be buried in the Vicksburg National Cemetery, where he rests today.* Adams, Indiana at Vicksburg.

The park commission continued to function as the major administrative entity throughout the majority of the 1920s, but its effectiveness was diminishing. One by one, the commissioners died away. Historian John S. Kountz died on June 14, 1909. Confederate representative Lewis Guion died on January 12, 1920, followed by Everest on April 17, 1924. In accordance with the 1912 legislation phasing out the various commissions, the secretary of war did not fill these positions, leaving only Rigby to manage the park.[68]

Some questioned whether Rigby could handle the management of the park as age became a concern. Yet auditors and inspectors verified his ability to maintain the park well into the mid-1920s. As he became more infirm, however, the War Department appointed a helper. L. C. Swett became "overseer" under Rigby, serving in much the same capacity as DeLong Rice at Shiloh and Richard Randolph at Chickamauga. Swett managed the park until 1931, when Major John B. Holt was appointed superintendent, holding the position until the shift to the National Park Service in 1933.

Rigby lived until May 10, 1929. The most influential man in Vicksburg National Military Park's history, indeed the father of the park, was fittingly laid to rest in the Vicksburg National Cemetery. Swett wrote lovingly of Rigby in his 1929 annual report: "In his death the service loses a most faithful administrative officer, this community an influential and valued citizen and his associates a dearly loved friend." Just six months before, on his eighty-seventh birthday, Rigby's friends had dedicated a "portrait bust" of the captain.[69]

Rigby's passing was another watershed event in the park's history. Only four short years after Rigby's death, the park became a part of the National Park Service, whose emphasis was on preservation and interpretation to the general public—something very different from the original establishment idea. The rumblings of such a move had been heard before, causing Rigby to cry at the thought of what he deemed a major mistake. Nevertheless, Vicksburg National Military Park was by then well established. A compromise between the competing Antietam and Chickamauga plans of the early 1890s, Vicksburg marked the best of both plans, something some in the War Department no doubt thought they could replicate in future parks. Unbeknownst to them, however, Vicksburg would prove to be the last of the original parks. By the time another American battlefield was preserved, all but a few thousand veterans would be gone, the nation would be changed culturally and demographically, and the nonveteran legislators on both the federal and state levels would be more interested in other projects. Thus Vicksburg was the last of five original battlefield parks, an accomplishment of preservation that has not been seen since in America.[70]

# 8

## THE GOLDEN AGE REASSESSED

AS THE DEVELOPMENT of the five military parks continued in the 1890s and the congressional and War Department reaction to them was debated and forgotten, a certain termination policy was nevertheless put into place. After 1899, instead of formulating a governing policy or setting guidelines for future parks, Congress did nothing, ushering in a period several decades long that resulted in no new Civil War parks and no comprehensive plan for governing the ones already established. No new Civil War parks or formulated policy emerged until the middle to late 1920s.

In the early 1900s, Congress reacted to the emergency need for a comprehensive plan by backing away from preservation. In the years after 1899 and Vicksburg's establishment, only a few small American Revolutionary War battlefields were begun, and no new Civil War parks emerged. The only action that could conceivably be called preservation was the 1917 legislation that allowed the government to accept title to some sixty privately held acres at the Kennesaw Mountain battlefield, but even that was not concluded until 1926. In each case, little or no preservation or interpretive work was done.[1]

By the mid-1920s, however, times had changed to the degree that battlefield preservation was again a possibility. The nation had endured another war, much larger that the Spanish-American War in 1898. World War I again infused patriotism into the nation, and the 1920s, after a short recession, was a fiscally abundant time in which Americans were doing well and wanted to flaunt it. A combination of these two factors resulted in an increased call for more military parks. Unfortunately, the veterans were no longer around in large numbers to mark the battlefields. Similarly, the battlefields themselves were no longer in pristine shape, having endured the second industrial revolution when cities and towns exploded into sprawling metropolises, forever destroying many of the battlefields. And most importantly, Congress and state legislatures were no longer dominated by veterans who would, despite some opposition, appropriate millions of dollars for battlefield preservation as those veterans of the 1890s had done. Their sons now appropriated only small amounts of money, and the result was a much leaner effort to preserve battlefields.[2]

As many as twenty-eight battlefield bills appeared in Congress in the mid-1920s, prompting the House Military Affairs Committee to hold hearings on the issue and to work out a plan by which they all could be preserved cheaply. The hearings were held in early 1926 and resulted in a broad study. Carried out by the War Department, this study developed a class system of battlefields, with various classes denoting priorities. Congress began to preserve the battlefields in the highest unpreserved tier: places such as Petersburg, Fredericksburg, Stones River, Fort Donelson, and some Revolutionary War battlefields. Later, they added a lower tier of battlefields such as Brices Crossroads, Tupelo, Appomattox, and several other Revolutionary War fields.[3]

In all, between 1906 and 1931, some thirteen parks were established—some with park amenities and some mere plots of ground. All, however, were patterned after George B. Davis' Antietam Plan. That officer, as well as several secretaries of war, had labored to develop an economical policy of battlefield preservation, but their initial defeated goals were finally realized. There would be no more large Boyntonesque national military parks like those in the 1890s, but instead more small parks like Antietam. Indeed, the parks that followed in the decades after the 1920s and 1930s were also mostly along those lines, parks such as Richmond and Manassas.[4]

There was at the same time another factor that would also have a direct impact on the original military parks as well as on those that came later. At the same time Congress was debating battlefield parks policy, it was also involved in the slow process of formulating a national historic preservation policy. The 1906 Antiquities Act had begun the effort, culminating with the birth of the National Park Service in 1916, overseeing such nature parks as Yellowstone, Yosemite, and Mammoth Cave. By the mid-1920s, with several new parks coming into the War Department, National Park Service leaders Horace Albright and Stephen T. Mather began to call for these parks to be placed under their jurisdiction. They argued that the War Department, with the passing of the veterans, was no longer capable or willing to interpret them properly. The War Department agreed, with several secretaries of war in the 1920s giving their support. Their arguments fell on fertile ears in 1933 with the arrival of President Franklin D. Roosevelt in the White House. His August 10, 1933, executive order took

*Franklin D. Roosevelt at Chattanooga. President Roosevelt made a major change in the military parks when he transferred them from the War Department to the National Park Service in 1933. Here, Roosevelt is seen at Point Park on Lookout Mountain. Chattanooga and the Tennessee River can be seen below. Chickamauga and Chattanooga National Military Park.*

the military parks from the War Department and placed them within the National Park Service of the Department of the Interior.[5]

The preservation path that the Golden Age parks had begun thus took a major turn, but not everyone was happy about the situation. Vicksburg commissioner William T. Rigby cried when he thought of the chances that the War Department might lose the battlefields. Congressmen in committee hearings on the transfer also voiced opposition, one blurting out that the National Park Service would fill the battlefields with "hot dog stands" and another saying the Interior agency did not "know what they [the battlefields] are or what they mean." Given the lack of attention from the War Department in later years, however, it was time for an agency that specialized in preservation and interpretation to take control of the battlefields. As historian Ed Bearss has said: "During the development at that stage, thank God the War Department had them. I hate to think what some of our planners would have thought of them." He admitted, however, that the National Park Service was the right agency to take control as the War Department "began to flunk on the educational mission because the veterans [were] getting older." A new age of post–Civil War veterans was dawning in America, and the federal government intended to keep up.[6]

❦ · ❧

An analysis of the first five military parks reveals some fascinating differences as well as similarities and shows just what those veterans who built the parks had in mind when they preserved their great fields of conflict. Each park was different, and it was a good thing they were. Complete uniformity would have driven away any reason to create all five parks. Some contemporary thinkers such as George B. Davis, in fact, wanted only one western and one eastern battlefield. Two parks, he said, would cover the needs of both the nation to remember and the military to study. The veterans themselves saw differently and ultimately established the five 1890s-era parks.[7]

The uniqueness of each park was in itself an outgrowth of the lack of central control over the various commissions' work. The War Department had administrative control over each, but beyond approving major work such as land acquisition and monument and tablet inscriptions, the department and secretaries of war rarely became involved in the day-to-day operations of the commissions (Vicksburg being somewhat of an exception). Lower-level officials were of course in contact, but it was mostly up to the different commissions to build the parks as they saw fit. With five different commissions and boards, the result was five very different parks.

Despite some cooperation and correspondence between the commissions, the final results on each battlefield were the result of an autonomous group of directors at each site. The uniqueness of the parks and the lack of an overall monumentation scheme can be noted. None of the regular army monuments, which seemed to be a major priority of Congress in establishing these parks, were even similar. Likewise, the commissions had complete freedom to develop their own headquarters and mortuary monuments. The headquarters monuments at Shiloh looked very similar to the mortuary monuments at Chickamauga, while the mortuary monuments at Antietam looked very similar to the headquarters monuments at Gettysburg. The Vicksburg commission chose not to become involved in monumenting all headquarters and mortuary monuments, allowing the states to mark the headquarters of famous officers, while simple tablets marked some of the mortuary positions.[8]

This thread of similarity, not uniformity, is seen in the types of parks themselves. Antietam, of course, is of a different character altogether, but serves as the forefather of most of the later parks such as Appomattox Court House, Kennesaw Mountain, Manassas, Petersburg, and many more. The Chattanooga end of Chickamauga and Chattanooga National Military Park resembles Antietam more than it resembles any other 1890s-era park.

The other four parks seemed to develop in two distinct ways. Shiloh and Chickamauga were both primarily rural—away from big cities that threatened their existence. As a result, they developed in almost pristine condition. Almost the entire battlefields were purchased, and the vast majority of the lines were marked. Gettysburg and Vicksburg developed differently. Sitting on the edge of cities, these two parks had to take expansion into account and thus were not willing or able to acquire the entire battlefields. Neither contained all the battlefields, but only the most important points, with secondary areas connected by drives and strips of land. In this way, Gettysburg and Vicksburg were somewhat similar to Antietam.

Shiloh and Chickamauga developed a much simpler monumentation scheme than Gettysburg and Vicksburg. Neither Shiloh nor Chickamauga had any equestrian statues, and their state monuments were below the size and cost of those at Gettysburg and Vicksburg. Perhaps even in their support for battlefield preservation, the veterans saw that Gettysburg and Vicksburg would see more visitation and wanted to put their money where more people would benefit from it.

There also developed a slight but important difference in the tablet and monumentation schemes at the various parks. An east and west dichotomy appeared in this respect, for the eastern parks were not nearly as well marked as the western parks. The Gettysburg and Antietam commissions primarily marked unit positions along roadways and lines of battle. Tablets at those two parks even today might tell of a unit that was engaged a certain number of yards away in a certain direction. At Chickamauga, Shiloh, and Vicksburg, the commissions tried to mark the *actual* positions held by each command. The majority of tablets and monuments at the three western parks were not necessarily along the roadways, although there is evidence that the western commissions wanted to utilize roadways in marking, when it was possible, to allow more casual visitors to see the tablets.

Even more fascinating, the western commissions took their monumenting schemes to deeper levels. The three western parks utilized colorcoding for the armies, something Gettysburg and Antietam did not do. Antietam's tablets were simple black tablets with white letters. Some of Gettysburg's were also, although they were later replaced with bronze tablets, which of course were not painted. But the western commissions used red for the Confederate tablets and blue for the Federals. In the case of Shiloh, where three armies fought, yellow was used for the second Federal army. As a result, a visitor at the western battlefields could immediately see which side the tablet in question represented, whereas at the eastern parks they had to read each tablet in detail.[9]

One park went beyond the color schemes. The Shiloh commission seemed to be the most progressive of all, using shapes to denote the different days of battle. Neither Gettysburg nor Chickamauga differentiated between the days of battle in their tablets, while Vicksburg could not because it was a forty-seven-day siege and Antietam was only a one-day battle. But Shiloh's commission used square tablets for first-day positions while using oval tablets for second-day areas.

The uniqueness of each park on a local and tactical level is different from the overarching similarities between the parks on an overall and strategic level. Overall, the parks have many similarities, which make them a unified series of historic parks. For instance, each of the five parks had very similar legislative histories, in that each gained broad support from the committees but endured some opposition in the Congress itself. (Of course, Antietam's legislative history, although similar to the others, never culminated in an outright enabling bill.) Similarly, the process of creating the various parks was related, with major and special emphases on map-making and regular army position marking. Even the monumentation process had similar results, with Federal states dominating the process— a free choice by less-interested Southern state legislatures, which would fund only a few Confederate monuments on the battlefields. In the same way, the state monuments were very similar on several of the battlefields, adding a type of uniformity. Distinct Illinois, Ohio, Pennsylvania, and New York monuments were readily discernable whether at Shiloh or Chickamauga or Antietam. Likewise, the idea of placing tablets and monuments to mark troop positions was a somewhat constant theme at all the parks. Even the major controversies were similar at each park, although some were more critical and divisive than others. The veterans themselves, aged and more hardheaded than ever, frequently fought over how the work should be done and displayed to future generations just how much they cared about their legacy—they wanted it to be accurate as they saw it. Unfortunately, others sometimes saw the same events in different ways.

One of the substantial similarities between the parks in those days of reconciliation and reunion was the role of the Confederates on the commissions. For the first time in history, former Confederates were an integral part of the process of preservation. And some made major differences. Stephen D. Lee actually served as commission chairman at Vicksburg for a time, although in reality William T. Rigby wielded as much power during Lee's tenure. The Confederate commissioners at Shiloh, Chickamauga, Antietam, and Gettysburg all served faithfully and in varying degrees of importance, some making major differences in how the parks developed. Alexander P. Stewart at Chickamauga oversaw some of the construction on the park, and William Robbins was involved at Gettysburg. Although other Confederates such as Lewis Guion at Vicksburg, Henry Heth at Antietam, William Forney at Gettysburg, Joseph Cumming at Chickamauga, or Robert Looney, Josiah Patterson, and Basil Duke at Shiloh all served in varying capacities, serve they did. The mere fact that there were even Confederates on the commissions is testament to the true reconciliation of the age, and there is little evidence that the Southerners were actively and purposely left out of the building process. It is also worth noting that the vast majority of the commission controversies were between fellow Union veterans, not between Union and Confederate veterans. And not only did the Confederate commissioners get involved; veteran's organizations such as the UCV readily lent their support and covered the progress of the parks in their various publications such as *Confederate Veteran* and *Southern Historical Society Papers.*[10]

Other important attributes also help to render the five parks a cohesive whole. There is no doubt that the parks were the outgrowth of the minds and hard work of the veterans themselves. Each of the five parks was the brainchild of a veteran association, was sponsored (except Antietam) by a veteran in Congress, was established by a Congress dominated by veterans, and was built and overseen by veterans. The old soldiers' rhetoric (North and South) makes it clear that these men wanted to preserve their scenes of conflict not only to remember their comrades who were no longer with them but also to allow future generations a glimpse of what they had done during the Civil War. They were writing their own generational autobiographies for later generations to read; they were telling us what they wanted us to know about them.

The veterans also wanted to keep safe the scenes of conflict so that many future groups could learn from them, whether they be future historians, future military leaders, or future Americans desiring to learn about the past. And it is abundantly clear that the veterans wanted the battlefields, unlike the national cemeteries, to be preserved in their original shape at the time of the battle, not landscaped and made into city-park-like recreational areas. The veterans felt a sincere emotional connection to the fields of conflict where they and their friends had fought and bled and where some had died. There was perhaps no greater shame to them than for one of their parks to be landscaped into a recreation park where the graves of their comrades would be trampled upon by visitors playing games.

The veterans also wanted to reconcile the sections through these parks. It had been on their watch that war had broken out and the United States had split. The veterans themselves had a keen interest in reconciling the two sections and making one nation again. Their rhetoric in support of the parks and their speeches and actions at the parks themselves make clear that the veterans were intent on putting the sectional past behind them and moving forward as united brethren.

Perhaps most important, the veterans used all the parks to memorialize. Their desire to remember what had occurred on those battlefields and to honor the memory of their dear comrades was a central driving force in the establishment of these five parks, and it produced the physical foundation of our collective Civil War memory. Something momentous had occurred on these sites, and many good men, North and South, had died there. By 1890, it was clear that they had not died in vain, but the veterans wanted to make sure that no one forgot their sacrifice. The veterans were no doubt preserving, restoring, and reuniting at these battlefields, but most of all they were memorializing.

# EPILOGUE

THE MASSIVE BATTLEFIELD preservation efforts begun so promisingly in the 1890s were seemingly spurned in the decades afterwards, but fortunately preservation efforts have revived in recent years. In the present day, many national, state, and local organizations are working hard to continue the task so gloriously begun, and those efforts have been blessed with varied levels of success.

The first three phases of battlefield preservation, the veterans' efforts, the Golden Age of the 1890s, and the New Deal–era parks, tell only a partial story of the entire 150-year history of the movement. After the parks' transfer to the National Park Service in 1933, several more battlefields saw some preservation, but nothing on the scale of the 1890s. And as time passed, the key components needed to create large Boyntonesque battlefield parks such as those at Chickamauga and Shiloh slipped forever away. No longer were the veterans alive to mark positions; no longer were most battlefields untainted from modernization and urbanization; and no longer were Congress and state legislatures interested in spending huge sums of money to preserve entire battlefields. The result was a list of federally preserved battlefields mostly on the Antietam Plan (an exception being Pea Ridge), and a corresponding number of smaller and seemingly even less-preserved state battlefield parks. As a result, despite a few successes, the era of battlefield preservation from the 1900s to the 1980s was anything but golden.

Fortunately, that drought began to change in the 1990s. A combination of several proponents came together to revive the preservation movement. Historical stalwarts pushed for preservation on sentimental and commemorative grounds; environmentalists promoted preservation on conservation grounds; politicians and tourism officials hoping to generate heritage-based tourism desired preservation on financial grounds. These varying groups, odd bedfellows in some cases, all agreed on a common goal, however, and some success has been evident.

As the movement began in earnest again in the 1990s, numerous city, state, and national organizations soon appeared out of nowhere, as everyone suddenly wanted to get in on the preservation. Groups such as the Friends of Raymond and the Siege and Battle of Corinth Commission pushed for their local projects, while state entities likewise began to redevelop their state-run sites by adding more land and modernizing interpretation at those sites. Perhaps the most substantial efforts came on the national level, however, with several organizations such as The Conservation Fund, the Association for the Preservation of Civil War Sites, and the Civil War Trust fighting for every piece of land they could preserve. In the last years of the 1990s, the latter two organizations combined into the mammoth Civil War Preservation Trust, the nation's leading battlefield preservation organization. The Trust has been able to accomplish many results in the effort to preserve our steadily disappearing battlefields.

And even the federal government has become involved again. In conjunction with the rebirth of the preservation movement, Congress again saw the need to study the battlefield preservation needs of America and funded the Civil War Sites Advisory Commission. Upon that commission's recommendation, Congress also created the American Battlefield Protection Program (ABPP) within the National Park Service and actually funded it generously (in part through selling commemorative postage stamps and minting silver and gold coins). The ABPP has saved thousands of acres of battlefield land since its inception. These federal entities have placed the stamp of the federal government on modern preservation efforts.

What is most ironic, however, is that with all the activity of the 1990s and into the twenty-first century, we are right back where we began in the 1890s. After a dearth of some nine decades, preservationists are again thinking in terms of preserving not just a small portion of a battlefield here and there, but of preserving *entire* battlefields. The Antietam Plan has seemingly been thrown on the trash heap of history, as modern-day preservationists are busy trying to buy up as much land as possible. There is no more ironic illustration of this phenomenon than at the Antietam National Battlefield itself, where the original Antietam Plan received its name. In recent years, the National Park Service has bought hundreds of acres of the battlefield that was purposely left in private hands in the 1890s. Now, we seem to be back to the Boyntonesque idea of preserving entire battlefields.

Yet there is a major difference. Today, we do not have the ability to preserve the way the veterans did in the 1890s, and we can only wish they had not stopped at five battlefields during that decade. They seemed to have had every factor lined up in their favor, with monies to appropriate, veterans returning to the scenes to mark specific spots, and battlefields still primarily untouched by modernization. Today, we have no such luxuries. Still, these disadvantages, trying though they are, make the difficult work currently being done all the more meaningful. They make the toils of the modern preservationist all the more satisfying. They make the money being spent all the more significant. Most importantly, however, they make the original efforts by the veterans in the 1890s all the more special.

# APPENDIX 1
## *Enabling Legislation*

CHICKAMAUGA-CHATTANOOGA NATIONAL MILITARY PARK

Be it enacted by the Senate and House of Representatives of the United States of America in Congress assembled, That for the purpose of preserving and suitably marking for historical and professional military study the fields of some of the most remarkable maneuvers and most brilliant fighting in the war of the rebellion, and upon the ceding of jurisdiction to the United States by the States of Tennessee and Georgia, respectively, and the report of the Attorney General of the United States that the title to the lands thus ceded is perfect, the following described highways in those States are hereby declared to be approaches to and parts of the Chickamauga and Chattanooga National Military Park as established by the second section of this act, to wit: First. The Missionary Ridge Crest road from Sherman Heights at the north end of Missionary Ridge, in Tennessee, where the said road enters upon the ground occupied by the Army of the Tennessee under Major-General William T. Sherman, in the military operations of November twenty-fourth and twenty-fifth, eighteen hundred and sixty-three; thence along said road through the positions occupied by the army of General Braxton Bragg on November twenty-fifth, eighteen hundred and sixty-three, and which were assaulted by the Army of the Cumberland under Major-General George H. Thomas on that date, to where the said road crosses the southern boundary of the State of Tennessee, near Rossville Gap, Georgia, upon the ground occupied by the troops of Major-General Joseph Hooker, from the Army of the Potomac, and thence in the State of Georgia to the junction of said road with the Chattanooga and Lafayette or State road at Rossville Gap; second, the Lafayette or State road from Rossville, Georgia, to Lee and Gordon's Mills, Georgia; third, the road from Lee and Gordon's Mills, Georgia, to Crawfish Springs, Georgia; fourth, the road from Crawfish Springs, Georgia, to the crossing of the Chickamauga at Glass' Mills, Georgia; fifth, the Dry Valley road from Rossville, Georgia, to the southern limits of McFarland's Gap in Missionary Ridge; sixth, the Dry Valley and Crawfish Springs road from McFarland's Gap to the intersection of the road from Crawfish Springs to Lee and Gordon's Mills; seventh, the road from Ringold, Geogia, to Reed's Bridge on the Chickamauga River; eighth, the roads from the crossing of Lookout Creek across the northern slope of Lookout Mountain and thence to the old Summertown Road and to the valley on the east slope of the said mountain, and thence by the route of General Joseph Hooker's troops to Rossville, Georgia, and each and all of these herein described roads shall, after the passage of this act, remain open as free public highways, and all rights of way now existing through the grounds of the said park and its approaches shall be continued.

SEC. 2. That upon the ceding of jurisdiction by the legislature of the State of Georgia, and the report of the Attorney-General of the United States that a perfect title has been secured under the provisions of the act approved August first, eighteen hundred and eighty-eight, entitled "An act to authorize condemnation of land for sites of public buildings, and for other purposes," the lands and roads embraced in the area bounded as herein described, together with the roads described in section one of this act, are hereby declared to be a national park, to be known as the Chickamauga and Chattanooga National Park; that is to say, the area inclosed by a line beginning on the Lafayette or State road, in Georgia, at a point where the bottom of the ravine next north of the house known on the field of Chickamauga as the Cloud House, and being about six hundred yards north of said house, due east to the Chickamauga River and due west to the intersection of the Dry Valley road at McFarland's Gap; thence along the west side of the Dry Valley and Crawfish Springs roads to the south side of the road from Crawfish Springs to Lee and Gordon's Mills; thence along the south side of the last named road to Lee and Gordon's Mills; thence along the channel of the Chickamauga River to the line forming the northern boundary of the park, as hereinbefore described, containing seven thousand six hundred acres, more or less.

SEC. 3. That the said Chickamauga and Chattanooga National Park, and the approaches thereto, shall be under the control of the Secretary of War, and it shall be his duty, immediately after the passage of this act to notify the Attorney-General of the purpose of the United States to acquire title to the roads and lands described in the previous sections of this act under the provisions of the act of August first, eighteen hundred and eighty eight; and the said Secretary, upon receiving notice from the Attorney-General of the United States that perfect titles have been secured to the said lands and roads, shall at once proceed to establish and substantially mark the boundaries of the said park.

SEC. 4. That the Secretary of War is hereby authorized to enter into agreements, upon such nominal terms as he may prescribe, with such present owners of the land as may desire to remain upon it, to occupy and cultivate their present holdings, upon condition that they will preserve the present buildings and roads, and the present outlines of field and forest, and that they will only cut trees or underbrush under such regulations as the Secretary may prescribe, and that they will assist in caring for and protecting all tablets, monuments, or such other artificial works as may from time to time be erected by proper authority.

SEC. 5. That the affairs of the Chickamauga and Chattanooga National Park shall, subject to the supervision and direction of the Secretary of War, be in charge of three commissioners, each of whom shall have actively participated in the battle of Chickamauga or one of the battles about Chattanooga, two to be appointed from civil life by the Secretary of War, and a third, who shall be detailed by the Secretary of War from among those officers of the Army best acquainted with the details of the battles of Chickamauga and Chattanooga, who shall act as Secretary of the Commission. The said commissioners and Secretary shall have an office in the War Department building, and while on actual duty shall be paid such compensation, out of the appropriation provided in this act, as the Secretary of War shall deem reasonable and just.

SEC. 6. That it shall be the duty of the commissioners named in the preceding section, under the direction of the Secretary of War, to superintend the opening of such roads as may be necessary to the purposes of the park, and the repair of the roads of the same, and to ascertain and definitely mark the lines of battle of all troops engaged in the battles of Chickamauga and Chattanooga, so far as the same shall fall within the lines of the park as defined in the previous sections of this act, and, for the purpose of assisting them in their duties and in ascertaining these lines, the Secretary of War shall have authority to employ, at such compensation as he may deem reasonable and just, to be paid out of the appropriation made by this act, some person recognized as well informed in regard to the details of the battles of Chickamauga and Chattanooga, and who shall have actively participated in one of those battles, and it shall be the duty of the Secretary of War from and after the passage of this act, through the commissioners, and their assistant in historical work, and under the act approved August first, eighteen hundred and eighty-eight, regulating the condemnation of land for public uses, to proceed with the preliminary work of establishing the park and its approaches as the same are defined in this act, and the expenses thus incurred shall be paid out of the appropriation provided by this act.

SEC. 7. That it shall be the duty of the commissioners, acting under the Secretary of War, to ascertain and substantially mark the locations of the regular troops, both infantry and artillery, within the boundaries of the park, and to erect monuments upon those positions as Congress may provide the necessary appropriations; and the Secretary of War in the same way may ascertain and mark all lines of battle within the boundaries of the park and erect plain and substantial historical tablets at such points in the vicinity of the Park and its approaches as he may deem fitting and necessary to clearly designate positions and movements, which, although without the limits of the Park, were directly connected with the battles of Chickamauga and Chattanooga.

SEC. 8. That it shall be lawful for the authorities of any State having troops engaged either at Chattanooga or Chickamauga, and for the officers and directors of the Chickamauga Memorial Association, a corporation chartered under the laws of Georgia, to enter upon the lands and approaches of the Chickamauga and Chattanooga National Park for the purpose of ascertaining and marking the lines of battle of troops engaged therein: *Provided*, That before any such lines are permanently designated the position of the lines and the proposed methods of marking them by monuments, tablets, or otherwise shall be submitted to the Secretary of War, and shall first receive the written approval of the Secretary, which approval shall be based upon formal written reports, which must be made to him in each case by the commissioners of the park.

SEC. 9. That the Secretary of War, subject to the approval of the President of the United States, shall have the power to make, and shall make, all needed regulations for the care of the park and for the establishment and marking of the lines of battle and other historical features of the park.

SEC. 10. That if any person shall willfully destroy, mutilate, deface, injure, or remove any monument, column, statue, memorial structure, or work of art that shall be erected or placed upon the grounds of the park by lawful authority, or shall willfully destroy or remove any fence, railing, inclosure, or other work for the protection or ornament of said park, or any portion thereof, or shall willfully destroy, cut, hack,

bark, break down, or otherwise injure any tree, bush, or shrubbery that may be growing upon said park, or shall cut down or fell or remove any timber, battle relic, tree
or trees growing or being upon such park, except by permission of the Secretary of
War, or shall willfully remove or destroy any breast-works, earth-works, walls, or other
defenses or shelter, on any part thereof, constructed by the armies formerly engaged
in the battles on the lands or approaches to the park, any person so offending and
found guilty thereof, before any justice of the peace of the county in which the offense
may be committed, shall for each and every such offense forfeit and pay a fine, in the
discretion of the justice, according to the aggravation of the offense, of not less than
five nor more than fifty dollars, one-half to the use of the park and the other half to
the informer, to be enforced and recovered, before such justice, in like manner as debts
of like nature are now by law recoverable in the several counties where the offense may
be committed.

    SEC. 11. That to enable the Secretary of War to begin to carry out the purposes of
this act, including the condemnation and purchase of the neces-sary land, marking the
boundaries of the park, opening or repairing necessary roads, maps and surveys, and
the pay and expenses of the commissioners and their assistant, the sum of one hundred and twenty-five thousand dollars, or such portion thereof as may be necessary, is
hereby appropriated, out of any moneys in the Treasury not otherwise appropriated,
and disbursements under this act shall require the approval of the Secretary of War,
and he shall make annual report of the same to Congress.

## ANTIETAM NATIONAL BATTLEFIELD

For the purpose of surveying, locating, and preserving the lines ofbattle of the
Army of the Potomac and of the Army of Northern Virginia at Antitam, and for
marking the same, and for locating and marking the position of each of the forty-
three different commands of the Regular Army engaged in the battle of Antietam,
and for the purchase of sites for tablets for the marking of such positions, fifteen
thousand dollars. And all lands acquired by the United States for this purpose,
whether by purchase, gift, or otherwise, shall be under the care and supervision of
the Secretary of War.

## SHILOH NATIONAL MILITARY PARK

Be it enacted by the Senate and House of Representatives of the United States of
America in Congress assembled, That in order that the armies of the southwest which
served in the civil war, like their comrades of the eastern armies at Gettysburg and
those of the central west at Chickamauga, may have the history of one of their memorable battles preserved on the ground where they fought, the battlefield of Shiloh, in
the State of Tennessee, is hereby declared to be a national military park, whenever
title to the same shall have been acquired by the United States and the usual jurisdiction over the lands and roads of the same shall have been granted to the United
States by the State of Tennessee; that is to say, the area inclosed by the following
lines, or so much thereof as the commissioners of the park may deem necessary, to

wit: Beginning at low-water mark on the north bank of Snake Creek where it emp-
ties into the Tennessee River; thence westwardly in a straight line to the point where
the river road to Crumps Landing, Tennessee, crosses Snake Creek; thence along the
channel of Owl Creek to the crossing of the road to Purdy, Tennessee; thence south-
wardly in a straight line to the intersection of an east and west line to the point where
the Hamburg Road crosses Lick Creek; thence along the channel of Lick Creek to the
Tennessee River; thence along low-water mark of the Tennessee River to the point of
beginning, containing three thousand acres, more or less, and the area thus inclosed
shall be known as the Shiloh National Military Park: *Provided,* That the boundaries of
the land authorized to be acquired may be changed by the said commissioners.

SEC. 2. That the establishment of Shiloh National Military Park shall be carried
forward under the control and direction of the Secretary of War, who, upon the passage of the Act, shall proceed to acquire title to the same either under the Act approved
August first, eighteen hundred and eighty-eight, entitled "An Act to authorize the condemnation of land for sites of public buildings, and for other purposes," or under the
Act approved February twenty-seventh, eighteen hundred and sixty-seven, entitled
"An Act to establish and protect national cemeteries," as he may select, and as title is
procured to any portion of the lands and roads within the legal boundaries of the park
he may proceed with the establishment of the park upon such portions as may thus
be acquired.

SEC. 3. That the Secretary of War is hereby authorized to enter into agreements
whereby he may lease, upon such terms as he may prescribe, with such present owners or tenants of the lands as may desire to remain upon it, to occupy and cultivate
their present holding upon condition that they will preserve the present buildings and
roads and the present outlines of field and forest, and that they only will cut trees
or underbrush under such regulations as the Secretary may prescribe, and that they
will assist in caring for and protecting all tablets, monuments, or such other artificial
works as may from time to time be erected by proper authority.

SEC. 4. That the affairs of the Shiloh National Military Park shall, subject to the
supervision and direction of the Secretary of War, be in charge of three commissioners, to be appointed by the Secretary of War, each of whom shall have served at the
time of the battle in one of the armies engaged therein, one of whom shall have served
in the Army of the Tennessee, commanded by General U. S. Grant, who shall be chairman of the commission; one in the Army of the Ohio, commanded by General D. C.
Buell; one in the Army of the Mississippi, commanded by General A. S. Johnston. The
said commissioners shall have an office in the War Department building, and while
on actual duty shall be paid such compensation out of the appropriations provided by
this Act as the Secretary of War shall deem reasonable and just; and for the purpose of
assisting them in their duties and in ascertaining the lines of battle of all troops engaged
and the history of their movements in the battle, the Secretary of War shall have authority to employ, at such compensation as he may deem reasonable, to be paid out of the
appropriations made by this Act, some person recognized as well informed concerning
the history of the several armies engaged at Shiloh, and who shall also act as secretary of
the commission.

SEC. 5. That it shall be the duty of the commission named in the preceding section, under the direction of the Secretary of War, to open or repair such roads as

may be necessary to the purpose of the park, and to ascertain and mark with historical tablets or otherwise, as the Secretary of War may determine, all lines of battle of the troops engaged in the battle of Shiloh and other historical points of interest pertaining to the battle within the park or its vicinity, and the said commission in establishing this military park shall also have authority, under the direction of the Secretary of War, to employ such labor and services and to obtain such supplies and material as may be necessary to the establishment of the said park under such regulations as he may consider best for the interest of the Government, and the Secretary of War shall make and enforce all needed regulations for the care of the park.

SEC. 6. That it shall be lawful for any State that had troops engaged in the battle of Shiloh to enter upon the lands of the Shiloh National Military Park for the purpose of ascertaining and marking the lines of battle of its troops engaged therein: *Provided*, That before any such lines are permanently designated the position of the lines and the proposed methods of marking them by monuments, tablets, or otherwise shall be submitted to and approved by the Secretary of War, and all such lines, designs and inscriptions for the same shall first receive the written approval of the Secretary, which approval shall be based upon formal written reports, which must be made to him in each case by the commissioners of the park: *Provided*, That no discrimination shall be made against any State as to the manner of designating lines, but any grant made to any State by the Secretary of War may be used by any other State.

SEC. 7. That if any person shall, excect by permission of the Secretary of War, destroy, mutilate, deface, injure, or remove any monument, column, statues, memorial structures, or work of art that shall be erected or placed upon the grounds of the park by lawful authority, or shall destroy or remove any fence, railing, inclosure, or other work for the protection or ornament of said park, or any portion thereof, or shrubbery that may be growing upon said park, or shall cut down or fell or remove any timber, battle relic, tree or trees growing or being upon said park, or hunt within the limits of the park, or shall remove or destroy any breastworks, earthworks, walls, or other defenses or shelter on any part thereof constructed by the armies formerly engaged in the battles on the lands or approaches to the park, any person so offending and found guilty thereof, before any justice of the peace of the county in which the offenses may be committed or any court of competent jurisdiction shall for each and every such offense forfeit and pay a fine, in the discretion of the justice, according to the aggravation of the offense, of not less than five nor more than fifty dollars, one-half for the use of the park and the other half to the informer, to be enforced and recovered before such justice in like manner as debts of like nature are now by law recoverable in the several counties where the offense may be committed.

SEC. 8. That to enable the Secretary of War to begin to carry out the purpose of this Act, including the condemnation or purchase of the necessary land, marking the boundaries of the park, opening or repairing necessary roads, restoring the field to its condition at the time of the battle, maps and surveys, and the pay and expenses of the commissioners and their assistant, the sum of seventy-five thousand dollars, or such portion thereof as may be necessary, is hereby appropriated, out of any moneys in the Treasury not otherwise appropriated, and disbursements under this Act shall require the approval of the Secretary of War, and he shall make annual report of the same to Congress.

## GETTYSBURG NATIONAL MILITARY PARK

Be it enacted by the Senate and House of Representatives of the Untied States of America in Congress assembled, That the Secretary of War is hereby authorized to receive from the Gettysburg Battlefield Memorial Association, a corporation chartered by the State of Pennsylvania, a deed of conveyance to the United States of all the lands belonging to said association, embracing about eight hundred acres, more or less, and being a considerable part of the battlefield of Gettysburg, together with all rights of way over avenues through said lands acquired by said association, and all improvements made by it in and upon the same. Upon the due execution and delivery to the Secretary of War of such deed of conveyance, the Secretary of War is authorized to pay to the said Battlefield Memorial Association the sum of two thousand dollars, or so much thereof as may be necessary to discharge the debts of said association, the amount of such debts to be verified by the officers thereof, and the sum of two thousand dollars is hereby appropriated out of any money in the Treasury not otherwise appropriated to meet and defray such charges.

SEC. 2. That as soon as the lands aforesaid shall be conveyed to the United States the Secretary of War shall take possession of the same, and such other lands on the battlefield as the United States have acquired, or shall hereafter acquire, by purchase or condemnation proceedings; and the lands aforesaid, shall be designated and known as the "Gettysburg National Park."

SEC. 3. That the Gettysburg national park shall, subject to the supervision and direction of the Secretary of War, be in charge of the commissioners heretofore appointed by the Secretary of War for the location and acquisition of lands at Gettysburg, and their successors; the said commissioners shall have their office at Gettysburg, and while on duty shall be paid such compensation out of the appropriation provided in this Act as the Secretary of War shall deem reasonable and just. And it shall be the duty of the said commissioners, under the direction of the Secretary of War, to superintend the opening of such additional roads as may be necessary for the purposes of the park and for the improvement of the avenues heretofore laid out therein, and to properly mark the boundaries of the said park, and to ascertain and definitely mark the lines of battle of all troops engaged in the battle of Gettysburg, so far as the same shall fall within the limits of the park.

SEC. 4. That the Secretary of War is hereby authorized and directed to acquire, at such times and in such manner as he may deem best calculated to serve the public interest, such lands in the vicinity of Gettysburg, Pennsylvania, not exceeding in area the parcels shown on the map prepared by Major-General Daniel E. Sickles, United States Army, and now on file in the office of the Secretary of War, which were occupied by the infantry, cavalry and artillery on the first, second and third days of July, eighteen hundred and sixty-three, and such other adjacent lands as he may deem necessary to preserve the important topographical features of the battlefield: *Provided,* That nothing contained in this Act shall be deemed and held to prejudice the rights acquired by any State or by any military organization to the ground on which its monuments or markers are placed, nor the right of way to the same.

SEC. 5. That for the purpose of acquiring the lands designated and described in the foregoing section not already acquired and owned by the United States, and such other adjacent land as may be deemed necessary by the Secretary of War for the preservation and marking of the lines of battle of the Union and Confederate armies at Gettysburg, the Secretary of War is authorized to employ the services of the commissioners heretofore appointed by him for the location, who shall proceed, in conformity with his instructions and subject in all things to his approval, to acquire such lands by purchase, or by condemnation proceedings, to be taken by the Attorney-General in behalf of the United States, in any case in which it shall be ascertained that the same can not be purchased at prices deemed reasonable and just by the said commissioners and approved by the Secretary of War. And such condemnation proceedings may be taken pursuant to the Act of Congress approved August first, eighteen hundred and eighty-eight, regulating the condemnation of land for public uses, or the Joint Resolution authorizing the purchase or condemnation of land in the vicinity of Gettysburg, Pennsylvania, approved June fifth, eighteen hundred and ninety-four.

SEC. 6. That it shall be the duty of the Secretary of War to establish and enforce proper regulations for the custody, preservation, and care of the monuments now erected or which may be hereafter erected within the limits of the said national military park; and such rules shall provide for convenient access by visitors to all such monuments within the park, and the ground included therein, on such days and within such hours as may be designated and authorized by the Secretary of War.

SEC. 7. That if any person shall destroy, mutilate, deface, injure, or remove, except by permission of the Secretary of War, any column, statue, memorial structure, or work of art that shall be erected or placed upon the grounds of the park by lawful authority, or shall destroy or remove any fence, railing, inclosure, or other work for the protection or ornament of said park or any portion thereof, or shall destroy, cut, hack, bark, break down, or otherwise injure any tree, bush, or shrubbery that may be growing upon said park, or shall cut down or fell or remove any timber, battle relic, tree or trees, growing or being upon said park, or hunt within the limits of the park, or shall remove or destroy any breastworks, earthworks, walls, or other defenses or shelter or any part thereof constructed by the armies formerly engaged in the battles on the land or approaches to the park, or shall violate any regulation made and published by the Secretary of War for the government of visitors within the limits of said park, any person so offending and found guilty thereof, before any justice of the peace of the county in which the offense may be committed, shall, for each and every such offense, forfeit and pay a fine, in the discretion of the justice, according to the aggravation of the offense, of not less than five nor more than five hundred dollars, one-half for the use of the park and the other half to the informer, to be enforced and recovered before such justice in like manner as debts of like nature are now by law recoverable in the county where the offense may be committed.

SEC. 8. That the Secretary of War is hereby authorized and directed to cause to be made a suitable bronze tablet, containing on it the address delivered by Abraham Lincoln, President of the United States, at Gettysburg on the nineteenth day of November, eighteen hundred and sixty-three, on the occasion of the dedication of the national cemetery at that place, and such tablet, having on it besides the address a medallion likeness of President Lincoln, shall be erected on the most suitable site within the limits of said park, which said address was in the following words, to wit: "Four score and seven years ago our fathers brought forth on this continent a new nation, conceived in liberty and dedicated to the proposition that all men are created equal. Now we are engaged in a great civil war, testing whether that nation, or any nation so conceived and so dedicated, can long endure. We are met on a great battle-field of that war. We have come to dedicate a portion of that field as a final resting place for those who here gave their lives that that nation might live. It is altogether fitting and proper that we should do this. But, in a larger sense, we can not dedicate, we can not consecrate, we can not hallow this ground. The brave men, living and dead, who struggled here, have consecrated it far above our poor power to add or detract. The world will little note, nor long remember, what we say here; but it can never forget what they did here. It is for us, the living, rather to be dedicated here to the unfinished work which they who fought here have thus far so nobly advanced. It is rather for us to be here dedicated to the great task remaining before us; that from these honored dead we take increased devotion to that cause for which they gave the last full measure of devotion; that we here highly resolve that these dead shall not have died in vain; that this nation, under God, shall have a new birth of freedom, and that government of the people, by the people, for the people, shall not perish from the earth." And the sum of five thousand dollars, or so much thereof as may be necessary, is hereby appropriated, out of any money in the Treasury not otherwise appropriated, to pay the cost of said tablet and medallion and pedestal.

SEC. 9. That, to enable the Secretary of War to carry out the purposes of this Act, including the purchase or condemnation of the land described in sections four and five of this Act, opening, improving, and repairing necessary roads and avenues, providing surveys and maps, suitably marking the boundaries of the park, and for the pay and expenses of the commissioners and their assistants, the sum of seventy-five thousand dollars, or so much thereof as may be necessary, is hereby appropriated, out of any money in the Treasury not otherwise appropriated; and all disbursements made under this Act shall require the approval of the Secretary of War, who shall make annual report of the same to Congress.

## VICKSBURG NATIONAL MILITARY PARK

Be it enacted by the Senate and House of Representatives of the United States of America in Congress assembled, That in order to commemorate the campaign and siege and defense of Vicksburg, and to preserve the history of the battles and opera-tions of the siege and defense on the ground where they were fought and were carried on, the battlefield of Vicksburg, in the State of Mississippi, is hereby declared to be a national military park whenever the title to the same shall have been acquired by the United States and the usual jurisdiction over the lands and roads of the same shall have been granted to the United States by the State of Mississippi; that is to say, the area inclosed by the following lines, or so much thereof as the commissioners of the park may deem necessary, to wit: Beginning near the point where the graveyard road, now known as the City Cemetery road, crosses the line of the Confederate earthworks, thence north about eighty rods, thence in an easterly direction about one hundred and twenty rods, thence in a southerly direction, and keeping as far from the line of the Confederate earthworks as the purposes of the park may require and as the park com-mission, to be hereinafter named, may determine, but not distant from the nearest point on said line of Confederate earthworks more than one hundred and sixty rods at any part, to a point about forty rods south and from eighty to one hundred and sixty rods east of Fort Garrott, also known as the "Square Fort;" thence in a westerly direction to a point in the rear of said Fort Garrott, thence in a northerly direction across the line of the Confederate earthworks and to a point about two hundred feet in the rear of the said line of Confederate earthworks, thence in a general northerly direction, and at an approximate distance of about two hundred feet in the rear of the line of Confederate earthworks as the conformation of the ground may require, to the place of beginning. This to constitute the main body of the park. In addition thereto a strip of land about two hundred and sixty-four feet in width along and including the remaining parts of the Confederate earthworks, namely, from the north part of said main body of the park to and including Fort Hill or Fort Nogales on the high hill over looking the national cemetery, and from the south part of said main body of the park to the edge of the bluff at the river below the city of Vicksburg; and also in addition thereto a strip of land about two hundred and sixty-four feet in width, as near as may be, along and including the Federal lines opposed to the Confederate lines here-in and above named and not included in the main body of the park; and in further addition thereto such points of interest as the commission may deem necessary, for the purposes of the park and the Secretary of War may approve; the whole containing about one thousand two hundred acres, and costing not to exceed forty thousand dollars.

SEC. 2. That the establishment of the Vicksburg national military park shall be carried forward under the control and direction of the Secretary of War; and the Secretary of War shall, upon the passage of this Act, proceed to acquire title to the same by voluntary conveyance or under the Act approved August first, eighteen hundred and eighty-eight, entitled "An Act to authorize the condemnation of land for sites of public buildings, and for other purposes," or under Act approved February twenty-second, eighteen hundred and sixty-seven, entitled "An Act to establish and protect national cemeteries," as he may elect or deem practicable; and when title is procured to all of the lands and roads within the boundaries of the proposed park, as described in section one of this Act, he may proceed with the establishment of the park; and he shall detail an officer of the Engineer Corps of the Army to assist the commissioners in establishing the Park.

SEC. 3. That the Secretary of War is hereby authorized to enter into agreements of leasing upon such terms as he may prescribe, with such occupants or tenants of the lands as may desire to remain upon it, to occupy and cultivate their present holdings upon condition that they will preserve the present buildings and roads and the present outlines of field and forest, and that they will only cut trees or underbrush under such regulations as the Secretary of War may prescribe, and that they will assist in caring for and protecting all tablets, monuments, or such other artificial works as may from time to time be erected by proper authority: *Provided,* That the United States shall at all times have and retain full right, power, and authority to take possession of any and all parts or portions of said premises and to remove and expel there from any such occupant, tenant, or other person or persons found thereon whenever the Secretary of War or the commissioners shall deem it proper or necessary; and such right, power, and authority shall be reserved in express terms in all leases and agreements giving or granting such occupant or tenant the right to remain in possession as herein contemplated; and thereupon said occupant or tenant or other persons who may be required to vacate said premises shall each and all at once surrender and deliver up the possession thereof.

SEC. 4. That the affairs of the Vicksburg national military park shall, subject to the supervision and direction of the Secretary of War, be in charge of three commissioners, to be appointed by the Secretary of War, each of whom shall have served at the time of the siege and defense in one of the armies engaged therein, two of whom shall have served in the army commanded by General Grant and one in the army commanded by General Pemberton. The commissioners shall elect one of their number chairman; they shall also elect, subject to the approval of the Secretary of War, a secretary, who shall also be historian, and who shall possess the requisite qualifications of a commissioner, and they and the secretary shall have an office in the city of Vicksburg, Mississippi, or on the grounds of the park, and be paid such compensation as the Secretary of War shall deem reasonable and just.

SEC. 5. That it shall be the duty of the commissioners named in the preceding section, under the direction of the Secretary of War, to restore the forts and the lines of fortification, the parallels and the approaches of the two armies, or so much thereof as may be necessary to the purposes of this park; to open and construct and to repair such roads as may be necessary to said purposes, and to ascertain and mark with historical tablets, or otherwise as the Secretary of War may determine, the lines of battle of the troops engaged in the assaults, and the lines held by the troops during the siege and defense of Vicksburg, the headquarters of General Grant and of General Pemberton, and other historical points of interest pertaining to the siege and defense of Vicksburg with-in the park or its vicinity; and the said commissioners in establishing this military park shall also have authority under the direction of the Secretary of War to do all things necessary to the purposes of the park, and for its establishment under such regulations as he may consider best for the interest of the Government, and the Secretary of War shall make and enforce all needful regulations for the care of the park.

SEC. 6. That it shall be lawful for any State that had troops engaged in the siege and defense of Vicksburg to enter upon the lands of the Vicksburg national military park for the purpose of ascertaining and marking the lines of battle of its troops engaged therein: *Provided,* That before any such lines are permanently designated the position of the lines and the proposed methods of marking them by monuments, tablets, or otherwise shall be submitted to and approved by the Secretary of War, and all such lines, designs, and inscriptions for the same shall first receive the written approval of the Secretary of War, which approval shall be based upon formal written reports which must be made to him in each case by the commissioners of the park; and no monument, tablet, or other designating indication shall be erected or placed within said park or vicinity without such written authority of the Secretary of War: *Provided,* That no discrimination shall be made against any State as to the manner of designating lines, but any grant made to any State by the Secretary of War may be used by any other State. The provisions of this section shall also apply to organizations and persons; and as the Vicksburg National Cemetery is on ground partly occupied by Federal lines during the siege of Vicksburg, the provisions of this section, as far as may be practicable, shall apply to monuments or tablets designating such lines within the limits of that cemetery.

SEC. 7. That if any person shall, except by permission of the Secretary of War, destroy, mutilate, deface, injure, or remove any monument, column, statue, memorial structure, tablet, or work of art that shall be erected or placed upon the grounds of the park by lawful authority, or shall destroy or remove any fence, railing, enclosure, or other work intended for the protection or ornamentation of said park, or any portion thereof, or shall destroy, cut, hack, bark, break down, or otherwise injure any tree, bush, or shrub that may be growing upon said park, or shall cut down or fell or remove any timber, battle relic, tree, or trees growing or being upon said park, or hunt within the limits of the park, or shall remove or destroy any breastworks, earthworks, walls, or other defenses or shelter on any part thereof constructed by the armies formerly engaged in the battles, on the lands or approaches to the park, any person so offending and found guilty thereof, before any United States commissioner or court, justice of the peace of the county in which the offense may be committed, or any court of competent jurisdiction, shall for each and every such offense forfeit and pay a fine in the discretion of the said commissioner or court of the United States or justice of the peace, according to the aggravation of the offense, of not less than five nor more than five hundred dollars, one-half for the use of the park and the other half to the informant, to be enforced and recovered before such United States commissioner or court or justice of the peace or other court in like manner as debts of like nature are now by law recoverable in the several counties where the offense may be committed.

SEC. 8. That to enable the Secretary of War to begin to carry out the purpose of this Act, including the condemnation or purchase of the necessary land, marking the boundaries of the park, opening or repairing necessary roads, restoring the field to its condition at the time of the battle, maps and surveys, material, labor, clerical, and all other necessary assistants, and the pay and expenses of the commissioners and their secretary and assistants, the sum of sixty-five thousand dollars, or such portion thereof as may be necessary, is hereby appropriated, out of any moneys in the Treasury not otherwise appropriated, and disbursements under this Act shall require the approval of the Secretary of War, and he shall make annual report of the same to Congress.

# APPENDIX 2
## Military Park Commissioners and Board Members

*Chickamauga and Chattanooga National Military Park*

| | |
|---|---|
| Joseph S. Fullerton (C) | 1890–1897 |
| Alexander P. Stewart | 1890–1908 |
| Sanford C. Kellogg | 1890–1893 |
| Frank G. Smith | 1893–1908 |
| Henry Van Ness Boynton (C) | 1897–1905 |
| Ezra A. Carman (C) | 1905–1909 |
| Charles H. Grosvenor (C) | 1910–1917 |
| Joseph B. Cumming (C) | 1908–1922 |
| John Tweedale | 1908–1910 |
| Webster J. Colburn | 1910–1911 |
| John T. Wilder | 1911–1917 |

*Antietam National Battlefield*

| | |
|---|---|
| Henry Heth | 1891–1898 |
| John C. Stearns | 1891–1894 |
| George B. Davis (C) | 1894–1895 |
| Ezra A. Carman | 1894–1896 |
| George W. Davis (C) | 1895–1898 |

*Shiloh National Military Park*

| | |
|---|---|
| Cornelius Cadle (C) | 1895–1910 |
| Don Carlos Buell | 1895–1898 |
| Robert F. Looney | 1895–1899 |
| Josiah Patterson | 1899–1904 |
| James H. Ashcraft | 1899–1920 |
| Basil W. Duke | 1904–1916 |
| David W. Reed (C) | 1910–1916 |

*Gettysburg National Military Park*

| | |
|---|---|
| John P. Nicholson (C) | 1893–1922 |
| John B. Bachelder | 1893–1894 |
| William H. Forney | 1893–1894 |
| Charles Richardson | 1895–1917 |
| William M. Robbins | 1894–1905 |
| Lunsford Lindsay Lomax | 1905–1913 |

*Vicksburg National Military Park*

| | |
|---|---|
| Stephen D. Lee (C) | 1899–1908 |
| William T. Rigby (C) | 1899–1929 |
| James G. Everest | 1899–1924 |
| Lewis Guion | 1908–1920 |

# NOTES

## ABBREVIATIONS

| | |
|---|---|
| ANTI | Antietam National Battlefield Archives |
| CHCH | Chickamauga and Chattanooga National Military Park Archives |
| FHS | Filson Historical Society |
| GNMP | Gettysburg National Military Park Archives |
| LC | Library of Congress |
| MHS | Massachusetts Historical Society |
| MSCPL | Memphis Shelby County Public Library |
| MDAH | Mississippi Department of Archives and History |
| NARA | National Archives and Records Administration |
| NYPL | New York Public Library |
| SNMP | Shiloh National Military Park Archives |
| UI | University of Iowa |
| VNMP | Vicksburg National Military Park |

## INTRODUCTION
### THE CONTEXT OF CIVIL WAR BATTLEFIELD PRESERVATION

1. *Illinois at Vicksburg* (n.p.: Illinois-Vicksburg Military Park Commission, 1907), 77; John R. Neff, *Honoring The Civil War Dead: Commemoration and the Problem of Reconciliation* (Lawrence: Univ. Press of Kansas, 2005).

2. D. W. Reed, "National Cemeteries and National Military Parks," in *War Sketches and Incidents As Related by Companions of the Iowa Commandery, Military Order of the Loyal Legion of the United States,* vol. 2 (Des Moines: n.p., 1898), 373; *Report of the Proceedings of the Society of the Army of the Tennessee at the Twenty-Eighth Meeting held at St. Louis, Mo., November 18–19, 1896* (Cincinnati: F. W. Freeman, 1897), 53.

3. *Society of the Army of the Cumberland: Twenty-Third Reunion, Chickamauga, Georgia, 1892* (Cincinnati: Robert Clarke and Co., 1892), 51.

4. A study of the members of the 51st Congress, 1889–1891, reveals that 47.86 percent of them were veterans of the Civil War.

5. Reed, "National Cemeteries and National Military Parks," 374; Edwin C. Bearss, Chief Historian Emeritus, National Park Service, interview by author, Aug. 11, 2004.

6. *Society of the Army of the Cumberland: Twenty-Third Reunion,* 57; Reed, "National Cemeteries and National Military Parks," 372.

7. *Illinois at Vicksburg,* 87.

8. Reed, "National Cemeteries and National Military Parks," 372.

9. Bearss, interview by author.

## 1. BATTLEFIELDS, CEMETERIES, AND EARLY PRESERVATION

1. O. Edward Cunningham, *Shiloh and the Western Campaign of 1862*, edited by Gary D. Joiner and Timothy B. Smith (New York: Savas Beatie, 2007); Wiley Sword, *Shiloh: Bloody April* (New York: William Morrow and Company, 1974); Larry J. Daniel, *Shiloh: The Battle That Changed the Civil War* (New York: Simon and Schuster, 1997).

2. Stephen W. Sears, *Landscape Turned Red: The Battle of Antietam* (New Haven: Ticknor and Fields, 1983); James M. McPherson, *Crossroads of Freedom: Antietam, The Battle That Changed the Course of the Civil War* (New York: Oxford Univ. Press, 2002).

3. Edwin C. Bearss, *The Vicksburg Campaign*, 3 vols. (Dayton, OH: Morningside House, 1985–86); Terrence J. Winschel, *Vicksburg: Fall of the Confederate Gibraltar* (Abilene: McWhiney Foundation Press, 1999); Warren E. Grabau, *Ninety-eight Days: A Geographer's View of the Vicksburg Campaign* (Knoxville: Univ. of Tennessee Press, 2000); Michael B. Ballard, *Vicksburg: The Campaign That Opened the Mississippi* (Chapel Hill: Univ. of North Carolina Press, 2004).

4. Edwin B. Coddington, *The Gettysburg Campaign: A Study in Command* (New York: Charles Scribner's Sons, 1968); Noah Andre Trudeau, *Gettysburg: A Testing of Courage* (New York: Harper Collins, 2002); Stephen W. Sears, *Gettysburg* (New York: Houghton Mifflin Company, 2003).

5. Glenn Tucker, *Chickamauga: Bloody Battle in the West* (Indianapolis: Bobbs-Merrill, 1961); Peter Cozzens, *This Terrible Sound: The Battle of Chickamauga* (Urbana: Univ. of Illinois Press, 1992).

6. Robert E. L. Krick, "The Civil War's First Monument: Bartow's Marker at Manassas," *Blue and Gray* 8, no. 4 (Apr. 1991): 33.

7. Daniel A. Brown, "Marked for Future Generations: the Hazen Brigade Monument, 1863–1929" (Murfreesboro: Stones River National Battlefield, 1985), 5–8.

8. Mary Munsell Abroe, "'All the Profound Scenes': Federal Preservation of Civil War Battlefields, 1861–1990," (Ph.D. diss., Loyola Univ. Chicago, 1996), 91–92.

9. Quoted in Dean W. Holt, *American Military Cemeteries: A Comprehensive Illustrated Guide to the Hollowed Grounds of the United States, Including Cemeteries Overseas* (Jefferson: McFarland and Company, Inc., Publishers, 1992), 2–3.

10. Ibid.

11. Ibid.

12. U.S. Quartermaster Department, *Roll of Honor: Names of Soldiers Who Died in Defense of the American Union Interred in the National Cemeteries*, 27 vols. (Washington, DC: Government Printing Office, 1869), 15:2.

13. Ibid.

14. Charles W. Snell and Sharon A. Brown, *Antietam National Battlefield and National Cemetery* (Washington, DC: National Park Service, 1986), 26; U.S. Quartermaster Department, *Roll of Honor*, 15:2; Holt, *American Military Cemeteries*, 429.

15. Holt, *American Military Cemeteries*, 65.

16. U.S. Quartermaster Department, *Roll of Honor*, 11:11–13; Holt, *American Military Cemeteries*, 67.

17. U.S. Quartermaster Department, *Roll of Honor*, 16:76.

18. Ibid.; Gary Wills, *Lincoln at Gettysburg: The Words That Remade America* (New York: Simon and Schuster, 1992).

19. Holt, *American Military Cemeteries*, 439; U.S. Quartermaster Department, *Roll of Honor*, 16:76.

20. G. Kurt Piehler, *Remembering War the American Way* (Washington, DC: Smithsonian Institution Press, 1995), 51.

21. David Charles Sloane, *The Last Great Necessity: Cemeteries in American History* (Baltimore: Johns Hopkins Univ. Press, 1991); James J. Farrell, *Inventing the American Way of Death, 1830–1920* (Philadelphia: Temple Univ. Press, 1980); Piehler, *Remembering War the American Way*, 6, 50. See also the various descriptions of the physical makeup of the cemeteries contained in *Roll of Honor*.

22. U.S. Quartermaster Department, *Roll of Honor*, 11:12; Piehler, *Remembering War the American Way*, 50.

23. U.S. Quartermaster Department, *Roll of Honor*, 24:7; Holt, *American Military Cemeteries*, 445.

24. Ephraim P. Abbott to Mother, July 11, 1867, Shiloh National Cemetery vertical file, SNMP; Timothy B. Smith, "'The Handsomest Cemetery in the South': Shiloh National Cemetery," *West Tennessee Historical Society Papers* 56 (2002): 1–16; U.S. Quartermaster Department, *Roll of Honor*, 20:119.

25. For the text of "An Act to Establish and Protect National Cemeteries," see Richard Myers, *The Vicksburg National Cemetery: An Administrative History* (Washington, DC: National Park Service, 1968), 200–201.

26. For commemorative efforts at Manassas, see Joan M. Zenzen, *Battling for Manassas: The Fifty-Year Preservation Struggle at Manassas National Battlefield Park* (University Park: Pennsylvania State Univ. Press, 1998); Abroe, "All the Profound Scenes," 92–93.

27. Snell and Brown, *Antietam National Battlefield*, 23–24.

28. Ibid., 360–63; Harlan D. Unrau, *Administrative History: Gettysburg National Military Park and National Cemetery* (Denver: National Park Service, 1991), 41–43; Minute Book Gettysburg Battlefield Memorial Association, 1872–1895, GNMP, 49, 51.

29. John M. Vanderslice, *Gettysburg, Then and Now, The Field of American Valor: Where and How Troops Fought and the Troops They Encountered; An Account of the Battle Giving Movements, Positions, and Losses of the Commands Engaged* (Philadelphia: Gettysburg Battlefield Memorial Association, 1899), 355–56; Unrau, *Administrative History*, 22, 25; Abroe, "All the Profound Scenes," 93–94.

30. Vanderslice, *Gettysburg, Then and Now*, 364.

31. Unrau, *Administrative History*, 44.

32. Vanderslice, *Gettysburg, Then and Now*, 363–64, 367; Unrau, *Administrative History*, 47.

33. Vanderslice, *Gettysburg, Then and Now*, 367–68.

34. *Annual Report of the Secretary of War*, 1895 (Washington, DC: Government Printing Office, 1866–1933), 31; Unrau, *Administrative History*, 47–48.

35. Vanderslice, *Gettysburg, Then and Now*, 368–71; Unrau, *Administrative History*, 50–51.

36. Vanderslice, *Gettysburg, Then and Now*, 371.

37. Ibid., 372–88; Unrau, *Administrative History*, 58. Ziegler's Grove would not be "restore[d] . . . as nearly as possible to the condition in which it was during the battle" until years later.

38. Unrau, *Administrative History*, 57, 59.
39. Ibid., 64.
40. Ibid., 58–59, 63.
41. Vanderslice, *Gettysburg, Then and Now*, 368, 372–379; Abroe, "All the Profound Scenes," 118, 125–28; Minute Book Gettysburg Battlefield Memorial Association, 1872–1895, GNMP, 135, 151–52.
42. Minute Book Gettysburg Battlefield Memorial Association, 1872–1895, GNMP, 146; John P. Nicholson, William M. Robbins, and C. A. Richardson to Secretary of War, Feb. 15, 1898, RG 92, E 711, Box 2, NARA.
43. Unrau, *Administrative History*, 61–62; Abroe, "All the Profound Scenes," 151.

## 2. CONGRESS, THE WAR DEPARTMENT, AND THE NATIONAL MILITARY PARKS

1. Eric Foner, *Reconstruction: America's Unfinished Revolution, 1863–1877* (New York: Harper Collins, 1989), 538–39.
2. Ibid., xv, 25–26.
3. Ibid., 564, 575–87; Piehler, *Remembering War the American Way*, 64.
4. Ronald F. Lee, *The Origin and Evolution of the National Military Park Idea* (Washington, DC: National Park Service, 1973), 7, 9–10, 12.
5. See David Blight, *Race and Reunion: The Civil War in Memory and Reunion* (Cambridge: Harvard Univ. Press, 2001); C. Vann Woodward, *The Strange Career of Jim Crow*, 3rd ed. (New York: Oxford Univ. Press, 1989).
6. Woodward, *The Strange Career of Jim Crow*.
7. Ibid.
8. For background see Nell Irvin Painter, *Standing at Armageddon: The United States, 1877–1919* (New York: W. W. Norton, 1987), and Vincent P. DeSantis, *The Shaping of Modern America, 1877–1920* (Wheeling: Forum Press, 1973).
9. Lee, *Origin and Evolution*, 13.
10. *Congressional Record*, 51st Cong., 1st sess., 21, pt. 9:8903.
11. For yearly reports of the work, see the Chickamauga and Chattanooga National Military Park Commission Annual Reports in *Annual Report of the Secretary of War*.
12. *Congressional Record*, 51st Cong., 1st sess., 21, pt. 6:5816; *United States Statutes at Large*, 26 (1889–1891): 371, 401; *Congressional Record*, 51st Congress, 1st Session, 21, pt. 10:9776; *House Reports*, 51st Cong., 2nd sess., H. Rept. 4019, 1–3.
13. Lee, *Origin and Evolution*, 40.
14. *Congressional Record*, 51st Cong., 2nd sess., 21, pt. 1:559; *House Reports*, 51st Cong., 2nd sess., report 3024:1–6; *Congressional Record*, 51st Cong., 2nd sess., pt. 21, 1:730, pt. 10:10,080; *House Reports*, 51st Cong., 2nd sess., H. Rept. 3296, 1; *House Reports*, 52nd Cong., 2nd sess., H. Rept. 2188, 1–4; *Congressional Record*, 52nd Cong., 2nd sess., 24, pt. 1:748–49; *Statutes at Large*, 27 (1893): 599–600.
15. *Annual Report of the Secretary of War* (1891), 19; William Gardner Bell, *Secretaries of War and Secretaries of the Army: Portraits and Biographical Sketches* (Washington, DC: Center of Military History, 1982), 92, 94.

16. Bell, *Secretaries of War*, 96.

17. *House Reports*, 59th Cong., 1st sess., H. Rept. 4431, 13; *Annual Report of the Secretary of War* (1895), 31–32; *Congressional Record*, 53rd Cong., 3rd sess., 27, pt. 1:651; *Congressional Record*, 53rd Cong., 3rd sess., 27, pt. 3:2109.

18. Daniel S. Lamont to Shiloh commission, Mar. 30, 1895, Early Park Road Development vertical file, SNMP. For a good study of the roadways at the various parks, see Timothy Davis, Todd A. Croteau, and Christopher H. Marston, eds., *America's National Park Roads and Parkways: Drawings from the Historic American Engineering Record* (Baltimore: Johns Hopkins Univ. Press, 2004).

19. Daniel S. Lamont to Shiloh commission, Mar. 30, 1895, Early Park Road Development vertical file, SNMP.

20. Smith, *This Great Battlefield of Shiloh: History, Memory, and the Establishment of a Civil War National Military Park* (Knoxville: Univ. of Tennessee Press, 2004), 97.

21. *Annual Report of the Secretary of War* (1895), 31–32.

22. *House Reports*, 54th Cong., 1st sess., H. Rept. 374, 1–3; *Senate Reports*, 54th Cong., 1st sess., S. Rept. 526, 1–3; *Congressional Record*, 54th Cong., 1st sess., 28, pt. 3:2443–44, 2491–92, pt. 6:5042, 5380.

23. "Protection of Military Parks," *Statutes at Large* (1897), 29:599–600.

24. "Father of Park Delighted with Progress," *Vicksburg Evening Post*, Nov. 30, 1908. Although nearly half of the congressmen were Civil War veterans in 1890, the number had dropped to 30.53 percent by 1899.

25. *House Reports*, 57th Cong., 1st sess., H. Rept. 771, 1–13; *Annual Report of the Secretary of War* (1899), 44–45; *House Reports*, 57th Cong., 1st sess., H. Rept. 2043, 18–88.

26. *United States v. Gettysburg Electric Railroad Company*, 160, *United States Reports* (1896), 668–86.

27. *Annual Report of the Secretary of War* (1897), 60; Bell, *Secretaries of War*, 98.

28. Bell, *Secretaries of War*, 100.

29. *House Reports*, 57th Cong., 1st sess., H. Rept. 2043, 5; Smith, *This Great Battlefield of Shiloh*, 53.

30. *House Reports*, 57th Cong., 1st sess., H. Rept. 2043, 5–7.

31. Francis B. Heitman, *Historical Register and Dictionary of the United States Army, From Its Organization, September 29, 1789, to Mar. 2, 1903*, 2 vols. (Washington, DC: Government Printing Office, 1903), 1:358.

32. *House Reports*, 59th Cong., 1st sess., H. Rept. 4431, 8–9.

33. Ibid., 8–9, 13–14.

34. Ibid., 13, 17.

35. *House Reports*, 57th Cong., 1st sess., H. Rept. 2043, 2.

36. H. V. Boynton to John P. Nicholson, Apr. 22, 1902, and Cornelius Cadle to D. W. Reed, Mar. 2, 1904, both in series 1, box 38, folder 628, SNMP.

37. *House Reports*, 57th Cong., 1st sess., H. Rept. 2043, 3–4.

38. Lee, *Origin and Evolution*, 44; *House Reports*, 59th Cong., 1st sess., H. Rept. 4431, 16; Cornelius Cadle to Josiah Patterson, Mar. 24, 1902, and Cornelius Cadle to D. W. Reed, Mar. 24, 1902, both in series 1, box 38, folder 628, SNMP.

39. *House Reports*, 59th Cong., 1st sess., H. Rept. 4431, 16; *Annual Report of the Secretary of War* (1904), 39; Bell, *Secretaries of War*, 100, 102.

40. *House Reports*, 58th Cong., 2nd sess., H. Rept. 2325, 1–5.

41. *House Reports*, 59th Cong., 1st sess., H. Rept. 4431, 1–5; *Annual Report of the Secretary of War* (1905), 39.

42. *Statutes at Large*, 37, pt. 1 (1912): 417–18.

43. *Annual Report of the Secretary of War* (1923), 161; *Annual Report of the Secretary of War* (1931), 21.

## 3. "A WESTERN GETTYSBURG"

1. *Society of the Army of the Cumberland: Nineteenth Reunion, Chicago, Illinois, 1888* (Cincinnati: Robert Clarke and Co., 1889), 53–55.

2. Jim Ogden, Historian, Chickamauga and Chattanooga National Military Park, interview by author, Oct. 20, 2003; *House Reports*, 59th Cong., 1st sess., H. Rept. 4431, 10; *Society of the Army of the Cumberland: Twenty-Second Reunion, Columbus, Ohio, 1891* (Cincinnati: Robert Clarke and Co., 1892), 18; *Society of the Army of the Cumberland: Twenty-Third Reunion*, 53; H. V. Boynton, *Dedication of the Chickamauga and Chattanooga National Military Park, September 18–20, 1895: Report of the Joint Committee to Represent the Congress at the Dedication of the Chickamauga and Chattanooga National Military Park* (Washington, DC: Government Printing Office, 1896), 318; H. V. Boynton, *The National Military Park, Chickamauga-Chattanooga: An Historical Guide, With Maps and Illustrations* (Cincinnati: The Robert Clarke Company, 1895), 219, 224; *Chickamauga Memorial Association Proceedings at Chattanooga, Tenn., and Crawfish Springs, Ga., September 19 and 20, 1889* (n.p.: Chattanooga Army of the Cumberland Reunion Entertainment Committee, n.d.), 8.

3. Boynton, *Dedication*, 317; H. V. Boynton, "The Chickamauga Memorial Association," *Southern Historical Society Papers*, 38 vols. (Richmond: Southern Historical Society, 1888), 16:339, 344; Boynton, *National Military Park*, 219, 225; Henry Van Ness Boynton, *Sherman's Historical Raid: The Memoirs in the Light of the Record* (Cincinnati: Wilstach, Baldwin, and Co., 1875). For more information on the Sherman controversy as well as others, see the scrapbooks and newspaper clippings in the Henry Van Ness Boynton Papers, MHS. For more Boynton correspondence, see box 4, folders 1–7, Ezra A. Carman Papers, Manuscripts and Archives Division, Humanities and Social Science Library, NYPL.

4. Boynton, *Dedication*, 317; Boynton, "Chickamauga Memorial Association," 339, 344; Boynton, *National Military Park*, 219, 225.

5. Boynton, "Chickamauga Memorial Association," 339–40.

6. Boynton, *Dedication*, 318; Boynton, "Chickamauga Memorial Association," 348–49. The Union committee consisted of Henry M. Cist, Charles F. Manderson, Russell A. Alger, Absolem Baird, and Boynton. The Confederates were William B. Bate, Alfred H. Colquitt, Edward C. Walthall, Joseph Wheeler, John T. Morgan, James B. Morgan, Marcus J. Wright, and John H. Bankhead. The formation committee was made up of Cist, Colquitt, Baird, Walthall, Wheeler, Wright, Boynton, and Kellogg.

7. Boynton, *Dedication*, 319–21; John C. Paige and Jerome A. Greene, *Administrative History of Chickamauga and Chattanooga National Military Park* (Denver: Denver Service Center, National Park Service, 1983), 14–15, 22; Boynton, *National Military Park*, 243, 247, 250; *Chickamauga Memorial Association Proceedings*, 27. The Society of the Army of the Cumberland nominated Wilder and Fullerton, while the United Confederate Veterans Association chose Wheeler and Wright. For a list of the board of directors see Boynton, *Dedication*, 321. The United Confederate Veterans also held reunions in Chattanooga, the first of which was in 1890.

8. *Chickamauga Memorial Association Proceedings*, 7, 29; Boynton, *National Military Park*, 222, 245.

9. *House Reports*, 51st Cong., 1st sess., H. Rept. 643, 3; Paige and Greene, *Administrative History*, 13; Boynton, *National Military Park*, 221. For the charter see Boynton, *Dedication*, 322–24 or *Chickamauga Memorial Association Proceedings*, 38–42; *The Middle Tennessee and Chattanooga Campaign of 1863, Including the Battle of Chickamauga* (n.p.: United States War Department, 1889). The petition for charter was handled by Atlanta lawyer Julius Brown, who declined any compensation.

10. Boynton, *Dedication*, 324; Paige and Greene, *Administrative History*, 17; Boynton, *National Military Park*, 247, 251 268–69.

11. *Congressional Record*, 51st Cong., 1st sess., 21, pt. 6:5393.

12. Ibid.

13. Ibid.

14. Ibid.

15. *Congressional Record*, 51st Cong., 1st sess., 21, pt. 1:281, pt. 2:1116.

16. *House Reports*, 51st Cong., 1st sess., H. Rept. 643, 1–5.

17. Ibid.

18. Ibid.

19. *Congressional Record*, 51st Cong., 1st sess., 21, pt. 6:5393; Boynton, *National Military Park*, 259. The bill was actually brought up during debate on a river and harbor bill, "which every member of the House was anxious to complete," Boynton wrote.

20. *Congressional Record*, 51st Cong., 1st sess., 21, pt. 6:5393–94; Boynton, *National Military Park*, 260.

21. *Congressional Record*, 51st Cong., 1st sess., 21, pt. 8:7318; *Senate Reports*, 51st Cong., 1st sess., S. Rept. 1297, 1. Boynton, *National Military Park*, 260. Boynton surmised that the faster time in the Senate was attributable to "the Senate clerk being a more rapid reader." The clerk was Brevet Brigadier General Anson McCook, a Chattanooga veteran.

22. *Congressional Record*, 51st Cong., 1st sess., 21, pt. 8:7335; *Congressional Record*, 51st Cong., 1st sess., 21, pt. 9:8473, 8693, 8695, 8903; Boynton, *Dedication*, 329; Boynton, *National Military Park*, 260. For more on the "Billion Dollar Congress," see Thomas Adams Upchurch, *Legislating Racism: The Billion Dollar Congress and the Birth of Jim Crow* (Lexington: Univ. Press of Kentucky, 2004). Additional legislation in the years that followed provided for the purchase of land in Chattanooga and on Missionary Ridge.

23. *Society of the Army of the Cumberland: Twenty-Second Reunion,* 17–18, 21.

24. *Annual Report of the Secretary of War* (1891), 24; Heitman, *Historical Register and Diction-ary,* 1:237, 440, 589, 924; Boynton, *National Military Park,* 272–73; *Society of the Army of the Cumberland: Twenty-Second,* 22:12. With the commission's appointment, the old associa-tion ceased to be a player, one member reporting they "did not see that there was any thing for them to do."

25. Paige and Greene, *Administrative History,* 21.

26. *Annual Report of the Secretary of War* (1891), 24–25; *Society of the Army of the Cumberland: Twenty-Third Reunion,* 23:52–53; Paige and Greene, *Administrative History of Chickamauga and Chattanooga National Military Park,* 25–26.

27. *Annual Report of the Secretary of War* (1891), 25; *Society of the Army of the Cumberland: Twenty-Second Reunion,* 22:13–14, 18; *Society of the Army of the Cumberland: Twenty-Third Reunion,* 23:52, 54.

28. "The Park Lands," *Chattanooga Times,* Feb. 4, 1892; *Annual Report of the Secretary of War* (1892), 19; *Annual Report of the Secretary of War* (1893), 33; *Annual Report of the Secretary of War* (1894), 27; Boynton, *Dedication,* 15.

29. Boynton, *Dedication,* 15–16; *Annual Report of the Secretary of War* (1892), 19; *Annual Report of the Secretary of War* (1893), 33.

30. Sanford Kellogg to E. E. Betts, Jan. 16, 1891 and Mar. 1, 1892, series 1, box 4, folder 104, CHCH; *Annual Report of the Secretary of War* (1894), 27–28; Boynton, *Dedication,* 16; Boynton, *National Military Park,* 3. The farmers in the area in 1863 had employed open-range grazing, allowing their animals to wander in the forest. The animals grazed on the undergrowth, which was soon nonexistent.

31. Joseph S. Fullerton, "Progress and Condition of the Work of Establishing the Chickamauga and Chattanooga National Military Park," Jan. 19, 1895, Chickamauga and Chattanooga National Military Park vertical files, Chattanooga Public Library, 9; *Annual Report of the Sec-retary of War* (1892), 19; *Annual Report of the Secretary of War* (1893), 33; *Annual Report of the Secretary of War* (1894), 28; Boynton, *Dedication,* 17–18; Boynton, *National Military Park,* 3–4, 273–74; *Annual Report of the Secretary of War* (1913), 175. Three of the towers were on Chickamauga battlefield at Hall's Ford, Jay's Mill, and Snodgrass Hill, and two on Mission-ary Ridge at Bragg's headquarters and the right of the Confederate line.

32. Boynton, *National Military Park,* 12, 273; *Annual Report of the Secretary of War* (1894), 28; Boynton, *Dedication,* 16.

33. A. P. Stewart to Secretary of War, May 31, 1893, series 4, box 1, folder 12, CHCH; Boynton, *National Military Park,* 12, 273; Boynton, *Dedication,* 16; Paige and Greene, *Administrative History,* 23, 46–47, 126, 142; Commission Meeting Minutes, Nov. 18, 1892, series 1, box 2, folder 48, CHCH.

34. Commission Meeting Minutes, Oct. 3, 1893, series 1, box 2, folder 49, CHCH; *Annual Report of the Secretary of War* (1900), 183; Paige and Greene, *Administrative History,* 31–32.

35. Boynton, *Dedication,* 7, 10; *Society of the Army of the Cumberland: Twenty-Fourth Reunion, Cleveland, Ohio, 1893* (Cincinnati: Robert Clarke Co., 1894), 50. The commission originally intended to dedicate the park in 1894, but was not far enough along to do so.

36. Boynton, *Dedication,* 14, 21; Official Souvenir Program, Chickamauga and Chattanooga National Military Park vertical file, Chattanooga Public Library.

37. Boynton, *Dedication,* 9–10, 12, 14; James W. Livingood, "Chickamauga and Chattanooga National Military Park," *Tennessee Historical Quarterly* 23, no. 1 (Mar. 1964): 17.

38. Boynton, *National Military Park,* 11; Boynton, *Dedication,* 11, 274, 341. The states placed monuments according to strict regulations issued by the commission in December 1893. The text of the regulations can be found in Boynton, *National Military Park,* 270–71.

39. Boynton, *Dedication,* 11.

40. Ibid., 12.

41. Ibid., 12.

42. Ibid., 13–14, 200–201.

43. Ibid., 28, 37–38, 46, 69.

44. A. P. Stewart to S. G. French, Mar. 25, 1897, Samuel G. French Papers, MDAH; Alonzo Abernathy, *Dedication of Monuments Erected by the State of Iowa* (Des Moines: Emory H. English, 1908), 43; *Annual Report of the Secretary of War* (1897), 57. It was some time before Fullereton's body was recovered from the wreckage.

45. *Annual Report of the Secretary of War* (1897), 56; *Annual Report of the Secretary of War* (1899), 324. For background on the process of acquiring the Lookout Mountain property, see Livingood, "Chickamauga and Chattanooga National Military Park," 19.

46. *Annual Report of the Secretary of War* (1896), 44; *Annual Report of the Secretary of War* (1897), 56–57; *Annual Report of the Secretary of War* (1899), 323–24; Boynton, *National Military Park,* 11.

47. *Annual Report of the Secretary of War* (1897), 56; *Annual Report of the Secretary of War* (1899), 322.

48. *Pennsylvania at Chickamauga and Chattanooga: Ceremonies at the Dedication of the Monuments Erected by the Commonwealth of Pennsylvania to Mark the Positions of the Pennsylvania Commands Engaged in the Battles* (n.p.: Wm. Stanley Ray, 1897), 46; Abernathy, *Dedication of Monuments Erected by the State of Iowa,* 175.

49. Lee, *Origin and Evolution,* 35–36.

50. H. V. Boynton to A. P. Stewart, Sep. 14, 1897, series 1, box 6, folder 159, CHCH; *Annual Report of the Secretary of War* (1897), 57; *Annual Report of the Secretary of War* (1898), 582; Paige and Greene, *Administrative History,* 44, 171. The park's nearness to the railroad was a key factor in sending troops there.

51. *Annual Report of the Secretary of War* (1898), 400–401, 532; Paige and Greene, *Administrative History,* 173–74. Major General James C. Breckinridge would command the post after Wade, but Boynton would soon take over.

52. *Annual Report of the Secretary of War* (1899), 321; Paige and Greene, *Administrative History,* 178.

53. *Annual Report of the Secretary of War* (1899), 321, 324.

54. Ibid., 321–22.

55. *Annual Report of the Secretary of War* (1900), 182, 9; *Annual Report of the Secretary of War* (1905), 130; *Annual Report of the Secretary of War* (1907), 317; *Annual Report of the Secretary*

*of War* (1918), 1461; *Annual Report of the Secretary of War* (1919), 5240; *Annual Report of the Secretary of War* (1920), 1945; Paige and Greene, *Administrative History*, 76, 184–85, 187–92.

56. *Annual Report of the Secretary of War* (1905), 129; *Annual Report of the Secretary of War* (1908), 161–62.

57. *Annual Report of the Secretary of War* (1900), 177; *Annual Report of the Secretary of War* (1901), 356.

58. *Annual Report of the Secretary of War* (1900), 175; *Annual Report of the Secretary of War* (1901), 354–55, 367; *Annual Report of the Secretary of War* (1902), 8.

59. *Annual Report of the Secretary of War* (1902), 8; *Annual Report of the Secretary of War* (1908), 164; Paige and Greene, *Administrative History*, 151.

60. "Empire State Warriors Here on Peace Mission," *Chattanooga Times*, Nov. 14, 1910; *Annual Report of the Secretary of War* (1904), 252; *Annual Report of the Secretary of War* (1913), 177; Paige and Greene, *Administrative History*, 127.

61. *Annual Report of the Secretary of War* (1900), 178.

62. "Commissioners Appointed by States For Inspection," Oct. 9–11, 1900, series 1, box 4, folder 103, CHCH; *Annual Report of the Secretary of War* (1900), 178–80; Paige and Greene, *Administrative History*, 150.

63. *Annual Report of the Secretary of War* (1900), 182; *Annual Report of the Secretary of War* (1900), 304–5.

64. H. V. Boynton, *Battles About Chickamauga, GA., September 19–20, 1863: Organization of the Army of the Cumberland and of the Army of Tennessee* (Washington, DC: Government Printing Office, 1895), copy found in RG 92, E 715, Box 1, NARA; H. V. Boynton, *Battles About Chattanooga, Tenn., November 23–25, 1863: Orchard Knob, Lookout Mountain, Missionary Ridge: Organization of the Union Forces and of the Confederate Forces* (Washington, DC: Government Printing Office, 1895), copy found in RG 92, E 715, Box 1, NARA; Boynton, *Dedication;* Boynton, *National Military Park; Atlas of the Battlefields Chickamauga, Chattanooga, and Vicinity* (Washington, DC: United States War Department, 1897; revised 1901); *Annual Report of the Secretary of War* (1901), 355–56; *Annual Report of the Secretary of War* (1902), 8; Louisiana Purchase Exposition Exhibit, series 1, box 4, folder 105, CHCH. The 1897 *Atlas* contained one Chattanooga and four Chickamauga maps, along with other western theater maps. The expanded 1901 version included seven Chickamauga and five Chattanooga maps, along with the other original western theater maps. The department printed four thousand copies in 1901.

65. *Annual Report of the Secretary of War* (1912), 171; *Annual Report of the Secretary of War* (1913), 178; *Annual Report of the Secretary of War* (1914), 629.

66. A. P. Stewart to E. Betts, Apr. 10, 1899, series 3, box 3, folder 34, CHCH; A. P. Stewart to L. Coleman, May 7, 1895, and L. Coleman to A. P. Stewart, May 8, 1895, series 4, box 7, folder 122, CHCH; Paige and Greene, *Administrative History*, 69; *Annual Report of the Secretary of War* (1899), 321; "Report Upon the Sanitary Conditions of Camp George H. Thomas From the Beginning of its Occupation until Vacated," Oct. 3, 1898, series 6, box 1, folder 1, CHCH.

67. *Indiana at Chickamauga, 1863–1900: Report of the Indiana Commission, Chickamauga and Chattanooga National Military Park* (Indianapolis: Wm. B. Burford, 1901); *Annual Report of the Secretary of War* (1897), 56; *Annual Report of the Secretary of War* (1901), 357; Dave Powell,

"The 96th Illinois and the Battles for Horseshoe Ridge, 1863 and 1895," *North and South* 8, no. 2 (Mar. 2005): 58; Laurence D. Conley, "The Truth about Chickamauga: A Ninth Indiana Regiment's Perspective," Indiana Magazine of History 98 (June 2002): 114–43; H. V. Boynton to James R. Carnahan, Feb. 18, 1902, series 1, box 2, folder 62, CHCH. For a case study of controversy between veterans and the commission, see James A. Kaser, *At the Bivouac of Memory: History, Politics, and the Battle of Chickamauga* (New York: Peter Lang, 1996).

68. Archibald Gracie, *The Truth About Chickamauga* (Dayton: Morningside, 1997), xl–xliv. Gracie later survived the *Titanic*'s maiden voyage. Ogden, interview by author, Oct. 20, 2003. Boynton's 35th Ohio has more monuments and markers than any other unit at Chickamauga, betraying Boynton's subjectivity.

69. *Annual Report of the Secretary of War* (1901), 357; Paige and Greene, *Administrative History*, 23, 145; Boynton, *Dedication*, 313; Boynton, *Sherman's Historical Raid*; Smith, *This Great Battlefield of Shiloh*, 85–87.

70. Kellogg to Secretary of War, Oct. 25, 1892, and A. P. Stewart to Secretary of War, Oct. 26, 1892, series 4, box 5, folder 88, CHCH; A. P. Stewart to Frank G. Smith, June 3, 1896 and A. P. Stewart to J. S. Fullerton, Jan. 3, 1896, series 1, box 4, folder 118, CHCH; "Major Gageby and Others 'Have It In for Engineer E. E. Betts,'" undated newspaper clipping, series 1, box 4, folder 118, CHCH; Paige and Greene, *Administrative History*, 128.

71. Frank G. Smith to E. E. Betts, Nov. 30, 1897, series 1, box 2, folder 60, CHCH; *Annual Report of the Secretary of War* (1900), 182; *Annual Report of the Secretary of War* (1901), 366; *Annual Report of the Secretary of War* (1913), 178; Paige and Greene, *Administrative History*, 80, 84.

72. "Memorandum of Inspection of the Chickamauga and Chattanooga National Park," series 1, box 5, folder 135, CHCH; *Annual Report of the Secretary of War* (1908), 164–65; *Annual Report of the Secretary of War* (1909), 24; *Annual Report of the Secretary of War* (1915), 860.

73. H. V. Boynton to E. E. Betts, Dec. 21, 1898, series 1, box 3, folder 72, CHCH; *Annual Report of the Secretary of War* (1901), 351; *Annual Report of the Secretary of War* (1902), 7; *Annual Report of the Secretary of War* (1912), 171; Paige and Greene, *Administrative History*, 49; untitled and undated newspaper clipping, series 1, box 4, folder 110, CHCH.

74. *Annual Report of the Secretary of War* (1905), 132.

75. Ezra A. Carman to E. E. Betts, Nov. 11 and 20, 1907, series 2, box 7, folder 118, CHCH; *Annual Report of the Secretary of War* (1910), 293; Richard B. Randolph to Joseph B. Cumming, Sep. 28, 1921, series 2, box 13, folder 208, CHCH; J. W. Colburn to John C. Scofield, Apr. 30, 1910, series 1, box 2, folder 65, CHCH; "Chickamauga Park Commission Thursday," *Chattanooga Times*, June 6, 1911; "My Severance From Park Commission Has Not Been Legally Accomplished," *Chattanooga Times*, Oct. 15, 1911; Paige and Greene, *Administrative History*, 44, 54. For more on Carman, see box 9, folders 5–8, Ezra A. Carman Papers, NYPL.

76. Baxter Smith Obituary, *Chattanooga News*, June 26, 1919; *Annual Report of the Secretary of War* (1909), 23.

77. "My Severance From Park Commission Has Not Been Legally Accomplished," *Chattanooga Times*, Oct. 15, 1911; "Disagreement in Park Commission Results in Removal of Maj. Colburn," *Chattanooga Times*, Oct. 6, 1911; W. J. Colburn to William Howard Taft, Nov. 1911, series 1, box 4, folder 120, CHCH; "Protest of W. J. Colburn," June 29, 1911, series 1, box 2, folder 52, CHCH; Commission Meeting Minutes, May 31 and June 30, 1911, series 1, b2, folder 52,

CHCH; *Annual Report of the Secretary of War* (1909), 23; *Annual Report of the Secretary of War* (1910), 293; *Annual Report of the Secretary of War* (1912), 171; *Annual Report of the Secretary of War* (1913), 175; Paige and Greene, *Administrative History*, 54, 153. Smith would die on Oct. 7, 1912.

78. Lee, *Origin and Evolution*, 44–45; *Annual Report of the Secretary of War* (1912), 171.

79. J. W. Colburn to John C. Scofield, May 13, 1910, series 1, box 2, folder 65, CHCH; *Annual Report of the Secretary of War* (1910), 293; Paige and Greene, *Administrative History*, 52. The park's enabling legislation, which required an office in Washington, had to be amended in order for the move to take place.

80. Commission Meeting Minutes, Dec. 11, 1918, series 1, box 2, folder 58, CHCH; *Annual Report of the Secretary of War* (1915), 859; *Annual Report of the Secretary of War* (1918), 1459; Charles Grosvenor obituary, *Columbus Evening Dispatch*, Oct. 30, 1917; Mary Wilder to R. B. Randolph, Oct. 20, 1917, series 1, box 5, folder 140, CHCH; John T. Wilder obituary, *Chattanooga Times*, Oct. 21, 1917; 1922 Annual Report, series 1, box 1, folder 31, CHCH.

81. "Famous Charge at Battle of Chickamauga Re-Enacted; Cry of 'Steam Roller' Resented by Commander Entenz," *Chattanooga Times*, Sep. 19, 1923; Paige and Greene, *Administrative History*, 56, 156, 201; Richard Randolph obituary, *Chattanooga Times*, Oct. 9, 1937. Some in the War Department opposed Chickamauga's transfer out of the department on the grounds of military occupation, its being so near Fort Oglethorpe. Randolph would remain superintendent until his death in October 1937.

82. *Annual Report of the Secretary of War* (1895), 31–32.

## 4. "THE EXPERIMENT AT ANTIETAM"

1. *House Reports,* 59th Cong., 1st sess., H. Rept. 4431, 9. For a history of Antietam National Battlefield, see Susan W. Trail, "Remembering Antietam: Commemoration and Preservation of a Civil War Battlefield," (Ph. D. diss., Univ. of Maryland, 2005).

2. *Keedysville Antietam Wavelet,* Oct. 15, 1887; "Antietam Memorial Association," *Keedysville Antietam Wavelet,* May 24, 1890; Reed, "National Cemeteries and National Military Parks," 371.

3. *Congressional Record,* 51st Cong., 1st sess., 21, pt. 6:5816; *Keedysville Antietam Wavelet,* June 21, 1890; *Statutes at Large,* 26 (1890): 371, 401.

4. *Congressional Record,* 51st Cong., 1st sess., 21, pt. 10:9776; *House Reports,* 51st Cong., 2nd sess., H. Rept. 4019, 1–3; Charles W. Snell and Brown, *Antietam National Battlefield,* 73.

5. For a brief bio of McComas, see his entry in the rare *Biographical Directory of the United States Congress.* Fortunately, the directory has been put online: for McComas, see http://bioguide.congress.gov/scripts/biodisplay.pl?index=M000351. Susan W. Trail, in her Ph.D. dissertation, "Remembering Antietam: Commemoration and Preservation of a Civil War Battlefield" (Univ. of Maryland, 2005), argues that the important policy decision to keep Antietam a small park was not made until the later 1894 reorganization..

6. Secretary of War Memo, June 11, 1891, RG 92, E 707, box 1, NARA.

7. L. E. McComas to Redfield Proctor, Oct. 17, 1890, W. Cogswell to Secretary of War, May 26, 1891, E. A. Carman to R. N. Bachelder, June 3, 1891, R. N. Bachelder to Secretary of War,

June 11, 1891, E. A. Carman to L. E. McComas, July 4, 1891, all in RG 92, E 707, box 1, NARA.

8. *Annual Report of the Secretary of War* (1892), 363; R. N. Bachelder to Depot Quartermaster, July 8, 1891, and Henry Heth to R. N. Bachelder, Aug. 12, 1891, both in RG 92, E 707, box 1, NARA; Snell and Brown, *Antietam National Battlefield*, 73; Ezra J. Warner, *Generals in Gray: Lives of the Confederate Commanders* (Baton Rouge: Louisiana State Univ. Press, 1959), 133; Trail, "Remembering Antietam," 184–85.

9. J. C. Stearns and H. Heth to Secretary of War, Oct. 19, 1891, Antietam Board to R. N. Bachelder, Jan. 18, 1892, J. C. Stearns and H. Heth to R. N. Bachelder, June 10, 1892, Sep. 26, 1892, and June 27, 1893, all in RG 92, E 707, Box 1, NARA; David A. Lilley, "The Antietam Battlefield Board and Its Atlas; Or the Genesis of the Carman-Cope Maps," Ezra Carman file, ANTI; *Annual Report of the Secretary of War* (1892), 364; *Annual Report of the Secretary of War* (1893), 223; Snell and Brown, *Antietam National Battlefield*, 76, 84; Lafayette McLaws to Henry Heth, Dec. 13, 1894, and Francis Barlow to Antietam Board, May 20, 1893, both in Ezra Carman file, ANTI.

10. *Annual Report of the Secretary of War* (1892), 364; *Keedysville Antietam Valley Record*, Oct. 5, 1894; J. C. Stearns and H. Heth to R. N. Bachelder, June 10, 1892, J. C. Stearns to R. N. Bachelder, Aug. 27, 1892, Antietam Board to R. N. Bachelder, Jan. 13, 1894, all in RG 92, E 707, Box 1, NARA.

11. Antietam Board to R. N. Bachelder, Jan. 13, 1894, and J. C. Stearns and H. Heth to R. N. Bachelder, June 27, 1893, both in RG 92, E 707, box 1, NARA; *Annual Report of the Secretary of War* (1893), 223.

12. Daniel S. Lamont to Quartermaster General, July 14, 1894, and R. N. Bachelder to J. C. Stearns, July 19, 1894, both in RG 92, E 707, box 1, NARA.

13. John C. Stearns to Daniel S. Lamont, July 26, 1894, H. C. Lodge to Daniel S. Lamont, Aug. 13, 1894, Henry Heth to R. N. Bachelder, Aug. 1, 1894, all in RG 92, E 707, box 1, NARA.

14. E. A. Carman to R. N. Bachelder, July 30, 1894, George B. Davis to Secretary of War, Oct. 4, 1894, Daniel S. Lamont to George B. Davis, Oct. 5, 1894, Daniel S. Lamont Memo, Oct. 8, 1894, Daniel S. Lamont to Quartermaster General, Oct. 8, 1894, Jed. Hotchkiss to George B. Davis, Oct. 15, 1894, all in RG 92, E 707, box 1, NARA; Heitman, *Historical Register and Dictionary*, 1:358; David A. Lilley, "The Antietam Battlefield Board and Its Atlas: Or the Genesis of the Carman-Cope Maps," Ezra Carman file, ANTI. On Carman, see John Connor Scully, "Ezra Carman: Soldier and Historian," M.A. thesis, George Mason Univ., 1997. For more on Carman at Antietam, see box 9, folders 1–4, Ezra A. Carman Papers, NYPL.

15. Daniel S. Lamont, memorandum, Oct. 8, 1894, and R. N. Bachelder to Chief Clerk, Oct. 15, 1894, both in RG 92, E 707, box 1, NARA; Daniel S. Lamont to Quartermaster General, Oct. 8, 1894, RG 92, E 89, file 10048, NARA.

16. *Annual Report of the Secretary of War* (1894), 29, 255–56.

17. Jed Hotchkiss to George B. Davis, Oct. 20 and Nov. 30, 1894, and George B. Davis to E. A. Carman, Nov. 27, 1894, all in RG 92, E 707, box 1, NARA.

18. E. A. Carman to George B. Davis, Oct. 23, 1894, RG 92, E 707, box 1, NARA.

19. George B. Davis to E. A. Carman, Oct. 13, 1894, RG 92, E 707, box 1, NARA.

20. George B. Davis to Jed Hotchkiss, Oct. 13 and 23, 1894, Joseph B. Doe to George B. Davis, Oct. 20, 1894, Jed Hotchkiss to George B. Davis, Oct. 20 and 25, 1894, all in RG 92, E 707, box 1, NARA; David A. Lilley, "The Antietam Battlefield Board and Its Atlas: Or the Genesis of the Carman-Cope Maps," Ezra Carman file, ANTI.

21. Jed Hotchkiss to George B. Davis, Nov. 5 and 27, 1894, both in RG 92, E 707, box 1, NARA; George B. Davis to Jed Hotchkiss, Feb. 23, 1895, and Jed Hotchkiss to George B. Davis, Feb. 27, 1895, both in RG 92, E 707, box 2, NARA.

22. George B. Davis to Jed Hotchkiss, Mar. 25, 1895, Jed Hotchkiss to George B. Davis, Apr. 30, 1895, George B. Davis to E. A. Carman, June 25, 1895, E. A. Carman to George B. Davis, June 27, 1895, E. A. Carman to George B. Davis, July 12, 1895, George B. Davis, memorandum, Aug. 2, 1895, all in RG 92, E 707, box 2, NARA.

23. George B. Davis to A. L. Crist, Oct. 22, 1894, and George B. Davis and Henry Heth to Secretary of War, Nov. 7, 1894, both in RG 92, E 707, box 1, NARA.

24. E. A. Carman to George B. Davis, Oct. 23 and 28 and Nov. 3 and 5, 1894, and Jed Hotchkiss to George B. Davis, Oct. 25, 1894, all in RG 92, E 707, box 1, NARA.

25. George B. Davis to E. A. Carman, Nov. 6, 1894, and George B. Davis to Jed Hotchkiss, Nov. 7, 1894, both in RG 92, E 707, box 1, NARA.

26. George B. Davis to H. V. Boynton, Nov. 17, 1894, George B. Davis to E. A. Carman, Nov. 26 and Dec. 7, 1894, George B. Davis to Otho Poffenberger, Dec. 7, 1894, E. A. Carman to George B. Davis, Dec. 10, 1894, all in RG 92, E 707, box 1, NARA; *Keedysville Antietam Valley Record,* Oct. 3, 1895.

27. E. A. Carman to George B. Davis, Dec. 12, 15, 18, and 19, 1894, George B. Davis to E. A. Carman, Dec. 13 and 20, 1894, Elmer E. Piper appointment, Dec. 14, 1894, George B. Davis to James Snyder, Jan. 29 and 31, 1895, all in RG 92, E 707, box 1, NARA; George B. Davis to James Snyder, Feb. 20, 1895, RG 92, E 707, box 2, NARA; *Keedysville Antietam Valley Record,* Aug. 20, 1896; *Keedysville Antietam Wavelet,* May 19, 1888.

28. George B. Davis to E. A. Carman, Jan. 21 and Apr. 12, 1895, Anna Newcomer to George B. Davis, Jan. 23, 1895, Charles H. Locher to George B. Davis, Jan. 26, 1895, Charles G. Biggs to George B. Davis, May 23, 1895, all in RG 92, E 707, box 1, NARA.

29. George B. Davis to E. A. Carman, Apr. 26, 1895, and E. A. Carman to George B. Davis, Apr. 27, 1895, both in RG 92, E 707, box 2, NARA.

30. *Keedysville Antietam Valley Record,* Mar. 22, 1895, E. A. Carman to George B. Davis, Mar. 9, Apr. 1, Apr. 11, and June 26, 1895, M. F. Smith appointment, Apr. 6, 1895, George B. Davis to James March and Co., Mar. 23 and 27, 1895, George B. Davis to James Snyder, May 30, 1895, George B. Davis to E. A. Carman, June 25, 1895, M. F. Smith to E. A. Carman, July 19, 1895, George W. Davis, memorandum, Jan. 17, 1896, all in RG 92, E 707, box 2, NARA.

31. George B. Davis to Otto Poffenberger, Dec. 7, 1894, E. A. Carman to George B. Davis, Dec. 15, 1894, George B. Davis to E. A. Carman, Dec. 20, 1894, all in RG 92, E 707, box 1, NARA; George B. Davis to Adam H. Baer, Feb. 21, 1895, and George B. Davis to Charles G. Biggs, Feb. 23, 1895, both in RG 92, E 707, box 2, NARA; Adam Baer contract, Mar. 27, 1895, Antietam National Battlefield Legislation and Administrative file, ANTI.

32. George B. Davis to Adam H. Baer, Feb. 21, Mar. 15, Apr. 29, and May 10, 1895 and Aug. 7, 1896, E. A. Carman to George B. Davis, Mar. 9 and 28 and Apr. 30, 1895, and May 1 and Sep. 12, 1896, George B. Davis to E. N. Gray, Mar. 23, 1895, George B. Davis to E. A. Carman, Apr. 6 and May 29, 1895, all in RG 92, E 707, box 2, NARA.

33. John P. Nicholson to George B. Davis, Oct. 15 and 22, 1894, and George B. Davis to E. A. Carman, Nov. 5, 1894, all in RG 92, E 707, box 1, NARA. See George R. Large and Joe A. Swisher, *Battle of Antietam: The Official History by the Antietam Battlefield Board* (Shippensburg, PA: Burd Street Press, 1998), for texts of Antietam's tablets.

34. George B. Davis to Jed. Hotchkiss, Oct. 31, 1894, George B. Davis to Ezra Carman, Oct. 31 and Nov. 5, 1894, Ezra Carman to George B. Davis, Nov. 10, 1894, George B. Davis to John P. Nicholson, Nov. 17, 1894, Jed Hotchkiss to George B. Davis, Nov. 27, 1894, all in RG 92, E 707, box 1, NARA.

35. George B. Davis to John P. Nicholson, Nov. 17, 1894, and George B. Davis to W. F. Rogers, Jan. 22, 1895, both in RG 92, E 707, box 1, NARA.

36. George B. Davis to H. V. Boynton, Nov. 17, 1894, George B. Davis to George D. Rise, Nov. 27, 1894, George B. Davis to J. E. Evans, Dec. 21, 1894, all in RG 92, E 707, box 1, NARA.

37. George B. Davis to J. E. Evans, Feb. 19 and 21, 1895, J. E. Evans to George B. Davis, Feb. 23, 1895, George B. Davis to Henry Edwards, Mar. 4, 1895, George B. Davis to L. M. Poffenberger, Mar. 4, 1895, George B. Davis to Board of County Commissioners, Mar. 4, 1895, Henry Edwards to George B. Davis, Mar. 9, 1895, John P. Nicholson to George B. Davis, Mar. 12, 1895, L. W. Poffenberger to George B. Davis, Mar. 12, 1895, George B. Davis to E. A. Carman, Mar. 19, 1895, George B. Davis to John P. Nicholson, Mar. 23, 1895, D. A. Staley to George B. Davis, Apr. 4, 1895, all in RG 92, E 707, box 2, NARA; *Keedysville Antietam Valley Record,* Mar. 29, 1895.

38. George B. Davis to J. E. Evans, Apr. 4 and 5, 1895, J. E. Evans to George B. Davis, Apr. 4 and 8, 1895, all in RG 92, E 707, box 2, NARA.

39. J. E. Evans to George B. Davis, May 4 and 8, and Aug. 7, 1895, George B. Davis to Secretary of War, May 1, 1895, E. A. Carman to George B. Davis, Apr. 11 and July 12, 1895, Allen R. Adams to J. E. Evans, July 19, 1895, J. E. Evans to Allen R. Adams, July 22, 1895, George B. Davis to J. E. Evans, Aug. 1, 1895, George W. Davis to J. E. Evans, Aug. 9, 1895, J. E. Evans to George W. Davis, Oct. 5, 1895, George W. Davis to George B. Davis, Oct. 9, 1895, E. A. Carman to George W. Davis, Dec. 4, 1895, all in RG 92, E 707, box 2, NARA; *Keedysville Antietam Valley Record,* Dec. 12, 1895.

40. George B. Davis and Henry Heth to Secretary of War, Nov. 7, 1894, George B. Davis to Secretary of War, Jan. 21, 1895, and George B. Davis to James Snyder, Jan. 26, 1895, all in RG 92, E 707, box 1, NARA; George W. Davis, memorandum, Jan. 17, 1896, George B. Davis to E. A. Carman, May 16, 1896, E. A. Carman to George W. Davis, Aug. 12, 1896, E. A. Carman to George B. Davis, Dec. 11, 1896, Henry Kyd Douglas to E. A. Carman, Sep. 14, 1896, all in RG 92, E 707, box 2, NARA; *Keedysville Antietam Valley Record,* Aug. 20, 1896; *Annual Report of the Secretary of War* (1897), 58; E. A. Carman to Henry Kyd Douglas, Sep. 12, 1896, Ezra Carman file, ANTI.

41. George B. Davis to E. A. Carman, Dec. 20, 1894, RG 92, E 707, box 1, NARA; E. A. Carman to George W. Davis, July 29, 1895, George W. Davis to Joseph G. Cannon, Mar. 24, 1896, George W. Davis to E. A. Carman, Sep. 9, 1896, all in RG 92, E 707, box 2, NARA; *Annual Report of the Secretary of War* (1896), 45.

42. E. A. Carman to George B. Davis, Dec. 12, 1894, and George B. Davis to E. A. Carman, Oct. 13, 1894, both in RG 92, E 707, box 1, NARA; George B. Davis to John P. Nicholson, Mar. 23, 1895, Charles G. Biggs to George B. Davis, Mar. 27, 1895, E. A. Carman to George B. Davis, June 7, 1895, George W. Davis to Nathan Eastbrook, Dec. 9, 1895, all in RG 92, E 707, box 2, NARA.

43. John W. Frazier to Daniel S. Lamont, Sep. 5, 1896, RG 92, E 707, box 2, NARA; Dedication of Philadelphia Brigade Monument, Sep. 17, 1896, Pennsylvania Monument file, ANTI.

44. *Annual Report of the Secretary of War* (1895), 32; *Keedysville Antietam Valley Record*, Sep. 19, 1895.

45. E. A. Carman to George B. Davis, July 31, 1895, George B. Davis, memorandum, Aug. 1, 1895, George W. Davis appointment, Aug. 1, 1895, Joseph B. Doe to E. A. Carman, Aug. 17, 1895, Joseph B. Doe to Henry Heth, Aug. 17, 1895, Daniel S. Lamont to E. A. Carman, Aug. 17, 1895, all in RG 92, E 707, box 2, NARA; Trail, "Remembering Antietam," 219.

46. George W. Davis to R. W. Grove, Sep. 13, 1895, and George W. Davis to Nathan Eastbrook, Dec. 9, 1895, both in RG 92, E 707, box 2, NARA; Heitman, *Historical Register and Dictionary*, 1:358.

47. *Keedysville Antietam Valley Record*, May 7, 1896; George W. Davis to E. A. Carman, May 19, 1896, George W. Davis to Daniel S. Lamont, June 27, 1896, and Jed Hotchkiss to Henry St. George Tucker, May 30 and June 23, 1896, all in RG 92, E 707, box 2, NARA.

48. David A. Lilley, "The Antietam Battlefield Board and Its Atlas: Or the Genesis of the Carman-Cope Maps," Ezra Carman file, ANTI; George W. Davis to John P. Nicholson, Nov. 27, 1896, John P. Nicholson to George W. Davis, Nov. 30, 1896, E. B. Cope to George W. Davis, Dec. 2, 1896, E. A. Carman to George W. Davis, Dec. 18, 1896, all in RG 92, E 707, box 3, NARA.

49. John P. Nicholson to George W. Davis, Dec. 31, 1896, Feb. 11, 1897, and June 14, 1897, George W. Davis to Secretary of War, Mar. 2 and May 28, 1897, George W. Davis to John P. Nicholson, June 14, 1897, George W. Davis to E. A. Carman, June 21, 1897, all in RG 92, E 707, box 3, NARA.

50. George W. Davis to Secretary of War, July 28, 1897; E. B. Cope to George W. Davis, Aug. 11 and Sep. 24, 1897; George W. Davis to E. B. Cope, Nov. 13, 1897, Jan. 22 and Feb. 2, 1898; George W. Davis to John P. Nicholson, Feb. 2, 1898, all in RG 92, E 707, box 3, NARA.

51. George W. Davis to Secretary of War, May 17 and Oct. 15, 1897, Henry Heth Appointment, July 31, 1897, George W. Davis to Acting Secretary of War, Jan. 31, 1898, all in RG 92, E 707, box 3, NARA.

52. George W. Davis to Secretary of War, July 12, 1898, and George W. Davis to George D. Meiklejohn, Mar. 28, 1898, both in RG 92, E 707, box 3, NARA; Snell and Brown, *Antietam National Battlefield*, 109, 111.

53. George W. Davis to F. A. Cummings, July 29, 1897, RG 92, E 707, box 3, NARA; Heitman, *Historical Register and Dictionary*, 1:358; Warner, *Generals in Gray*, 133.

54. M. J. Ludington to Depot Quartermaster, Mar. 30, 1898, and Assistant Quartermaster to Depot Quartermaster, Apr. 7, 1898, both in RG 92, E 89, file 109863, NARA.

55. Depot Quartermaster to Quartermaster General, Apr. 27, 1900, and J. M. Ludington to Secretary of War, May 3, 1900, both in RG 92, E 89, file 109863, NARA.

56. M. J. Ludington to Depot Quartermaster, June 22, 1900, RG 92, E 89, file 109863, NARA; Elihu Root to Charles W. Adams, June 14, 1900, RG 92, E 89, file 152827, NARA.

57. Charles W. Adams to H. L. Pettus, Apr. 1, 1912, George W. Graham to J. E. Normoyle, Sep. 13, 1912, John L. Cook to Depot Quartermaster, Dec. 2, 1913, all in RG 92, E 89, file 362360, NARA; Thomas A. Poffenberger to David J. Lewis, June 13, 1913, and Assistant Secretary of War to David J. Lewis, July 3, 1913, both in RG 92, E 89, file 463850, NARA.

58. Quartermaster General to Depot Quartermaster, June 1, 1904, and E. A. Carman to C. F. Humphrey, Sep. 23, 1904, both in RG 92, E 89, file 109863, NARA; Charles W. Adams to E. A. Carman, Dec. 19, 1909, and E. H. Humphrey to Charles W. Adams, Jan. 6, 1910, both in RG 92, E 89, file 256732, NARA; David A. Lilley, "The Antietam Battlefield Board and Its Atlas; Or the Genesis of the Carman-Cope Maps," Ezra Carman file, ANTI; C. F. Humphrey to Secretary of War, May 24, 1905; Robert Shaw Oliver to Charles W. Adams, May 27, 1905, George A. Pearre to William Howard Taft, May 29, 1905, C. F. Humphrey to Charles W. Adams, May 31, 1905, all in RG 92, E 89, File 109863, NARA.

59. W. N. Pickerill to Quartermaster General, Nov. 1, 1909, RG 92, E 89, file 256732, NARA; Charles W. Adams to Depot Quartermaster, May 2, 1910, and John C. Scofield to Secretary of War, Aug. 15, 1910, both in RG 92, E 89, file 262450, NARA.

60. *Pennsylvania at Antietam: Report of the Antietam Battlefield Memorial Commission of Pennsylvania and Ceremonies at the Dedication of the Monuments Erected by the Commonwealth of Pennsylvania to Mark the Position of Thirteen of the Pennsylvania Commands Engaged in the Battle* (Harrisburg, PA: Harrisburg Publishing Company, 1906), 47, 203.

61. D. Cunningham and W. W. Miller, *Antietam: Report of the Ohio Antietam Battlefield Commission* (Springfield, OH: Springfield Publishing Company, 1904), 110, 127. For more information see the Ohio Monument file, ANTI.

62. *Dedication of the New York State Monument on the Battlefield of Antietam* (Albany: J. B. Lyon Company, 1923), 38, 52. For more information see the New York Monument file, ANTI.

63. J. M. Dalzell to General, Oct. 19, 1903, and A. W. Butt to Quartermaster General, Nov. 14, 1903, both in RG 92, E 89, file 109863, NARA; J. L. Pettus to Quartermaster General, June 7, 1912, and John L. Cook to Depot Quartermaster, June 6, 1912, both in RG 92, E 89, file 370969, NARA; Snell and Brown, *Antietam National Battlefield*, 123–24; Trail, "Remembering Antietam," 297.

64. J. L. Pettus to Captain Humphrey, June 8, 1912, RG 92, E 89, file 370969, NARA; George W. Graham oath, Aug. 5, 1912, RG 92, E 89, file 371906, NARA.

65. Quartermaster General to Secretary of War, June 22, 1912, statement of Patterson Roulette, Apr. 11, 1913, statement of Harriet Highberger, Apr. 12, 1913, statement of Jennie Graham, Apr. 13, 1913, statement of E. S. Cummings, Apr. 13, 1913, all in RG 92, E 89, file 371906, NARA; John W. Carroll to Woodrow Wilson, May 7, 1913, RG 92, E 89, file 457776, NARA.

66. C. P. Spence to Depot Quartermaster, Apr. 14, 1913, statement of Hezekiah Thomas, Apr. 11, 1913, statement of C. P. Spence, Apr. 11, 1913, all in RG 92, E 89, file 371906, NARA; C. P. Spence to Depot Quartermaster, Apr. 12, 1913, and Chief Quartermaster Corps to Secretary of War, May 14, 1913, both in RG 92, E 89, file 457776, NARA.

67. George W. Graham to David J. Lewis, RG 92, E 89, file 371906, NARA; Henry Breckinridge, memorandum, Aug. 1, 1913, RG 92, E 89, file 457776, NARA.

68. Snell and Brown, *Antietam National Battlefield*, 129, 561. For a later description of the battlefield, see the 1921-era Fred Cross file in the Antietam National Battlefield Archives. Cross returned and spent many days on the battlefield, ultimately producing a short monograph entitled "Antietam, September 17, 1862," which is a general description of his exploration of the field.

## 5. "THIS GREAT BATTLEFIELD"

1. *Report of the Proceedings of the Society of the Army of the Tennessee at the Twenty-Fifth Meeting held at Chicago, Ills. September 12th and 13th, 1893* (Cincinnati: F. W. Freeman, 1893), 58, 60–61.

2. Ibid., 59–61.

3. Ibid., 59, 62.

4. Ibid., 60–61. At least some of the vice presidents were named without their prior knowledge or consent.

5. *Report of the Twenty-Fifth Meeting*, 59; *Report of the Proceedings of the Society of the Army of the Tennessee at the Twenty-Sixth Meeting held at Council Bluffs, Iowa. October 3rd and 4th, 1894* (Cincinnati: F. W. Freeman, 1895), 126; *Memphis Commercial Appeal*, Dec. 5, 1894, 1.

6. *Report of the Twenty-Fifth Meeting*, 59.

7. "List of Lands Optioned to John A. McClernand, President, E. T. Lee, Secretary, and J. W. Coleman, Treasurer, of the Shiloh Battlefield Association" and "Copy of Option Form," blank and undated, both in series 1, box 19, folder 268, SNMP; "Memorandum of Agreement," Mar. 26, 1895, series 1, box 21, folder 295, SNMP; *Report of the Twenty-Sixth Meeting*, 125.

8. *Report of the Twenty-Fifth Meeting*, 59.

9. David B. Henderson compiled service record, NARA; *Biographical Directory of the United States Congress* (Washington, DC: Government Printing Office, 1989), 1170; David W. Reed, *Campaigns and Battles of the Twelfth Regiment Iowa Veteran Volunteer Infantry: From Organization, September, 1861, to Muster-Out, January 20, 1866* (n.p.: n.p., n.d.), 64.

10. *Report of the Twenty-Sixth Meeting*, 127.

11. *Congressional Record*, 53rd Cong., 3rd sess., 27, pt. 1:19–20.

12. Ibid., 19; *Congressional Record*, 53rd Cong., 2nd sess., 26, pt. 4:3368, pt. 7:6722; *House Reports*, 53rd Cong., 2nd sess., H. Rept. 1139, 1–5.

13. *House Reports*, 53rd Cong., 2nd sess., H. Rept. 1139, 1–5.

14. Ibid.

15. *Report of the Twenty-Sixth Meeting*, 127–28.

16. *Congressional Record*, 53rd Cong., 3rd sess., 27, pt. 1:20.

17. Ibid.

18. Ibid.

19. Ibid., 21.

20. Ibid.

21. Ibid., 73, 270; *Senate Reports*, 53rd Cong., 3rd sess., S. Rept. 722, 1–4.

22. *Congressional Record,* 53rd Cong., 3rd sess., 27, pt. 1:393. Of course, Bate and Harris were interested in the project because the proposed park was in their state.

23. *Congressional Record,* 53rd Cong., 3rd sess., 27, pt. 1:430.

24. Ibid., 651. Grover Cleveland was not a stranger to Civil War memory controversy. In his first term, he had returned Confederate battle flags to southern states, earning the ire of many northern Republicans.

25. E. C. Dawes to George B. Davis, Dec. 29, 1894, RG 92, E 712, box 1, NARA; J. W. Irwin compiled service record, NARA; F. A. Large appointment, Sep. 24, 1897, RG 92, E 712, box 1, NARA; J. M. Riddell appointment, June 1, 1895, series 1, box 37, folder 618, SNMP.

26. George B. Davis to R. F. Looney, Apr. 16, 1895, series 1, box 37, folder 618, SNMP.

27. George B. Davis to D. B. Henderson, Feb. 20, 1895, RG 92, E 713, NARA; D. B. Henderson to Cornelius Cadle, Mar. 29, 1895, series 1, box 35, folder 531, SNMP; D. B. Henderson to Cornelius Cadle, July 7, 1895, series 1, box 13, folder 153, SNMP; D. B. Henderson to D. W. Reed, Jan. 13, 1895, series 1, box 35, folder 555, SNMP.

28. Daniel S. Lamont to Cornelius Cadle, Mar. 12, 1895, RG 92, E 713, NARA; George B. Davis to Secretary of War, Mar. 18, 1895, series 1, box 19, folder 267, SNMP.

29. George B. Davis to Cornelius Cadle, Mar. 28, 1895, series 1, box 37, folder 618, SNMP.

30. George B. Davis to Cornelius Cadle, May 6, 1895, series 1, box 37, folder 618, SNMP; Daniel S. Lamont Order, Feb. 11, 1895; George B. Davis to Cornelius Cadle, Mar. 26, 1895, Daniel S. Lamont to Cornelius Cadle, Mar. 26, 1895, Daniel S. Lamont to Cornelius Cadle, Apr. 20, 1895, Daniel S. Lamont to Cornelius Cadle, May 10, 1895; all in RG 92, E 713, NARA; George B. Davis to Cornelius Cadle, Apr. 8, 1895, series 1, box 37, folder 618, SNMP.

31. George B. Davis to Cornelius Cadle, Apr. 27, 1895 and May 13, 1895, series 1, box 37, folder 618, SNMP; Clayton Hart to John L. Clem, Apr. 17, 1895, series 4, Letters Sent, vol. 1, SNMP, 157; Otis H. Jones, "Building Shiloh Park," vertical file, SNMP, 6.

32. Isabell Borgeson, "Character Sketch of Colonel E. T. Lee," series 1, box 13, folder 153, SNMP; "Feel Indignant," newspaper clipping, no date, no heading, series 1, box 39, folder 635, SNMP.

33. D. C. Buell to Robert F. Looney, June 9, 1895, Robert F. Looney Collection, folder 64, MSCPL; R. F. Looney to Cornelius Cadle, Aug. 21, 1895, series 1, box 39, folder 635, SNMP; John A. McClernand to Cornelius Cadle, Sep. 26 and Oct. 11, 1895, series 1, box 39, folder 635, SNMP.

34. George B. Davis to Cornelius Cadle, Apr. 17 and June 25, 1895, "Letter Book of the Shiloh National Military Park Commission," RG 92, E 713, NARA. As the majority of the association's officers, Lee and Coleman held the fate of the land in their hands.

35. George B. Davis to Cornelius Cadle, Sep. 24, 1895, RG 92, E 713, NARA.

36. Daniel S. Lamont to Cornelius Cadle, Apr. 20, 1895, and Daniel S. Lamont to George B. Davis, Mar. 19, 1895, both in RG 92, E 713, NARA; George B. Davis to Cornelius Cadle, Mar. 23, 1895, series 1, box 35, folder 570, SNMP.

37. Atwell Thompson to Cornelius Cadle, July 9, 1895, series 1, box 17, folder 249, SNMP; Atwell Thompson to Shiloh National Military Park Commission, July 10, 1896, series 1, box 40, folder 640, SNMP.

38. "Preliminary Map, Battlefield of Shiloh," Dec. 1, 1895, series 7, drawer 1, folder 7, SNMP; Atwell Thompson to Shiloh National Military Park Commission, July 10, 1896, series 1, box 40, folder 640, SNMP.

39. Elihu Root to Cornelius Cadle, Mar. 26, 1902, series 1, box 37, folder 601, SNMP; J. W. Irwin to Cornelius Cadle, Sep. 3, 1896, series 1, box 18, folder 265, SNMP; Atwell Thompson to Cornelius Cadle, Dec. 8, 1898, series 1, box 40, folder 641, SNMP.

40. "Boundary Description: By Metes and Bounds," undated, series 1, box 40, folder 644, SNMP; W. C. Meeks Land Acquisition folder, series 1, box 22, folder 312, SNMP.

41. Cornelius Cadle to J. G. Cannon, Jan. 22, 1897, series 1, box 40, folder 641, SNMP.

42. Cornelius Cadle to J. G. Cannon, Jan. 22, 1897, series 1, box 40, folder 641, SNMP; "Boundary Description: By Metes and Bounds," undated, series 1, box 40, folder 644, SNMP.

43. "Boundary Description: By Metes and Bounds," undated, series 1, box 40, folder 644, SNMP; list of land owned by SNMP, May 28, 1903, series 1, box 18, folder 265, SNMP; "List of Lands Optioned to . . . Shiloh Battlefield Association," undated, series 1, box 19, folder 268, SNMP.

44. D. C. Buell to George W. Davis, Oct. 18, 1897, RG 92, E 713, NARA; D. C. Buell to George W. Davis, June 24, 1896, series 1, box 37, folder 621, SNMP; Cornelius Cadle to D. W. Reed, Mar. 6, 1896, series 1, box 37, folder 621, SNMP; Cornelius Cadle to D. W. Reed, Nov. 9, 1897, series 1, box 38, folder 624, SNMP; George W. Davis to Cornelius Cadle, June 30, 1896, series 1, box 37, folder 621, SNMP.

45. Rules of action for the Shiloh Battlefield Commission, July 20, 1896, series 1, box 38, folder 624, SNMP; Cornelius Cadle to D. W. Reed, Aug. 6, 1896, series 1, box 38, folder 622, SNMP.

46. "Regulations Governing the Erection of Monuments, Tablets, and Markers in the Chickamauga and Chattanooga National Park," Dec. 14, 1895, series 1, box 37, folder 620, SNMP; "Rules to be Observed in Preparing the Battle Map," Apr. 8, 1896, Shiloh Battlefield Commission vertical file, SNMP.

47. "Rules to be Observed in Preparing the Battle Map," Apr. 8, 1896, Shiloh Battlefield Commission vertical file, SNMP.

48. "Regulations," undated, series 1, box 38, folder 624, SNMP.

49. Jones, "Building Shiloh Park," vertical file, SNMP, 13.

50. D. W. Reed to Cornelius Cadle, Jan. 30, 1897, series 1, box 38, folder 623, SNMP; D. W. Reed to Cornelius Cadle, June 1, 1897, series 1, box 38, folder 624, SNMP; Shiloh National Military Park Commission Daily Events, May 20 and June 4, 1901, SNMP, 29, 31; "Federal Veterans at Shiloh," *Confederate Veteran* 3, no. 4 (Apr. 1895): 104.

51. D. W. Reed to Basil W. Duke, July 20, 1906, series 1, box 13, folder 140, SNMP.

52. Cornelius Cadle to Secretary of War, Feb. 23, 1901, Shiloh National Military Park Commission Daily Events, Feb. 20, 1901, SNMP, 23; Cornelius Cadle to Robert F. Looney, Aug. 10, 1895, Robert F. Looney Collection, MSCPL; Atwell Thompson to Cornelius Cadle, Jan. 27, 1896, series 1, box 37, folder 620, SNMP; D. W. Reed to Cornelius Cadle, Mar. 4, 1896, series 1, box 37, folder 621, SNMP; Atwell Thompson to Shiloh National Military Park Commission, July 10, 1896, series 1, box 40, folder 640, SNMP.

53. D. C. Buell to George W. Davis, Nov. 13, 1897, RG 92, E 712, box 1, NARA; D. C. Buell to George W. Davis, Nov. 10, 1897, RG 92, E 713, NARA; Atwell Thompson to D. W. Reed, Nov. 14, 1900, series 1, box 25, folder 369, SNMP; *Annual Report of the Secretary of War* (1901), 384.

54. Atwell Thompson to D. W. Reed, Mar. 8, 1901, series 1, box 25, folder 369, SNMP; Atwell Thompson to D. W. Reed, June 23, 1899, Cornelius Cadle to John C. Scofield, Nov. 11, 1899, D. W. Reed to Cornelius Cadle, July 12, 1899, all in series 1, box 25, folder 368, SNMP.

55. Atwell Thompson to D. W. Reed, June 11, 1901, series 1, box 25, folder 369; SNMP; *Annual Report of the Secretary of War* (1900), 213; *Annual Report of the Secretary of War* (1901), 384; *Annual Report of the Secretary of War* (1902), 23; *Annual Report of the Secretary of War* (1903), 236; *Annual Report of the Secretary of War* (1904), 267; *Annual Report of the Secretary of War* (1905), 150; *Annual Report of the Secretary of War* (1906), 318; *Annual Report of the Secretary of War* (1908), 178; Shiloh National Military Park Commission Daily Events, Feb. 10, 1902, 85, 113, SNMP; *Annual Report of the Secretary of War* (1904), 268–69; *Annual Report of the Secretary of War* (1905), 150.

56. J. E. Evans to Cornelius Cadle, Sep. 9, 1902, series 1, box 25, folder 370, SNMP; Shiloh National Military Park Commission Daily Events, Nov. 23, 1900, Jan. 9, 1901, and Oct. 23, 1901, SNMP, 9, 16, 39; Shiloh National Military Park Commission Annual Report, Oct. 31, 1899, series 1, box 40, folder 641, SNMP. Reed even made the foundry correct the misspelling of Prentiss's name as "Prentice" on the 61st Illinois monument.

57. J. W. Irwin to J. M. Riddell, Mar. 5, 1897, series 1, box 25, folder 361, SNMP; Cornelius Cadle to Secretary of War, Nov. 14, 1896, RG 92, E 713, NARA; "List of Cannon to be turned over to the Shiloh Battlefield Commission," undated, series 1, box 24, folder 359, SNMP; George W. Davis to Cornelius Cadle, Mar. 13, 1897, series 1, box 25, folder 361, SNMP; Atwell Thompson to Cornelius Cadle, Dec. 8, 1898, series 1, box 40, folder 641, SNMP.

58. John P. Nicholson to Cornelius Cadle, Apr. 23, 1897, series 1, box 38, folder 623, SNMP; J. E. Evans to Cornelius Cadle, Apr. 10, 1897, and Calvin Gilbert to Cornelius Cadle, Apr. 27, 1897, both in series 1, box 24, folder 360, SNMP.

59. "Request to Publish Advertisement," various newspapers, Dec. 29, 1900, series 1, box 25, folder 361, SNMP; Cornelius Cadle to Atwell Thompson, Jan. 29, 1901, series 1, box 25, folder 361, SNMP; Cornelius Cadle to J. W. Foley and Co., Feb. 18, 1901, series 1, box 25, folder 361, SNMP.

60. Cornelius Cadle to Ross-Meehan Foundry Company, Dec. 12, 1901, series 1, box 25, folder 361, SNMP; Shiloh National Military Park Commission Daily Events, July 13 and Aug. 10, 1901, Jan. 2, 5, 17, 18, 28, Feb. 10, Mar. 22, Nov. 17, and Dec. 27, 1902, and Jan. 13 and 31, May 1, Aug. 1, and Sep. 18, 1903, SNMP, 34–35, 59–60, 150, 161, 163, 164, 172, 176, 178.

61. Reed Map, First and Second Days, 1900, series 6, boxes 1 and 2, SNMP; David W. Reed, *The Battle of Shiloh and the Organizations Engaged* (Washington, DC: Government Printing Office, 1902); "First Reunion of Iowa Hornet's Nest Brigade," Oct. 12–13, 1887, series 3, box 4, folder 216, SNMP; "12th Iowa Veteran Volunteer Infantry," series 3, box 4, folder 218, SNMP.

62. Reed, *Battle of Shiloh*, 19, 23, 62–63.

63. T. J. Lindsey, *Ohio at Shiloh: Report of the Commission* (Cincinnati: C. J. Krehbiel and Co., 1903), 195, 200, 210.

64. John W. Coons, *Indiana at Shiloh: Report of the Commission* (Indianapolis: William B. Burford, 1904), 296; *The Seventy-seventh Pennsylvania at Shiloh: History of the Regiment* (Harrisburg, PA: Harrisburg Publishing Co., 1905), 50; Abernathy, *Dedication of Monuments Erected by the*

*State of Iowa,* 256; George Mason, *Illinois at Shiloh* (Chicago: M. A. Donohue and Co., n.d.), 177; F. H. Magdeburg, *Wisconsin at Shiloh: Report of the Commission* (Milwaukee: Riverside Ptg. Co., 1909), 236–37.

65. "Alabama's Shiloh Monument," *Confederate Veteran* 15, no. 6 (June 1907): 249; "The Confederate Monument at Shiloh," *Confederate Veteran* 13, no. 10 (Oct. 1905): 441; "Dedication of the Monument at Shiloh," *Confederate Veteran* 25, no. 6 (June 1917): 251–52; Joe Gillis, *The Confederate Monument: Shiloh National Military Park* (n.p.: n.p., 1994), 16.

66. Smith, *This Great Battlefield of Shiloh,* 81–85.

67. D. C. Buell to Cornelius Cadle, Feb. 9, 1896, Robert F. Looney Collection, folder 66, MSCPL; D. C. Buell to H. V. Boynton, Jan. 9, 1895, series 9, CHCH; Robert F. Looney to D. C. Buell, Mar. 11, 1896, Don Carlos Buell Papers, FHS.

68. Paige and Greene, *Administrative History,* 10.

69. D. W. Reed to Cornelius Cadle, Feb. 20, 1905, series 1, box 11, folder 91, SNMP.

70. H. V. Boynton to Secretary of War, Mar. 7, 1905, series 1, box 12, folder 92, SNMP.

71. H. V. Boynton to Secretary of War, Mar. 25, 1905, series 1, box 12, folder 92, SNMP.

72. D. W. Reed to Cornelius Cadle, Mar. 27, 1905, and Robert Shaw Oliver to Cornelius Cadle, Mar. 30, 1905, both in series 1, box 12, folder 93, SNMP; D. W. Reed to Cornelius Cadle, Apr. 13, 1905, series 1, box 12, folder 94, SNMP.

73. D. W. Reed to Cornelius Cadle, Apr. 1, 1905, series 1, box 12, folder 94, SNMP; H. V. Boynton to Assistant Secretary of War, Apr. 27, 1905, series 1, box 12, folder 95, SNMP; Robert Shaw Oliver to Cornelius Cadle, May 5, 1905, series 1, box 12, folder 95, SNMP; W. W. Wotherspoone, memorandum, Sep. 2, 1909, series 1, box 39, folder 630, SNMP.

74. Smith, *This Great Battlefield of Shiloh,* 68–70; Timothy B. Smith, *The Untold Story of Shiloh: The Battle and the Battlefield* (Knoxville: Univ. of Tennessee Press, 2006), 139–55.

75. Cornelius Cadle to Allen R. Adams, Oct. 24, 1898, RG 92, E 712, box 1, NARA; Atwell Thompson to J. M. Riddell, Nov. 27, 1898, series 1, box 38, folder 626, SNMP. Buell replacement James H. Ashcraft attended Robert F. Looney's funeral in 1899, and Cadle himself attended Looney replacement Josiah Patterson's funeral in 1904. See Shiloh National Military Park Commission Daily Events, n.d., SNMP, 185; *Annual Report of the Secretary of War* (1900), 216.

76. J. H. Ashcraft compiled service record, NARA; Cornelius Cadle to J. H. Ashcraft, Mar. 1, 1901, and J. H. Ashcraft appointment, Jan. 12, 1899, both in series 1, box 34, folder 470, SNMP.

77. "Col. R. F. Looney," *Confederate Veteran* 8, no. 1 (Jan. 1900): 36; Cornelius Cadle to Secretary of War, Nov. 27, 1899, RG 79, box 11, "Press Copies of Letters Sent," NARA Southeast Region, Atlanta; *Biographical Directory of the United States Congress,* 1619; James D. Porter, *Tennessee,* vol. 10 of *Confederate Military History: A Library of Confederate States History in Seventeen Volumes,* ed. Clement A. Evans (1899; reprint, Wilmington, NC: Broadfoot Publishing Company, 1987), 662–67; Cornelius Cadle to D. W. Reed, Jan. 23, 1899, series 1, box 38, folder 626, SNMP; *Biographical Directory of the United States Congress,* 1619.

78. Basil W. Duke Compiled Service Record, NARA; Warner, *Generals in Gray,* 76–77; *Annual Report of the Secretary of War* (1904), 268.

79. Cornelius Cadle to D. W. Reed, Nov. 13, 1905, and Cornelius Cadle to John C. Scofield, Oct. 15, 1906, both in series 1, box 35, folder 570, SNMP; D. W. Reed to Cornelius Cadle, June 23,

1905, series 1, box 38, folder 629, SNMP; Atwell Thompson obituary, *Chattanooga Daily Times*, Feb. 2, 1912.

80. "Mt. Vinson–Shiloh Illustrated Account of the Cyclone, Oct. 14, 1909," Cyclone – 1909, vertical file, SNMP; Robert Shaw Oliver to Cornelius Cadle, Dec. 22, 1909, RG 107, E 82, vol. 44, NARA; Cornelius Cadle to Sydney E. Smith, Nov. 25, 1909, series 1, box 4, folder 28, SNMP; "An Act Making Appropriations to Supply Deficiencies in Appropriations for the Fiscal Year Nineteen Hundred and Ten, for other purposes," undated, series 1, box 5, folder 32, SNMP; John C. Scofield to D. W. Reed, Feb. 28, 1910, series 1, box 4, folder 28, SNMP; *Annual Report of the Secretary of War* (1910), 308.

81. Jacob Dickinson to Cornelius Cadle, Jan. 15, 1910, RG 107, E 82, vol. 44, NARA; D. W. Reed et al to John B. Randolph, July 5, 1911, series 1, box 36, folder 589, SNMP; Cornelius Cadle to D. W. Reed, Jan. 31, 1910, series 1, box 39, folder 630, SNMP; Thomas McAdory Owen, *History of Alabama and Dictionary of Alabama Biography*, 4 vols. (1921; reprint, Spartanburg, SC: Reprint Company, 1978), 3:279.

82. J. M. Riddell to J. H. Ashcraft, May 5, 1908, series 1, box 13, folder 116, SNMP; Stacy D. Allen to Charles E. Adams, Dec. 14, 1998, in "Cornelius Cadle, Jr.," vertical files, SNMP; Frank W. Mahin, *Genealogy of the Cadle Family Including English Decent* (n.p.: n.p., 1915), 95–100; *Cincinnati Commercial Tribune*, Jan. 16, 1913; Assistant and Chief Clerk to D. W. Reed, Dec. 6, 1909, RG 107, E 82, vol. 44, NARA; Minutes of Commission Meeting, Oct. 26, 1911, in Shiloh National Military Park Commission Daily Events, SNMP.

83. D. W. Reed et al to John B. Randolph, July 5, 1911, series 1, box 36, folder 589, SNMP; Cornelius Cadle to D. W. Reed, Jan. 31, 1910, series 1, box 39, folder 630, SNMP.

84. John T. Wilder compiled service record, NARA; "Invoices" ledger book, RG 79, box 5, NARA Southeast Region; Shiloh National Military Park Daily Events, Oct. 1911, Dec. 1912, and May 1913, SNMP, 14, 26, 29; *Annual Report of the Secretary of War* (1912), 196; *Annual Report of the Secretary of War* (1913), 200.

85. *Annual Report of the Secretary of War* (1914), 659.

86. Commission Minutes, Apr. 6, 1912, in Shiloh National Military Park Commission Daily Events, Apr. 1912, SNMP, 20; Shiloh National Military Park Commission Daily Events, May 1913, SNMP, 29; *Annual Report of the Secretary of War* (1917), 1008; "David Wilson Reed," in *Memorials of Deceased Companions of the Commandery of the State of Illinois, Military Order of the Loyal Legion of the United States* (1901; reprint, Wilmington: Broadfoot, 1993), 353; *Annual Report of the Secretary of War* (1920), 1963.

87. Labor Roll, Aug. 1916, in Time Books, RG 79, box 5, NARA Southeast Region; *Annual Report of the Secretary of War* (1920), 1963; *Annual Report of the Secretary of War* (1918), 1480.

88. Smith, *This Great Battlefield of Shiloh*, 126.

## 6. "A SPLENDID MONUMENT TO AMERICAN VALOR"

1. For a broader look at Gettysburg, see Jim Weeks, *Gettysburg: Memory, Market, and an American Shrine* (Princeton: Princeton Univ. Press, 2003) and Amy Kinsel, "'From These Honored Dead': Gettysburg in American Culture, 1863–1938," Ph.D. diss., Cornell Univ., 1992.

2. *Congressional Record,* 51st Cong., 2nd sess., 21, pt. 1:559; *House Reports,* 51st Cong., 2nd sess., H. Rept. 3024, 1–6.

3. *Congressional Record,* 51st Cong., 2nd sess., 21, pt. 1:730; *Congressional Record,* 51st Cong., 2nd sess., 21, pt. 10:10,080; *House Reports,* 51st Cong., 2nd sess., H. Rept. 3296, 1.

4. *House Reports,* 52nd Cong., 2nd sess., H. Rept. 2188, 1–4.

5. *Congressional Record,* 52nd Cong., 2nd sess., 24, pt. 1:748–49.

6. *Statutes at Large,* 27 (1893): 599–600.

7. Minute Book Gettysburg Battlefield Memorial Association, 1872–1895, Gettysburg National Military Park Archives, GNMP, 251; W. C. Storrick, *Gettysburg: The Place, The Battles, The Outcome* (Harrisburg, PA: J. Horace McFarland Company, 1932), 112, 144; Gettysburg National Military Park Commission, *Annual Reports to the Secretary of War, 1893–1901* (Washington, DC: Government Printing Office, 1902), 5; Warner, *Generals in Gray,* 91; Nicholson Journals, vol. 1, GNMP, 1.

8. Storrick, *Gettysburg,* 144; Gettysburg Commission, *Annual Reports,* 5, 9; Nicholson Journals, vol. 1, GNMP, 2–3; E. B. Cope to Assistant Secretary of War, Dec. 9, 1904, RG 92, E 711, box 2, NARA.

9. John P. Nicholson, William M. Robbins, and C. A. Richardson to Secretary of War, Feb. 15, 1898, RG 92, E 711, box 2, NARA; Gettysburg Commission, *Annual Reports,* 5; George B. Davis to Secretary of War, May 25, 1893, Nicholson Journals, vol. 1, GNMP, 13.

10. Secretary of War to Justice Department, Nicholson Journals, vol. 1, GNMP, 19; Daniel S. Lamont to Attorney General, May 1, 1895, RG 92, E 709, NARA; Gettysburg Commission, *Annual Reports to the Secretary of War,* 8, 11; John P. Nicholson to G. W. Davis, Feb. 5, 1895, RG 92, E 710, NARA; Unrau, *Administrative History,* 75–76.

11. Gettysburg Commission, *Annual Reports,* 5–6.

12. Ibid., 7, 10.

13. Minute Book Gettysburg Battlefield Memorial Association, 1872–1895, GNMP, 249; Gettysburg Commission, *Annual Reports,* 7–8, 11.

14. Gettysburg Commission, *Annual Reports,* 10.

15. *Annual Report of the Secretary of War* (1893), 32, 326–27; *Annual Report of the Secretary of War* (1894), 28, 58. Congress passed laws on Mar. 3, 1887, Oct. 2, 1888, and Mar. 2, 1889, for the marking of regular army sites.

16. Gettysburg Commission, *Annual Reports,* 9, 11–12; *Annual Report of the Secretary of War* (1893), 32–33.

17. Gettysburg Commission, *Annual Reports,* 9, 11–12; *Annual Report of the Secretary of War,* (1893), 32–33.

18. *Annual Report of the Secretary of War* (1894), 29; *Congressional Record,* 53rd Cong., 3rd sess., 27, pt. 1:105, 402; Thomas A. Desjardin, *These Honored Dead: How the Story of Gettysburg Shaped American Memory* (Cambridge, MA: Da Capo, 2003), 80.

19. *Congressional Record,* 53rd Cong., 3rd sess., 27, pt. 2:1038–39.

20. Ibid., 1226–27.

21. Ibid., 1278, 1607, 1715, 1815; *Congressional Record,* 53rd Cong., 3rd sess., 27, pt. 3:2109. The language actually created the Gettysburg National Park, but for conformity's sake I will refer to it as a national military park.

22. *Statutes at Large,* 28 (1895): 651–53.

23. Ibid.

24. Edwin C. Bearss, Chief Historian Emeritus, National Park Service, interview by author, Aug. 11, 2004; Allen R. Adams to George B. Davis, Nov. 23, 1895, and George W. Davis to John P. Nicholson, Feb. 27, 1897, both in RG 92, E 709, NARA; "Regulations for the Government of the Gettysburg National Park, Gettysburg, Pennsylvania, 1895," RG 92, E 711, box 2, NARA.

25. Gettysburg Commission, *Annual Reports to the Secretary of War,* 21.

26. Ibid., 15, 27.

27. Ibid., 15. The roads were indeed very substantial and form the foundation of the park's roads today.

28. Ibid., 32, 51.

29. Ibid., 16, 27, 53.

30. Gettysburg Commission to G. W. Davis, Dec. 16, 1895, and G. W. Davis to John P. Nicholson, Jan. 3, 1896, both in RG 92, E 710, NARA; *Senate Reports,* 54th Cong., 1st sess., S. Rept. 527, 1–2; Gettysburg Commission, *Annual Reports to the Secretary of War,* 37, 38. The commission had specified the language it wanted in the additional road legislation, but it was not acceptable to the judge advocate general, who devised a compromise bill.

31. Gettysburg Commission, *Annual Reports to the Secretary of War,* 46; *Annual Report of the Secretary of War* (1904), 258.

32. John P. Nicholson, William M. Robbins, and C. A. Richardson to Secretary of War, Feb. 15, 1898, RG 92, E 711, box 2, NARA.

33. Land Syndicate press release, Aug. 19, 1893, Nicholson Journals, vol. 1, GNMP, 29; John P. Nicholson, William M. Robbins, and C. A. Richardson to Secretary of War, Feb. 15, 1898, RG 92, E 711, box 2, NARA.

34. John P. Nicholson, William M. Robbins, and C. A. Richardson to Secretary of War, Feb. 15, 1898, RG 92, E 711, box 2, NARA.

35. *United States v. Gettysburg Electric Railroad Company,* 160, *United States Reports,* 668–86 (1896); John P. Nicholson to G. W. Davis, Apr. 2, 1895, RG 92, E 710, NARA; Unrau, *Administrative History,* 76; John P. Nicholson, William M. Robbins, and C. A. Richardson to Secretary of War, Feb. 15, 1898, RG 92, E 711, box 2, NARA.

36. Gettysburg Commission, *Annual Reports to the Secretary of War,* 32; John P. Nicholson, William M. Robbins, and C. A. Richardson to Secretary of War, Feb. 15, 1898, RG 92, E 711, box 2, NARA.

37. John P. Nicholson, William M. Robbins, and C. A. Richardson to Secretary of War, Feb. 15, 1898, RG 92, E 711, box 2, NARA; *Annual Report of the Secretary of War* (1904), 258, 261.

38. *Annual Report of the Secretary of War* (1904), 259; Nicholson Journals, vol. 4, GNMP, 152.

39. Elihu Root to Secretary of Agriculture, Mar. 6, 1903, Nicholson Journals, vol. 11, GNMP, 14; Commission, *Annual Reports to the Secretary of War,* 16–17, 23, 28–29; *Annual Report of the Secretary of War* (1903), 229; *Annual Report of the Secretary of War* (1904), 259; John P. Nicholson to F. McMahon, July 8, 1895, Nicholson Journals, vol. 3, GNMP, 68.

40. Allen R. Adams to John P. Nicholson, Apr. 31, 1895, RG 92, E 709, NARA; Gettysburg Commission, *Annual Reports to the Secretary of War,* 3.

41. Gettysburg Commission, *Annual Reports to the Secretary of War*, 17, 28–29, 46, 53; *Annual Report of the Secretary of War* (1904), 260.

42. Minute Book Gettysburg Battlefield Memorial Association, 1872–1895, GNMP, 138, 146; Commission, *Annual Reports to the Secretary of War*, 17. See George R. Large, comp., *Battle of Gettysburg: The Official History by the Gettysburg National Military Park Commission* (Shippensburg, PA: Burd Street Press, 1999), for texts of Gettysburg's tablets.

43. Gettysburg Commission, *Annual Reports to the Secretary of War*, 22, 33–34.

44. John P. Nicholson to Secretary of War, Oct. 4, 1904, Nicholson Journals, vol. 12, GNMP, 147; Gettysburg Commission, *Annual Reports to the Secretary of War*, 33, 44–45, 53; *Annual Report of the Secretary of War* (1902), 14; *Annual Report of the Secretary of War* (1903), 226; *Annual Report of the Secretary of War* (1904), 259.

45. Minute Book Gettysburg Battlefield Memorial Association, 1872–1895, GNMP, 128, 231; Gettysburg Commission, *Annual Reports to the Secretary of War*, 16, 22.

46. Gettysburg Commission, *Annual Reports to the Secretary of War*, 22, 53; *Annual Report of the Secretary of War* (1902), 15; *Annual Report of the Secretary of War* (1904), 258.

47. *Philadelphia Inquirer,* June 8, 1899; Storrick, *Gettysburg,* 132; Gettysburg Commission, *Annual Reports to the Secretary of War*, 29, 32–33, 39, 52; *Annual Report of the Secretary of War* (1902), 16; *Annual Report of the Secretary of War* (1903), 228; *Annual Report of the Secretary of War* (1904), 258–59.

48. William F. Fox, *New York at Gettysburg,* 3 vols. (Albany: J. B. Lyon Company, 1900), 1:235–40; *Pennsylvania at Gettysburg: Ceremonies at the Dedication of the Monuments Erected by the Commonwealth of Pennsylvania to Major-General George G. Meade, Major General Winfield S. Hancock, Major General John F. Reynolds, and to Mark the Positions of the Pennsylvania Commands Engaged in the Battle,* 3 vols. (Harrisburg, PA: Wm. Stanley Ray, 1914), 2:44–46.

49. "North Carolina at Gettysburg," *Confederate Veteran* 37, no. 8 (Aug. 1929): 288; Gettysburg Commission, *Annual Reports to the Secretary of War*, 39.

50. Gettysburg Commission, *Annual Reports to the Secretary of War*, 46; *Annual Report of the Secretary of War* (1903), 227.

51. Nicholson Journals, vol. 12, GNMP, 31; *Annual Report of the Secretary of War* (1904), 260.

52. Desjardin, *These Honored Dead,* 94; Garry E. Adelman, *The Myth of Little Round Top: Gettysburg, PA* (Gettysburg: Thomas Publications, 2003), 37–84. See also Carol Reardon, *Pickett's Charge in History and Memory* (Chapel Hill: Univ. of North Carolina Press, 1997), and Kent Masterson Brown, *Retreat from Gettysburg: Lee, Logistics, and the Pennsylvania Campaign* (Chapel Hill: Univ. of North Carolina Press, 2005).

53. Postmaster General to Secretary of War, Oct. 17, 1903, RG 92, E 711, box 2, NARA; G. D. Meiklejohn to Gettysburg Commission, Feb. 23, 1898, RG 92, E 711, box 1, NARA; *Annual Report of the Secretary of War* (1904), 257; John P. Nicholson to Secretary of War, May 20, 1902, RG 92, E 711, box 2, NARA; Robert Shaw Oliver to J. R. Dickson, Nov. 16, 1908, RG 92, E 711, box 2, NARA; Gettysburg Town Counsel to Gettysburg Commission, June 30, 1908, RG 92, E 711, box 2, NARA.

54. Nicholson Journals, vol. 9, GNMP, 110; Gettysburg Commission, *Annual Reports to the Secretary of War*, 54; *Annual Report of the Secretary of War* (1904), 259; *Gettysburg Star Sentinel,* July 24, 1907; *Annual Report of the Secretary of War* (1913), 185; *Annual Report of the Secretary of War* (1920), 5251.

55. Gettysburg Commission to Secretary of War, Sep. 30, 1897, Nicholson Journals, vol. 5, GNMP, 81; G. D. Meiklejohn to Gettysburg Commission, Feb. 23, 1898, RG 92, E 711, box 1, NARA; John P. Nicholson to Secretary of War, May 20, 1902, RG 92, E 711, box 2, NARA.

56. Oliver Wendell Holmes to [?], Jan. 17, 1913, John P. Nicholson to Secretary of War, Dec. 31, 1912, and Jan. 2, 1913, Robert Shaw Oliver, Memorandum, July 6, 1912, all in RG 92, E 711, box 2, NARA; Nicholson Journals, vol. 1, GNMP, 40.

57. Daniel Sickles to Secretary of War, July 31, 1902, and Daniel Sickles to Secretary of War, Nov. 13, 1902, both in RG 92, E 711, box 1, NARA; Elihu Root to Daniel Sickles, July 8, 1902, Elihu Root Papers, Correspondence June 7 to Dec. 18, 1902, folder 176, part 1, LC; Desjardin, *These Honored Dead*, 80–81, 194; Nicholson Journals, vol. 12, GNMP, 37.

58. W. C. Oates to William M. Robbins, Dec. 10, 1902, Joshua Lawrence Chamberlain to John P. Nicholson, Aug. 17, 1903, John P. Nicholson to Joshua Lawrence Chamberlain, Apr. 21, 1903, W. C. Oates to John P. Nicholson, Nov. 4, 1903, SJR 530, John P. Nicholson to John C. Scofield, Feb. 26, 1903, William M. Robbins to John P. Nicholson, Feb. 26, 1903, John P. Nicholson to Secretary of War, Nov. 16, 1901, "Regulations for the Government of the Gettysburg National Park, Gettysburg, Pennsylvania, 1904," all in RG 92, E 711, box 1, NARA; Gettysburg Commission to Secretary of War, Jan. 18, 1904, Nicholson Journals, vol. 12, GNMP, 1–2; Elihu Root to "Gentlemen," Jan. 22, 1904, and William Robbins to [?], Jan. 1904, Oates Correspondence, GNMP; Edwin C. Bearss, Chief Historian Emeritus, National Park Service, interview by author, Aug. 11, 2004. For later controversies in the 1920s and 1930s, see Unrau, *Administrative History*, 133–34. Also see the voluminous correspondence on the matter in the Oates Correspondence, GNMP. For Oates, see Glenn W. LaFantasie, *Gettysburg Requiem: The Life and Lost Causes of Confederate Colonel William C. Oates* (New York: Oxford Univ. Press, 2006).

59. Unrau, *Administrative History*, 95–96.

60. Gettysburg Commission, *Annual Reports to the Secretary of War*, 23, 47; *Annual Report of the Secretary of War* (1904), 261.

61. *Annual Report of the Secretary of War* (1904), 261.

62. Nicholson Journals, vol. 13, GNMP, 34; Storrick, *Gettysburg*, 131; *Annual Report of the Secretary of War* (1907), 327; *Annual Report of the Secretary of War* (1915), 871; *Annual Report of the Secretary of War* (1919), 5245; Unrau, *Administrative History*, 91; Warner, *Generals in Gray*, 191.

63. Nicholson Journals, vol. 13, GNMP, 34; Storrick, *Gettysburg*, 131; *Annual Report of the Secretary of War* (1907), 327; *Annual Report of the Secretary of War* (1915), 871; *Annual Report of the Secretary of War* (1919), 5245; Unrau, *Administrative History*, 91; Warner, *Generals in Gray*, 191.

64. *Annual Report of the Secretary of War* (1905), 142–43; *Annual Report of the Secretary of War* (1914), 640, 642–43.

65. "Statement of Rents paid by Lessees of land of the Gettysburg National Park from June 10, 1904, the date of last report, to May 27, 1905," RG 92, E 711, box 1, NARA; *Annual Report of the Secretary of War* (1919), 5250; Unrau, *Administrative History*, 87; *Annual Report of the Secretary of War* (1920), 1955.

66. Gettysburg Commission to Secretary of War, Oct. 16, 1906, RG 92, E 711, box 1, NARA; *Annual Report of the Secretary of War* (1909), 33–34; *Annual Report of the Secretary of War* (1911), 325; *Annual Report of the Secretary of War* (1913), 189–90; *Annual Report of the Secretary of War* (1918), 1472.

67. *Annual Report of the Secretary of War* (1908), 169; *Annual Report of the Secretary of War* (1920), 1952–53.

68. *Annual Report of the Secretary of War* (1908), 170; *Annual Report of the Secretary of War* (1914), 641.

69. *Annual Report of the Secretary of War* (1906), 311; *Annual Report of the Secretary of War* (1907), 325; *Annual Report of the Secretary of War* (1908), 173; *Annual Report of the Secretary of War* (1910), 301; *Annual Report of the Secretary of War* (1911), 319; *Annual Report of the Secretary of War* (1912), 181–82; *Annual Report of the Secretary of War* (1914), 868.

70. *Annual Report of the Secretary of War* (1910), 301.

71. *Annual Report of the Secretary of War* (1905), 138; *Annual Report of the Secretary of War* (1908), 171; *Annual Report of the Secretary of War* (1909), 32–34; *Annual Report of the Secretary of War* (1910), 322; *Annual Report of the Secretary of War* (1913), 184; *Annual Report of the Secretary of War* (1917), 994; *Annual Report of the Secretary of War* (1920), 1951–52.

72. Nicholson Journals, vol. 12, GNMP, 31; *Annual Report of the Secretary of War* (1905), 139; *Annual Report of the Secretary of War* (1910), 302; *Annual Report of the Secretary of War* (1914), 641; *Annual Report of the Secretary of War* (1915), 869; *Annual Report of the Secretary of War* (1916), 1233–34; Unrau, *Administrative History*, 114; *The Location of the Monuments, Markers, and Tablets on the Battlefield of Gettysburg*, E 711, box 1, NARA. The relief map is still on display at Gettysburg.

73. *Annual Report of the Secretary of War* (1909), 34; *Annual Report of the Secretary of War* (1911), 326–27.

74. *Annual Report of the Secretary of War* (1911), 326;

75. *Annual Report of the Secretary of War* (1912), 185–86; *Annual Report of the Secretary of War* (1913), 183, 190.

76. "At a Meeting of the Ex-Confederates at Gettysburg, July 2, 1913, Presided over by General Andrew J. West, of Georgia, the Following Resolutions Were Unanimously Adopted," RG 92, E 711, box 2, NARA; *Annual Report of the Secretary of War* (1913), 190–91.

77. *Pennsylvania at Gettysburg*, 3: 174.

78. John P. Nicholson to Secretary of War, Sep. 13, 1910, RG 92, E 711, box 2, NARA; *Annual Report of the Secretary of War* (1905), 139; *Annual Report of the Secretary of War* (1907), 328; *Annual Report of the Secretary of War* (1909), 33; *Annual Report of the Secretary of War* (1910), 303; *Annual Report of the Secretary of War* (1911), 323–24; *Annual Report of the Secretary of War* (1913), 189; *Annual Report of the Secretary of War* (1916), 1233–34; Unrau, *Administrative History*, 103; W. P. Hall to Superintendent, United States Military Academy, Mar. 14, 1904, Nicholson Journals, vol. 12, GNMP, 35; John P. Nicholson to Robert Shaw Oliver, Apr. 28, 1910, RG 92, E 711, box 2, NARA.

79. *Annual Report of the Secretary of War* (1917), 997–98.

80. *Annual Report of the Secretary of War* (1918), 1472; *Annual Report of the Secretary of War* (1919), 5248; Unrau, *Administrative History*, 117. The camp was not designated by name, since it was at such a famous place as Gettysburg.

81. Storrick, *Gettysburg*, 135; *Annual Report of the Secretary of War* (1918), 1472; *Annual Report of the Secretary of War* (1919), 5248–49.

82. *Annual Report of the Secretary of War* (1918), 1472; *Annual Report of the Secretary of War* (1919), 5248–51; *Annual Report of the Secretary of War* (1920), 1955.

83. Storrick, *Gettysburg,* 134.

84. *Annual Report of the Secretary of War* (1920), 1957–58; Storrick, *Gettysburg,* 131.

85. Storrick, *Gettysburg,* 131, 144.

7. "A VALUABLE CONTRIBUTION TO MILITARY SCIENCE"

1. James R. McConaghie and Daniel J. Keeffe, "A History of Vicksburg National Military Park," 1954, Edwin C. Bearss series, box 2, folder 49, VNMP, 12.

2. H. C. Landru, "The Vicksburg National Military Park—Its Origin, Growth and Future Development," 1936, Edwin C. Bearss series, box 2, folder 49, VNMP, 1; McConaghie and Keeffe, "History of Vicksburg National Military Park," 13.

3. Terrence J. Winschel, "Stephen D. Lee and the Making of an American Shrine," *Journal of Mississippi History* 63, no. 1 (2001): 21; McConaghie and Keeffe, "History of Vicksburg National Military Park," 14; *Vicksburg Evening Post,* Feb. 10, 1899, Administrative series, box 6, folder 145, VNMP; Landru, "Vicksburg National Military Park," 2; *Vicksburg Evening Post,* Nov. 23, 1895, Administrative series, box 7, folder 158, VNMP.

4. William T. Rigby report, Dec. 7, 1899, Administrative series, box 7, folder 158, VNMP; "Veterans are Back," undated newspaper article, Administrative series, box 7, folder 158, VNMP; Landru, "Vicksburg National Military Park," 2; McConaghie and Keeffe, "History of Vicksburg National Military Park," 14–15; W. T. Rigby, "History and Views of The Vicksburg National Military Park," *Vicksburg Monday Morning Democrat,* Sep. 6, 1909, Administrative series, box 6, folder 128, VNMP; "The Vicksburg National Military Park Association," Administrative series, box 7, folder 158, VNMP.

5. "Charter of Incorporation of the Vicksburg National Military Park Association," Administrative series, box 7, folder 158, VNMP; William T. Rigby report, Dec. 7, 1899, Administrative series, box 7, folder 158, VNMP; McConaghie and Keeffe, "History of Vicksburg National Military Park," 15; *Report of the Proceedings of the Society of the Army of the Tennessee at the Thirty-First Meeting held at Chicago, Ills., October 10–11, 1899* (Cincinnati: F. W. Freeman, 1900), 41. For more information on the association's proceedings, see the Vicksburg National Military Park Association's minutes dated Nov. 22–23, 1895, Jan. 10 and Dec. 16, 1896, Dec. 28, 1898, Dec. 7, 1899, and Nov. 28, 1900, all in Administrative series, box 7, folder 158, VNMP.

6. "Veterans are Back," undated newspaper article, Administrative series, box 7, folder 158, VNMP; Landru, "Vicksburg National Military Park," 3; *Report of the Twenty-Eighth Meeting,* 53, 56, 124; *Report of the Thirty-First Meeting,* 43–44; J. M. McCloud to William T. Rigby, Jan. 24, 1896, Administrative series, box 1, folder 1, VNMP. Even the Corps of Engineers became involved in supporting the proposed Vicksburg park.

7. William T. Rigby report, Dec. 7, 1899, Administrative series, box 7, folder 158, VNMP; McConaghie and Keeffe, "A History of Vicksburg National Military Park," 15; *Report of the Twenty-Eighth Meeting,* 55; *Report of the Thirty-First Meeting,* 31: 44; "Father of Park

Delighted With Progress," *Vicksburg Evening Post,* Nov. 30, 1908. The city of Vicksburg itself gave five hundred dollars to pay for the officers' travel to Washington.

8. *House Reports,* 55th Cong., 2nd sess., H. Rept. 596, 1–4.

9. Ibid., 2–3.

10. Ibid., 2, 4.

11. Landru, "Vicksburg National Military Park," 3; William T. Rigby report, Dec. 7, 1899, Administrative series, box 7, folder 158, VNMP; *Vicksburg Evening Post,* Feb. 7, 1899, Administrative series, box 6, folder 145, VNMP.

12. *Congressional Record,* 55th Cong., 3rd sess., 32, pt. 2:1518; William T. Rigby report, Dec. 7, 1899, Administrative series, box 7, folder 158, VNMP; *Vicksburg Evening Post,* Feb. 10, 1899, Administrative series, box 6, folder 145, VNMP.

13. *Congressional Record,* 55th Cong., 3rd sess., 32, pt. 2:1529, 1640, 1678.

14. Ibid., 1760; *Annual Report of the Secretary of War* (1899), 341.

15. *Congressional Record,* 55th Cong., 3rd sess., 32, pt.. 2:1518.

16. D. B. Henderson to J. F. Merry, Nov. 6, 1896, box 2, William T. Rigby Papers, UI; *Report of the Thirty-First Meeting,* 44.

17. D. B. Henderson to W. O. Mitchell, Feb. 14, 1899, box 3, William T. Rigby Papers, UI; William T. Rigby appointment, Mar. 1, 1899, William T. Rigby series, box 1, folder 7, VNMP; *Report of the Thirty-First Meeting,* 41; *Annual Report of the Secretary of War* (1899), 341.

18. W. T. Rigby, "History and Views of The Vicksburg National Military Park," *Vicksburg Monday Morning Democrat,* Sep. 6, 1909, Administrative series, box 6, folder 128, VNMP.

19. "Facts Concerning Early Park Personalities," Administrative series, box 6, folder 145, VNMP; *Annual Report of the Secretary of War* (1899), 341–42; Josiah Patterson to Stephen D. Lee, Aug. 18, 1900, RG 79, Letters Received—Vicksburg National Military Park Commission, box 1, NARA Southeast. The engineers' appointments dated from May 22, 1899, while Weightman's came on May 28. The secretary of war appointed Haydon at Willard's request. Shiloh commissioner Josiah Patterson unsuccessfully recommended that park's laborer M. A. Kirby for the position.

20. Stephen D. Lee to William T. Rigby, Apr. 27, 1899, Frank G. Smith to William T. Rigby, Aug. 1, 1899, Cornelius Cadle to William T. Rigby, Aug. 23, 1899, all in RG 79, Letters Received—Vicksburg National Military Park Commission, box 1, NARA Southeast.

21. Robert Shaw Oliver to William T. Rigby, Mar. 21, 1905, Administrative series, box 1, folder 4, VNMP; *Annual Report of the Secretary of War* (1899), 341–43.

22. Undated memorandum describing land acquisition at Vicksburg, Administrative series, box 6, folder 127, VNMP; *Annual Report of the Secretary of War* (1899), 341–42; *Report of the Thirty-First Meeting,* 41.

23. *Annual Report of the Secretary of War* (1899), 342.

24. Ibid., 342–43.

25. Ibid., 342–43; *Annual Report of the Secretary of War* (1900), 221.

26. *Annual Report of the Secretary of War* (1899), 343.

27. Ibid., 343–44.

28. *Annual Report of the Secretary of War* (1900), 219

29. Ibid., 219–21.

30. *Annual Report of the Secretary of War* (1901), 389, 392; *Annual Report of the Secretary of War* (1902), 27–28; *Annual Report of the Secretary of War* (1903), 241–42; *Annual Report of the Secretary of War* (1904), 273, 275; *Annual Report of the Secretary of War* (1905), 153; *Annual Report of the Secretary of War* (1906), 323; *Annual Report of the Secretary of War* (1907), 337; *Annual Report of the Secretary of War* (1908), 183.

31. *Annual Report of the Secretary of War* (1900), 221–22; *Annual Report of the Secretary of War* (1901), 390; *Annual Report of the Secretary of War* (1902), 28; *Annual Report of the Secretary of War* (1903), 241; *Annual Report of the Secretary of War* (1904), 273–74.

32. "Agreement for the Lease of the 'Shirley House,'" no date, Administrative series, box 1, folder 4, VNMP; *Annual Report of the Secretary of War* (1900), 222; *Annual Report of the Secretary of War* (1902), 28; *Annual Report of the Secretary of War* (1903), 242. The Culver Family lived in the Shirley House while J. S. Culver oversaw the work on the nearby Illinois memorial.

33. *Annual Report of the Secretary of War* (1900), 222.

34. Ibid., 222; John S. Kountz to William T. Rigby, Jan. 11 and 16, 1901, both in RG 79, Letters Received—Vicksburg National Military Park Commission, box 2, folder 1, NARA Southeast.

35. *Annual Report of the Secretary of War* (1901), 390.

36. Secretary of War to H. V. Boynton, Apr. 24, 1901, RG 92, E 715, box 1, NARA; *Annual Report of the Secretary of War* (1901), 391.

37. S. D. Lee to William T. Rigby, July 29, 1901, William T. Rigby series, box 1, folder 33, VNMP; *Annual Report of the Secretary of War* (1901), 391; Secretary of War to H. V. Boynton, May 20, 1902, and E. E. Betts to Secretary of War, Apr. 12, 1902, both in RG 92, E 715, box 1, NARA.

38. G. C. Haydon to William T. Rigby, June 2, 1902, RG 79, Letters Received—Vicksburg National Military Park Commission, box 3, NARA Southeast; G. C. Haydon to William T. Rigby, Feb. 10, 1902, William T. Rigby series, box 2, folder 34, VNMP; *Annual Report of the Secretary of War* (1901), 391.

39. H. V. Boynton to William T. Rigby, May 9, 1901, RG 79, Letters Received—Vicksburg National Military Park Commission, box 2, folder 1, NARA Southeast; S. D. Lee to William T. Rigby, July 29 31, and Oct. 31, 1901, William T. Rigby series, box 1, folder 33, VNMP.

40. Andrew Hickenlooper to G. M. Dodge, Apr. 19, 1902, William T. Rigby to Andrew Hickenlooper, May 8, 1902, and Secretary of War to H. V. Boynton, May 20, 1902, all in RG 92, E 715, box 1, NARA.

41. *Annual Report of the Secretary of War* (1901), 391; James G. Everest to William T. Rigby, Feb. 28, 1902, RG 79, Letters Received—Vicksburg National Military Park Commission, box 3, NARA Southeast.

42. William T. Rigby to Secretary of War, Dec. 22, 1903, Administrative series, box 1, folder 2, VNMP; *Annual Report of the Secretary of War* (1901), 351, 367; *Annual Report of the Secretary of War* (1902), 28; *Annual Report of the Secretary of War* (1903), 241.

43. Elihu Root to William T. Rigby, Mar. 22, 1902, Administrative series, box 1, folder 1, VNMP; S. D. Lee to William T. Rigby, Mar. 11, 1902, William T. Rigby series, box 2, folder 34, VNMP; Herman Hattaway, *General Stephen D. Lee* (Jackson: Univ. Press of Mississippi, 1976), 227, 229–30; James G. Everest to William T. Rigby, Mar. 7, 1902, RG 79, Letters Received—Vicksburg National Military Park Commission, box 3, NARA Southeast.

44. Andrew Hickenlooper to D. B. Henderson, May 10, 1902, Administrative series, box 1, folder 1, VNMP; John S. Kountz to William T. Rigby, Mar. 13, 1902, William T. Rigby series, box 2, folder 34, VNMP; D. B. Henderson to Elihu Root, May 20, 1902, and John P. Nicholson to Secretary of War, May 15, 1902, both in RG 92, E 715, box 1, NARA.

45. G. C. Haydon to William T. Rigby, Feb. 27, 1902, RG 79, Letters Received—Vicksburg National Military Park Commission, box 3, NARA Southeast; *Annual Report of the Secretary of War* (1901), 367; *Annual Report of the Secretary of War* (1902), 27–28.

46. William T. Rigby to Secretary of War, Aug. 11, 1902, William T. Rigby series, box 2, folder 34, VNMP; John C. Scofield to William T. Rigby, Feb. 19, 1903, Administrative series, box 1, folder 2, VNMP; E. E. Betts to William T. Rigby, June 11, 1902, RG 79, Letters Received— Vicksburg National Military Park Commission, box 3, NARA Southeast; E. E. Betts to Vicksburg National Military Park Commission, Sep. 19, 1901, RG 92, E 715, box 1, NARA.

47. Hattaway, *General Stephen D. Lee*, 229; *Annual Report of the Secretary of War* (1903), 241–42; *Annual Report of the Secretary of War* (1904), 274.

48. William T. Rigby to Secretary of War, Nov. 21, 1906, Administrative series, box 1, folder 5, VNMP; *Annual Report of the Secretary of War* (1905), 154; *Annual Report of the Secretary of War* (1906), 323; *Annual Report of the Secretary of War* (1907), 337; *Annual Report of the Secretary of War* (1908), 183; Memorandum, May 27, 1904, Administrative series, box 1, folder 3, VNMP.

49. W. T. Bell to Secretary of War, May 14, 1911, Administrative series, box 1, folder 10, VNMP; Robert Shaw Oliver to William T. Rigby, Jan. 8, 1904, Administrative series, box 1, folder 3, VNMP; John C. Scofield to William T. Rigby, June 4, 1903, Administrative series, box 1, folder 2, VNMP; Robert Shaw Oliver to William T. Rigby, Apr. 30, 1904, Administrative series, box 1, folder 3, VNMP; Hattaway, *General Stephen D. Lee*, 226.

50. *Annual Report of the Secretary of War* (1901), 391.

51. John S. Kountz to William T. Rigby, Mar. 9, 1901, RG 79, Letters Sent—Vicksburg National Military Park Commission, box 2, folder 1, NARA Southeast; John S. Kountz, *Record of the Organizations Engaged in the Campaign, Siege, and Defense of Vicksburg* (Washington, DC: Government Printing Office, 1901); *Annual Report of the Secretary of War* (1903), 243; *Annual Report of the Secretary of War* (1904), 275–76; *Annual Report of the Secretary of War* (1905), 156; William T. Rigby, *Historic Vicksburg: An Epitome of the Campaign, Siege, and Defense of Vicksburg, March 29–July 4, 1863* (Vicksburg: n.p., 1906); *Vicksburg For the Tourist*, 1911, William T. Rigby series, box 1, folder 2, VNMP.

52. William T. Rigby to Secretary of War, Oct. 31, 1902, and S. D. Lee to William T. Rigby, no date, both in Administrative series, box 1, folder 1, VNMP; S. D. Lee to William T. Rigby, Mar. 31, 1903, Administrative series, box 1, folder 2, VNMP; Hattaway, *General Stephen D. Lee*, 230–31.

53. "Facts Concerning Early Park Personalities," undated, Administrative series, box 6, folder 145, VNMP; W. T. Rigby, "History and Views of The Vicksburg National Military Park," *Vicksburg Monday Morning Democrat*, Sep. 6, 1909, Administrative series, box 6, folder 128, VNMP; Hattaway, *General Stephen D. Lee*, 228.

54. H. V. Boynton to William T. Rigby, May 31, 1902, and D. W. Reed to William T. Rigby, Aug. 23, 1902, both in RG 79, Letters Received—Vicksburg National Military Park Commission, box 3, NARA Southeast; "Regulations for the Government of the Vicksburg National

Military Park" (1904), "Regulations for the Government of the Gettysburg National Military Park," "Regulations Governing the Erection of Monuments, Tablets, and Markers in the Chickamauga and Chattanooga National Military Park," all in Administrative series, box 1, folder 3, VNMP; *Annual Report of the Secretary of War* (1901), 392.

55. William Cary Sanger to Chairman, June 25, 1903, Administrative series, box 1, folder 2, VNMP; *Annual Report of the Secretary of War* (1903), 242; *Annual Report of the Secretary of War* (1904), 274; *Annual Report of the Secretary of War* (1905), 154.

56. William T. Rigby to Secretary of War, Nov. 21, 1906, Administrative series, box 1, folder 5, VNMP; *Annual Report of the Secretary of War* (1906), 324; *Annual Report of the Secretary of War* (1907), 338; *Annual Report of the Secretary of War* (1908), 183–84.

57. *Annual Report of the Secretary of War* (1904), 274; *Annual Report of the Secretary of War* (1905), 154–55; *Annual Report of the Secretary of War* (1907), 338.

58. *Annual Report of the Secretary of War* (1907), 338; *Annual Report of the Secretary of War* (1908), 184.

59. *Annual Report of the Secretary of War* (1904), 275; *Annual Report of the Secretary of War* (1905), 155; *Annual Report of the Secretary of War* (1906), 325; *Annual Report of the Secretary of War* (1907), 338; *Annual Report of the Secretary of War* (1908), 184.

60. *Annual Report of the Secretary of War* (1904), 275; *Annual Report of the Secretary of War* (1905), 155; *Annual Report of the Secretary of War* (1907), 338.

61. *Illinois at Vicksburg,* 456, 460; W. P. Gault, *Ohio at Vicksburg: Report of the Ohio Vicksburg Battlefield Commission* (n.p.: n.p., 1906), 334; Henry C. Adams, *Indiana at Vicksburg* (Indianapolis: Wm. B. Burford, 1911), 448, 455; Abernathy, *Dedication of Monuments Erected by the State of Iowa,* 36, 49; Benjamin Humphreys speech, Nov. 12, 1909, Administrative series, box 6, folder 128, VNMP.

62. W. T. Younger to William T. Rigby, Nov. 30, 1906, Administrative series, box 1, folder 5, VNMP; *Annual Report of the Secretary of War* (1907), 339; *Annual Report of the Secretary of War* (1908), 185.

63. John C. Scofield to William T. Rigby, June 9, 1908, Administrative series, box 1, folder 7, VNMP; *Annual Report of the Secretary of War* (1908), 185; "Facts Concerning Early Park Personalities," Administrative series, box 6, folder 145, VNMP; B. W. Griffith to President, May 28, 1908, and William Loeb Jr. to William Howard Taft, May 29, 1908, both in RG 92, E 715, box 2, NARA.

64. *Annual Report of the Secretary of War* (1909), 41; *Annual Report of the Secretary of War* (1910), 315; *Annual Report of the Secretary of War* (1913), 203; *Annual Report of the Secretary of War* (1920), 1969–70.

65. William T. Rigby to Secretary of War, Jan. 4, 1910, Administrative series, box 1, folder 9, VNMP; Robert Shaw Oliver to William T. Rigby, Feb. 1, 1911, Administrative series, box 1, folder 10, VNMP; *Annual Report of the Secretary of War* (1909), 42–44; *Annual Report of the Secretary of War* (1910), 316–17; *Annual Report of the Secretary of War* (1911), 338; *Annual Report of the Secretary of War* (1912), 201; *Annual Report of the Secretary of War* (1918), 1488; *Annual Report of the Secretary of War* (1920), 1970; "Annual Report of the Vicksburg National Military Park Commission," July 14, 1921, Administrative series, box 6, folder 125, VNMP; "Vicksburg Park Work, Statement by States," Feb. 15,

1924, Administrative series, box 2, folder 29, VNMP; Commission Minutes, Jan. 20 and May 23, 1911, RG 79, Commission Minutes—Vicksburg National Military Park Commission, NARA Southeast; P. C. Hall to Secretary of War, June 14, 1907, and Robert Shaw Oliver to P. C. Hall, June 27, 1907, both in RG 92, E 715, box 2, NARA. A monument to black troops in the Vicksburg campaign was eventually dedicated in February 2004.

66. "Annual Report of the Vicksburg National Military Park Commission," July 14, 1921, Administrative series, box 6, folder 125, VNMP; *Annual Report of the Secretary of War* (1918), 1488; *Vicksburg Evening Post,* Nov. 12, 1909, and Oct. 12, 1927, copies found in Administrative series, box 6, folder 128, VNMP; Arthur Fridge to William T. Rigby, June 19, 1911, and William T. Rigby to Arthur Fridge, July 3, 1911, both in Administrative series, box 1, folder 10, VNMP; William T. Rigby to Assistant Secretary of War, May 8, 1916, and William M. Ingraham to Chairman, V.N.M.P. Commission, May 10, 1916, both in Administrative series, box 1, folder 20, VNMP; *Report of the Proceedings of the Society of the Army of the Tennessee at the Thirty-Seventh Meeting held at Vicksburg, Mississippi, November 7–8, 1907* (Cincinnati: Press of The Chas. O. Ebel Printing Co., 1908). The park required a five-hundred-dollar "bond" from the Mississippi National Guard to protect against any damaged the soldiers might inflict upon the park. It also required one from the film company.

67. "Vicksburg National Memorial Celebration," *Confederate Veteran* 25, no. 11 (Nov. 1917): 489–90.

68. William T. Rigby to Quartermaster General of the Army, Apr. 23, 1924, Administrative series, box 2, folder 29, VNMP; *Annual Report of the Secretary of War* (1909), 44; "Facts Concerning Early Park Personalities," Administrative series, box 6, folder 145, VNMP.

69. William T. Rigby Resident Commissioner Appointment, Mar. 1, 1922, William T. Rigby series, box 1, folder 7, VNMP; "Annual Report of the Vicksburg National Military Park Commission," July 30, 1929, Administrative series, box 6, folder 125, VNMP; H. A. Brsback to William T. Rigby, Jan. 12, 1924, Administrative series, box 2, folder 29, VNMP; "Facts Concerning Early Park Personalities," Administrative series, box 6, folder 145, VNMP.

70. Terry Winschel, Historian, Vicksburg National Military Park, interview by author, Aug. 18, 2004.

## 8. THE GOLDEN AGE REASSESSED

1. For Kennesaw Mountain, see Michael A. Capps, *Kennesaw Mountain National Battlefield Park: Administrative History* (Washington, DC: National Park Service, 1994).

2. Lee, *Origin and Evolution,* 46.

3. Ibid., 47–52.

4. Ibid., 51–52.

5. Edwin C. Bearss, Chief Historian Emeritus, National Park Service, interview by author, Aug. 11, 2004; Abroe, "All the Profound Scenes," 234, 284–88, 313; Snell and Brown, *Antietam National Battlefield,* 141.

6. Terry Winschel, Historian, Vicksburg National Military Park, interview by author, Aug. 18, 2004; Snell and Brown, *Antietam National Battlefield,* 141; Edwin C. Bearss, Chief Historian Emeritus, National Park Service, interview by author, Aug. 11, 2004.

7. *House Reports,* 59th Cong., 1st sess., H. Rept. 4431, 8–9.

8. Nicholson Journals, vol. 3, GNMP, 122; Nicholson Journals, vol. 9, GNMP, 43.

9. The western and eastern split in tablet schemes introduces a larger and more interesting debate between historians over which theater was more important. It seems that today, the majority of attention is focused on the eastern theater (although this is changing). In the 1890s, however, the veterans established three western parks and only two eastern ones. Likewise, a cursory glance at memoirs and books published by veterans reveals no eastern slant. It may well be that the eastern domination of Civil War historiography did not develop until after the passing of the veterans. One can perhaps look at the arrival of Douglas Southall Freeman as the advent of the eastern domination in Civil War study.

10. Boynton, "Chickamauga Memorial Association," 339, 344; "Alabama's Shiloh Monument," 249; "Confederate Monument at Shiloh," 441; "Dedication of the Monument at Shiloh," 251–52.

# BIBLIOGRAPHY

## *PRIMARY SOURCES*

MANUSCRIPTS

Antietam National Battlefield, Sharpsburg, Maryland
    Antietam National Battlefield Legislation and Administrative File
    Ezra A. Carman File
    Fred Cross File
    New York Monument File
    Ohio Monument File
    Pennsylvania Monument File
Chattanooga–Hamilton County Bicentennial Library, Chattanooga, Tennessee
    Vertical File
        Chickamauga and Chattanooga National Military Park
Chickamauga and Chattanooga National Military Park, Ft. Oglethorpe, Georgia
    Series 1—General Administration
    Series 2—Monuments, Tablets, Markers, and Historical Tablets
    Series 3—Park Maintenance
    Series 4—Land Acquisition and Leases
    Series 5—Personnel and Payroll
    Series 6—Military Occupation
    Series 9—Shiloh Battlefield Commission, 1881–1906
The Filson Historical Society, Louisville, Kentucky
    Don Carlos Buell Papers
Gettysburg National Military Park, Gettysburg, Pennsylvania
    Minute Book Gettysburg Battlefield Memorial Association, 1872–1895
    John P. Nicholson Journals
    William C. Oates Correspondence
Library of Congress, Washington, DC
    William Howard Taft Papers
    Daniel S. Lamont Papers
    Elihu Root Papers
Massachusetts Historical Society
    Henry Van Ness Boynton Papers
Memphis Shelby County Public Library
    Robert F. Looney Collection
Mississippi Department of Archives and History, Jackson, Mississippi
    Samuel G. French Papers
National Archives and Records Administration, Washington, DC
    RG 92—Records of the Office of the Quartermaster General

E 89 —General Correspondence, 1890–1914

E 225 —Consolidated Correspondence File, 1794–1890

E 576 —General Correspondence and Reports Relating to National and Post Cemeteries, 1865–1890

E 588 —Correspondence, Maps, and Other Papers of the Mail and Record Division, Office of the Secretary of War, Relating to National Battlefield Parks at Chickamauga-Chattanooga, Vicksburg, and Other Battlefield Parks, 1913–1923

E 707 —Antietam Battlefield Commission—General Correspondence, Mainly Letters Received, 1894–1898

E 709 —Gettysburg National Military Park Commission—Press Copies of Letters Sent, Related to the Gettysburg Battlefield Commission, 1895–1898

E 710 —Gettysburg National Military Park Commission—Register of Letters Received by the Gettysburg Battlefield Commission, 1895–1897

E 711 —Gettysburg National Military Park Commission—General Correspondence, Mainly Letters, 1898–1913

E712 —Shiloh National Military Park—General Correspondence, Chiefly Letters Received, 1895–1911

E713 —Shiloh National Military Park—Press Copies of Letters Sent, February 1895-Apr. 1899

E 714 —Shiloh National Military Park—Register of Letters Received, February 1895-July 1899

E 715 —Vicksburg National Military Park—General Correspondence and Reports, 1899–1913

RG94 —Records of the Adjutant General's Office, 1780s–1917

E 2 —Document File, 1890–1917

RG 107 —Records of the Office of the Secretary of War

E 82 —Press Copies of Letters Sent, January 1896-July 1913

National Archives and Records Administration, Southeast Region, Atlanta, GA

RG 79 —Records of the National Park Service

Shiloh National Military Park, Tennessee, 1869–1950

Vicksburg National Military Park, Mississippi, 1865–1949

New York Public Library, Manuscripts and Archives Division, Astor, Lenox and Tilden Foundations

Ezra A. Carman Papers

Shiloh National Military Park, Shiloh, Tennessee

Series 1 —Administration #1

Series 2 —Administration #2

Series 3 —D. W. Reed Papers

Series 4 —National Cemetery

Series 5 —Civil War Items

Series 6 —Maps #1

Series 7 —Maps #2

Series 8 —Blueprints/Plans

Series 9 —Photographs

Vertical Files

Cornelius Cadle, Jr.

Cyclone—1909

Early Park Road Development

Jones, Otis H. "Building Shiloh Park."

Shiloh Battlefield Commission

Shiloh National Cemetery

University of Iowa, Iowa City, Iowa
    William T. Rigby Papers
Vicksburg National Military Park, Vicksburg, Mississippi
    Administrative Series
    Edwin C. Bearss Series
    William T. Rigby Series


NEWSPAPERS

*Chattanooga News*, June 26, 1919.
*Chattanooga Daily Times*, Feb. 2, 1912.
*Chattanooga Times*, Feb. 4, 1892–Oct. 9, 1937.
*Cincinnati Commercial Tribune*, Jan. 16, 1913.
*Columbus Evening Dispatch*, Oct. 30, 1917.
*Gettysburg Star Sentinel*, July 24, 1907.
*Keedysville Antietam Valley Record*, Oct. 5, 1894–Aug. 20, 1896.
*Keedysville Antietam Wavelet*, Oct. 15, 1887–June 21, 1890.
*Memphis Commercial Appeal*, Dec. 5, 1894.
*Philadelphia Inquirer*, June 8, 1899.
*Vicksburg Evening Post*, Nov. 23, 1895–Oct. 12, 1927.
*Vicksburg Monday Morning Democrat*, Sep. 6, 1909.


PUBLISHED PRIMARY SOURCES

Abernathy, Alonzo. *Dedication of Monuments Erected by the State of Iowa*. Des Moines: Emory H. English, 1908.
Adams, Henry C. *Indiana at Vicksburg*. Indianapolis: Wm. B. Burford, 1911.
"Alabama's Shiloh Monument." *Confederate Veteran* 15, no. 6 (June 1907): 247–50.
*Annual Report of the Secretary of War*. Washington, DC: Government Printing Office, 1866–1933.
*Atlas of the Battlefields Chickamauga, Chattanooga, and Vicinity*. Washington, DC: United States War Department, 1897; revised 1901.
Boynton, H. V. *Sherman's Historical Raid: The Memoirs in the Light of the Record*. Cincinnati: Wilstach, Baldwin, and Co., 1875.
———. "The Chickamauga Memorial Association." *Southern Historical Society Papers* 16:339–49. Richmond: Southern Historical Society, 1888,.
———. *The National Military Park, Chickamauga-Chattanooga: An Historical Guide, With Maps and Illustrations*. Cincinnati: Robert Clarke Company, 1895.
———. *Battles About Chattanooga, Tenn., November 23–25, 1863: Orchard Knob, Lookout Mountain, Missionary Ridge: Organization of the Union Forces and of the Confederate Forces*. Washington, DC: Government Printing Office, 1895.
———. *Battle of Chickamauga, GA., September 19–20, 1863: Organization of the Army of the Cumberland and of the Army of Tennessee*. Washington, DC: Government Printing Office, 1895.
———. *Dedication of the Chickamauga and Chattanooga National Military Park, September 18–20, 1895: Report of the Joint Committee to Represent the Congress at the Dedication of the Chickamauga and Chattanooga National Military Park*. Washington, DC: Government Printing Office, 1896.
*Chickamauga Memorial Association Proceedings at Chattanooga, Tenn., and Crawfish Springs, Ga., September 19 and 20, 1889*. N.p.: Chattanooga Army of the Cumberland Reunion Entertainment Committee, n.d.
Clarke, Joseph Ignatius Constantine. *New York at Antietam*. N.p.: n.p., 1920.
"Col. R. F. Looney." *Confederate Veteran* 8, no. 1 (Jan. 1900): 36–37.

"The Confederate Monument at Shiloh." *Confederate Veteran* 13, no. 10 (Oct. 1905): 437–43.

*Congressional Record.* 51st–59th Congress. Washington, DC.

Coons, John W. *Indiana at Shiloh: Report of the Commission.* Indianapolis: William B. Burford, 1904.

Cunningham, D., and W. W. Miller. *Antietam: Report of the Ohio Antietam Battlefield Commission.* Springfield, OH: Springfield Publishing Company, 1904.

"David Wilson Reed." In *Memorials of Deceased Companions of the Commandery of the State of Illinois, Military Order of the Loyal Legion of the United States.* 1901. Reprint, Wilmington, N.C.: Broadfoot, 1993.

"Dedication of the Monument at Shiloh." *Confederate Veteran* 25, no. 6 (June 1917): 250–252.

*Dedication of the New York State Monument on the Battlefield of Antietam.* Albany: J. B. Lyon Company, 1923.

"Federal Veterans at Shiloh." *Confederate Veteran* 3, no. 4 (Apr. 1895): 104–5.

Fox, William F. *New York at Gettysburg.* 3 vols. Albany: J. B. Lyon Company, 1900.

Gault, W. P. *Ohio at Vicksburg: Report of the Ohio Vicksburg Battlefield Commission.* N.p.: n.p., 1906.

Gettysburg National Military Park Commission. *Annual Reports to the Secretary of War, 1893–1901.* Washington, DC: Government Printing Office, 1902.

Gracie, Archibald. *The Truth About Chickamauga.* 1911. Reprint, Dayton: Morningside, 1997.

Heitman, Francis B. *Historical Register and Dictionary of the United States Army, From Its Organization, September 29, 1789, to March 2, 1903.* 2 vols. Washington, DC: Government Printing Office, 1903.

Hood, John B. "The Defense of Atlanta." In *Battles and Leaders of the Civil War,* vol. 4: 336–44. New York: Century Co., 1884–87.

*House Reports.* 51st Cong., 1st sess., H. Rept. 643.

*House Reports.* 51st Cong., 2nd sess., H. Rept. 3024.

*House Reports.* 51st Cong., 2nd sess., H. Rept. 3296.

*House Reports.* 51st Cong., 2nd sess., H. Rept. 4019.

*House Reports.* 52nd Cong., 2nd sess., H. Rept. 2188.

*House Reports.* 53rd Cong., 2nd sess., H. Rept. 1139.

*House Reports.* 54th Cong., 1st sess., H. Rept. 374.

*House Reports.* 55th Cong., 2nd sess., H. Rept. 596.

*House Reports.* 57th Cong., 1st sess., H. Rept. 771.

*House Reports.* 57th Cong., 1st sess., H. Rept. 2043.

*House Reports.* 58th Cong., 2nd sess., H. Rept. 2325.

*House Reports.* 59th Cong., 1st sess., H. Rept. 4431.

*Illinois at Vicksburg.* N.p.: Illinois-Vicksburg Military Park Commission, 1907.

*Indiana at Chickamauga, 1863–1900: Report of the Indiana Commission, Chickamauga and Chattanooga National Military Park.* Indianapolis: Wm. B. Burford, 1901.

Kniffin, G. C. "The Battle of Stones River." In *Battles and Leaders of the Civil War,* vol. 3: 613–32. New York: Century Co., 1884–87.

Kountz, John S. *Record of the Organizations Engaged in the Campaign, Siege, and Defense of Vicksburg.* Washington, DC: Government Printing Office, 1901.

Lindsey, T. J. *Ohio at Shiloh: Report of the Commission.* Cincinnati: C. J. Krehbiel and Co., 1903.

Magdeburg, F. H. *Wisconsin at Shiloh: Report of the Commission.* Milwaukee: Riverside Ptg. Co., 1909.

Mahin, Frank W. *Genealogy of the Cadle Family Including English Decent.* N.p.: n.p., 1915.

Mason, George. *Illinois at Shiloh.* Chicago: M. A. Donohue and Co., n.d.

*The Middle Tennessee and Chattanooga Campaign of 1863, Including the Battle of Chickamauga.* N.p.: United States War Department, 1889.

"North Carolina at Gettysburg." *Confederate Veteran* 37, no. 8 (Aug. 1929): 288.

*Pennsylvania at Antietam: Report of the Antietam Battlefield Memorial Commission of Pennsylvania and Ceremonies at the Dedication of the Monuments Erected by the Commonwealth of Pennsylvania to Mark the Position of Thirteen of the Pennsylvania Commands Engaged in the Battle.* Harrisburg, PA: Harrisburg Publishing Company, 1906.

*Pennsylvania at Chickamauga and Chattanooga: Ceremonies at the Dedication of the Monuments Erected by the Commonwealth of Pennsylvania to Mark the Positions of the Pennsylvania Commands Engaged in the Battles.* N.p.: Wm. Stanley Ray, 1897.

*Pennsylvania at Gettysburg: Ceremonies at the Dedication of the Monuments Erected by the Commonwealth of Pennsylvania to Major-General George G. Meade, Major General Winfield S. Hancock, Major General John F. Reynolds, and to Mark the Positions of the Pennsylvania Commands Engaged in the Battle.* 3 vols. Harrisburg, PA: Wm. Stanley Ray, 1914.

Porter, James D. *Tennessee.* Vol. 10 of *Confederate Military History: A Library of Confederate States History in Seventeen Volumes,* edited by Clement A. Evans. 1899. Reprint, Wilmington, NC: Broadfoot Publishing Company, 1987.

Reed, David W. *Campaigns and Battles of the Twelfth Regiment Iowa Veteran Volunteer Infantry: From Organization, September, 1861, to Muster-Out, January 20, 1866.* N.p.: n.p., n.d.

———. "National Cemeteries and National Military Parks." In *War Sketches and Incidents As Related by Companions of the Iowa Commandery, Military Order of the Loyal Legion of the United States* 2: 355–74. Des Moines: n.p., 1898.

———. *The Battle of Shiloh and the Organizations Engaged.* Washington, DC: Government Printing Office, 1902.

———. *The Battle of Shiloh and the Organizations Engaged.* 2nd edition. Washington, DC: Government Printing Office, 1909.

*Report of the Proceedings of the Society of the Army of the Tennessee at the Twenty-Fifth Meeting held at Chicago, Ills. September 12th and 13th, 1893.* Cincinnati: F. W. Freeman, 1893.

*Report of the Proceedings of the Society of the Army of the Tennessee at the Twenty-Sixth Meeting held at Council Bluffs, Iowa. October 3rd and 4th, 1894.* Cincinnati: F. W. Freeman, 1895.

*Report of the Proceedings of the Society of the Army of the Tennessee at the Twenty-Eighth Meeting held at St. Louis, Mo., November 18–19, 1896.* Cincinnati: F. W. Freeman, 1897.

*Report of the Proceedings of the Society of the Army of the Tennessee at the Thirty-First Meeting held at Chicago, Ills., October 10–11, 1899.* Cincinnati: F. W. Freeman, 1900.

*Report of the Proceedings of the Society of the Army of the Tennessee at the Thirty-Seventh Meeting held at Vicksburg, Mississippi, November 7–8, 1907.* Cincinnati: Press of The Chas. O. Ebel Printing Co., 1908.

Rigby, William T. *Historic Vicksburg: An Epitome of the Campaign, Siege, and Defense of Vicksburg, March 29–July 4, 1863.* Vicksburg: n.p., 1906.

*Senate Reports.* 51st Cong., 1st sess., S. Rept. 1297.

*Senate Reports.* 53rd Cong., 3rd sess., S. Rept. 722.

*Senate Reports.* 54th Cong., 1st sess., S. Rept. 526.

*Senate Reports.* 54th Cong., 1st sess., S. Rept. 527.

*The Seventy-seventh Pennsylvania at Shiloh: History of the Regiment.* Harrisburg, PA: Harrisburg Publishing Co., 1905.

*Society of the Army of the Cumberland: Nineteenth Reunion, Chicago, Illinois, 1888.* Cincinnati: Robert Clarke and Co., 1889.

*Society of the Army of the Cumberland: Twenty-Second Reunion, Columbus, Ohio, 1891.* Cincinnati: Robert Clarke and Co., 1892.

*Society of the Army of the Cumberland: Twenty-Third Reunion, Chickamauga, Georgia, 1892.* Cincinnati: Robert Clarke and Co., 1892.

*Society of the Army of the Cumberland: Twenty-Fourth Reunion, Cleveland, Ohio, 1893.* Cincinnati: Robert Clarke Co., 1894.

Storrick, W. C. *Gettysburg: The Place, The Battles, The Outcome.* Harrisburg, PA: J. Horace McFarland Company, 1932.

*United States v. Gettysburg Electric Railroad Company*, 160, United States Reports (1896).
U.S. Quartermaster Department. *Roll of Honor: Names of Soldiers Who Died in Defense of the American Union Interred in the National Cemeteries.* 27 vols. Washington, DC: Government Printing Office, 1869.
Vanderslice, John M. *Gettysburg, Then and Now, The Field of American Valor: Where and How Troops Fought and the Troops They Encountered; An Account of the Battle Giving Movements, Positions, and Losses of the Commands Engaged.* Philadelphia: Gettysburg Battlefield Memorial Association, 1899.
"Vicksburg National Memorial Celebration." *Confederate Veteran* 25, no. 11 (Nov. 1917): 489–90.

## PRIMARY SOURCES

Abroe, Mary Munsell. "'All the Profound Scenes': Federal Preservation of Civil War Battlefields, 1861–1990." Ph.D. diss., Loyola Univ. Chicago, 1996.
Adelman, Garry E. *The Myth of Little Round Top: Gettysburg, PA.* Gettysburg: Thomas Publications, 2003.
Ballard, Michael B. *Vicksburg: The Campaign That Opened the Mississippi.* Chapel Hill: Univ. of North Carolina Press, 2004.
Bearss, Edwin C. *The Vicksburg Campaign.* 3 vols. Dayton, OH: Morningside House, 1985.
Bell, William Gardner. *Secretaries of War and Secretaries of the Army: Portraits and Biographical Sketches.* Washington, DC: Center of Military History, 1982.
*Biographical Directory of the United States Congress.* Washington, DC: Government Printing Office, 1989.
Blair, William A. *Cities of the Dead: Contesting the Memory of the Civil War in the South, 1865–1914.* Chapel Hill: Univ. of North Carolina Press, 2003.
Blight, David. *Race and Reunion: The Civil War in Memory and Reunion.* Cambridge: Harvard Univ. Press, 2001.
———. *Beyond the Battlefield: Race, Memory, and the American Civil War.* Amherst: Univ. of Massachusetts Press, 2002.
Bodnar, John. *Remaking America: Public Memory, Commemoration, and Patriotism in the Twentieth Century.* Princeton: Princeton Univ. Press, 1992.
Brown, Daniel A. *Marked for Future Generations: The Hazen Brigade Monument, 1863–1929.* Murfreesboro, TN: Stones River National Battlefield, 1985.
Brown, Kent Masterson. *Retreat from Gettysburg: Lee, Logistics, and the Pennsylvania Campaign.* Chapel Hill: Univ. of North Carolina Press, 2005.
Capps, Michael A. *Kennesaw Mountain National Battlefield Park: Administrative History.* Washington, DC: National Park Service, 1994.
Coddington, Edwin B. *The Gettysburg Campaign: A Study in Command.* New York: Charles Scribner's Sons, 1968.
Conley, Laurence D. "The Truth about Chickamauga: A Ninth Indiana Regiment's Perspective." *Indiana Magazine of History* 98 (June 2002): 114–43.
Cozzens, Peter. *This Terrible Sound: The Battle of Chickamauga.* Urbana: Univ. of Illinois Press, 1992.
Cunningham, O. Edward. *Shiloh and the Western Campaign of 1862.* Edited by Gary D. Joiner and Timothy B. Smith. New York: Savas Beatie, 2007.
Daniel, Larry J. *Shiloh: The Battle That Changed the Civil War.* New York: Simon and Schuster, 1997.

Davis, Timothy, Todd A. Croteau, and Christopher H. Marston, eds. *America's National Park Roads and Parkways: Drawings from the Historic American Engineering Record*. Baltimore: Johns Hopkins Univ. Press, 2004.

DeSantis, Vincent P. *The Shaping of Modern America, 1877–1920*. Wheeling: Forum Press, 1973.

Desjardin, Thomas A. *These Honored Dead: How the Story of Gettysburg Shaped American Memory*. Cambridge, MA: Da Capo, 2003.

Fahs, Alice, and Joan Waugh, eds. *The Memory of the Civil War in American Culture*. Chapel Hill: Univ. of North Carolina Press, 2004.

Farrell, James J. *Inventing the American Way of Death, 1830–1920*. Philadelphia: Temple Univ. Press, 1980.

Foner, Eric. *Reconstruction: America's Unfinished Revolution, 1863–1877*. New York: Harper Collins, 1989.

Gillis, Joe. *The Confederate Monument: Shiloh National Military Park*. N.p.: n.p., 1994.

Grabau, Warren E. *Ninety-eight Days: A Geographer's View of the Vicksburg Campaign*. Knoxville: Univ. of Tennessee Press, 2000.

Hattaway, Herman. *General Stephen D. Lee*. Jackson: Univ. Press of Mississippi, 1976.

———— and A. J. Meek. *Gettysburg to Vicksburg: The Five Original Civil War Battlefield Parks*. Columbia: Univ. of Missouri Press, 2001.

Holt, Dean W. *American Military Cemeteries: A Comprehensive Illustrated Guide to the Hollowed Grounds of the United States, Including Cemeteries Overseas*. Jefferson, NC: McFarland and Company, 1992.

Kammen, Michael. *Mystic Chords of Memory: The Transformation of Tradition in American Culture*. New York: Vintage Books, 1991.

Kaser, James A. *At the Bivouac of Memory: History, Politics, and the Battle of Chickamauga*. New York: Peter Lang, 1996.

Kinsel, Amy. "'From These Honored Dead': Gettysburg in American Culture, 1863–1938." Ph.D. diss., Cornell Univ., 1992.

Krick, Robert E. L. "The Civil War's First Monument: Bartow's Marker at Manassas." *Blue and Gray* 8, no. 4 (Apr. 1991): 33.

LaFantasie, Glenn W. *Gettysburg Requiem: The Life and Lost Causes of Confederate Colonel William C. Oates*. New York: Oxford Univ. Press, 2006.

Large, George R., and Joe A. Swisher. *Battle of Antietam: The Official History by the Antietam Battlefield Board*. Shippensburg, PA: Burd Street Press, 1998.

————. comp. *Battle of Gettysburg: The Official History by the Gettysburg National Military Park Commission*. Shippensburg, PA: Burd Street Press, 1999.

Lee, Ronald F. *The Origin and Evolution of the National Military Park Idea*. Washington, DC: National Park Service, 1973.

Linenthal, Edward T. *Sacred Ground: Americans and Their Battlefields*. Urbana: Univ. of Illinois Press, 1991.

Livingood, James W. "Chickamauga and Chattanooga National Military Park." *Tennessee Historical Quarterly* 23, no. 1 (Mar. 1964): 3–23.

McPherson, James M. *Crossroads of Freedom: Antietam, The Battle That Changed the Course of the Civil War*. New York: Oxford Univ. Press, 2002.

Myers, Richard. *The Vicksburg National Cemetery: An Administrative History*. Washington, DC: National Park Service, 1968.

Neff, John R. *Honoring The Civil War Dead: Commemoration and the Problem of Reconciliation*. Lawrence: Univ. Press of Kansas, 2005.

Owen, Thomas McAdory. *History of Alabama and Dictionary of Alabama Biography*. 4 vols. 1921. Reprint, Spartanburg, SC: Reprint Company, 1978.

Paige, John C., and Jerome A. Greene. *Administrative History of Chickamauga and Chattanooga National Military Park*. Denver: Denver Service Center, National Park Service, 1983.

Painter, Nell Irvin. *Standing at Armageddon: The United States, 1877–1919*. New York: W. W. Norton, 1987.

Panhorst, Michael W. "Lest We Forget: Monuments and Memorial Sculpture in National Military Parks on Civil War Battlefields, 1861–1917." Ph.D. diss., Univ. of Delaware, 1988.

Piehler, G. Kurt. *Remembering War the American Way*. Washington, DC: Smithsonian Institution Press, 1995.

Powell, Dave. "The 96th Illinois and the Battles for Horseshoe Ridge, 1863 and 1895." *North and South* 8, no. 2 (Mar. 2005): 48–59.

Reardon, Carol. *Pickett's Charge in History and Memory*. Chapel Hill: Univ. of North Carolina Press, 1997.

Scully, John Connor. "Ezra Carman: Soldier and Historian." M.A. thesis, George Mason Univ., 1997.

Sears, Stephen W. *Landscape Turned Red: The Battle of Antietam*. New Haven: Ticknor and Fields, 1983.

———. *Gettysburg*. New York: Houghton Mifflin Company, 2003.

Sellars, Richard W. "Pilgrim Places: Civil War Battlefields, Historic Preservation, and America's First National Military Parks, 1863–1900." *CRM: The Journal of Heritage Stewardship* 2, no. 1 (Winter 2005): 22–52.

———. *Pilgrim Places: Civil War Battlefields, Historic Preservation, and America's First National Military Parks, 1863–1900*. Fort Washington, PA: Eastern National, 2005.

Shedd, Charles E. *A History of Shiloh National Military Park, Tennessee*. Washington, DC: Government Printing Office, 1954.

Sloane, David Charles. *The Last Great Necessity: Cemeteries in American History*. Baltimore: Johns Hopkins Univ. Press, 1991.

Smith, Timothy B. "'The Handsomest Cemetery in the South': Shiloh National Cemetery." *West Tennessee Historical Society Papers* 56 (2002): 1–16.

———. *This Great Battlefield of Shiloh: History, Memory, and the Establishment of a Civil War National Military Park*. Knoxville: Univ. of Tennessee Press, 2004.

———. *The Untold Story of Shiloh: The Battle and the Battlefield*. Knoxville: Univ. of Tennessee Press, 2006.

Snell, Charles W., and Sharon A. Brown. *Antietam National Battlefield and National Cemetery*. Washington, DC: National Park Service, 1986.

Sword, Wiley. *Shiloh: Bloody April*. New York: William Morrow and Company, 1974.

Trail, Susan W. "Remembering Antietam: Commemoration and Preservation of a Civil War Battlefield." Ph.D. diss., Univ. of Maryland, 2005.

Trudeau, Noah Andre. *Gettysburg: A Testing of Courage*. New York: HarperCollins, 2002.

Tucker, Glenn. *Chickamauga: Bloody Battle in the West*. Indianapolis: Bobbs-Merrill, 1961.

Unrau, Harlan D. *Administrative History: Gettysburg National Military Park and National Cemetery*. Denver: National Park Service, 1991.

Upchurch, Thomas Adams. *Legislating Racism: The Billion Dollar Congress and the Birth of Jim Crow*. Lexington: Univ. Press of Kentucky, 2004.

Waldrep, Christopher. *Vicksburg's Long Shadow: The Civil War Legacy of Race and Remembrance*. New York: Rowman and Littlefield, 2005.

Warner, Ezra J. *Generals in Gray: Lives of the Confederate Commanders*. Baton Rouge: Louisiana State Univ. Press, 1959.

Weeks, Jim. *Gettysburg: Memory, Market, and an American Shrine*. Princeton: Princeton Univ. Press, 2003.

Wills, Gary. *Lincoln at Gettysburg: The Words That Remade America*. New York: Simon and Schuster, 1992.

Winschel, Terrence J. *Vicksburg: Fall of the Confederate Gibraltar*. Abilene, TX: McWhiney Foundation Press, 1999.

———. "Stephen D. Lee and the Making of an American Shrine." *Journal of Mississippi History* 63, no. 1 (2001): 17–32.

Woodward, C. Vann. *The Strange Career of Jim Crow*. 3rd edition. New York: Oxford Univ. Press, 1989.

Zenzen, Joan M. *Battling for Manassas: The Fifty-Year Preservation Struggle at Manassas National Battlefield Park*. Univ. Park: Pennsylvania State Univ. Press, 1998.


## WEB SITE

http://bioguide.congress.gov/scripts/biodisplay.pl?index=M000351. "McComas, Louis Emory (1846–1907)." Biographical Directory of the United States Congress.


## PERSONAL INTERVIEWS

Alexander, Ted (Historian, Antietam National Battlefield). Interview by author. May 25, 2001.

Bearss, Edwin C. (Chief Historian Emeritus, National Park Service). Interview by author. August 11, 2004.

Hartwig, D. Scott (Historian, Gettysburg National Military Park). Interview by author. May 22, 2001.

Ogden, Jim (Historian, Chickamauga and Chattanooga National Military Park). Interview by author. May 21, 2001.

———. Interview by author. October 20, 2003.

Winschel, Terry (Historian, Vicksburg National Military Park). Interview by author. May 21, 2001.

———. Interview by author, August 18, 2004.

# INDEX

*The Golden Age of Battlefield Preservation* was designed and typeset on a Macintosh computer system using Adobe InDesign software. The body text is set in 10.5 / 13.25 Chaparral and display type is set in Minion. This book was designed and typeset by Tom Helleberg and manufactured by Thomson-Shore, Inc.